Everyman, I will go with thee, and be thy guide,
In thy most need to go by thy side.

EVERYMAN'S LIBRARY
EDITED BY ERNEST RHYS

POETRY & THE DRAMA

POEMS, SELECT LETTERS & ESSAYS
BY THOMAS GRAY · INTRODUCTION
BY JOHN DRINKWATER

THOMAS GRAY, born in 1716, the son of a London scrivener. Educated at Cambridge, and lived there most of his life, accepting in 1768 a university professorship in history and modern languages. Declined poet-laureate-ship, 1757. Died in 1771 at Cambridge, and buried at Stoke Poges.

POEMS, LETTERS, AND ESSAYS

THOMAS GRAY

LONDON: J. M. DENT & SONS LTD.
NEW YORK: E. P. DUTTON & CO. INC.

INTRODUCTION

(THOMAS GRAY, 1716-1771)

THE acute power of observation that Alexander Pope applied so admirably to the manners of his time and the foibles of humanity was not wholly set aside in his contemplation of man's spiritual life and the beauty of the natural world. A tradition, not false in itself, but false in him because he accepted it without a poet's conviction, was, indeed, continually set between him and the thing seen. He could not see a woodland without pretending to himself that he also saw it peopled by " coy nymphs," and a flock of sheep outraged his sense of decency unless it was accompanied by Pan. But, in spite of this imaginative trickery, he had moments when he came near to seeing the loveliness of earth with undistracted vision, and they are moments that afford a striking commentary on the essential weakness of his poetry and that of his age. Whilst it is true that the sublime is but a step from the ridiculous, it is equally true that the greatest poets, those who have most often encompassed the sublime, are also those who have had least fear of the false step that should lead them to disaster. They have not infrequently taken it, and been utterly unashamed, probably not even conscious of their lapse. Great poetry is never self-conscious; however carefully it may be wrought, the care is a concession to the poet's desire to express fully the thing that he has discovered, and not to his sense of propriety. The profoundest imaginative truth in poetry is often embodied in an utterance quite unable to bear examination by common standards of fact. A level-headed lawyer, who carried truth in a nutshell, reading Shelley's " Skylark," came to the phrase " Now scorner of the ground." " Nonsense," he exclaimed, " the bird makes its nest on the ground." The besetting sin of the temper in poetry for which Pope stood was precisely this self-consciousness, this distrust of poetic truth, this fear of the ridiculous. So that Pope, looking out on to distant hills and seeing that they were blue, was troubled. He knew that they were really green or brown, in any case not blue. And then he began to doubt whether even in appearance they were quite blue after all, and finally suppressed the poet that was in him and wrote—

" There wrapt in clouds the *blueish* hills ascend."

Propriety was unoffended, and we were given an epitome in one line of the twist that did so much to devitalise the poetry of the age.

As if to emphasise the essential unity of matter and manner in art, this timorousness of spirit found its exact parallel in the form into which poetry was shaped. The prevalence of the heroic couplet cannot have been due to any conviction in the minds of the poets that this was indisputably the form best fitted for the language. But it was capable of a balance, a regularity, a precision that commended it with peculiar force to men to whom these things were of first-rate importance in their reading of life. Once it had been handled by a master technician, it was thenceforth easy to determine at a glance whether the versification was correct, and the appeal to correctness was sacrosanct. Any departure from recognised rules could be instantly detected: a most comfortable privilege to men who valued rule more than adventure. Rejecting blank verse as sorting ill with that elegance which was a plaything for polite society, the poets were not disposed to surrender those qualities of blank verse most suited to their formal habit of mind. The five foot line was established as the staple of English verse, and by stripping it of variety and lending it the adornment of rhyme they found a vehicle as rigid as their own perceptions and at the same time not devoid of authority. To have experimented with more flexible lyrical forms would have been, in their eyes, wilful folly, for flexibility meant a confusion of standards, a license that would have destroyed the simple code of reference to which they were used. The relationship of early eighteenth century poetry in England to classicism is extremely remote. In great classic art, as in great art of every kind, the supreme arbiter is the imagination, and it was the radical flaw of that phase of English poetry that the imagination was subjected not merely to the reason, but to a reason that continually argued back to formal standards and not forward to discoveries. The poets were not even progressive in their science.

To praise a poet because he achieved in spite of great difficulties rather than for his achievement itself is to serve him ill. The external circumstance of John Clare's poverty adds nothing to the worth of his lyrics. We may be astonished at the spectacle of a penniless and untutored labourer adding to the store of authentic poetry, but our astonishment has nothing to do with our understanding of art. It is not our concern, in seeking for the beauty that is the gift of art, to remember that Milton was blind or Beethoven deaf. We may acclaim Chaucer because he shaped a language, but we love him because he was a poet, and it is by our love that he is immortal. It is the function of poetry to impart to us strong exaltation, to free our imaginations and quicken our spiritual perceptions, and if it fails to do this no plea of disabilities or obstacles will serve the poet. That he might have done better under other circumstances, or that he did well considering this thing or that, does not matter. The poet's revelation alone can move us, and his written word is the only revelation that we can accept. If he fails to reveal we may still be interested in the failure, but for reasons remote from the divine curiosity that leads us to poetry.

There are, however, circumstances that, whilst not increasing the positive value of a poet's work, may throw his achievement into greater relief. Thomas Gray, who was born when Pope was twenty-eight years old, holds his place among the poets because he had something to reveal, and with whatever uncertainty and in however small a compass, found fit expression for the thing that he had to say, and for no other reason. But he arrests particular attention in the course of English poetry because he was the first man of importance to revolt against the formalism of the poets of the age into which he was born. The distinction was shared by Collins, who heralded the great romantic revival with a note of purer poetry than that of the poet who is more widely known, but the two men were working independently to the same end. Gray certainly owed nothing to Collins; he might, indeed, have done so with gain. His judgment was not at any time as sound in this matter of contemporary poetry as his instinct. He worked away from the things that he praised and towards the things in which he professed to see no virtue. We find him speaking highly of Shenstone and Beattie and Mason, and yet writing to his friend, Wharton, " Have you seen the works of two young authors, a Mr. Warton and Mr. Collins, both writers of odes? it is odd enough, but each is the half of a considerable man, and one the counterpart of the other.

The first has but little invention, very poetical choice of expression, and a good ear. The second, a fine fancy, modelled upon the antique, a bad ear, great variety of words and images, with no choice at all. They both deserve to last some years, but will not." But the denial of the false tradition by which he was surrounded was no less emphatic because it was more or less unconscious. Gray's habitual outlook upon the world was rather of the scholarly observer than that of the creative seer, but he had moments of genuinely imaginative vision, and his instinct impelled him to allow these free and not unadventurous expression. Lyrical verse during the hundred years that followed him attained a variety and colour that would have seemed even to his independent mind the merest vagary and licentiousness, but in his rather formally constructed odes, and even in the simple stanzas of the " Elegy," he made a definite and memorable departure from the rigidity that was threatening to deprive poetry of all its suppleness and finer expression. In his diction he was unable to escape with any certainty from the constraint of his age. Poetry in his hands was still too often concerned with hearsay instead of vision, and, save at times when he gave himself up wholly to his better impulse, he was ready to lend his authority to the fustian rhetoric that did duty for style. We still have the " attic warbler " and the " fury Passions," " melting strains," and the " enchanting shell," and we still find poetry masquerading in such dress as this—

> " What idle progeny succeed
> To chase the rolling circle's speed,
> Or urge the flying ball? "

There are, in short, many traces in Gray's poetry of a tradition against which he revolted but which he could not be expected to overcome at a stroke. But there are, scattered through his small volume of work, many instances of the poet's determination to express himself completely and with indifference to current standards. He could rival Pope himself on occasion in precision and the sublimation of mere reason, as for example in—

> " all are men
> Condemned alike to groan,
> The tender for another's pain,
> The unfeeling for his own. . . ."

or—

> " where ignorance is bliss
> 'Tis folly to be wise,"

or again in such a phrase as " leave us leisure to be good."
But he could also reach true dignity of style, a thing new to
his time—

> " Nor the pride, nor ample pinion
> That the Theban Eagle bear,
> Sailing with supreme dominion
> Thro' the azure deep of air,"

and—

> " In gallant trim the gilded vessel goes;
> Youth on the prow and Pleasure at the helm,"

are notes for which he could find no example among his
contemporaries save Collins. And he could, further, touch
the pure simplicity of manner that he found discredited and
rejected in the practice of the men that were then accepted
as controllers of taste, and is yet the highest triumph of the
poet's expression. He did this not only in such isolated
passages as—

> " The meanest floweret of the vale,
> The simplest note that swells the gale,
> The common sun, the air, the skies,
> To him are opening Paradise."

but also, with very few lapses, throughout a whole poem. The
" Elegy written in a Country Churchyard " has the distinction
of being one of the few excellent poems in the language that
are really popular. The qualities that have made it popular
have, of course, nothing to do with Gray's position as a
pioneer. They are those of tenderness and of clear distinction
between sentiment and sentimentality, of intimacy with
the beauty and change of earth, all set down without affectation and yet never meanly. It is a chapter of simple things
which once again have gripped a poet by their loveliness and
poignancy, and it is by virtue of this that it has won the
affection of so many men; but it does, nevertheless, take on
a new distinction when we realise that it was written at a
time when these qualities were most grudgingly served by
poetry. Gray had not a particularly rich imagination, but
he was willing at times to allow what imaginative faculty he
had free play. His power of vision was not of the highest,
but in his more inspired moments he was careful to allow
nothing to come between his vision and the thing seen. It
has been charged against him that " he never spoke out."
The criticism would not seem to be well considered. He did
not, it is true, speak often, and he sometimes spoke without

conviction. But it is not the least of his distinctions that at
other times, when he was really moved to follow the guidance
of his instinct, he was one of two men in his age who did speak
out. He was not afraid to put on record the evidence of his
imagination. If Gray saw blue hills he called them blue and
not bluish.

Wordsworth did Gray an injustice by placing him " at the
head of those who, by their reasonings, have attempted to
widen the space of separation betwixt prose and metrical
composition," and adding that he was " more than any other
man curiously elaborate in the structure of his own poetic
diction." Even in his elaboration Gray was doing something
to escape from a precision numbing in its formality, and,
although Wordsworth rightly protested against much in the
earlier poet's diction, he might have drawn his examples as
aptly from almost any of Gray's contemporaries, who could
not have defended themselves by an " Elegy " or the passages of
perfectly sincere and imaginative diction that are to be found
in the Odes. Although Gray was not at all times a profitable
servant, he was ever ready to acknowledge the lordship of
the imagination, and it was not quite generous of Wordsworth
to omit this fact from his reckoning. Johnson complained
that he was " tall by walking on tiptoe," but the desire to be
tall was in itself laudable, and not always unrewarded.

The poet's letters are not only delightful in their revelation
of a most companionable personality, but they also contain
many passages that show a clear-sightedness as to the general
principles of his craft. It was natural enough that he should
be mistaken as to Collins, and confused in his judgments of
the work that was being done in his own day, even that he
should at times be disloyal to his instincts in his own creation.
The influence of Pope was too great for any man to resist
without much stumbling. But as soon as he began to consider
the abstract nature of poetry he did so with admirable balance
and insight His professed essays on the art are concerned
rather with the evolution of language and metrical form than
with the cosmic spirit of poetry, but his correspondents might
profit, if they were able, by many swift words of profound
critical understanding. Speaking of description, he says, " I
have always thought that it made the most graceful ornament
of poetry, but never ought to make the subject," and his
letters to Mason about that industrious writer's work abound
in observations that are worthy of a better subject. It is

clear from these flashes of criticism scattered through the letters that he had a finer understanding of his art than, perhaps, any man of his age, however inconsistently he may have applied his understanding in practice, and although this, again, does not add to his stature as poet, it gives some new distinction to his place in the history of letters.

The chief defect in his positive contribution to poetry is its unconcern with humanity. He peoples his poems with personages that are but rarely warm with life. Gray was not commonly fortunate in his choice of subjects. The odes, which form the greater part of his work, each contain incidental and isolated passages that by their sudden rise to excellence of style or their clarity and intimacy of feeling are made memorable, but they do not command our interest either by their unity of conception, their sustained beauty of expression, or their nearness to our own experience. In the "Elegy" alone among his more serious poems did he take a subject that by its simplicity and universality enabled him to write in complete accord with the impulse that was in him for direct and unstrained expression, and it is the "Elegy" that we treasure as a complete poem, reading it from beginning to end when we turn back to it, not hastening forward for some rare glimpse of splendour that we know awaits us. In his lighter poems, notably "The Long Story," he attained something of this same warmth. His humour was always one of his most lovable qualities, and when he brings it to his poetry it is some compensation for the naturalness and depth that we miss in the odes save at long intervals; nearly related as it is to the quick humanity that stirred him to utterance in the poem that popular affection has agreed with Dr. Johnson in proclaiming as his highest achievement.

JOHN DRINKWATER.

BIRMINGHAM, 1912.

The following is a list of the works of Thomas Gray:—

SINGLE POEMS: Ode on a Distant Prospect of Eton College, 1747; Ode to Spring, Ode on the Death of a Favourite Cat, 1748; Elegy written in a Country Churchyard, 1751; A Long Story, Hymn to Adversity, 1753; The Progress of Poetry, The Bard, 1757; The Fatal Sisters, The Descent of Odin, The Triumphs of Owen, 1768; Ode at the Installation of the Duke of Grafton, 1769; Ode on the Pleasure arising from Vicissitude, 1775; De principiis cogitandi, 1839.

TRANSLATIONS: Elegia Inglese del Signor T. Gray sopra un Cimitero di Campagna (English, Latin, and Italian), by G. Gennari and G. Costa, 1772; Tes Elegias en Thomas Graies en Koimeterio agroiko (English and Greek), by C. Coote, 1794; Poésies de Gray (French), by A. J. Lemierre d'Argy, 1798; Myfyrdod ar Einioes ac Angeu a ysgrifenwyd mewn Mynwent yn y wlad, ym mrig yr hwyr (Welsh), by D. Davies, 1798; Ode sobre o Progreço da Poezia; hymno a Adversidade; Ode . . . vendo ao longe o Colegio de Eton (Portuguese), by A. de Aranja, 1799; O Cemiterio de Aldea (Portuguese), by Almeida Coutinho, 1837; Elégie dans un cimetière de Campagna; Le Barde (French), by M. A. Elwall, 1887.

PROSE WORKS: A Catalogue of Antiquities in England and Wales, 1774 (?); Supplement, 1787; The Traveller's Companion, 1799. Many of his Letters have been published: Mr. Gray's Journal in a Letter to Dr. Wharton, 1803; The Correspondence of T. G. and Wm. Mason, edited by. T. Mitford, 1853; Gray and his Friends, edited by D. C. Tovey, 1890; Letters of T. G., edited by D. C. Tovey (Bohn's Standard Library), 1900-1907.

COLLECTED WORKS: Poems, published by Dodsley, 1748, 1757, 1768; by Foulis, 1768. Designs for Six Poems by R. Bentley, 1753. Poems, edited by W. Mason, 1775; other editions, 1775, 1776, 1778, 1807; edited by G. Wakefield, 1786. Works, edited by T. J. Mathias, 1814; by J. Mitford, 1816, 1836, 1835-43. Poems, edited by J. Mitford, 1816; Poetical Works, Eng. and Latin, edited by J. Moultrie and J. Mitford, 1847; Poetical Works (Aldine edition), 1853; Works in Prose and Verse, edited by E. Gosse, 1884; Poems, edited by J. Bradshaw, 1891.

BIOGRAPHY AND CRITICISM: Lives and Memoirs are to be found in most of the collected editions of Gray's Works, the best being those of Bradshaw, Mason, Mathias, and Tovey. Johnson's sketch in the Lives of the Poets (1779) shows haste, while Matthew Arnold's, in T. H. Ward's English Poets (1880-1881) is a gem of literature; Edmund Gosse's Life of Gray appeared in the English Men of Letters series, 1889. Consult also C. E. Norton's The Poet Gray as a Naturalist, 1903; A. S. Cook's Concordance to Eng. Poems of Thos. Gray, 1908; C. S. Northrup's Addison and Gray as Travellers, 1910; W. H. Hudson's Gray and his Poetry, 1911.

CONTENTS

POEMS

POSTHUMOUS POEMS AND FRAGMENTS

EXTRACTS

POEMATA

EXTRACTS

A SELECTION OF LETTERS

Contents

Contents

Contents

Contents

APPENDIX

METRUM

GRAY'S POEMS AND LETTERS

ODES

I. ON THE SPRING

The original manuscript title given by Gray to this Ode was " Noontide." It appeared for the first time in Dodsley's *Collection*, vol. ii. p. 271, under the title of " Ode." See Meleager's " Ode to Spring," and Jones, *Comm. Poes. Asiaticæ*, p. 411. This Ode is formed on Horace's Ode " Ad Sestium," I. iv. Translated into Latin in *Musæ Etonens.* vol. ii. p. 60.

Lo! where the rosy-bosom'd Hours,
 Fair Venus' train, appear,
Disclose the long-expecting flowers,
 And wake the purple year!
The Attic warbler pours her throat,
Responsive to the cuckoo's note,
 The untaught harmony of spring:
While, whisp'ring pleasure as they fly,
Cool Zephyrs thro' the clear blue sky
 Their gather'd fragrance fling.

Where'er the oak's thick branches stretch
 A broader browner shade,
Where'er the rude and moss-grown beech
 O'er-canopies the glade,
Beside some water's rushy brink
With me the Muse shall sit, and think
 (At ease reclin'd in rustic state)
How vain the ardour of the crowd,
How low, how little are the proud,
 How indigent the great!

Still is the toiling hand of Care;
 The panting herds repose:
Yet hark, how thro' the peopled air
 The busy murmur glows!

The insect-youth are on the wing,
Eager to taste the honied spring,
   And float amid the liquid noon:
Some lightly o'er the current skim,
Some show their gayly-gilded trim
   Quick-glancing to the sun.

To Contemplation's sober eye
   Such is the race of Man:
And they that creep, and they that fly,
   Shall end where they began.
Alike the Busy and the Gay
But flutter thro' life's little day,
   In Fortune's varying colours drest:
Brush'd by the hand of rough Mischance,
Or chill'd by Age, their airy dance
   They leave, in dust to rest.

Methinks I hear, in accents low,
   The sportive kind reply:
Poor moralist! and what art thou?
   A solitary fly!
Thy joys no glittering female meets,
No hive hast thou of hoarded sweets,
   No painted plumage to display:
On hasty wings thy youth is flown;
Thy sun is set, thy spring is gone—
   We frolic while 'tis May.

II. ON THE DEATH OF A FAVOURITE CAT

DROWNED IN A TUB OF GOLD FISHES

On a favourite cat called Selima, that fell into a China Tub with
gold fishes in it, and was drowned, MS. Wharton. Walpole, after
the death of Gray, placed the China Vase on a pedestal at Strawberry Hill, with a few lines of the Ode for its inscription.

'Twas on a lofty vase's side,
Where China's gayest art had dy'd
   The azure flowers, that blow;
Demurest of the tabby kind,
The pensive Selima, reclin'd,
   Gaz'd on the lake below.

Her conscious tail her joy declar'd;
The fair round face, the snowy beard,
 The velvet of her paws,
Her coat, that with the tortoise vies,
Her ears of jet, and emerald eyes,
 She saw; and purr'd applause.

Still had she gaz'd; but 'midst the tide
Two angel forms were seen to glide,
 The Genii of the stream:
Their scaly armour's Tyrian hue
Through richest purple to the view
 Betray'd a golden gleam.

The hapless nymph with wonder saw:
A whisker first, and then a claw,
 With many an ardent wish,
She stretch'd, in vain, to reach the prize.
What female heart can gold despise?
 What Cat's averse to fish?

Presumptuous maid! with looks intent
Again she stretch'd, again she bent,
 Nor knew the gulf between.
(Malignant Fate sat by, and smil'd)
The slipp'ry verge her feet beguil'd,
 She tumbled headlong in.

Eight times emerging from the flood
She mew'd to ev'ry wat'ry God,
 Some speedy aid to send.
No Dolphin came, no Nereid stirr'd:
Nor cruel Tom, nor Susan heard.
 A fav'rite has no friend!

From hence, ye beauties, undeceiv'd,
Know, one false step is ne'er retriev'd,
 And be with caution bold.
Not all that tempts your wand'ring eyes
And heedless hearts is lawful prize,
 Nor all that glisters, gold.

III. ON A DISTANT PROSPECT OF
ETON COLLEGE

Ἀνθρωπος, ἱκανὴ πρόφασις εἰς τὸ δυστυχεῖν.
Menander, Incert. Fragm. ver. 382, ed. Cler. p. 245.

See *Musæ Etonenses*, vol. i. p. 229, and *Brit. Bibliographer*,
vol. ii. p. 214.

YE distant spires, ye antique towers,
  That crown the wat'ry glade,
Where grateful Science still adores
  Her Henry's holy shade;
And ye, that from the stately brow
Of Windsor's heights th' expanse below
  Of grove, of lawn, of mead survey,
Whose turf, whose shade, whose flowers among
Wanders the hoary Thames along
  His silver-winding way:

Ah, happy hills! ah, pleasing shade!
  Ah, fields belov'd in vain!
Where once my careless childhood stray'd,
  A stranger yet to pain!
I feel the gales that from ye blow
A momentary bliss bestow,
  As waving fresh their gladsome wing,
My weary soul they seem to soothe,
And, redolent of joy and youth,
  To breathe a second spring.

Say, father Thames, for thou hast seen
  Full many a sprightly race
Disporting on thy margent green,
  The paths of pleasure trace;
Who foremost now delight to cleave,
With pliant arm, thy glassy wave?
  The captive linnet which enthral?
What idle progeny succeed
To chase the rolling circle's speed,
  Or urge the flying ball?

While some on earnest business bent
  Their murm'ring labours ply
'Gainst graver hours that bring constraint
  To sweeten liberty:
Some bold adventurers disdain
The limits of their little reign,
  And unknown regions dare descry:
Still as they run they look behind,
They hear a voice in every wind,
  And snatch a fearful joy.

Gay hope is theirs by fancy fed,
  Less pleasing when possest;
The tear forgot as soon as shed,
  The sunshine of the breast:
Theirs buxom health, of rosy hue,
Wild wit, invention ever new,
  And lively cheer, of vigour born;
The thoughtless day, the easy night,
The spirits pure, the slumbers light,
  That fly th' approach of morn.

Alas! regardless of their doom
  The little victims play;
No sense have they of ills to come,
  Nor care beyond to-day:
Yet see, how all around 'em wait
The ministers of human fate,
  And black Misfortune's baleful train!
Ah, show them where in ambush stand,
To seize their prey, the murth'rous band!
  Ah, tell them, they are men!

These shall the fury Passions tear,
  The vultures of the mind,
Disdainful Anger, pallid Fear,
  And Shame that sculks behind;
Or pining Love shall waste their youth,
Or Jealousy, with rankling tooth,
  That inly gnaws the secret heart;
And Envy wan, and faded Care,
Grim-visag'd comfortless Despair,
  And Sorrow's piercing dart.

Ambition this shall tempt to rise,
  Then whirl the wretch from high,
To bitter Scorn a sacrifice,   -
  And grinning Infamy.
The stings of Falsehood those shall try,
And hard Unkindness' alter'd eye,
  That mocks the tear it forc'd to flow;
And keen Remorse with blood defil'd,
And moody Madness laughing wild
  Amid severest woe.

Lo! in the vale of years beneath
  A griesly troop are seen,
The painful family of Death,
  More hideous than their queen:
This racks the joints, this fires the veins,
That every labouring sinew strains,
  Those in the deeper vitals rage:
Lo! Poverty, to fill the band,
That numbs the soul with icy hand,
  And slow-consuming Age.

To each his suff'rings: all are men,
  Condemn'd alike to groan;
The tender for another's pain,
  Th' unfeeling for his own.
Yet, ah! why should they know their fate,
Since sorrow never comes too late,
  And happiness too swiftly flies?
Thought would destroy their paradise.
No more;—where ignorance is bliss,
  'Tis folly to be wise.

HYMN TO ADVERSITY

—Ζῆνα—

. . . .
Τὸν φρονεῖν βροτοὺς ὁδώ-
σαντα, τῷ πάθει μαθὼν
Θέντα κυρίῳ ἔχειν.—Æsch. *Agam.* ver. 181.

DAUGHTER of Jove, relentless power,
  Thou tamer of the human breast,
Whose iron scourge and tort'ring hour
  The bad affright, afflict the best!

Bound in thy adamantine chain,
The proud are taught to taste of pain,
And purple tyrants vainly groan
With pangs unfelt before, unpitied and alone.

When first thy sire to send on earth
   Virtue, his darling child, design'd,
To thee he gave the heav'nly birth,
   And bade to form her infant mind.
Stern rugged nurse! thy rigid lore
With patience many a year she bore:
What sorrow was, thou bad'st her know,
And from her own she learn'd to melt at others' woe.

Scar'd at thy frown terrific, fly
   Self-pleasing Folly's idle brood,
Wild Laughter, Noise, and thoughtless Joy,
   And leave us leisure to be good.
Light they disperse, and with them go
The summer friend, the flattering foe;
   By vain Prosperity receiv'd,
To her they vow their truth, and are again believ'd.

Wisdom in sable garb array'd,
   Immers'd in rapt'rous thought profound,
And Melancholy, silent maid,
   With leaden eye that loves the ground,
Still on thy solemn steps attend:
Warm Charity, the gen'ral friend,
   With Justice, to herself severe,
And Pity, dropping soft the sadly-pleasing tear.

Oh! gently on thy suppliant's head,
   Dread goddess, lay thy chast'ning hand!
Not in thy Gorgon terrors clad,
   Not circled with the vengeful band
(As by the impious thou art seen)
With thund'ring voice, and threat'ning mien,
   With screaming Horror's fun'ral cry,
Despair, and fell Disease, and ghastly Poverty:

Thy form benign, oh goddess, wear,
   Thy milder influence impart,

Thy philosophic train be there
  To soften, not to wound, my heart.
The gen'rous spark extinct revive
Teach me to love, and to forgive,
Exact my own defects to scan,
What others are to feel, and know myself a Man.

THE PROGRESS OF POESY

A PINDARIC ODE

Φωνᾶντα συνετοῖσιν. ἐς
Δὲ τὸ πᾶν ἑρμηνέων
Χατίζει.—PINDAR, Ol. ii. v. 152.

I. 1.

AWAKE, Æolian lyre, awake,
And give to rapture all thy trembling strings.
From Helicon's harmonious springs
  A thousand rills their mazy progress take:
The laughing flowers that round them blow,
Drink life and fragrance as they flow.
Now the rich stream of music winds along,
Deep, majestic, smooth, and strong,
Thro' verdant vales, and Ceres' golden reign:
Now rolling down the steep amain,
Headlong, impetuous, see it pour;
The rocks and nodding groves rebellow to the roar.

I. 2.

  Oh! Sov'reign of the willing soul,
Parent of sweet and solemn-breathing airs,
Enchanting shell! the sullen Cares
  And frantic Passions hear thy soft controul.
On Thracia's hills the Lord of War
Has curb'd the fury of his car,
And dropt his thirsty lance at thy command.
Perching on the scept'red hand
Of Jove, thy magic lulls the feather'd king
With ruffled plumes and flagging wing:
Quench'd in dark clouds of slumber lie
The terror of his beak, and lightnings of his eye.

I. 3.

Thee the voice, the dance, obey,
Temper'd to thy warbled lay.
O'er Idalia's velvet-green
The rosy-crowned Loves are seen
On Cytherea's day;
With antic Sport, and blue-eyed Pleasures,
Frisking light in frolic measures;
Now pursuing, now retreating,
   Now in circling troops they meet:
To brisk notes in cadence beating,
   Glance their many-twinkling feet.
Slow melting strains their Queen's approach declare:
   Where'er she turns, the Graces homage pay.
With arm sublime, that float upon the air,
   In gliding state she wins her easy way:
O'er her warm cheek, and rising bosom, move
The bloom of young Desire and purple light of Love.

II. 1.

   Man's feeble race what ills await!
Labour, and Penury, the racks of Pain,
Disease, and Sorrow's weeping train,
   And Death, sad refuge from the storms of fate!
The fond complaint, my song, disprove,
And justify the laws of Jove.
Say, has he giv'n in vain the heav'nly Muse?
Night and all her sickly dews,
Her spectres wan, and birds of boding cry,
He gives to range the dreary sky;
Till down the eastern cliffs afar
Hyperion's march they spy, and glitt'ring shafts of war.

II. 2.

   In climes beyond the solar road,
Where shaggy forms o'er ice-built mountains roam,
The Muse has broke the twilight gloom
   To cheer the shivering native's dull abode.
And oft, beneath the od'rous shade
Of Chili's boundless forests laid,

She deigns to hear the savage youth repeat,
In loose numbers wildly sweet,
Their feather-cinctur'd chiefs, and dusky loves.
Her track, where'er the goddess roves,
Glory pursue, and gen'rous Shame,
Th' unconquerable Mind, and freedom's holy flame.

II. 3.

Woods, that wave o'er Delphi's steep,
Isles, that crown th' Ægean deep,
     Fields, that cool Ilissus laves,
     Or where Mæander's amber waves
In lingering lab'rinths creep,
     How do your tuneful echoes languish,
     Mute, but to the voice of anguish!
Where each old poetic mountain
     Inspiration breath'd around;
Ev'ry shade and hallow'd fountain
     Murmur'd deep a solemn sound:
Till the sad Nine, in Greece's evil hour,
     Left their Parnassus for the Latian plains.
Alike they scorn the pomp of tyrant Power,
     And coward Vice, that revels in her chains.
When Latium had her lofty spirit lost,
They sought, oh Albion! next thy sea-encircled coast.

III. I.

Far from the sun and summer-gale,
In thy green lap was Nature's Darling laid,
     What time, where lucid Avon stray'd,
     To him the mighty mother did unveil
Her awful face: the dauntless child
Stretch'd forth his little arms and smil'd,
" This pencil take (she said), whose colours clear
Richly paint the vernal year:
Thine too these golden keys, immortal Boy!
This can unlock the gates of joy;
Of horror that, and thrilling fears,
Or ope the sacred source of sympathetic tears."

III. 2.

Nor second He, that rode sublime
Upon the seraph-wings of Extasy,

The secrets of th' abyss to spy.
　He pass'd the flaming bounds of place and time:
The living throne, the sapphire blaze,
Where angels tremble while they gaze,
He saw; but, blasted with excess of light,
Clos'd his eyes in endless night.
Behold, where Dryden's less presumptuous car,
Wide o'er the fields of glory bear
Two coursers of ethereal race,
With necks in thunder cloth'd, and long-resounding pace.

III. 3.

　Hark, his hands the lyre explore!
Bright-eyed Fancy, hov'ring o'er,
Scatters from her pictur'd urn
Thoughts that breathe, and words that burn.
But ah! 'tis heard no more—
　Oh! lyre divine, what daring spirit
　Wakes thee now? Tho' he inherit
Nor the pride, nor ample pinion,
　That the Theban eagle bear,
Sailing with supreme dominion
　Thro' the azure deep of air:
Yet oft before his infant eyes would run
　Such forms as glitter in the Muse's ray,
With orient hues, unborrow'd of the sun:
　Yet shall he mount, and keep his distant way
Beyond the limits of a vulgar fate,
Beneath the Good how far——but far above the Great.

THE BARD

A PINDARIC ODE

I. I.

" Ruin seize thee, ruthless King!
　Confusion on thy banners wait;
Tho' fann'd by Conquest's crimson wing,
　They mock the air with idle state.
Helm, nor hauberk's twisted mail,
Nor e'en thy virtues, Tyrant, shall avail

To save thy secret soul from nightly fears,
　　From Cambria's curse, from Cambria's tears!"
Such were the sounds that o'er the crested pride
　　Of the first Edward scatter'd wild dismay,
As down the steep of Snowdon's shaggy side
　　He wound with toilsome march his long array.
Stout Glo'ster stood aghast in speechless trance:
"To arms!" cried Mortimer, and couch'd his quiv'ring
　　lance.

I. 2.

On a rock, whose haughty brow
Frowns o'er cold Conway's foaming flood,
　　Robed in the sable garb of woe,
With haggard eyes the poet stood;
(Loose his beard, and hoary hair
Stream'd, like a meteor, to the troubled air)
And with a master's hand, and prophet's fire,
Struck the deep sorrows of his lyre.
　　" Hark, how each giant-oak, and desert cave,
Sighs to the torrent's awful voice beneath!
O'er thee, oh King! their hundred arms they wave,
　　Revenge on thee in hoarser murmurs breathe;
Vocal no more, since Cambria's fatal day,
To high-born Hoel's harp, or soft Llewellyn's lay.

I. 3.

" Cold is Cadwallo's tongue,
　　That hush'd the stormy main:
Brave Urien sleeps upon his craggy bed:
　　Mountains, ye mourn in vain
　　Modred, whose magic song
Made huge Plinlimmon bow his cloud-topt head.
　　On dreary Arvon's shore they lie,
Smear'd with gore, and ghastly pale:
Far, far aloof th' affrighted ravens sail;
　　The famish'd eagle screams, and passes by.
Dear lost companions of my tuneful art,
　　Dear as the light that visits these sad eyes,
Dear as the ruddy drops that warm my heart,
　　Ye died amidst your dying country's cries—
No more I weep.　They do not sleep.

On yonder cliffs, a griesly band,
I see them sit, they linger yet,
   Avengers of their native land:
With me in dreadful harmony they join,
And weave with bloody hands the tissue of thy line.

II. I.

  " Weave the warp, and weave the woof,
The winding-sheet of Edward's race.
   Give ample room, and verge enough
The characters of hell to trace.
Mark the year, and mark the night,
When Severn shall re-echo with affright
The shrieks of death, thro' Berkley's roof that ring,
Shrieks of an agonising king!
   She-wolf of France, with unrelenting fangs,
That tear'st the bowels of thy mangled mate,
   From thee be born, who o'er thy country hangs
The scourge of heav'n.   What terrors round him wait!
Amazement in his van, with flight combin'd,
And sorrow's faded form, and solitude behind.

II. 2.

  " Mighty victor, mighty lord!
Low on his funeral couch he lies!
   No pitying heart, no eye, afford
A tear to grace his obsequies.
   Is the sable warrior fled?
Thy son is gone.   He rests among the dead.
The swarm, that in thy noontide beam were born?
Gone to salute the rising morn.
Fair laughs the morn, and soft the zephyr blows,
   While proudly riding o'er the azure realm
In gallant trim the gilded vessel goes;
   Youth on the prow, and Pleasure at the helm;
Regardless of the sweeping whirlwind's sway,
That, hush'd in grim repose, expects his ev'ning prey.

II. 3.

  " Fill high the sparkling bowl,
The rich repast prepare,
   Reft of a crown, he yet may share the feast:
Close by the regal chair

Fell Thirst and Famine scowl
A baleful smile upon their baffled guest.
Heard ye the din of battle bray,
Lance to lance, and horse to horse?
Long years of havock urge their destined course,
And thro' the kindred squadrons mow their way.
Ye towers of Julius, London's lasting shame,
With many a foul and midnight murder fed,
Revere his consort's faith, his father's fame,
And spare the meek usurper's holy head.
Above, below, the rose of snow,
Twin'd with her blushing foe, we spread:
The bristled boar in infant-gore
Wallows beneath the thorny shade.
Now, brothers, bending o'er the accursed loom,
Stamp we our vengeance deep, and ratify his doom.

III. 1.

" Edward, lo! to sudden fate
(Weave we the woof.   The thread is spun.)
Half of thy heart we consecrate.
(The web is wove.   The work is done.)
Stay, oh stay! nor thus forlorn
Leave me unbless'd, unpitied, here to mourn:
In yon bright track, that fires the western skies,
They melt, they vanish from my eyes.
But oh! what solemn scenes on Snowdon's height
Descending slow their glittering skirts unroll?
Visions of glory, spare my aching sight!
Ye unborn ages, crowd not on my soul!
No more our long-lost Arthur we bewail.
All hail, ye genuine kings, Britannia's issue, hail!

III. 2.

" Girt with many a baron bold
Sublime their starry fronts they rear;
And gorgeous dames, and statesmen old
In bearded majesty, appear.
In the midst a form divine!
Her eye proclaims her of the Briton-line;
Her lion-port, her awe-commanding face,
Attemper'd sweet to virgin-grace.

What strings symphonious tremble in the air,
  What strains of vocal transport round her play.
Hear from the grave, great Taliessin, hear;
  They breathe a soul to animate thy clay.
Bright Rapture calls, and soaring as she sings,
Waves in the eye of heav'n her many-colour'd wings.

III. 3.

" The verse adorn again
  Fierce war, and faithful love,
And truth severe, by fairy fiction drest.
  In buskin'd measures move
Pale grief, and pleasing pain,
With horror, tyrant of the throbbing breast.
  A voice, as of the cherub-choir,
Gales from blooming Eden bear;
And distant warblings lessen on my ear,
  That lost in long futurity expire.
Fond impious man, think'st thou yon sanguine cloud,
  Rais'd by thy breath, has quench'd the orb of day?
To-morrow he repairs the golden flood,
  And warms the nations with redoubled ray.
Enough for me; with joy I see
  The diff'rent doom our fates assign.
Be thine despair, and scept'red care,
  To triumph, and to die, are mine."
He spoke, and headlong from the mountain's height
Deep in the roaring tide he plunged to endless night.

ODE FOR MUSIC

(IRREGULAR)

This Ode was performed in the Senate-House at Cambridge,
July 1, 1769, at the Installation of His Grace Augustus-Henry
Fitzroy, Duke of Grafton, Chancellor of the University. (This
Ode is printed with the divisions adopted by the Composer, Dr.
Randall, then Professor of Music at Cambridge. On Dr. Burney's
disappointment that he did not set this Ode to music, see Miss
Burney's *Mem.* i. 212; and Cradock's *Mem.* i. p. 107.)

I. AIR

" HENCE, avaunt ('tis holy ground),
  Comus, and his midnight-crew,
And Ignorance with looks profound,
  And dreaming Sloth of pallid hue,

Mad Sedition's cry profane,
Servitude that hugs her chain,
Nor in these consecrated bowers,
Let painted Flatt'ry hide her serpent-train in flowers.

CHORUS

" Nor Envy base, nor creeping Gain,
Dare the Muse's walk to stain,
While bright-eyed Science watches round:
Hence, away, 'tis holy ground!"

II. RECITATIVE

From yonder realms of empyrean day
　　Bursts on my ear th' indignant lay:
There sit the sainted sage, the bard divine,
　　The few, whom genius gave to shine
Thro' every unborn age, and undiscover'd clime.
　　Rapt in celestial transport they:
　　Yet hither oft a glance from high
　　They send of tender sympathy
To bless the place, where on their opening soul
　　First the genuine ardour stole.
'Twas Milton struck the deep-ton'd shell,
And, as the choral warblings round him swell,
Meek Newton's self bends from his state sublime
And nods his hoary head, and listens to the rhyme.

III. AIR

" Ye brown o'er-arching groves,
　　That contemplation loves,
Where willowy Camus lingers with delight!
　　Oft at the blush of dawn
　　I trod your level lawn,
Oft woo'd the gleam of Cynthia silver-bright
In cloisters dim, far from the haunts of Folly,
With Freedom by my side, and soft-eyed Melancholy."

IV. RECITATIVE

But hark! the portals sound, and pacing forth
    With solemn steps and slow,
High potentates, and dames of royal birth,
And mitred fathers in long order go:
Great Edward, with the lilies on his brow
    From haughty Gallia torn,
And sad Chatillon, on her bridal morn
That wept her bleeding Love, and princely Clare,
And Anjou's heroine, and the paler rose,
The rival of her crown and of her woes,
    And either Henry there,
The murder'd saint, and the majestic lord,
    That broke the bonds of Rome.
    (Their tears, their little triumphs o'er,
   Their human passions now no more,
Save Charity, that glows beyond the tomb.)

ACCOMPANIED

All that on Granta's fruitful plain
    Rich streams of regal bounty pour'd,
And bad these awful fanes and turrets rise,
To hail their Fitzroy's festal morning come;
    And thus they speak in soft accord
    The liquid language of the skies:

V. QUARTETTO

" What is grandeur, what is power?
    Heavier toil, superior pain.
    What the bright reward we gain?
    The grateful memory of the good.
    Sweet is the breath of vernal shower,
    The bee's collected treasures sweet,
    Sweet music's melting fall, but sweeter yet
    The still small voice of gratitude."

VI. RECITATIVE

Foremost and leaning from her golden cloud
    The venerable Marg'ret see!
   *B 628

" Welcome, my noble son (she cries aloud),
　To this, thy kindred train, and me:
Pleas'd in thy lineaments we trace
A Tudor's fire, a Beaufort's grace.

AIR

" Thy liberal heart, thy judging eye,
The flow'r unheeded shall descry,
And bid it round heav'n's altars shed
The fragrance of its blushing head:
Shall raise from earth the latent gem
To glitter on the diadem.

VII. RECITATIVE

" Lo! Granta waits to lead her blooming band,
　Not obvious, not obtrusive, she
No vulgar praise, no venal incense flings;
　Nor dares with courtly tongue refin'd
Profane thy inborn royalty of mind:
　She reveres herself and thee.
With modest pride to grace thy youthful brow,
The laureate wreath, that Cecil wore, she brings,
　And to thy just, thy gentle hand,
　Submits the fasces of her sway,
While spirits blest above and men below
Join with glad voice the loud symphonious lay.

VIII. GRAND CHORUS

" Thro' the wild waves as they roar,
　With watchful eye and dauntless mien,
　Thy steady course of honour keep,
Nor fear the rocks, nor seek the shore:
　The star of Brunswick smiles serene,
　And gilds the horrors of the deep."

THE FATAL SISTERS

AN ODE.   FROM THE NORSE TONGUE

To be found in the *Orcades* of Thormodus Torfæus; Hafniæ, 1697, folio; and also in Bartholinus, p. 617, lib. iii. c. 1, 4to. (The song of the " Weird Sisters," translated from the Norwegian, written about 1029. Wharton MS.)

Vitt er orpit fyrir valfalli, etc.

In the eleventh century, *Sigurd*, earl of the Orkney Islands, went with a fleet of ships and a considerable body of troops into Ireland, to the assistance of *Sictryg with the Silken Beard*, who was then making war on his father-in-law, *Brian*, king of Dublin. The earl and all his forces were cut to pieces, and *Sictryg* was in danger of a total defeat; but the enemy had a greater loss by the death of *Brian* their king, who fell in the action. On Christmas day (the day of the battle), a native of Caithness in Scotland, of the name of Darrud, saw at a distance a number of persons on horseback riding full speed towards a hill, and seeming to enter into it. Curiosity led him to follow them, till looking through an opening in the rocks, he saw twelve gigantic figures resembling women. They were all employed about a loom, and as they wove, they sung the following dreadful song, which when they had finished, they tore the web into twelve pieces, and (each taking her portion) galloped six to the north, and as many to the south. These were the *Valkyriur*, female divinities, Parcæ Militares, servants of *Odin* (or *Woden*) in the Gothic mythology. Their name signifies *Chusers of the Slain*. They were mounted on swift horses, with drawn swords in their hands; and in the throng of battle selected such as were destined to slaughter, and conducted them to *Valhalla*, the hall of *Odin*, or paradise of the brave; where they attended the banquet, and served the departed heroes with horns of mead and ale. Their numbers are not agreed upon, some authors representing them as *six*, some as *four*. See " Magni Beronii diss. de Eddis Islandicis," p. 145, in Ælrichs' *Dan et Sued lit. opuscula*, vol. i.

Now the storm begins to lower
    (Haste, the loom of hell prepare),
Iron sleet of arrowy shower
    Hurtles in the darken'd air.

Glitt'ring lances are the loom,
    Where the dusky warp we strain,
Weaving many a soldier's doom,
    Orkney's woe, and Randver's bane.

See the griesly texture grow!
    ('Tis of human entrails made)
And the weights, that play below,
    Each a gasping warrior's head.

Shafts for shuttles, dipt in gore,
  Shoot the trembling cords along.
Sword, that once a monarch bore,
  Keep the tissue close and strong.

Mista, black terrific maid,
  Sangrida, and Hilda, see,
Join the wayward work to aid:
  'Tis the woof of victory.

Ere the ruddy sun be set,
  Pikes must shiver, javelins sing,
Blade with clattering buckler meet,
  Hauberk crash, and helmet ring.

(Weave the crimson web of war)
  Let us go, and let us fly,
Where our friends the conflict share,
  Where they triumph, where they die.

As the paths of fate we tread,
  Wading through th' ensanguin'd field,
Gondula, and Geira, spread
  O'er the youthful king your shield.

We the reins to slaughter give,
  Ours to kill, and ours to spare:
Spite of danger he shall live.
  (Weave the crimson web of war.)

They, whom once the desert-beach
  Pent within its bleak domain,
Soon their ample sway shall stretch
  O'er the plenty of the plain.

Low the dauntless earl is laid,
  Gor'd with many a gaping wound:
Fate demands a nobler head;
  Soon a king shall bite the ground.

Long his loss shall Eirin weep,
  Ne'er again his likeness see;
Long her strains in sorrow steep:
  Strains of immortality!

Horror covers all the heath,
   Clouds of carnage blot the sun.
Sisters, weave the web of death;
   Sisters, cease; the work is done.

Hail the task, and hail the hands!
   Songs of joy and triumph sing!
Joy to the victorious bands;
   Triumph to the younger king.

Mortal, thou that hear'st the tale,
   Learn the tenour of our song.
Scotland, thro' each winding vale
   Far and wide the notes prolong.

Sisters, hence with spurs of speed:
   Each her thundering faulchion wield;
Each bestride her sable steed.
   Hurry, hurry to the field!

THE VEGTAM'S KIVITHA

OR THE DESCENT OF ODIN

AN ODE.   FROM THE NORSE TONGUE

The original is to be found in Sæmund's *Edda*, and in Bartholinus'
De Causis contemnendæ Mortis ; Hafniæ, 1689, quarto, lib. iii. c. ii.
p. 632. (See Warton, *Hist. of E. Poetry*, vol. i. p. xli. and **Warton's**
Pope, vol. ii. p. 70. " This Ode, I think with Lord Orford, equal
to any of Gray's.")

Upreis Odinn allda gautr, etc.

UPROSE the king of men with speed,
And saddled straight his coal-black steed;
Down the yawning steep he rode,
That leads to Hela's drear abode.
Him the dog of darkness spied;
His shaggy throat he open'd wide
(While from his jaws, with carnage fill'd,
Foam and human gore distill'd):
Hoarse he bays with hideous din,
Eyes that glow, and fangs that grin:

And long pursues with fruitless yell,
The father of the powerful spell.
Onward still his way he takes
(The groaning earth beneath him shakes),
Till full before his fearless eyes
The portals nine of hell arise.

Right against the eastern gate,
By the moss-grown pile he sate;
Where long of yore to sleep was laid
The dust of the prophetic maid.
Facing to the northern clime,
Thrice he trac'd the Runic rhyme;
Thrice pronounc'd, in accents dread,
The thrilling verse that wakes the dead:
Till from out the hollow ground
Slowly breath'd a sullen sound.

PROPHETESS

What call unknown, what charms presume
To break the quiet of the tomb?
Who thus afflicts my troubled sprite,
And drags me from the realms of night?
Long on these mould'ring bones have beat
The winter's snow, the summer's heat,
The drenching dews, and driving rain!
Let me, let me sleep again.
Who is he, with voice unblest,
That calls me from the bed of rest?

ODIN

A traveller, to thee unknown,
Is he that calls, a warrior's son.
Thou the deeds of light shalt know;
Tell me what is done below,
For whom yon glitt'ring board is spread,
Dress'd for whom yon golden bed?

PROPHETESS

Mantling in the goblet see
The pure bev'rage of the bee:

O'er it hangs the shield of gold;
'Tis the drink of Balder bold:
Balder's head to death is giv'n.
Pain can reach the sons of heav'n!
Unwilling I my lips unclose:
Leave me, leave me to repose.

ODIN

Once again my call obey,
Prophetess, arise, and say,
What dangers Odin's child await,
Who the author of his fate?

PROPHETESS

In Hoder's hand the hero's doom;
His brother sends him to the tomb.
Now my weary lips I close:
Leave me, leave me to repose.

ODIN

Prophetess, my spell obey,
Once again arise, and say,
Who th' avenger of his guilt,
By whom shall Hoder's blood be spilt?

PROPHETESS

In the caverns of the west,
By Odin's fierce embrace comprest,
A wond'rous boy shall Rinda bear,
Who ne'er shall comb his raven-hair,
Nor wash his visage in the stream,
Nor see the sun's departing beam,
Till he on Hoder's corse shall smile
Flaming on the fun'ral pile.
Now my weary lips I close:
Leave me, leave me to repose.

ODIN

Yet a while my call obey;
Prophetess, awake, and say,
What virgins these, in speechless woe,
That bend to earth their solemn brow,

That their flaxen tresses tear,
And snowy veils that float in air?
Tell me whence their sorrows rose:
Then I leave thee to repose.

PROPHETESS

Ha! no traveller art thou,
King of men, I know thee now;
Mightiest of a mighty line——

ODIN

No boding maid of skill divine
Art thou, nor prophetess of good;
But mother of the giant brood!

PROPHETESS

Hie thee hence, and boast at home,
That never shall enquirer come
To break my iron-sleep again;
Till Lok has burst his tenfold chain;
Never, till substantial night
Has reassum'd her ancient right;
Till wrapt in flames, in ruin hurl'd,
Sinks the fabric of the world.

THE TRIUMPHS OF OWEN

A FRAGMENT. FROM THE WELSH

From Evans' *Spec. of the Welsh Poetry*, 1764, quarto, p. 25,
where is a prose version of this poem, and p. 127. Owen succeeded
his father Griffith app Cynan in the principality of N. Wales, A.D.
1137. This battle was fought in the year 1157. Jones, *Relics*,
vol. ii. p. 36.

Owen's praise demands my song,
Owen swift, and Owen strong;
Fairest flower of Roderic's stem,
Gwyneth's shield, and Britain's gem.

He nor heaps his brooded stores,
Nor on all profusely pours;
Lord of every regal art,
Liberal hand, and open heart.
Big with hosts of mighty name,
Squadrons three against him came;
This the force of Eirin hiding,
Side by side as proudly riding,
On her shadow long and gay
Lochlin plows the wat'ry way;
There the Norman sails afar
Catch the winds and join the war:
Black and huge along they sweep,
Burthens of the angry deep.

Dauntless on his native sands
The dragon-son of Mona stands;
In glitt'ring arms and glory drest,
High he rears his ruby crest.
There the thund'ring strokes begin,
There the press, and there the din;
Talymalfra's rocky shore
Echoing to the battle's roar.
Check'd by the torrent-tide of blood,
Backward Meinai rolls his flood;
While, heap'd his master's feet around,
Prostrate warriors gnaw the ground.
Where his glowing eye-balls turn,
Thousand banners round him burn:
Where he points his purple spear,
Hasty, hasty rout is there,
Marking with indignant eye
Fear to stop, and shame to fly.
There confusion, terror's child,
Conflict fierce, and ruin wild,
Agony, that pants for breath,
Despair and honourable death.

.   .   .   .   .

THE DEATH OF HOEL

AN ODE. SELECTED FROM THE "GODODIN"

See S. Turner's *Vindication of Ancient British Poems*, p. 50;
Warton's *Engl. Poetry*, vol. i. p. lxiii.

HAD I but the torrent's might,
With headlong rage and wild affright
Upon Deïra's squadrons hurl'd
To rush, and sweep them from the world!
　　Too, too secure in youthful pride,
By them, my friend, my Hoel, died,
Great Cian's son: of Madoc old
He ask'd no heaps of hoarded gold;
Alone in nature's wealth array'd,
He ask'd and had the lovely maid.

　　To Cattraeth's vale in glitt'ring row
Thrice two hundred warriors go:
Every warrior's manly neck
Chains of regal honour deck,
Wreath'd in many a golden link:
From the golden cup they drink
Nectar that the bees produce,
Or the grape's extatic juice.
Flush'd with mirth and hope they burn:
But none from Cattraeth's vale return,
Save Aëron brave, and Conan strong,
(Bursting through the bloody throng)
And I, the meanest of them all,
That live to weep and sing their fall.

　　Have ye seen the tusky boar,
Or the bull, with sullen roar,
On surrounding foes advance?
So Caràdoc bore his lance.

　　Conan's name, my lay, rehearse,
Build to him the lofty verse,
Sacred tribute of the bard,
Verse, the hero's sole reward.

As the flame's devouring force;
As the whirlwind in its course;
As the thunder's fiery stroke,
Glancing on the shiver'd oak;
Did the sword of Conan mow
The crimson harvest of the foe.

SONNET

ON THE DEATH OF MR. RICHARD WEST

See *W. S. Landori Poemata*, p. 186.

In vain to me the smiling mornings shine,
  And redd'ning Phœbus lifts his golden fire:
The birds in vain their amorous descant join;
  Or cheerful fields resume their green attire:
These ears, alas! for other notes repine
  A different object do these eyes require:
My lonely anguish melts no heart but mine;
  And in my breast the imperfect joys expire.
Yet morning smiles the busy race to cheer,
  And new-born pleasure brings to happier men:
The fields to all their wonted tribute bear:
  To warm their little loves the birds complain:
I fruitless mourn to him that cannot hear,
  And weep the more, because I weep in vain.

EPITAPH ON MRS. JANE CLARKE

See Woty's *Poetical Calendar*, part viii. p. 121; Nicoll's *Select Poems*, vol. vii. p. 331.
  This lady, the wife of Dr. John Clarke, physician at Epsom, died April 27, 1757, and was buried in the church of Beckenham, Kent.

Lo! where this silent marble weeps,
A friend, a wife, a mother sleeps:
A heart, within whose sacred cell
The peaceful virtues lov'd to dwell.
Affection warm, and faith sincere,
And soft humanity were there.
In agony, in death resign'd,
She felt the wound she left behind,

Her infant image here below,
Sits smiling on a father's woe:
Whom what awaits, while yet he strays
Along the lonely vale of days?
A pang, to secret sorrow dear;
A sigh; an unavailing tear;
Till time shall every grief remove,
With life, with memory, and with love.

EPITAPH ON SIR WILLIAM WILLIAMS

This Epitaph was written at the request of Mr. Frederick Montagu, who intended to have inscribed it on a monument at Bellisle, at the siege of which Sir W. Williams was killed, 1761. See Mason's *Memoirs*, vol. i. p. 73; and vol. iv. p. 76, and H. Walpole's Lett. to G. Montagu, p. 244. See account of Sir W. P. Williams, in Brydges' *Restituta*, vol. iii. p. 53; and in *Clubs of London*, vol. ii. p. 13. " In the recklessness of a desponding mind, he approached too near the enemy's sentinels, and was shot through the body."

" Valiant in arms, courteous and gay in peace,
See *Williams* snatch'd to an untimely tomb."
HALL STEVENSON'S *Poems*, ii. p. 49.

HERE, foremost in the dangerous paths of fame,
  Young Williams fought for England's fair renown;
His mind each Muse, each Grace adorn'd his frame,
  Nor envy dar'd to view him with a frown.

At Aix, his voluntary sword he drew,
  There first in blood his infant honour seal'd;
From fortune, pleasure, science, love, he flew,
  And scorn'd repose when Britain took the field.

With eyes of flame, and cool undaunted breast,
  Victor he stood on Bellisle's rocky steeps—
Ah, gallant youth! this marble tells the rest,
  Where melancholy friendship bends, and weeps.

ELEGY WRITTEN IN A COUNTRY CHURCH-YARD

THE curfew tolls the knell of parting day,
  The lowing herd winds slowly o'er the lea,
The ploughman homeward plods his weary way,
  And leaves the world to darkness and to me.

Now fades the glimmering landscape on the sight,
  And all the air a solemn stillness holds,
Save where the beetle wheels his droning flight,
  And drowsy tinklings lull the distant folds:

Save that from yonder ivy-mantled tow'r,
  The moping owl does to the moon complain
Of such as, wand'ring near her secret bow'r,
  Molest her ancient solitary reign.

Beneath those rugged elms, that yew-tree's shade,
  Where heaves the turf in many a mould'ring heap,
Each in his narrow cell for ever laid,
  The rude forefathers of the hamlet sleep.

The breezy call of incense-breathing morn,
  The swallow twitt'ring from the straw-built shed,
The cock's shrill clarion, or the echoing horn,
  No more shall rouse them from their lowly bed.

For them no more the blazing hearth shall burn,
  Or busy housewife ply her evening care;
No children run to lisp their sire's return,
  Or climb his knees the envied kiss to share.

Oft did the harvest to their sickle yield,
  Their furrow oft the stubborn glebe has broke:
How jocund did they drive their team afield!
  How bow'd the woods beneath their sturdy stroke!

Let not ambition mock their useful toil,
  Their homely joys, and destiny obscure;
Nor grandeur hear with a disdainful smile
  The short and simple annals of the poor.

The boast of heraldry, the pomp of pow'r,
  And all that beauty, all that wealth e'er gave,
Awaits alike th' inevitable hour.
  The paths of glory lead but to the grave.

Nor you, ye proud, impute to these the fault,
  If memory o'er their tomb no trophies raise,
Where through the long-drawn aisle and fretted vault
  The pealing anthem swells the note of praise.

Can storied urn, or animated bust,
    Back to its mansion call the fleeting breath?
Can honour's voice provoke the silent dust,
    Or flatt'ry soothe the dull cold ear of death?

Perhaps in this neglected spot is laid
    Some heart once pregnant with celestial fire;
Hands, that the rod of empire might have sway'd,
    Or wak'd to extasy the living lyre.

But knowledge to their eyes her ample page
    Rich with the spoils of time did ne'er unroll;
Chill penury repress'd their noble rage,
    And froze the genial current of the soul.

Full many a gem of purest ray serene
    The dark unfathom'd caves of ocean bear:
Full many a flower is born to blush unseen,
    And waste its sweetness on the desert air.

Some village Hampden, that, with dauntless breast,
    The little tyrant of his fields withstood,
Some mute inglorious Milton here may rest,
    Some Cromwell guiltless of his country's blood.

Th' applause of list'ning senates to command,
    The threats of pain and ruin to despise,
To scatter plenty o'er a smiling land,
    And read their history in a nation's eyes,

Their lot forbad: nor circumscrib'd alone
    Their growing virtues, but their crimes confined;
Forbad to wade thro' slaughter to a throne,
    And shut the gates of mercy on mankind,

The struggling pangs of conscious truth to hide,
    To quench the blushes of ingenuous shame,
Or heap the shrine of luxury and pride
    With incense kindled at the Muse's flame.

Far from the madding crowd's ignoble strife,
    Their sober wishes never learn'd to stray;
Along the cool sequester'd vale of life
    They kept the noiseless tenour of their way.

Yet ev'n these bones from insult to protect
   Some frail memorial still erected nigh,
With uncouth rhymes and shapeless sculpture deck'd,
   Implores the passing tribute of a sigh.

Their name, their years, spelt by th' unletter'd Muse,
   The place of fame and elegy supply:
And many a holy text around she strews,
   That teach the rustic moralist to die.

For who, to dumb forgetfulness a prey,
   This pleasing anxious being e'er resign'd,
Left the warm precincts of the cheerful day,
   Nor cast one longing ling'ring look behind?

On some fond breast the parting soul relies,
   Some pious drops the closing eye requires;
E'en from the tomb the voice of nature cries,
   E'en in our ashes live their wonted fires.

For thee, who, mindful of th' unhonour'd dead,
   Dost in these lines their artless tale relate;
If chance, by lonely contemplation led,
   Some kindred spirit shall enquire thy fate,—

Haply some hoary-headed swain may say,
   " Oft have we seen him at the peep of dawn
Brushing with hasty steps the dews away,
   To meet the sun upon the upland lawn.

" There at the foot of yonder nodding beech,
   That wreathes its old fantastic roots so high,
His listless length at noontide would he stretch,
   And pore upon the brook that babbles by.

" Hard by yon wood, now smiling as in scorn,
   Mutt'ring his wayward fancies he would rove;
Now drooping, woful-wan, like one forlorn,
   Or craz'd with care, or cross'd in hopeless love.

" One morn I miss'd him on the custom'd hill,
   Along the heath, and near his fav'rite tree;
Another came; nor yet beside the rill,
   Nor up the lawn, nor at the wood was he:

" The next, with dirges due in sad array
   Slow through the church-way path we saw him borne:—
Approach and read (for thou can'st read) the lay
   Grav'd on the stone beneath yon aged thorn."

THE EPITAPH

Here rests his head upon the lap of earth
   A youth, to fortune and to fame unknown:
Fair science frown'd not on his humble birth,
   And melancholy mark'd him for her own.

Large was his bounty, and his soul sincere,
   Heaven did a recompense as largely send:
He gave to mis'ry (all he had) a tear,
   He gain'd from heav'n ('twas all he wish'd) a friend.

No farther seek his merits to disclose,
   Or draw his frailties from their dread abode
(There they alike in trembling hope repose),
   The bosom of his Father and his God.

A LONG STORY

See Mason's *Memoirs*, vol. iii. p. 130, and Pennant's *Life*, p. 23.
Gray's " Elegy in a Country Churchyard," previous to its publication, was handed about in manuscript; and had amongst other
admirers the Lady Cobham, who resided at the mansion-house at
Stoke Pogeis. The performance inducing her to wish for the
author's acquaintance, her relation, Miss Speed, and Lady Schaub,
then at her house, undertook to effect it. These two ladies waited
upon the author at his aunt's solitary habitation, where he at that
time resided; and not finding him at home, they left a card behind
them. Mr. Gray, surprised at such a compliment, returned the
visit. And as the beginning of this acquaintance bore some
appearance of romance, he soon after gave a humorous account of
it in the following copy of verses, which he entitled " A Long
Story." Printed in 1753 with Mr. Bentley's designs, and repeated
in a second edition. MS.

IN Britain's isle, no matter where,
   An ancient pile of building stands:
The Huntingdons and Hattons there
   Employ'd the pow'r of fairy hands

To raise the ceiling's fretted height,
  Each pannel in achievements clothing,
Rich windows that exclude the light,
  And passages, that lead to nothing.

Full oft within the spacious walls,
  When he had fifty winters o'er him,
My grave Lord-Keeper led the brawls;
  The seals and maces danc'd before him.

His bushy beard, and shoe-strings green,
  His high-crown'd hat, and satin doublet,
Mov'd the stout heart of England's queen,
  Though Pope and Spaniard could not trouble it.

What, in the very first beginning!
  Shame of the versifying tribe!
Your hist'ry whither are you spinning!
  Can you do nothing but describe?

A house there is (and that's enough)
  From whence one fatal morning issues
A brace of warriors, not in buff,
  But rustling in their silks and tissues.

The first came cap-a-pee from France,
  Her conqu'ring destiny fulfilling,
Whom meaner beauties eye askance,
  And vainly ape her art of killing.

The other amazon kind heav'n
  Had arm'd with spirit, wit, and satire;
But Cobham had the polish giv'n,
  And tipp'd her arrows with good-nature.

To celebrate her eyes, her air—
  Coarse panegyrics would but tease her;
Melissa is her " nom de guerre."
  Alas, who would not wish to please her!

With bonnet blue and capuchine,
  And aprons long, they hid their armour;
And veil'd their weapons, bright and keen,
  In pity to the country farmer.

Fame, in the shape of Mr. P—t
   (By this time all the parish know it),
Had told that thereabouts there lurk'd
   A wicked imp they call a poet:

Who prowl'd the country far and near,
   Bewitch'd the children of the peasants,
Dried up the cows, and lam'd the deer,
   And suck'd the eggs, and kill'd the pheasants.

My lady heard their joint petition,
   Swore by her coronet and ermine,
She'd issue out her high commission
   To rid the manor of such vermin.

The heroines undertook the task,
   Thro' lanes unknown, o'er stiles they ventur'd,
Rapp'd at the door, nor stay'd to ask,
   But bounce into the parlour enter'd.

The trembling family they daunt,
   They flirt, they sing, they laugh, they tattle,
Rummage his mother, pinch his aunt,
   And upstairs in a whirlwind rattle:

Each hole and cupboard they explore,
   Each creek and cranny of his chamber,
Run hurry-scurry round the floor,
   And o'er the bed and tester clamber;

Into the drawers and china pry,
   Papers and books, a huge imbroglio!
Under a tea-cup he might lie,
   Or creased, like dogs-ears, in a folio.

On the first marching of the troops,
   The Muses, hopeless of his pardon,
Convey'd him underneath their hoops
   To a small closet in the garden.

So rumour says (who will, believe);
   But that they left the door ajar,
Where, safe and laughing in his sleeve,
   He heard the distant din of war.

Short was his joy.   He little knew
  The pow'r of magic was no fable;
Out of the window, wisk, they flew,
  But left a spell upon the table.

The words too eager to unriddle,
  The poet felt a strange disorder;
Transparent bird-lime form'd the middle,
  And chains invisible the border.

So cunning was the apparatus,
  The powerful pot-hooks did so move him,
That, will he, nill he, to the great house
  He went, as if the devil drove him.

Yet on his way (no sign of grace,
  For folks in fear are apt to pray)
To Phœbus he preferr'd his case,
  And begg'd his aid that dreadful day.

The godhead would have back'd his quarrel;
  But with a blush, on recollection,
Own'd that his quiver and his laurel
  'Gainst four such eyes were no protection.

The court was sate, the culprit there,
  Forth from their gloomy mansions creeping,
The lady Janes and Joans repair,
  And from the gallery stand peeping:

Such as in silence of the night
  Come (sweep) along some winding entry
(Styack has often seen the sight),
  Or at the chapel-door stand sentry:

In peaked hoods and mantles tarnish'd,
  Sour visages, enough to scare ye,
High dames of honour once, that garnish'd
  The drawing-room of fierce Queen Mary.

The peeress comes.   The audience stare,
  And doff their hats with due submission:
She curtsies, as she takes her chair,
  To all the people of condition.

The bard, with many an artful fib,
    Had in imagination fenc'd him,
Disprov'd the arguments of Squib,
    And all that Groom could urge against him.

But soon his rhetoric forsook him,
    When he the solemn hall had seen;
A sudden fit of ague shook him,
    He stood as mute as poor Macleane.

Yet something he was heard to mutter,
    " How in the park beneath an old tree,
(Without design to hurt the butter
    Or any malice to the poultry),

" He once or twice had penn'd a sonnet;
    Yet hop'd, that he might save his bacon:
Numbers would give their oaths upon it,
    He ne'er was for a conj'rer taken."

The ghostly prudes with hagged face
    Already had condemn'd the sinner.
My lady rose, and with a grace—
    She smil'd, and bid him come to dinner.

" Jesu-Maria! Madam Bridget,
    Why, what can the Viscountess mean? "
(Cried the square-hoods in woful fidget)
    " The times are alter'd quite and clean!

" Decorum's turn'd to mere civility;
    Her air and all her manners show it.
Commend me to her affability!
    Speak to a commoner and poet! "

[Here five hundred stanzas are lost.]

And so God save our noble king,
    And guard us from long-winded lubbers,
That to eternity would sing,
    And keep my lady from her rubbers.

POSTHUMOUS POEMS AND FRAGMENTS

ODE ON THE PLEASURE ARISING FROM
VICISSITUDE

Now the golden morn aloft
    Waves her dew-bespangled wing,
With vermeil cheek and whisper soft
    She wooes the tardy spring:
Till April starts, and calls around
The sleeping fragrance from the ground;
And lightly o'er the living scene
Scatters his freshest, tenderest green.

New-born flocks, in rustic dance,
    Frisking ply their feeble feet;
Forgetful of their wintry trance
    The birds his presence greet:
But chief, the sky-lark warbles high
His trembling thrilling extasy;
And, lessening from the dazzled sight,
Melts into air and liquid light.

Rise, my soul! on wings of fire,
    Rise the rapt'rous choir among;
Hark! 'tis nature strikes the lyre,
    And leads the gen'ral song:
·   ·   ·   ·   ·   ·

Yesterday the sullen year
    Saw the snowy whirlwind fly;
Mute was the music of the air,
    The herd stood drooping by:
Their raptures now that wildly flow,
No yesterday nor morrow know;
'Tis man alone that joy descries
With forward, and reverted eyes.

Smiles on past misfortune's brow
    Soft reflection's hand can trace;
And o'er the cheek of sorrow throw
    A melancholy grace;

While hope prolongs our happier hour,
Or deepest shades, that dimly lower
And blacken round our weary way,
Gilds with a gleam of distant day.

Still, where rosy pleasure leads,
    See a kindred grief pursue;
Behind the steps that misery treads,
    Approaching comfort view:
The hues of bliss more brightly glow,
Chastis'd by sabler tints of woe;
And blended form, with artful strife,
The strength and harmony of life.

See the wretch, that long has tost
    On the thorny bed of pain,
At length repair his vigour lost,
    And breathe and walk again:
The meanest floweret of the vale,
The simplest note that swells the gale,
The common sun, the air, the skies,
To him are opening paradise.

Humble quiet builds her cell,
    Near the source whence pleasure flows;
She eyes the clear crystalline well,
    And tastes it as it goes.[1]

TRANSLATION OF A PASSAGE FROM STATIUS

Theb. lib. vi. ver. 704-724.

THIRD in the labours of the disc came on,
With sturdy step and slow, Hippomedon;
Artful and strong he pois'd the well-known weight
By Phlegyas warn'd, and fir'd by Mnestheus' fate,
That to avoid, and this to emulate.
His vigorous arm he tried before he flung,
Brac'd all his nerves, and every sinew strung;

[1] This ode was not completed, and the few fragments that were written of the concluding lines have been omitted.

To such a mother owes; the world, you gave him,
Suffices not to pay the obligation.
  I well remember too (for I was present)
When in a secret and dead hour of night,
Due sacrifice perform'd with barb'rous rites
Of mutter'd charms, and solemn invocation,
You bade the Magi call the dreadful powers,
That read futurity, to know the fate
Impending o'er your son: their answer was,
If the son reign, the mother perishes.
Perish (you cried) the mother! reign the son!
He reigns, the rest is heav'n's; who oft has bade,
Ev'n when its will seem'd wrote in lines of blood,
Th' unthought event disclose a whiter meaning.
Think too how oft in weak and sickly minds
The sweets of kindness lavishly indulg'd
Rankle to gall; and benefits too great
To be repaid, sit heavy on the soul,
As unrequited wrongs. The willing homage
Of prostrate Rome, the senate's joint applause,
The riches of the earth, the train of pleasures
That wait on youth, and arbitrary sway:
These were your gift, and with them you bestow'd
The very power he has to be ungrateful.
  AGRIP. Thus ever grave and undisturb'd reflection
Pours its cool dictates in the madding ear
Of rage, and thinks to quench the fire it feels not.
Say'st thou I must be cautious, must be silent,
And tremble at the phantom I have raised?
Carry to him thy timid counsels. He
Perchance may heed 'em: tell him too, that one
Who had such liberal power to give, may still
With equal power resume that gift, and raise
A tempest that shall shake her own creation
To its original atoms—tell me! say
This mighty emperor, this dreaded hero,
Has he beheld the glittering front of war?
Knows his soft ear the trumpet's thrilling voice,
And outcry of the battle? Have his limbs
Sweat under iron harness? Is he not
The silken son of dalliance, nurs'd in ease
And pleasure's flow'ry lap? Rubellius lives,
And Sylla has his friends, though school'd by fear

To bow the supple knee, and court the times
With shows of fair obeisance; and a call,
Like mine, might serve belike to wake pretensions
Drowsier than theirs, who boast the genuine blood
Of our imperial house.

    ACER. Did I not wish to check this dangerous passion,
I might remind my mistress that her nod
Can rouse eight hardy legions, wont to stem
With stubborn nerves the tide, and face the rigour
Of bleak Germania's snows.   Four, not less brave,
That in Armenia quell the Parthian force
Under the warlike Corbulo, by you
Mark'd for their leader: these, by ties confirm'd,
Of old respect and gratitude, are yours.
Surely the Masians too, and those of Egypt,
Have not forgot your sire: the eye of Rome,
And the Prætorian camp have long rever'd
With custom'd awe, the daughter, sister, wife,
And mother of their Cæsars.

    AGRIP.   Ha! by Juno,
It bears a noble semblance.   On this base
My great revenge shall rise; or say we sound
The trump of liberty; there will not want,
Even in the servile senate, ears to own
Her spirit-stirring voice; Soranus there,
And Cassius; Vetus too, and Thrasea,
Minds of the antique cast, rough, stubborn souls,
That struggle with the yoke.   How shall the spark
Unquenchable, that glows within their breasts,
Blaze into freedom, when the idle herd
(Slaves from the womb, created but to stare,
And bellow in the Circus) yet will start,
And shake 'em at the name of liberty,
Stung by a senseless word, a vain tradition,
As there were magic in it?   Wrinkled beldams
Teach it their grandchildren, as somewhat rare
That anciently appear'd, but when, extends
Beyond their chronicle—oh! 'tis a cause
To arm the hand of childhood, and rebrace
The slacken'd sinews of time-wearied age.

    Yes, we may meet, ungrateful boy, we may!
Again the buried Genius of old Rome
Shall from the dust uprear his reverend head,

Rous'd by the shout of millions: there before
His high tribunal thou and I appear.
Let majesty sit on thy awful brow,
And lighten from thy eye: around thee call
The gilded swarm that wantons in the sunshine
Of thy full favour; Seneca be there
In gorgeous phrase of labour'd eloquence
To dress thy plea, and Burrhus strengthen it
With his plain soldier's oath, and honest seeming.
Against thee, liberty and Agrippina:
The world, the prize; and fair befall the victors.

   But soft! why do I waste the fruitless hours
In threats unexecuted? Haste thee, fly
These hated walls that seem to mock my shame,
And cast me forth in duty to their lord.

   Acer. 'Tis time to go, the sun is high advanc'd,
And, ere mid-day, Nero will come to Baiæ.

   Agrip. My thought aches at him; not the basilisk
More deadly to the sight, than is to me
The cool injurious eye of frozen kindness.
I will not meet its poison. Let him feel
Before he sees me.

   Acer.   Why then stays my sovereign,
Where he so soon may—

   Agrip.   Yes, I will be gone,
But not to Antium—all shall be confess'd,
Whate'er the frivolous tongue of giddy fame
Has spread among the crowd; things, that but whisper'd
Have arch'd the hearer's brow, and riveted
His eyes in fearful extasy: no matter
What; so't be strange, and dreadful.—Sorceries,
Assassinations, poisonings—the deeper
My guilt, the blacker his ingratitude.

   And you, ye manes of ambition's victims,
Enshrined Claudius, with the pitied ghosts
Of the Syllani, doom'd to early death,
(Ye unavailing horrors, fruitless crimes!)
If from the realms of night my voice ye hear,
In lieu of penitence, and vain remorse,
Accept my vengeance. Though by me ye bled,
He was the cause. My love, my fears for him,
Dried the soft springs of pity in my heart,
And froze them up with deadly cruelty.

Yet if your injur'd shades demand my fate,
If murder cries for murder, blood for blood,
Let me not fall alone; but crush his pride,
And sink the traitor in his mother's ruin.   [*Exeunt*.

SCENE II. OTHO, POPPÆA

OTHO. Thus far we're safe. Thanks to the rosy queen
Of amorous thefts: and had her wanton son
Lent us his wings, we could not have beguil'd
With more elusive speed the dazzled sight
Of wakeful jealousy. Be gay securely;
Dispel, my fair, with smiles, the tim'rous cloud
That hangs on thy clear brow. So Helen look'd,
So her white neck reclin'd, so was she borne
By the young Trojan to his gilded bark
With fond reluctance, yielding modesty,
And oft reverted eye, as if she knew not
Whether she fear'd, or wish'd to be pursued.

.   .   .   .

HYMN TO IGNORANCE

A FRAGMENT

HAIL, horrors, hail! ye ever gloomy bowers,
Ye gothic fanes, and antiquated towers,
Where rushy Camus' slowly-winding flood
Perpetual draws his humid train of mud:
Glad I revisit thy neglected reign,
Oh take me to thy peaceful shade again.
But chiefly thee, whose influence breathed from high,
Augments the native darkness of the sky;
Ah, ignorance! soft salutary power!
Prostrate with filial reverence I adore.
Thrice hath Hyperion roll'd his annual race,
Since weeping I forsook thy fond embrace.
Oh say, successful dost thou still oppose
Thy leaden ægis 'gainst our ancient foes?
Still stretch, tenacious of thy right divine,

The massy sceptre o'er thy slumb'ring line?
And dews Lethean through the land dispense
To steep in slumbers each benighted sense?
If any spark of wit's delusive ray
Break out, and flash a momentary day,
With damp, cold touch forbid it to aspire,
And huddle up in fogs the dang'rous fire.

Oh say—she hears me not, but, careless grown,
Lethargic nods upon her ebon throne.
Goddess! awake, arise! alas, my fears!
Can powers immortal feel the force of years?
Not thus of old, with ensigns wide unfurl'd,
She rode triumphant o'er the vanquish'd world;
Fierce nations own'd her unresisted might,
And all was ignorance, and all was night.

Oh! sacred age! Oh! times for ever lost!
(The schoolman's glory, and the churchman's boast.)
For ever gone—yet still to fancy new,
Her rapid wings the transient scene pursue,
And bring the buried ages back to view.

High on her car, behold the grandam ride
Like old Sesostris with barbaric pride;
. . . a team of harness'd monarchs bend

.   .   .   . •

THE ALLIANCE OF
EDUCATION AND GOVERNMENT

A FRAGMENT

ESSAY I

Πόταγ', ὦ 'γαθέ· τὰν γὰρ ἀοιδὰν
Οὔτι πα εἰς Ἀίδαν γε τὸν ἐκλελάθοντα φυλαξεῖς.
THEOCRITUS, Id. I. 63.

As sickly plants betray a niggard earth,
Whose barren bosom starves her generous birth,
Nor genial warmth, nor genial juice retains,
Their roots to feed, and fill their verdant veins:
And as in climes, where winter holds his reign,
The soil, though fertile, will not teem in vain,

Forbids her gems to swell, her shades to rise,
Nor trusts her blossoms to the churlish skies:
So draw mankind in vain the vital airs,
Unform'd, unfriended, by those kindly cares,
That health and vigour to the soul impart,
Spread the young thought, and warm the opening heart:
So fond instruction on the growing powers
Of nature idly lavishes her stores,
If equal justice with unclouded face
Smile not indulgent on the rising race,
And scatter with a free, though frugal hand,
Light golden showers of plenty o'er the land:
But tyranny has fix'd her empire there,
To check their tender hopes with chilling fear,
And blast the vernal promise of the year.

   This spacious animated scene survey,
From where the rolling orb, that gives the day,
His sable sons with nearer course surrounds
To either pole, and life's remotest bounds,
How rude so e'er th' exterior form we find,
Howe'er opinion tinge the varied mind,
Alike to all, the kind, impartial heav'n
The sparks of truth and happiness has giv'n:
With sense to feel, with memory to retain,
They follow pleasure, and they fly from pain;
Their judgment mends the plan their fancy draws,
The event presages, and explores the cause;
The soft returns of gratitude they know,
By fraud elude, by force repel the foe;
While mutual wishes, mutual woes endear
The social smile, the sympathetic tear.

   Say, then, through ages by what fate confin'd
To different climes seem different souls assign'd?
Here measur'd laws and philosophic ease
Fix, and improve the polish'd arts of peace;
There industry and gain their vigils keep,
Command the winds, and tame th' unwilling deep:
Here force and hardy deeds of blood prevail;
There languid pleasure sighs in every gale.
Oft o'er the trembling nations from afar
Has Scythia breath'd the living cloud of war;
And, where the deluge burst, with sweepy sway
Their arms, their kings, their gods were roll'd away.

As oft have issued, host impelling host,
The blue-eyed myriads from the Baltic coast.
The prostrate south to the destroyer yields
Her boasted titles, and her golden fields:
With grim delight the brood of winter view
A brighter day, and heav'ns of azure hue;
Scent the new fragrance of the breathing rose,
And quaff the pendant vintage as it grows.
Proud of the yoke, and pliant to the rod,
Why yet does Asia dread a monarch's nod,
While European freedom still withstands
Th' encroaching tide that drowns her lessening lands;
And sees far off, with an indignant groan,
Her native plains, and empires once her own?
Can opener skies and suns of fiercer flame
O'erpower the fire, that animates our frame;
As lamps, that shed at eve a cheerful ray,
Fade and expire beneath the eye of day?
Need we the influence of the northern star
To string our nerves and steel our hearts to war?
And, where the face of nature laughs around,
Must sick'ning virtue fly the tainted ground?
Unmanly thought! what seasons can control,
What fancied zone can circumscribe the soul,
Who, conscious of the source from whence she springs,
By reason's light, on resolution's wings,
Spite of her frail companion, dauntless goes
O'er Libya's deserts and through Zembla's snows?
She bids each slumb'ring energy awake,
Another touch, another temper take,
Suspends th' inferior laws that rule our clay:
The stubborn elements confess her sway;
Their little wants, their low desires, refine,
And raise the mortal to a height divine.
  Not but the human fabric from the birth
Imbibes a flavour of its parent earth:
As various tracts enforce a various toil,
The manners speak the idiom of their soil.
An iron-race the mountain-cliffs maintain,
Foes to the gentler genius of the plain:
For where unwearied sinews must be found
With side-long plough to quell the flinty ground,
To turn the torrent's swift-descending flood,

To brave the savage rushing from the wood,
What wonder if to patient valour train'd,
They guard with spirit, what by strength they gain'd?
And while their rocky ramparts round they see,
The rough abode of want and liberty,
(As lawless force from confidence will grow)
Insult the plenty of the vales below?
What wonder, in the sultry climes, that spread
Where Nile redundant o'er his summer-bed
From his broad bosom life and verdure flings,
And broods o'er Egypt with his wat'ry wings,
If with advent'rous oar and ready sail
The dusky people drive before the gale;
Or on frail floats to neighb'ring cities ride,
That rise and glitter o'er the ambient tide

.   .   .   .

[The following couplet, which was intended to have been introduced in the poem on the " Alliance of Education and Government,"
is much too beautiful to be lost.   Mason, vol. iii. p. 114.]

When love could teach a monarch to be wise,
And gospel-light first dawn'd from Bullen's eyes.

STANZAS TO MR. BENTLEY

A FRAGMENT

See Mason's *Memoirs*, vol. iii. p. 148.

These were in compliment to Bentley, who drew a set of designs
for Gray's poems, particularly a head-piece to the " Long Story."
The original drawings are in the library at Strawberry Hill. See
H. Walpole's *Works*, vol. ii. p. 447.

IN silent gaze the tuneful choir among,
    Half pleas'd, half blushing, let the Muse admire,
While Bentley leads her sister-art along,
    And bids the pencil answer to the lyre.

See, in their course, each transitory thought
    Fix'd by his touch a lasting essence take;
Each dream, in fancy's airy colouring wrought
    To local symmetry and life awake!

The tardy rhymes that us'd to linger on,
    To censure cold, and negligent of fame,
In swifter measures animated run,
    And catch a lustre from his genuine flame,

Ah! could they catch his strength, his easy grace,
    His quick creation, his unerring line;
The energy of Pope they might efface,
    And Dryden's harmony submit to mine,

But not to one in this benighted age
    Is that diviner inspiration giv'n,
That burns in Shakespeare's or in Milton's page,
    The pomp and prodigality of heav'n.

As when conspiring in the diamond's blaze,
    The meaner gems that singly charm the sight,
Together dart their intermingled rays,
    And dazzle with a luxury of light.

Enough for me, if to some feeling breast
    My lines a secret sympathy " impart; "
And as their pleasing influence " flows confest,"
    A sigh of soft reflection " heaves the heart."

.   .   .   .

SKETCH OF HIS OWN CHARACTER

WRITTEN IN 1761, AND FOUND IN ONE OF HIS
POCKET-BOOKS

Too poor for a bribe, and too proud to importune;
He had not the method of making a fortune:
Could love, and could hate, so was thought somewhat
    odd;
No very great wit, he believed in a God:
A post or a pension he did not desire,
But left church and state to Charles Townshend and
    Squire.

AMATORY LINES

WITH beauty, with pleasure surrounded, to languish—
To weep without knowing the cause of my anguish:
To start from short slumbers, and wish for the morning—
To close my dull eyes when I see it returning;
Sighs sudden and frequent, looks ever dejected—
Words that steal from my tongue, by no meaning connected!
Ah! say, fellow-swains, how these symptoms befell me?
They smile, but reply not—Sure Delia will tell me!

SONG

THYRSIS, when we parted, swore
    Ere the spring he would return—
Ah! what means yon violet flower!
    And the bud that decks the thorn!
'Twas the lark that upward sprung!
'Twas the nightingale that sung!

Idle notes! untimely green!
    Why this unavailing haste?
Western gales and skies serene
    Speak not always winter past.
Cease, my doubts, my fears to move,
    Spare the honour of my love.

TOPHET

AN EPIGRAM

THUS Tophet look'd; so grinn'd the brawling fiend,
Whilst frighted prelates bow'd and call'd him friend.[1]
Our mother-church, with half-averted sight,
Blush'd as she blessed her griesly proselyte;
Hosannas rung through hell's tremendous borders,
And Satan's self had thoughts of taking orders.

[1] Mr. Gosse inserts two lines here, as follows:—

"I saw them bow, and while they wished him dead,
With servile simper nod the mitred head."

IMPROMPTU

SUGGESTED BY A VIEW, IN 1766, OF THE SEAT AND RUINS
OF A DECEASED NOBLEMAN, AT KINGSGATE, KENT

OLD, and abandon'd by each venal friend,
   Here Holland form'd the pious resolution
To smuggle a few years, and strive to mend
   A broken character and constitution.

On this congenial spot he fix'd his choice;
   Earl Goodwin trembled for his neighbouring sand;
Here sea-gulls scream, and cormorants rejoice,
   And mariners, though shipwreck'd, dread to land.

Here reign the blustering North and blighting East,
   No tree is heard to whisper, bird to sing;
Yet Nature could not furnish out the feast,
   Art he invokes new horrors still to bring.

Here mouldering fanes and battlements arise,
   Turrets and arches nodding to their fall,
Unpeopled monast'ries delude our eyes,
   And mimic desolation covers all.

" Ah! " said the sighing peer, " had Bute been true,
   Nor Mungo's, Rigby's, Bradshaw's friendship vain,
Far better scenes than these had blest our view,
   And realis'd the beauties which we feign:

" Purg'd by the sword, and purified by fire,
   Then had we seen proud London's hated walls;
Owls would have hooted in St. Peter's choir,
   And foxes stunk and litter'd in St. Paul's."

THE CANDIDATE

OR, THE CAMBRIDGE COURTSHIP

See character of Lord Sandwich in " Chrysal." See Scott's
Lives of the Novelists, i. p. 169; Davies, *Biog. and Lit. Anecdotes* ;
Churchill's verses on " Lord Sandwich " in *Candidate and Duellist;*
" From his youth upwards," etc.   Cradock's *Memoirs*, vol. i. p. 117,
148; vol. iv. p. 163, 223; Miss Hawkins's *Anecdotes*, p. 239; Bell's
Fugitive Poetry, v. xvi. p. 93, 172; Wilkes' *Letters*, i. p. 211; ii. p.
220; Walpole, *Letters to Lord Hertford*, p. 51-65, 102, by which it
appears that Warburton had dedicated his Sermons to Lord
Sandwich, but expunged his name for Pitt's.   I have seen " A
letter of advice from Alma Mater to her beloved son, Jemmy
Twitcher, 1764."

WHEN sly Jemmy Twitcher had smugg'd up his face,
With a lick of court white-wash, and pious grimace,
A wooing he went, where three sisters of old
In harmless society guttle and scold.
    " Lord! sister," says Physic to Law, " I declare,
Such a sheep-biting look, such a pick-pocket air!
Not I for the Indies:—You know I'm no prude,—
But his nose is a shame,—and his eyes are so lewd!
Then he shambles and straddles so oddly—I fear—
No—at our time of life 'twould be silly, my dear."
    " I don't know," says Law, " but methinks for his
        look,
'Tis just like the picture in Rochester's book;
Then his character, Phyzzy—his morals—his life—
When she died, I can't tell, but he once had a wife.
They say he's no Christian, loves drinking and w——g,
And all the town rings of his swearing and roaring!
His lying and filching, and Newgate-bird tricks;—
Not I—for a coronet, chariot and six."
    Divinity heard, between waking and dozing,
Her sisters denying, and Jemmy proposing:
From table she rose, and with bumper in hand,
She strok'd up her belly, and strok'd down her band—
" What a pother is here about wenching and roaring!
Why, David lov'd catches, and Solomon w——g:
Did not Israel filch from th' Egyptians of old
Their jewels of silver and jewels of gold?
The prophet of Bethel, we read, told a lie:
He drinks—so did Noah;—he swears—so do I:

To reject him for such peccadillos, were odd;
Besides, he repents—for he talks about G**—
                    [*To* Jemmy]
' Never hang down your head, you poor penitent elf,
Come buss me—I'll be Mrs. Twitcher myself.' "

.   .   .   .   .   .

[The concluding couplet is too gross to give.—MITFORD.]

EXTRACTS

PROPERTIUS, LIB. III. ELEG. V. v. 19

" Me juvat in primâ coluisse Helicona juventâ," etc.

IMITATED

LONG as of youth the joyous hours remain,
Me may Castalia's sweet recess detain,
Fast by the umbrageous vale lull'd to repose,
Where Aganippe warbles as it flows;
Or roused by sprightly sounds from out the trance,
I'd in the ring knit hands, and join the Muses' dance.
Give me to send the laughing bowl around,
My soul in Bacchus' pleasing fetters bound;
Let on this head unfading flowers reside,
There bloom the vernal rose's earliest pride;
And when, our flames commission'd to destroy,
Age step 'twixt Love and me, and intercept the joy;
When my changed head these locks no more shall know,
And all its jetty honours turn to snow;
Then let me rightly spell of Nature's ways;
To Providence, to HIM my thoughts I'd raise,
Who taught this vast machine its steadfast laws,
That first, eternal, universal cause;
Search to what regions yonder star retires,
That monthly waning hides her paly fires,
And whence, anew revived, with silver light
Relumes her crescent orb to cheer the dreary night:
How rising winds the face of ocean sweep,
Where lie the eternal fountains of the deep,

And whence the cloudy magazines maintain
Their wintry war, or pour the autumnal rain;
How flames perhaps, with dire confusion hurl'd,
Shall sink this beauteous fabrick of the world;
What colours paint the vivid arch of Jove;
What wondrous force the solid earth can move,
When Pindus' self approaching ruin dreads,
Shakes all his pines, and bows his hundred heads;
Why does yon orb, so exquisitely bright,
Obscure his radiance in a short-liv'd night;
Whence the Seven-Sisters' congregated fires,
And what Bootes' lazy waggon tires;
How the rude surge its sandy bounds control;
Who measured out the year, and bade the seasons roll;
If realms beneath those fabled torments know,
Pangs without respite, fires that ever glow,
Earth's monster brood stretch'd on their iron bed,
The hissing terrors round Alecto's head,
Scarce to nine acres Tityus' bulk confined,
The triple dog that scares the shadowy kind,
All angry heaven inflicts, or hell can feel,
The pendent rock, Ixion's whirling wheel,
Famine at feasts, or thirst amid the stream;
Or are our fears the enthusiast's empty dream,
And all the scenes, that hurt the grave's repose,
But pictured horror and poetic woes.
  These soft inglorious joys my hours engage;
Be love my youth's pursuit, and science crown my age.
You whose young bosoms feel a nobler flame,
Redeem what Crassus lost, and vindicate his name.

                                    1738.   Æt. 22.

PROPERTIUS, LIB. II. ELEG. I. v. 17

" Quod mihi si tantum, Mæcenas, fata dedissent," etc.

YET would the tyrant Love permit me raise
My feeble voice, to sound the victor's praise,
To paint the hero's toil, the ranks of war,
The laurell'd triumph and the sculptured car;
No giant race, no tumult of the skies,
No mountain-structures in my verse should rise.

Nor tale of Thebes, nor Ilium there should be,
Nor how the Persian trod the indignant sea;
Not Marius' Cimbrian wreaths would I relate,
Nor lofty Carthage struggling with her fate.
Here should Augustus great in arms appear,
And thou Mecænas, be my second care;
Here Mutina from flames and famine free,
And there the ensanguined wave of Sicily,
And scepter'd Alexandria's captive shore,
And sad Philippi, red with Roman gore:
Then, while the vaulted skies loud ïos rend,
In golden chains should loaded monarchs bend,
And hoary Nile with pensive aspect seem
To mourn the glories of his sevenfold stream,
While prows, that late in fierce encounter met,
Move through the sacred way and vainly threat,
Thee too the Muse should consecrate to fame,
And with her garlands weave thy ever-faithful name.

   But nor Callimachus' enervate strain
May tell of Jove, and Phlegra's blasted plain;
Nor I with unaccustomed vigour trace
Back to its source divine the Julian race.
Sailors to tell of winds and seas delight,
The shepherd of his flocks, the soldier of the fight,
A milder warfare I in verse display;
Each in his proper art should waste the day:
Nor thou my gentle calling disapprove,
To die is glorious in the bed of Love.

   Happy the youth, and not unknown to fame,
Whose heart has never felt a second flame.
Oh, might that envied happiness be mine!
To Cynthia all my wishes I confine;
Or if, alas! it be my fate to try
Another love, the quicker let me die:
But she, the mistress of my faithful breast,
Has oft the charms of constancy confest,
Condemns her fickle sex's fond mistake,
And hates the tale of Troy for Helen's sake.
Me from myself the soft enchantress stole;
Ah! let her ever my desires control,
Or if I fall the victim of her scorn,
From her loved door may my pale corse be borne.
The power of herbs can other harms remove,

And find a cure for every ill, but love.
The Lemnian's hurt Machaon could repair,
Heal the slow chief, and send again to war;
To Chiron Phœnix owed his long-lost sight,
And Phœbus' son recall'd Androgeon to the light.
Here arts are vain, e'en magic here must fail,
The powerful mixture and the midnight spell;
The hand that can my captive heart release,
And to this bosom give its wonted peace,
May the long thirst of Tantalus allay,
Or drive the infernal vulture from his prey.
For ills unseen what remedy is found?
Or who can probe the undiscover'd wound?
The bed avails not, nor the leech's care,
Nor changing skies can hurt, nor sultry air.
'Tis hard th' elusive symptoms to explore:
To-day the lover walks, to-morrow is no more;
A train of mourning friends attend his pall,
And wonder at the sudden funeral.
　　When then the fates that breath they gave shall claim,
And the short marble but preserve a name,
A little verse my all that shall remain;
Thy passing courser's slacken'd speed restrain;
(Thou envied honour of thy poet's days,
Of all our youth the ambition and the praise!)
Then to my quiet urn awhile draw near,
And say, while o'er that place you drop the tear,
Love and the fair were of his youth the pride;
He lived, while she was kind; and when she frown'd, he
　　died.

April 1742.　*Æt.* 26.

TASSO, "GERUS. LIB." CANT. XIV. ST. 32.

" Preser commiato, e sì 'l desio gli sprona," etc.

DISMISS'D at length, they break through all delay
To tempt the dangers of the doubtful way;
And first to Ascalon their steps they bend,
Whose walls along the neighbouring sea extend,
Nor yet in prospect rose the distant shore;
Scarce the hoarse waves from far were heard to roar,

When thwart the road a river roll'd its flood
Tempestuous, and all further course withstood;
The torrent stream his ancient bounds disdains,
Swoll'n with new force, and late-descending rains.
Irresolute they stand; when lo, appears
The wondrous Sage: vigorous he seem'd in years,
Awful his mien, low as his feet there flows
A vestment unadorn'd, though white as new-fall'n snows;
Against the stream the waves secure he trod,
His head a chaplet bore, his hand a rod.
      As on the Rhine, when Boreas' fury reigns,
And winter binds the floods in icy chains,
Swift shoots the village-maid in rustic play
Smooth, without step, adown the shining way,
Fearless in long excursion loves to glide,
And sports and wantons o'er the frozen tide.
      So mov'd the Seer, but on no harden'd plain;
The river boil'd beneath, and rush'd toward the main.
Where fix'd in wonder stood the warlike pair,
His course he turn'd, and thus relieved their care:
      " Vast, oh my friends, and difficult the toil
To seek your hero in a distant soil!
No common helps, no common guide ye need,
Art it requires, and more than winged speed.
What length of sea remains, what various lands,
Oceans unknown, inhospitable sands!
For adverse fate the captive chief has hurl'd
Beyond the confines of our narrow world:
Great things and full of wonder in your ears
I shall unfold; but first dismiss your fears;
Nor doubt with me to tread the downward road
That to the grotto leads, my dark abode."
      Scarce had he said, before the warriors' eyes
When mountain-high the waves disparted rise;
The flood on either hand its billows rears,
And in the midst a spacious arch appears.
Their hands he seized, and down the steep he led
Beneath the obedient river's inmost bed;
The watery glimmerings of a fainter day
Discover'd half, and half conceal'd their way;
As when athwart the dusky woods by night
The uncertain crescent gleams a sickly light.
Through subterraneous passages they went,

Earth's inmost cells, and caves of deep descent;
Of many a flood they view'd the secret source,
The birth of rivers rising to their course,
Whate'er with copious train its channel fills,
Floats into lakes, and bubbles into rills;
The Po was there to see, Danubius' bed,
Euphrates' fount, and Nile's mysterious head.
Further they pass, where ripening minerals flow,
And embryon metals undigested glow,
Sulphureous veins and living silver shine,
Which soon the parent sun's warm powers refine,
In one rich mass unite the precious store,
The parts combine and harden into ore:
Here gems break through the night with glittering beam,
And paint the margin of the costly stream,
All stones of lustre shoot their vivid ray,
And mix attemper'd in a various day;
Here the soft emerald smiles of verdant hue,
And rubies flame, with sapphire's heavenly blue,
The diamond there attracts the wondrous sight,
Proud of its thousand dies and luxury of light.

1738.   Æt. 22.

POEMATA

HYMENEAL

ON THE MARRIAGE OF HIS ROYAL HIGHNESS
THE PRINCE OF WALES

IGNARÆ nostrûm mentes, et inertia corda,
Dum curas regum, et sortem miseramur iniquam,
Quæ solio affixit, vetuitque calescere flammâ
Dulci, quæ dono divûm, gratissima serpit
Viscera per, mollesque animis lene implicat æstus;
Nec teneros sensus, Veneris nec præmia nôrunt,
Eloquiumve oculi, aut facunda silentia linguæ:
　　Scilicet ignorant lacrymas, sævosque dolores,
Dura rudimenta, et violentæ exordia flammæ;
Scilicet ignorant, quæ flumine tinxit amaro

Tela Venus, cæcique armamentaria Divi,
Irasque, insidiasque, et tacitum sub pectore vulnus;
Namque sub ingressu, primoque in limine Amoris
Luctus et ultrices posuere cubilia Curæ;
Intus habent dulces Risus, et Gratia sedem,
Et roseis resupina toris, roseo ore Voluptas:
Regibus huc faciles aditus; communia spernunt
Ostia, jamque expers duris custodibus istis
Panditur accessus, penetraliaque intima Templi.

Tuque Oh! Angliacis, Princeps, spes optima regnis,
Ne tantum, ne finge metum: quid imagine captus
Hæres, et mentem pictura pascis inani?
Umbram miraris: nec longum tempus, et ipsa
Ibit in amplexus, thalamosque ornabit ovantes.
Ille tamen tabulis inhians longum haurit amorem,
Affatu fruitur tacito, auscultatque tacentem
Immemor artificis calami, risumque, ruboremque
Aspicit in fucis, pictæque in virginis ore:
Tanta Venus potuit; tantus tenet error amantes.

Nascere, magna Dies, qua sese AUGUSTA Britanno
Committat Pelago, patriamque relinquat amœnam;
Cujus in adventum jam nunc tria regna secundos
Attolli in plausus, dulcique accensa furore
Incipiunt agitare modos, et carmina dicunt:
Ipse animo sedenim juvenis comitatur euntem
Explorat ventos, atque auribus aëra captat,
Atque auras, atque astra vocat crudelia; pectus
Intentum exultat, surgitque arrecta cupido;
Incusat spes ægra fretum, solitoque videtur
Latior effundi pontus, fluctusque morantes.

Nascere, Lux major, qua sese AUGUSTA Britanno
Committat juveni totam, propriamque dicabit;
At citius (precor) Oh! cedas melioribus astris;
Nox finem pompæ, finemque imponere curis
Possit, et in thalamos furtim deducere nuptam;
Sufficiat requiemque viris, et amantibus umbras:
Adsit Hymen, et subridens cum matre Cupido
Accedant, sternantque toros, ignemque ministrent;
Ilicet haud pictæ incandescit imagine formæ
Ulterius juvenis, verumque agnoscit amorem.

Sculptile sicut ebur, faciemque arsisse venustam
Pygmaliona canunt: ante hanc suspiria ducit,
Alloquiturque amens, flammamque et vulnera narrat;
Implorata Venus jussit cum vivere signum,
Fœmineam inspirans animam; quæ gaudia surgunt,
Audiit ut primæ nascentia murmura linguæ,
Luctari in vitam, et paulatim volvere ocellos
Sedulus, aspexitque novâ splendescere flammâ;
Corripit amplexu vivam, jamque oscula jungit
Acria confestim, recipitque rapitque; prioris
Immemor ardoris, Nymphæque oblitus eburneæ.

> THO. GRAY, Pet. Coll.

LUNA HABITABILIS

DUM Nox rorantes, non incomitata per auras
Urget equos, tacitoque inducit sidera lapsu;
Ultima, sed nulli soror inficianda sororum,
Huc mihi, Musa; tibi patet alti janua cœli,
Astra vides, nec te numeri, nec nomina fallunt.
Huc mihi, Diva veni; dulce est per aperta serena
Vere frui liquido, campoque errare silenti;
Vere frui dulce est; modo tu dignata petentem
Sis comes, et mecum gelidâ spatiere sub umbrâ.
Scilicèt hos orbes, cœli hæc decora alta putandum est,
Noctis opes, nobis tantum lucere; virûmque
Ostentari oculis, nostræ laquearia terræ,
Ingentes scenas, vastique aulæa theatri?
Oh! quis me pennis æthræ super ardua sistet
Mirantem, propiusque dabit convexa tueri;
Teque adeo, undè fluens reficit lux mollior arva
Pallidiorque dies, tristes solata tenebras?
  Sic ego, subridens Dea sic ingressa vicissim:
Non pennis opus hìc, supera ut simul illa petamus:
Disce, Puer, potiùs cœlo deducere Lunam;
Neu crede ad magicas te invitum accingier artes,
Thessalicosve modos; ipsam descendere Phœben
Conspicies novus Endymion; seque offeret ultrò
Visa tibi ante oculos, et notâ major imago.
  Quin tete admoveas (tumuli super aggere spectas),

Compositum tubulo; simul imum invade canalem
Sic intentâ acie, cœli simul alta patescent
Atria; jamque, ausus Lunaria visere regna,
Ingrediêre solo, et caput inter nubila condes.
    Ecce autem! vitri se in vertice sistere Phœben
Cernis, et Oceanum, et crebris Freta consista terris
Panditur *ille* atram faciem caligine condens
Sublustri; refugitque oculos, fallitque tuentem;
Integram Solis lucem quippe haurit aperto
Fluctu avidus radiorum, et longos imbibit ignes:
Verum *his*, quæ, maculis variata nitentibus, auro
Cœrula discernunt, celso sese insula dorso
Plurima protrudit, prætentaque littora saxis;
Liberior datur his quoniàm natura, minusque
Lumen depascunt liquidum; sed tela diei
Detorquent, retròque docent se vertere flammas.
    Hinc longos videas tractus, terrasque jacentes
Ordine candenti, et claros se attollere montes;
Montes queîs Rhodope assurgat, quibus Ossa nivali
Vertice: tum scopulis infrà pendentibus antra
Nigrescunt clivorum umbrâ, nemorumque tenebris.
Non rores illi, aut desunt sua nubila mundo;
Non frigus gelidum, atque herbis gratissimus imber;
His quoque nota ardet picto Thaumantias arcu,
Os roseum Auroræ, propriique crepuscula cœli.
    Et dubitas tantum certis cultoribus orbem
Destitui? exercent agros, sua mœnia condunt
Hi quoque, vel Martem invadunt, curantque triumphos
Victores: sunt hic etiam sua præmia laudi;
His metus, atque amor, et mentem mortalia tangunt.
Quin, uti nos oculis jam nunc juvat ire per arva,
Lucentesque plagas Lunæ, pontumque profundum;
Idem illos etiàm ardor agit, cum se aureus effert
Sub sudum globus, et terrarum ingentior orbis;
Scilicèt omne æquor tum lustrant, scilicèt omnem
Tellurem, gentesque polo sub utroque jacentes;
Et quidam æstivi indefessus ad ætheris ignes
Pervigilat, noctem exercens, cœlumque fatigat;
Jam Galli apparent, jam se Germania latè
Tollit, et albescens pater Apenninus ad auras;
Jam tandem in Borean, en! parvulus Anglia nævus
(Quanquam aliis longè fulgentior) extulit oras;
Formosum extemplò lumen, maculamque nitentem

Invisunt crebri Proceres, serùmque tuendo;
Hærent, certatimque suo cognomine signant:
Forsitan et Lunæ longinquus in orbe Tyrannus
Se dominum vocat, et nostrâ se jactat in aulâ.
Terras possim alias propiori sole calentes
Narrare, atque alias, jubaris queîs parcior usus,
Lunarum chorus, et tenuis penuria Phœbi;
Nî, meditans eadem hæc audaci evolvere cantu,
Jam pulset citharam soror, et præludia tentet.

  Non tamen has proprias laudes, nec facta silebo
Jampridèm in fatis, patriæque oracula famæ.
Tempus erit, sursùm totos contendere cœtus
Quo cernes longo excursu, primosque colonos
Migrare in lunam, et notos mutare Penates:
Dum stupet obtutu tacito vetus incola, longèque
Insolitas explorat aves, classemque volantem.

  Ut quondàm ignotum marmor, camposque na tantes
Tranavit Zephyros visens, nova regna, Columbus;
Litora mirantur circùm, mirantur et undæ
Inclusas acies ferro, turmasque biformes,
Monstraque fœta armis, et non imitabile fulmen.
Fœdera mox icta, et gemini commercia mundi,
Agminaque assueto glomerata sub æthere cerno.
Anglia, quæ pelagi jamdudum torquet habenas,
Exercetque frequens ventos, atque imperat undæ;
Aëris attollet fasces, veteresque triumphos
Hùc etiam feret, et victis dominabitur auris.

SAPPHIC ODE: TO MR. WEST

BARBARAS ædes aditure mecum
Quas Eris semper fovet inquieta,
Lis ubi latè sonat, et togatum
          Æstuat agmen;

Dulcius quanto, patulis sub ulmi
Hospitæ ramis temerè jacentem
Sic libris horas, tenuique inertes
          Fallere Musâ?

Sæpe enim curis vagor expeditâ
Mente; dum, blandam meditans Camænam,
Vix malo rori, meminive seræ
                    Cedere nocti;

Et, pedes quò me rapiunt, in omni
Colle Parnassum videor videre
Fertilem sylvæ, gelidamque in omni
                    Fonte Aganippen,

Risit et Ver me, facilesque Nymphæ
Nare captantem, nec ineleganti,
Manè quicquid de violis eundo
                    Surripit aura:

Me reclinatum teneram per herbam;
Quà leves cursus aqua cunque ducit,
Et moras dulci strepitu lapillo
                    Nectit in omni,

Hæ novo nòstrum ferè pectus anno
Simplices curæ tenuere, cœlum
Quamdiù sudum explicuit Favonî
                    Purior hora:

Otia et campos nec adhuc relinquo,
Nec magis Phœbo Clytie fidelis;
(Ingruant venti licet, et senescat
                    Mollior æstas.)

Namque, seu, lætos hominum labores
Prataque et montes recreante curru
Purpurâ tractus oriens Eoos
                    Vestit, et auro;

Sedulus servo veneratus orbem
Prodigum splendoris; amœniori
Sive dilectam meditatur igne
                    Pingere Calpen;

Usque dum, fulgore magìs magìs jam
Languido circum, variata nubes
Labitur furtim, viridisque in umbras
                    Scena recessit.

O ego felix, vice si (nec unquam
Surgerem rursus) simili cadentem
Parca me lenis sineret quieto
     Fallere Letho!

Multa flagranti radiisque cincto
Integris ah! quam nihil inviderem,
Cum Dei ardentes medius quadrigas
     Sentit Olympus.

ALCAIC FRAGMENT

O LACRYMARUM fons, tenero sacros
Ducentium ortus ex animo; quater
 Felix! in imo qui scatentem
  Pectore te, pia Nympha, sensit.

LATIN LINES

ADDRESSED TO MR. WEST, FROM GENOA

HORRIDOS tractus, Boreæque linquens
Regna Taurini fera, molliorem
Advehor brumam, Genuæque amantes
     Litora soles.

ELEGIAC VERSES

OCCASIONED BY THE SIGHT OF THE PLAINS WHERE THE BATTLE OF TREBIA WAS FOUGHT

QUA Trebie glaucas salices intersecat undâ,
 Arvaque Romanis nobilitata malis.
Visus adhuc amnis veteri de clade rubere,
 Et suspirantes ducere mœstus aquas;
Maurorumque ala, et nigræ increbescere turmæ,
 Et pulsa Ausonidum ripa sonare fugâ.

CARMEN AD C. FAVONIUM ZEPHYRINUM

MATER rosarum, cui teneræ vigent
Auræ Favonî, cui Venus it comes
    Lasciva, Nympharum choreis
        Et volucrum celebrata cantu!
Dic, non inertem fallere quâ diem
Amat sub umbrâ, seu sinit aureum
    Dormire plectrum, seu retentat
        Pierio Zephyrinus antro
Furore dulci plenus, et immemor
Reptantis inter frigora Tusculi
    Umbrosa, vel colles Amici
        Palladiæ superantis Albæ.
Dilecta Fauno, et capripedum choris
Pineta, testor vos, Anio minax
    Quæcunque per clivos volutus
        Præcipiti tremefecit amne,
Illius altum Tibur, et Æsulæ
Audîsse sylvas nomen amabiles,
    Illius et gratas Latinis
        Naisin ingeminâsse rupes;
Nam me Latinæ Naides uvidâ
Vidêre ripâ, quâ niveas levi
    Tam sæpe lavit rore plumas
        Dulcè canens Venusinus ales;
Mirum! canenti conticuit nemus,
Sacrique fontes, et retinent adhuc
    (Sic Musa jussit) saxa molles
        Docta modos, veteresque lauri.
Mirare nec tu me citharæ rudem
Claudis laborantem numeris: loca
    Amœna, jucundumque ver in-
        compositum docuere carmen;
Hærent sub omni nam folio nigri
Phœbea lucî (credite) somnia,
    Argutiusque et lympha et auræ
        Nescio quid solito loquuntur.

FRAGMENT OF LATIN POEM ON THE GAURUS

Nec procul infelix se tollit in æthera Gaurus,
Prospiciens vitreum lugenti vertice pontum:
Tristior ille diu, et veteri desuetus olivâ
Gaurus, pampineæque eheu jam nescius umbræ;
Horrendi tam sæva premit vicinia montis,
Attonitumque urget latus, exuritque ferentem.
  Nam fama est olim, mediâ dum rura silebant
Nocte, Deo victa, et molli perfusa quiete,
Infremuisse æquor ponti, auditamque per omnes
Latè tellurem surdùm immugire cavernas:
Quo sonitu nemora altra tremunt: tremit excita tuto
Parthenopæa sinu, flammantisque ora Vesevi.
At subitò se aperire solum, vastosque recessus
Pandere sub pedibus, nigrâque voragine fauces;
Tum piceas cinerum glomerare sub æthere nubes
Vorticibus rapidis, ardentique imbre procellam.
Præcipites fugere feræ, perque avia longè
Sylvarum fugit pastor, juga per deserta,
Ah, miser! increpitans sæpè altâ voce per umbram
Nequicquam natos, creditque audire sequentes.
Atque ille excelso rupis de vertice solus
Respectans notasque domos, et dulcia regna,
Nil usquàm videt infelix præter mare tristi
Lumine percussum, et pallentes sulphure campos
Fumumque, flammasque, rotataque turbine saxa.
  Quin ubi detonuit fragor, et lux reddita cœlo;
Mæstos confluere agricolas, passuque videres
Tandem iterum timido deserta requirere tecta:
Sperantes, si forte oculis, si forte darentur
Uxorum cineres, miserorumve ossa parentum
(Tenuia, sed tanti saltem solatia luctûs)
Unà colligere et justâ componere in urnâ.
Uxorum nusquam cineres, nusquam ossa parentum
(Spem miseram!) assuetosve Lares, aut rura videbunt.
Quippe ubi planities campi diffusa jacebat;
Mons novus: ille supercilium, frontemque favillâ
Incanum ostentans, ambustis cautibus, æquor
Subjectum, stragemque suam, mæsta arva, minaci
Despicit imperio, soloque in littore regnat.
  Hinc infame loci nomen, multosque per annos

Immemor antiquæ laudis, nescire labores
Vomeris, et nullo tellus revirescere cultu.
Non avium colles, non carmine matutino
Pastorum resonare; adeò undique dirus habebat
Informes latè horror agros saltusque vacantes.
Sæpius et longè detorquens navita proram
Monstrabat digito littus, sævæque revolvens
Funera narrabat noctis, veteremque ruinam.
   Montis adhuc facies manet hirta atque aspera saxis:
Sed furor extinctus jamdudum, et flamma quievit,
Quæ nascenti aderat; seu fortè bituminis atri
Defluxere olim rivi, atque effœta lacuna
Pabula sufficere ardori, viresque recusat;
Sive in visceribus meditans incendia jam nunc
(Horrendùm) arcanis glomerat genti esse futuræ
Exitio, sparsos tacitusque recolligit ignes.
   Raro per clivos haud secius ordine vidi
Canescentem oleam: longum post tempus amicti
Vite virent tumuli; patriamque revisere gaudens
Bacchus in assuetis tenerum caput exerit arvis
Vix tandem, infidoque audet se credere cœlo.

A FAREWELL TO FLORENCE

    . . . Oh Fæsulæ amœna
Frigoribus juga, nec nimiùm spirantibus auris!
Alma quibus Tusci Pallas decus Apennini
Esse dedit, glaucâque suâ canescere sylvâ!
Non ego vos posthàc Arni de valle videbo
Porticibus circum, et candenti cincta coronâ
Villarum longè nitido consurgere dorso,
Antiquamve Ædem, et veteres præferre Cupressus
Mirabor, tectisque super pendentia tecta.

IMITATION OF AN ITALIAN SONNET

OF SIGNIOR ABBATE BUONDELMONTE

        Spesso Amor sotto la forma
        D'amistà ride, e s'asconde:
        Poi si mischia, e si confonde
        Con lo sdegno, e col rancor.

In Pietade ei si trasforma;
Par trastullo, e par dispetto;
Mà nel suo diverso aspetto
Sempr' egli, è l' istesso Amor.

Lusit amicitiæ interdum velatus amictu,
 Et benè compositâ veste fefellit Amor.
Mox iræ assumpsit cultus, faciemque minantem,
 Inque odium versus, versus et in lacrymas:
Ludentem fuge, nec lacrymanti, aut crede furenti;
 Idem est dissimili semper in ore Deus.

ALCAIC ODE

WRITTEN IN THE ALBUM OF THE GRANDE CHARTREUSE,
IN DAUPHINY, AUGUST 1741

Oh Tu, severi Religio loci,
Quocunque gaudes nomine (non leve
 Nativa nam certè fluenta
  Numen habet, veteresque sylvas;
Præsentiorem et conspicimus Deum
Per invias rupes, fera per juga,
 Clivosque præruptos, sonantes
  Inter aquas, nemorumque noctem;
Quàm si repostus sub trabe citreâ
Fulgeret auro, et Phidiacâ manu)
 Salve vocanti ritè, fesso et
  Da placidam juveni quietem.
Quod si invidendis sedibus, et frui
Fortuna sacrâ lege silentii
 Vetat volentem, me resorbens
  In medios violenta fluctus:
Saltem remoto des, Pater, angulo
Horas senectæ ducere liberas;
 Tutumque vulgari tumultu
  Surripias, hominumque curis.

PART OF AN HEROIC EPISTLE

FROM SOPHONISBA TO MASINISSA

EGREGIUM accipio promissi Munus amoris,
  Inque manu mortem, jam fruitura, fero:
Atque utinam citius mandasses, luce vel unâ;
  Transieram Stygios non inhonesta lacus.
Victoris nec passa toros, nova nupta, mariti,
  Nec fueram fastus, Roma superba, tuos.
Scilicet hæc partem tibi, Masinissa, triumphi
  Detractam, hæc pompæ jura minora suæ
Imputat, atque uxor quòd non tua pressa catenis,
  Objecta et sævæ plausibus orbis eo:
Quin tu pro tantis cepisti præmia factis,
  Magnum Romanæ pignus amicitiæ!
Scipiadæ excuses, oro, si, tardius utar
  Munere.   Non nimiùm vivere, crede, velim.
Parva mora est, breve sed tempus mea fama requirit:
  Detinet hæc animam cura suprema meam.
Quæ patriæ prodesse meæ Regina ferebar,
  Inter Elisæas gloria prima nurus,
Ne videar flammæ nimis indulsisse secundæ,
  Vel nimis hostiles extimuisse manus.
Fortunam atque annos liceat revocare priores,
  Gaudiaque heu! quantis nostra repensa malis.
Primitiasne tuas meministi atque arma Syphacis
  Fusa, et per Tyrias ducta trophæa vias?
(Laudis at antiquæ forsan meminisse pigebit,
  Quodque decus quondam causa ruboris erit.)
Tempus ego certe memini, felicia Pœnis
  Quo te non puduit solvere vota deis;
Mœniaque intrantem vidi: longo agmine duxit
  Turba salutantum, purpureique patres.
Fœminea ante omnes longe admiratur euntem
  Hæret et aspectu tota caterva tuo.
Jam flexi, regale decus, per colla capilli,
  Jam decet ardenti fuscus in ore color!
Commendat frontis generosa modestia formam,
  Seque cupit laudi surripuisse suæ.
Prima genas tenui signat vix flore juventas,
  Et dextræ soli credimus esse virum.

Dum faciles gradiens oculos per singula jactas,
  (Seu rexit casus lumina, sive Venus)
In me (vel certè visum est) conversa morari
  Sensi; virgineus perculit ora pudor.
Nescio quid vultum molle spirare tuendo,
  Credideramque tuos lentius ire pedes.
Quærebam, juxta æqualis si dignior esset,
  Quæ poterat visus detinuisse tuos:
Nulla fuit circum æqualis quæ dignior esset,
  Asseruitque decus conscia forma suum.
Pompæ finis erat. Totâ vix nocte quievi,
  Sin premat invitæ lumina victa sopor,
Somnus habet pompas, eademque recursat imago;
  Atque iterum hesterno munere victor ades.

. . . .

DIDACTIC POEM UNFINISHED

ENTITLED

DE PRINCIPIIS COGITANDI

LIBER PRIMUS. AD FAVONIUM

Unde Animus scire incipiat; quibus inchoet orsa
Principiis seriem rerum, tenuemque catenam
Mnemosyne: Ratio unde rudi sub pectore tardum
Augeat imperium; et primum mortalibus ægris
Ira, Dolor, Metus, et Curæ nascantur inanes,
Hinc canere aggredior. Nec dedignare canentem
O decus! Angliacæ certe O lux altera gentis!
Si quà primus iter monstras, vestigia conor
Signare incertâ, tremulâque insistere plantâ.
Quin potius duc ipse (potes namque omnia) sanctum
Ad limen (si ritè adeo, si pectore puro,)
Obscuræ reserans Naturæ ingentia claustra.
Tu cæcas rerum causas, fontemque severum
Pande, Pater; tibi enim, tibi, veri magne Sacerdos,
Corda patent hominum, atque altæ penetralia Mentis.
    Tuque aures adhibe vacuas, facilesque, Favonî,
(Quod tibi crescit opus) simplex nec despice carmen,
Nec vatem: non illa leves primordia motus,

Quanquam parva, dabunt. Lætum vel amabile quicquid
Usquam oritur, trahit hinc ortum; nec surgit ad auras,
Quin ea conspirent simul, eventusque secundent.
Hinc variæ vitaï artes, ac mollior usus,
Dulce et amicitiæ vinclum: Sapientia dia
Hinc roseum accendit lumen, vultuque sereno
Humanas aperit mentes, nova gaudia monstrans,
Deformesque fugat curas, vanosque timores:
Scilicet et rerum crescit pulcherrima Virtus.
Illa etiam, quæ te (mirùm) noctesque diesque
Assiduè fovet inspirans, linguamque sequentem
Temperat in numeros, atque horas mulcet inertes;
Aurea non aliâ se jactat origine Musa.

    Principio, ut magnum fœdus Natura creatrix
Firmavit, tardis jussitque inolescere membris
Sublimes animas; tenebroso in carcere partem
Noluit ætheream longo torpere veterno:
Nec per se proprium passa exercere vigorem est,
Ne sociæ molis conjunctos sperneret artus,
Ponderis oblita, et cœlestis conscia flammæ.
Idcircó innumero ductu tremere undique fibras
Nervorum instituit: tum toto corpore miscens
Implicuit latè ramos, et sensile textum,
Implevitque humore suo (seu lympha vocanda,
Sive aura est) tenuis certè, atque levissima quædam
Vis versatur agens, parvosque infusa canales
Perfluit; assiduè externis quæ concita plagis,
Mobilis, incussique fidelis nuntia motûs,
Hinc indè accensâ contage relabitur usque
Ad superas hominis sedes, arcemque cerebri.
Namque illìc posuit solium, et sua templa sacravit
Mens animi: hanc circum coëunt, densoque feruntur
Agmine notitiæ, simulacraque tenuia rerum:
Ecce autem naturæ ingens aperitur imago
Immensæ, variique patent commercia mundi.

    Ac uti longinquis descendunt montibus amnes
Velivolus Tamisis, flaventisque Indus arenæ,
Euphratesque, Tagusque, et opimo flumine Ganges,
Undas quisque suas volvens, cursuque sonoro
In mare prorumpunt: hos magno acclinis in antro
Excipit Oceanus, natorumque ordine longo
Dona recognoscit venientûm, ultròque serenat
Cæruleam faciem, et diffuso marmore ridet.

Haud aliter species properant se inferre novellæ
Certatim menti, atque aditus quino agmine complent.
   Primas tactus agit partes, primusque minutæ
Laxat iter cæcum turbæ, recipitque ruentem.
Non idem huic modus est, qui fratribus: amplius ille
Imperium affectat senior, penitusque medullis,
Visceribusque habitat totis, pellîsque recentem
Funditur in telam, et latè per stamina vivit.
Necdum etiam matris puer eluctatus ab alvo
Multiplices solvit tunicas, et vincula rupit;
Sopitus molli somno, tepidoque liquore
Circumfusus adhuc: tactus tamen aura lacessit
Jamdudum levior sensus, animamque reclusit.
Idque magis simul, ac solitum blandumque calorem
Frigore mutavit cœli, quod verberat acri
Impete inassuetos artus: tum sævior adstat
Humanæque comes vitæ Dolor excipit; ille
Cunctantem frustrà et tremulo multa ore querentem
Corripit invadens, ferreisque amplectitur ulnis.
Tum species primùm patefacta est candida Lucis
(Usque vices adeò Natura bonique, malique,
Exæquat, justâque manu sua damna rependit)
Tum primùm, ignotosque bibunt nova lumina soles.
   Carmine quo, Dea, te dicam, gratissima cœli
Progenies, ortumque tuum; gemmantia rore
Ut per prata levi lustras, et floribus halans
Purpureum Veris gremium, scenamque virentem
Pingis, et umbriferos colles, et cærula regna?
Gratia te, Venerisque Lepos, et mille Colorum,
Formarumque chorus sequitur, motusque decentes.
At caput invisum Stygiis Nox atra tenebris
Abdidit, horrendæque simul Formidinis ora,
Pervigilesque æstus Curarum, atque anxius Angor.
Undique lætitiâ florent mortalia corda,
Purus et arridet largis fulgoribus Æther.
   Omnia nec tu ideò invalidæ se pandere Menti
(Quippe nimis teneros posset vis tanta diei
Perturbare, et inexpertos confundere visus)
Nec capere infantes animos; neu cernere credas
Tam variam molem, et miræ spectacula lucis:
Nescio quâ tamen hæc oculos dulcedine parvos
Splendida percussit novitas, traxitque sequentes;
Nonne videmus enim, latis inserta fenestris

Sicubi se Phœbi dispergant aurea tela,
Sive lucernarum rutilus colluxerit ardor,
Extemplo hùc obverti aciem, quæ fixa repertos
Haurit inexpletum radios, fruiturque tuendo.

Altior huic verò sensu, majorque videtur
Addita, Judicioque arctè connexa potestas,
Quod simul atque ætas volventibus auxerit annis,
Hæc simul, assiduo depascens omnia visu,
Perspiciet, vis quanta loci, quid polleat ordo,
Juncturæ quis honos, ut res accendere rebus
Lumina conjurant inter se, et mutua fulgent.

Nec minor in geminis viget auribus insita virtus,
Nec tantum in curvis quæ pervigil excubet antris
Hinc atque hinc (ubi Vox tremefecerit ostia pulsu
Aëriis invecta rotis) longèque recurset:
Scilicet Eloquio hæc sonitus, hæc fulminis alas,
Et mulcere dedit dictis et tollere corda,
Verbaque metiri numeris, versuque ligare
Repperit, et quicquid discant Libethrides undæ,
Calliope quotiès, quotiès Pater ipse canendi
Evolvat liquidum carmen, calamove loquenti
Inspiret dulces animas, digitisque figuret.

At medias fauces, et linguæ humentia templa
Gustus habet, quà se insinuet jucunda saporum
Luxuries, dona Autumni, Bacchique voluptas.

Naribus interea consedit odora hominum vis,
Docta leves captare auras, Panchaïa quales
Vere novo exhalat, Floræve quod oscula fragrant,
Roscida, cum Zephyri furtìm sub vesperis horâ
Respondet votis, mollemque aspirat amorem.

Tot portas altæ capitis circumdedit arci
Alma Parens, sensûsque vias per membra reclusit;
Haud solas: namque intùs agit vivata facultas,
Quâ sese explorat, contemplatusque repentè
Ipse suas animus vires, momentaque cernit.
Quid velit, aut possit, cupiat, fugiatve, vicissìm
Percipit imperio gaudens; neque corpora fallunt
Morigera ad celeres actus, ac numina mentis.

Qualis Hamadryadum quondam si fortè sororum
Una, novos peragrans saltus, et devia rura;
(Atque illam in viridi suadet procumbere ripâ
Fontis pura quies, et opaci frigoris umbra)
Dum prona in latices speculi de margine pendet,

Mirata est subitam venienti occurrere Nympham:
Mox eosdem, quos ipsa, artus, eadem ora gerentem
Unà inferre gradus, unà succedere sylvæ
Aspicit alludens; seseque agnoscit in undis.
Sic sensu interno rerum simulacra suarum
Mens ciet, et proprios observat conscia vultus.
Nec verò simplex ratio, aut jus omnibus unum
Constat imaginibus.   Sunt quæ bina ostia nôrunt;
Hæ privos servant aditus; sine legibus illæ
Passìm, quà data porta, ruunt, animoque propinquant.
Respice, cui à cunis tristes extinxit ocellos,
Sæva et in eternas mersit natura tenebras:
Illi ignota dies lucet, vernusque colorum
Offusus nitor est, et vivæ gratia formæ.
Corporis at filum, et motus, spatiumque, locique
Intervalla datur certo dignoscere tactu:
Quandoquidem his iter ambiguum est, et janua duplex,
Exclusæque oculis species irrumpere tendunt
Per digitos.   Atqui solis concessa potestas
Luminibus blandæ est radios immittere lucis.

    Undique proporrò sociis, quacunque patescit
Notitiæ campus, mistæ lasciva feruntur
Turba voluptatis comites, formæque dolorum
Terribiles visu, et portâ glomerantur in omni.
Nec vario minus introïtu magnum ingruit Illud,
Quo facere et fungi, quo res existere circùm
Quamque sibi proprio cum corpore scimus, et ire
Ordine, perpetuoque per ævum flumine labi.

    Nunc age quo valeat pacto, quâ sensilis arte
Affectare viam, atque animi tentare latebras
Materies (dictis aures adverte faventes)
Exsequar.   Imprimìs spatii quam multa per æquor
Millia multigenis pandant se corpora seclis,
Expende.   Haud unum invenies, quod mente licebit
Amplecti, nedum propriùs deprendere sensu,
Molis egens certæ, aut solido sine robore, cujus
Denique mobilitas linquit, texturave partes,
Ulla nec orarum circumcæsura coërcet.
Hæc conjuncta adeò totâ compage fatetur
Mundus, et extremo clamant in limine rerum,
Si rebus datur extremum) primordia.   Firmat
Hæc eadem tactus (tactum quis dicere falsum
Audeat?) hæc oculi nec lucidus arguit orbis.

Inde potestatum enasci densissima proles;
Nam quodcunque ferit visum, tangive laborat,
Quicquid nare bibis, vel concava concipit auris,
Quicquid lingua sapit, credas hoc omne, necesse est
Ponderibus, textu, discursu, mole, figurâ
Particulas præstare leves, et semina rerum.
Nunc oculos igitur pascunt, et luce ministrâ
Fulgere cuncta vides, spargique coloribus orbem,
Dum de sole trahunt alias, aliasque supernè
Detorquent, retròque docent se vertere flammas.
Nunc trepido inter se fervent corpuscula pulsu,
Ut tremor æthera per magnum, latèque natantes
Aurarum fluctus avidi vibrantia claustra
Auditûs queat allabi, sonitumque propaget.
Cominùs interdum non ullo interprete per se
Nervorum invadunt teneras quatientia fibras,
Sensiferumque urgent ultrò per viscera motum.

.   .   .   .

LIBER QUARTUS

HACTENUS haud segnis Naturæ arcana retexi
Musarum interpres, primusque Britanna per arva
Romano liquidum deduxi flumine rivum.
Cum Tu opere in medio, spes tanti et causa laboris,
Linquis, et æternam fati te condis in umbram!
Vidi egomet duro graviter concussa dolore
Pectora, in alterius non unquam lenta dolorem;
Et languere oculos vidi, et pallescere amantem
Vultum, quo nunquam Pietas nisi rara, Fidesque,
Altus amor Veri, et purum spirabat Honestum.
Visa tamen tardi demùm inçlementia morbi
Cessare est, reducemque iterum roseo ore Salutem
Speravi, atque unà tecum, dilecte Favoni!
Credulus heu longos, ut quondàm, fallere Soles:
Heu spes nequicquam dulces, atque irrita vota!
Heu mæstos Soles, sine te quos ducere flendo
Per desideria, et questus jam cogor inanes!
    At Tu, sancta anima, et nostri non indiga luctûs,
Stellanti templo, sincerique ætheris igne,

Unde orta es, fruere; atque ô si secura, nec ultra
Mortalis, notos olìm miserata labores
Respectes, tenuesque vacet cognoscere curas;
Humanam si fortè altâ de sede procellam
Contemplêre, metus, stimulosque cupidinis acres,
Gaudiaque et gemitus, parvoque in corde tumultum
Irarum ingentem, et sævos sub pectore fluctus;
Respice et has lacrymas, memori quas ictus amore
Fundo; quod possum, juxtà lugere sepulchrum
Dum juvat, et mutæ vana hæc jactare favillæ.

* * * * * * * * *

GREEK EPIGRAM

'Αζόμενος πολύθηρον ἐκηβόλου ἄλσος ἀνάσσας,
  Τᾶς δεινᾶς τεμένη λεῖπε κυναγὲ θεᾶς,
Μοῦνοι ἄρ' ἔνθα κύνων ζαθέων κλαγγεῦσιν ὑλάγμοι,
  'Ανταχεῖς Νυμφᾶν ἀγροτερᾶν κελάδῳ.

EXTRACTS

PETRARCA, PART I. SONETTO 170

" Lasso ch' i ardo, ed alti non mel crede," etc.

IMITATED

Uror, io; veros at nemo credidet ignes:
  Quin credunt omnes; dura sed illa negat,
Illa negat, soli volumus cui posse probare;
  Quin videt, et visos improba dissimulat.
Ah, durissima mî, sed et, ah, pulcherrima rerum!
  Nonne animam in miserâ, Cynthia, fronte vides?
Omnibus illa pia est; et, si non fata vetâssent,
  Tam longas mentem flecteret ad lacrymas.
Sed tamen has lacrymas, hunc tu, quem spreveris, ignem,
  Carminaque auctori non bene culta suo,
Turba futurorum non ignorabit amantûm:
  Nos duo, cumque erimus parvus uterque cinis,

Jamque faces, eheu! oculorum, et frigida lingua,
    Hæ sine luce jacent, immemor illa loqui;
Infelix musa æternos spirabit amores,
    Ardebitque urnâ multa favilla meâ.

FROM THE "ANTHOLOGIA GRÆCA"

EDIT. HEN. STEPH. 1566

IN BACCHÆ FURENTIS STATUAM

CREDITE, non viva est Mænas; non spirat imago:
    Artificis rabiem miscuit ære manus.

IN ALEXANDRUM, ÆRE EFFICTUM

QUANTUM audet, Lysippe, manus tua! surgit in ære
    Spiritus, atque oculis bellicus ignis adest:
Spectate hos vultus, miserisque ignoscite Persis:
    Quid mirum, imbelles si leo sparsit oves?

IN MEDEÆ IMAGINEM, NOBILE TIMOMACHI OPUS

EN ubi Medeæ varius dolor æstuat ore,
    Jamque animum nati, jamque maritus, habent!
Succenset, miseret, medio exardescit amore,
    Dum furor inque oculo gutta minante tremit.
Cernis adhuc dubiam; quid enim? licet impia matris
    Colchidos, at non sit dextera Timomachi.

IN NIOBES STATUAM

FECERAT e vivâ lapidem me Jupiter; at me
    Praxiteles vivam reddidit e lapide.

A NYMPH OFFERING A STATUE OF HERSELF TO VENUS

TE tibi, sancta, fero nudam; formosius ipsa
    Cum tibi, quod ferrem, te, Dea, nil habui.

III.—MR. GRAY TO MR. WEST

YOU must know that I do not take degrees, and, after this term, shall have nothing more of college impertinencies to undergo, which I trust will be some pleasure to you, as it is a great one to me. I have endured lectures daily and hourly since I came last, supported by the hopes of being shortly at full liberty to give myself up to my friends and classical companions, who, poor souls! though I see them fallen into great contempt with most people here, yet I cannot help sticking to them, and out of a spirit of obstinacy (I think) love them the better for it; and indeed, what can I do else? Must I plunge into metaphysics? Alas, I cannot see in the dark; nature has not furnished me with the optics of a cat. Must I pore upon mathematics? Alas, I cannot see in too much light; I am no eagle. It is very possible that two and two make four, but I would not give four farthings to demonstrate this ever so clearly; and if these be the profits of life, give me the amusements of it. The people I behold all around me, it seems, know all this and more, and yet I do not know one of them who inspires me with any ambition of being like him. Surely it was of this place, now Cambridge, but formerly known by the name of Babylon, that the prophet spoke when he said, "the wild beasts of the desert shall dwell there, and their houses shall be full of doleful creatures, and owls shall build there, and satyrs shall dance there; their forts and towers shall be a den for ever, a joy of wild asses; there shall the great owl make her nest, and lay and hatch and gather under her shadow; it shall be a court of dragons; the screech owl also shall rest there, and find for herself a place of rest." You see here is a pretty collection of desolate animals, which is verified in this town to a tittle, and perhaps it may also allude to your habitation, for you know all types may be taken by abundance of handles; however, I defy your owls to match mine.

If the default of your spirits and nerves be nothing but the effect of the hyp, I have no more to say. We all must submit to that wayward queen; I too in no small degree own her sway,

I feel her influence while I speak her power.

But if it be a real distemper, pray take more care of your health, if not for your own at least for our sakes, and do not be so soon weary of this little world. I do not know what refined friendships you may have contracted in the other, but pray do not be in a hurry to see your acquaintance above; among your terrestrial familiars, however, though I say it that should not say it, there positively is not one that has a greater esteem for you than—Yours most sincerely, etc.

PETERHOUSE, *Dec.* 1736.

IV.—MR. GRAY TO MR. WALPOLE

YOU can never weary me with the repetition of anything that makes me sensible of your kindness; since that has been the only idea of any social happiness that I have almost ever received and which (begging your pardon for thinking so differently from you in such cases) I would by no means have parted with for an exemption from all the uneasiness mixed with it. But it would be unjust to imagine my taste was any rule for yours; for which reason my letters are shorter and less frequent than they would be, had I any materials but myself to entertain you with. Love and brown sugar must be a poor regale for one of your *goût*, and, alas! you know I am by trade a grocer.[1] Scandal (if I had any) is a merchandise you do not profess dealing in; now and then, indeed, and to oblige a friend, you may perhaps slip a little out of your pocket, as a decayed gentlewoman would a piece of right mecklin, or a little quantity of run tea, but this only now and then, not to make a practice of it. Monsters appertaining to this climate you have seen already, both wet and dry. So you perceive within how narrow bounds my pen is circumscribed, and the whole contents of my share in our correspondence may be reduced under the two heads of first, You, secondly, I; the first is, indeed, a subject to expatiate upon, but you might laugh at me for talking about what I do not understand; the second is so tiny, so tiresome, that you shall hear no more of it, than that it is ever—Yours.

PETERHOUSE, *Dec.* 23, 1736.

[1] *i.e.* A man who deals only in coarse and ordinary wares. To these he compares the plain sincerity of his own friendship, undisguised by flattery, which, had he chosen to carry on the allusion, he might have termed the trade of a confectioner.—*Mason.*

V.—MR. GRAY TO MR. WEST

AFTER a month's expectation of you, and a fortnight's despair, at Cambridge, I am come to town, and to better hopes of seeing you. If what you sent me last [1] be the product of your melancholy, what may I not expect from your more cheerful hours? For by this time the ill-health that you complain of is (I hope) quite departed; though, if I were self-interested, I ought to wish for the continuance of anything that could be the occasion of so much pleasure to me. Low spirits are my true and faithful companions; they get up with me, go to bed with me, make journeys and returns as I do; nay, and pay visits, and will even affect to be jocose, and force a feeble laugh with me; but most commonly we sit alone together, and are the prettiest insipid company in the world. However, when you come, I believe they must undergo the fate of all humble companions, and be discarded. Would I could turn them to the same use that you have done, and make an Apollo of them. If they could write such verses with me, not hartshorn, nor spirit of amber, nor all that furnishes the closet of an apothecary's widow, should persuade me to part with them. But, while I write to you, I hear the bad news of Lady Walpole's death on Saturday night last. Forgive me if the thought of what my poor Horace must feel on that account, obliges me to have done in reminding you that I am—Yours, etc.

LONDON, *Aug.* 22, 1737.

VI.—MR. GRAY TO MR. WALPOLE

I WAS hindered in my last, and so could not give you all the trouble I would have done. The description of a road, which your coach wheels have so often honoured, it would be needless to give you; suffice it that I arrived safe [2] at my uncle's, who is a great hunter in imagination; his dogs take up every chair in the house, so I am forced to stand at this present writing; and though the gout forbids him galloping after them in the field, yet he continues still to regale his ears and nose with their comfortable noise and stink. He holds me mighty cheap, I perceive, for walking when I should ride, and reading when I should hunt. My comfort amidst all this is, that I have at the distance of half

---

[1] An imitation of Tibullus.   [2] At Burnham, in Buckinghamshire.

a mile, through a green lane, a forest (the vulgar call it a common) all my own, at least as good as so, for I spy no human thing in it but myself. It is a little chaos of mountains and precipices; mountains, it is true, that do not ascend much above the clouds, nor are the declivities quite so amazing as Dover cliff; but just such hills as people who love their necks as well as I do may venture to climb, and craggs that give the eye as much pleasure as if they were more dangerous. Both vale and hill are covered with most venerable beeches, and other very reverend vegetables, that, like most other ancient people are always dreaming out their old stories to the winds,

> And as they bow their hoary tops relate,
> In murm'ring sounds, the dark decrees of fate;
> While visions, as poetic eyes avow,
> Cling to each leaf and swarm on every bough.

At the foot of one of these squats ME I [1] (*il penseroso*) and there grow to the trunk for a whole morning. The timorous hare and sportive squirrel gambol around me like Adam in paradise before he had an Eve; but I think he did not use to read Virgil, as I commonly do there. In this situation I often converse with my Horace, aloud too, that is talk to you, but I do not remember that I ever heard you answer me. I beg pardon for taking all the conversation to myself, but it is entirely your own fault. We have old Mr. Southern at a gentleman's house a little way off, who often comes to see us; he is now seventy-seven years old, and has almost wholly lost his memory; but is as agreeable as an old man can be, at least I persuade myself so when I look at him, and think of Isabella and Oroonoko. I shall be in town in about three weeks. Adieu.

September 1737.

VII.—MR. GRAY TO MR. WALPOLE [2]

I SYMPATHISE with you in the sufferings which you foresee are coming upon you. We are both at present, I imagine, in no very agreeable situation; for my part I am under the misfortune of having nothing to do, but it is a misfortune which, thank my

---

[1] The same ludicrous expression is met with in Foote's " Play of the Knights," p. 27, from the mouth of Sir Penurious Trifle,—" And what does *me I*, but take a trip to a coffee-house in St. Martin's-lane," etc.— *Mitford*.

[2] At this time with his father at Houghton. Mr. Gray writes from the same place as he did before, from his uncle's house in Buckinghamshire.— *Mason*.

which was only eighteen miles further. This chaise is a strange
sort of conveyance, of much greater use than beauty, resembling
an ill-shaped chariot, only with the door opening before instead
of the side; three horses draw it, one between the shafts, and
the other two on each side, on one of which the postillion rides,
and drives too. This vehicle will, upon occasion, go fourscore
miles a-day, but Mr. Walpole, being in no hurry, chooses to make
easy journies of it, and they are easy ones indeed; for the motion
is much like that of a sedan, we go about six miles an hour, and
commonly change horses at the end of it. It is true they are no
very graceful steeds, but they go well, and through roads which
they say are bad for France, but to me they seem gravel walks
and bowling-greens; in short it would be the finest travelling in
the world, were it not for the inns, which are mostly terrible
places indeed. But to describe our progress somewhat more
regularly, we came into Boulogne when it was almost dark, and
went out pretty early on Tuesday morning; so that all I can
say about it is, that it is a large, old, fortified town, with more
English in it than French. On Tuesday we were to go to Abbéville, seventeen leagues, or fifty-one short English miles; but
by the way we dined at Montreuil, much to our hearts' content,
on stinking mutton cutlets, addled eggs, and ditch water.
Madame the hostess made her appearance in long lappets of bone
lace and a sack of linsey-woolsey. We supped and lodged
pretty well at Abbéville, and had time to see a little of it before
we came out this morning. There are seventeen convents in it,
out of which we saw the chapels of Minims and the Carmelite
nuns. We are now come further thirty miles to Amiens, the
chief city of the province of Picardy. We have seen the
cathedral which is just what that of Canterbury[1] must have
been before the reformation. It is about the same size, a huge
Gothic building, beset on the outside with thousands of small
statues, and within adorned with beautiful painted windows,

---

[1] On this passage Mr. Whittington remarks, in his elegant essay on
"Gothic Architecture," 4to. p. 156:—"It is extraordinary that Gray
should have compared this church (Amiens) to Canterbury. No two
structures of the same sort were ever more totally and in every respect
different." To the truth of Mr. Whittington's statement I can bear
witness; nor can I at all account for the comparison drawn by Gray,
except by supposing that he concluded it to be accurate enough to furnish
his mother with an idea of what he had seen. In his letter to West, when
he mentions the church at Amiens, he does *not* compare it to Canterbury.
And in a letter to his mother of a subsequent date, he describes the cathedral at Rheims in almost the same words which he used in his former
letter from Amiens. He attempted, I should suppose, only to give a very
general resemblance of size and splendour.—*Mitford.*

and a vast number of chapels dressed out in all their finery of altar-pieces, embroidery, gilding, and marble. Over the high altar are preserved, in a very large wrought shrine of massy gold, the relicks of St. Firmin, their patron saint. We went also to the chapels of the Jesuits and Ursuline nuns, the latter of which is very richly adorned. To-morrow we shall lie at Clermont, and next day reach Paris. The country we have passed through hitherto has been flat, open, but agreeably diversified with villages, fields well-cultivated, and little rivers. On every hillock is a wind-mill, a crucifix, or a Virgin Mary dressed in flowers, and a sarcenet robe; one sees not many people or carriages on the road; now and then indeed you meet a strolling friar, a countryman with his great muff, or a woman riding astride on a little ass, with short petticoats, and a great head-dress of blue wool. . . .

X.—MR. GRAY TO MR. WEST

PARIS, *April* 12, 1739.

Enfin donc me voici à Paris. Mr. Walpole is gone out to supper at Lord Conway's, and here I remain alone, though invited too. Do not think I make a merit of writing to you preferably to a good supper; for these three days we have been here, have actually given me an aversion to eating in general. If hunger be the best sauce to meat, the French are certainly the worst cooks in the world; for what tables we have seen have been so delicately served, and so profusely, that, after rising from one of them, one imagines it impossible ever to eat again. And now, if I tell you all I have in my head, you will believe me mad, *mais n'importe, courage, allons!* for if I wait till my head grow clear and settle a little, you may stay long enough for a letter. Six days have we been coming hither, which other people do in two; they have not been disagreeable ones; through a fine, open country, admirable roads, and in an easy conveyance; the inns not absolutely intolerable, and images quite unusual presenting themselves on all hands. At Amiens we saw the fine cathedral, and eat *paté de perdrix;* passed through the park of Chantilly by the Duke of Bourbon's palace, which we only beheld as we passed; broke down at Lusarche; stopt at St. Denis, saw all the beautiful monuments of the kings of France, and the vast treasures of the abbey, rubies, and emeralds as big as small eggs, crucifixes, and

vows, crowns and reliquaries, of inestimable value; but of all
their curiosities the thing the most to our tastes, and which they
indeed do the justice to esteem the glory of their collection,
was a vase of an entire onyx, measuring at least five inches
over, three deep, and of great thickness. It is at least two
thousand years old, the beauty of the stone and sculpture upon
it (representing the mysteries of Bacchus) beyond expression
admirable; we have dreamed of it ever since. The jolly old
Benedictine, that showed us the treasures, had in his youth
been ten years a soldier; he laughed at all the relicks, was very
full of stories, and mighty obliging. On Saturday evening we
got to Paris, and were driving through the streets a long while
before we knew where we were. The minute we came, *voilà*
Milors Holdernesse, Conway, and his brother; all stayed supper,
and till two o'clock in the morning, for here nobody ever sleeps;
it is not the way. Next day go to dine at my Lord Holdernesse's,
there was the Abbé Prevôt, author of the "Cleveland," and
several other pieces much esteemed: The rest were English. At
night we went to the "Pandore;" a spectacle literally, for it is
nothing but a beautiful piece of machinery of three scenes. The
first represents the chaos, and by degrees the separation of the
elements. The second, the temple of Jupiter, the giving of the
box to Pandora. The third, the opening of the box, and all
the mischiefs that ensued. An absurd design, but executed in
the highest perfection, and that in one of the finest theatres in
the world; it is the *grande sale des machines* in the Palais des
Tuileries. Next day dined at Lord Waldegrave's; then to the
opera. Imagine to yourself for the drama four acts [1] entirely
unconnected with each other, each founded on some little history,
skilfully taken out of an ancient author, *e.g.* Ovid's *Metamorphoses*, etc., and with great address converted into a French
piece of gallantry. For instance, that which I saw, called the
"Ballet de la Paix," had its first act built upon the story of
Nireus. Homer having said he was the handsomest man of
his time, the poet, imagining such a one could not want a
mistress, has given him one. These two come in and sing
sentiment in lamentable strains, neither air nor recitative;
only, to one's great joy, they are every now and then interrupted by a dance, or (to one's great sorrow) by a chorus that
borders the stage from one end to the other, and screams, past

---

[1] The French opera has only three acts, but often a prologue on a different
subject, which (as Mr. Walpole informs me, who saw it at the same time)
was the case in this very representation.—*Mason.*

all power of simile to represent. The second act was Baucis and Philemon. Baucis is a beautiful young shepherdess, and Philemon her swain. Jupiter falls in love with her, but nothing will prevail upon her; so it is all mighty well, and the chorus sing and dance the praises of Constancy. The two other acts were about Iphis and Ianthe, and the judgment of Paris. Imagine, I say, all this transacted by cracked voices, trilling divisions upon two notes and a half, accompanied by an orchestra of humstrums, and a whole house more attentive than if Farinelli sung, and you will almost have formed a just notion of the thing.[1] Our astonishment at their absurdity you can never conceive; we had enough to do to express it by screaming an hour louder than the whole *dramatis personæ*. We have also seen twice the Comedie Françoise; first, the "Mahomet Second," a tragedy that has had a great run of late; and the thing itself does not want its beauties, but the actors are beyond measure delightful. Mademoiselle Gaussin (M. Voltaire's Zara) has with a charming (though little) person the most pathetic tone of voice, the finest expression in her face, and most proper action imaginable. There is also a Dufrêne, who did the chief character, a handsome man and a prodigious fine actor. The second we saw was the "Philosophe marié," and here they performed as well in comedy; there is a Mademoiselle Quinault, somewhat in Mrs. Clive's way, and a Monsieur Grandval, in the nature of Wilks, who is the genteelest thing in the world. There are several more would be much admired in England, and many (whom we have not seen) much celebrated here. Great part of our time is spent in seeing churches and palaces full of fine pictures, etc., the quarter of which is not yet exhausted. For my part, I could entertain myself this month merely with the common streets and the people in them. . . .

XI.—Mr. GRAY to Mr. WEST

PARIS, *May 22,* 1739.

AFTER the little particulars aforesaid I should have proceeded to a journal of our transactions for this week past, should have carried you post from hence to Versailles, hurried you through

---

[1] Our author's sentiments here seem to correspond entirely with those which J. J. Rousseau afterwards published in his famous "Lettre sur la Musique Françoise." In a French letter also, which Mr. Gray writ to his friend soon after this, he calls their music "des miaulemens & des heurlemens effroyables, melés avec un tintamarre due diable; voilà la musique Françoise en abregé."—*Mason.*

the gardens to Trianon, back again to Paris, so away to Chantilly. But the fatigue is perhaps more than you can bear, and moreover I think I have reason to stomach your last piece of gravity. Supposing you were in your soberest mood, I am sorry you should think me capable of ever being so *dissipé*, so *evaporé*, as not to be in a condition of relishing anything you could say to me. And now, if you have a mind to make your peace with me, arouse ye from your megrims and your melancholies, and (for exercise is good for you) throw away your night-cap, call for your jack-boots, and set out with me, last Saturday evening, for Versailles — and so at eight o'clock, passing through a road speckled with vines, and villas, and hares, and partridges, we arrive at the great avenue, flanked on either hand with a double row of trees about half a mile long, and with the palace itself to terminate the view; facing which, on each side of you is placed a semi-circle of very handsome buildings, which form the stables. These we will not enter into, because you know we are no jockies. Well! and is this the great front of Versailles? What a huge heap of littleness! it is composed, as it were, of three courts, all open to the eye at once, and gradually diminishing till you come to the royal apartments, which on this side present but half a dozen windows and a balcony. This last is all that can be called a front, for the rest is only great wings. The hue of all this mass is black, dirty red, and yellow; the first proceeding from stone changed by age; the second, from a mixture of brick; and the last, from a profusion of tarnished gilding. You cannot see a more disagreeable *tout-ensemble;* and, to finish the matter, it is all stuck over in many places with small busts of a tawny hue between every two windows. We pass through this to go into the garden, and here the case is indeed altered; nothing can be vaster and more magnificent than the back front; before it a very spacious terrace spreads itself, adorned with two large basons; these are bordered and lined (as most of the others) with white marble, with handsome statues of bronze reclined on their edges. From hence you descend a huge flight of steps into a semi-circle formed by woods, that are cut all around into niches, which are filled with beautiful copies of all the famous antique statues in white marble. Just in the midst is the bason of Latona; she and her children are standing on the top of a rock in the middle, on the sides of which are the peasants, some half, some totally changed into frogs, all which throw out water at her in great plenty. From this place runs on the great alley, which brings you into a complete round, where is the bason of Apollo, the biggest in the gardens. He is rising in his car out of the water, surrounded by nymphs and tritons, all in bronze, and finely executed, and these, as they play, raise a perfect storm about him; beyond this is the great canal, a prodigious long piece of water, that terminates the whole, All this you have at one *coup d'œil* in entering the garden, which is truly great. I cannot say as much of the general taste of the place; everything you behold savours too much of art; all is forced, all is constrained about you; statues and vases sowed everywhere without distinction; sugar-loaves and minced pies of yew; scrawl work of box, and little squirting *jet-d'eau*, besides a great sameness in the walks, cannot help striking one at first sight, not to mention the silliest of labyrinths, and all Æsop's fables in water; since these were designed *in usum Delphini* only. Here then we walk by moonlight, and hear the ladies and the nightingales sing. Next morning, being Whitsunday, make ready to go to the installation of nine Knights du Saint Esprit, Cambis is one :[1] high mass celebrated with music, great crowd, much incense, king, queen, dauphin, mesdames, cardinals, and court: knights arrayed by his majesty; reverences before the altar, not bows, but curtsies; stiff hams; much tittering among the ladies; trumpets, kettledrums and fifes. My dear West, I am vastly delighted with Trianon, all of us with Chantilly; if you would know why, you must have patience, for I can hold my pen no longer, except to tell you that I saw " Britannicus " last night; all the characters, particularly Agrippina and Nero, done to perfection; to-morrow " Phædra and Hippolitus." We are making you a little bundle of *petites pièces*; there is nothing in them, but they are acting at present; there are too Crebillon's " Letters," and " Amusemens sur le langage des Bêtes," said to be of one Bougeant, a Jesuit; they are both esteemed, and lately come out. This day se'nnight we go to Rheims.

XII.—MR. GRAY TO HIS MOTHER

RHEIMS, *June* 21, *N.S.* 1739.

WE have now been settled almost three weeks in this city which is more considerable upon account of its size and antiquity, than from the number of its inhabitants, or any advan

---

[1] The Comte de Cambis was lately returned from his embassy in England.—*Mason*.

tages of commerce. There is little in it worth a stranger's curiosity, besides the cathedral church, which is a vast Gothic building of a surprising beauty and lightness, all covered over with a profusion of little statues, and other ornaments. It is here the kings of France are crowned by the Archbishop of Rheims, who is the first peer, and the primate of the kingdom. The holy vessel made use of on that occasion, which contains the oil, is kept in the church of St. Nicasius hard by, and is believed to have been brought by an angel from heaven at the coronation of Clovis, the first Christian king. The streets in general have but a melancholy aspect, the houses all old; the public walks run along the side of a great moat under the ramparts, where one hears a continual croaking of frogs; the country round about is one great plain covered with vines, which at this time of the year afford no very pleasing prospect, as being not above a foot high. What pleasures the place denies to the sight, it makes up for to the palate; since you have nothing to drink but the best champaigne in the world, and all sort of provisions equally good. As to other pleasures, there is not that freedom of conversation among the people of fashion here, that one sees in other parts of France; for though they are not very numerous in this place, and consequently must live a good deal together, yet they never come to any great familiarity with one another. As my Lord Conway had spent a good part of his time among them, his brother, and we with him, were soon introduced into all their assemblies. As soon as you enter, the lady of the house presents each of you a card, and offers you a party at quadrille; you sit down, and play forty deals without intermission, excepting one quarter of an hour, when everybody rises to eat of what they call the *goûter*, which supplies the place of our tea, and is a service of wine, fruits, cream, sweetmeats, crawfish and cheese. People take what they like, and sit down again to play; after that, they make little parties to go to the walks together, and then all the company retire to their separate habitations. Very seldom any suppers or dinners are given; and this is the manner they live among one another; not so much out of any aversion they have to pleasure, as out of a sort of formality they have contracted by not being much frequented by people who have lived at Paris. It is sure they do not hate gaiety any more than the rest of their country-people, and can enter into diversions, that are once proposed, with a good grace enough; for instance, the other evening we happened to be got together in

a company of eighteen people, men and women of the best
fashion here, at a garden in the town to walk; when one of the
ladies bethought herself of asking, " Why should not we sup
here? " Immediately the cloth was laid by the side of a
fountain under the trees, and a very elegant supper served up;
after which another said, " Come, let us sing; " and directly
began herself. From singing we insensibly fell to dancing,
and singing in a round; when somebody mentioned the violins,
and immediately a company of them was ordered. Minuets
were begun in the open air, and then came country-dances,
which held till four o'clock next morning; at which hour the
gayest lady there proposed, that such as were weary should
get into their coaches, and the rest of them should dance before
them with the music in the van; and in this manner we paraded
through all the principal streets of the city, and waked everybody in it. Mr. Walpole had a mind to make a custom of the
thing, and would have given a ball in the same manner next
week; but the women did not come into it; so I believe it will
drop, and they will return to their dull cards, and usual formalities. We are not to stay above a month longer here, and shall
then go to Dijon, the chief city of Burgundy, a very splendid
and very gay town; at least such is the present design.

XIII.—Mr. GRAY to his FATHER

DIJON, *Friday, Sept.* 11, *N.S.* 1739.

WE have made three short days' journey of it from Rheims
hither, where we arrived the night before last. The road we
have passed through has been extremely agreeable; it runs
through the most fertile part of Champaigne by the side of the
river Marne, with a chain of hills on each hand at some distance,
entirely covered with woods and vineyards, and every now and
then the ruins of some old castle on their tops; we lay at St.
Dizier the first night, and at Langres the second, and got hither
the next evening time enough to have a full view of this city
in entering it. It lies in a very extensive plain covered with
vines and corn, and consequently is plentifully supplied with
both. I need not tell you that it is the chief city of Burgundy,
nor that it is of great antiquity; considering which one should
imagine it ought to be larger than one finds it. However, what
it wants in extent, is made up in beauty and cleanliness, and in

rich convents and churches, most of which we have seen. The palace of the states is a magnificent new building, where the Duke of Bourbon is lodged when he comes every three years to hold that assembly, as governor of the province. A quarter of a mile out of the town is a famous abbey of Carthusians, which we are just returned from seeing. In their chapel are the tombs of the ancient dukes of Burgundy, that were so powerful, till at the death of Charles the Bold, the last of them, this part of his dominions was united by Lewis XI. to the crown of France. To-morrow we are to pay a visit to the abbot of the Cistercians, who lives a few leagues off, and who uses to receive all strangers with great civility; his abbey is one of the richest in the kingdom; he keeps open house always, and lives with great magnificence. We have seen enough of this town already to make us regret the time we spent at Rheims; it is full of people of condition, who seem to form a much more agreeable society than we found in Champaigne; but as we shall stay here but two or three days longer, it is not worth while to be introduced into their houses. On Monday or Tuesday we are to set out for Lyons, which is two days' journey distant, and from thence you shall hear again from me.

XIV.—Mr. GRAY to Mr. WEST

LYONS, *Sept.* 18, *N.S.* 1739.

Scavez vous bien, mon cher ami, que je vous hais, que je vous deteste ? voilà des termes un peu forts; and that will save me, upon a just computation, a page of paper and six drops of ink; which, if I confined myself to reproaches of a more moderate nature, I should be obliged to employ in using you according to your deserts. What! to let anybody reside three months at Rheims, and write but once to them? Please to consult Tully, *de Amicit*, page 5, line 25, and you will find it said in express terms, " Ad amicum inter Remos relegatum mense uno quinquies scriptum esto; " nothing more plain, or less liable to false interpretations. Now because, I suppose, it will give you pain to know we are in being, I take this opportunity to tell you that we are at the ancient and celebrated Lugdunum, a city situated upon the confluence of the Rhône and Saône (Arar, I should say), two people, who though of tempers extremely unlike, think fit to join hands here, and make a little party to travel to the Mediterranean in company; the lady comes gliding along through the fruitful plains of Burgundy, *incredibili lenitate, ita ut oculis in utram partem fluit judicari non possit;* the gentleman runs all rough and roaring down from the mountains of Switzerland to meet her; and with all her soft airs she likes him never the worse; she goes through the middle of the city in state, and he passes *incog.* without the walls, but waits for her a little below. The houses here are so high, and the streets so narrow, as would be sufficient to render Lyons the dismallest place in the world, but the number of people, and the face of commerce diffused about it, are, at least, as sufficient to make it the liveliest. Between these two sufficiencies, you will be in doubt what to think of it; so we shall leave the city and proceed to its environs, which are beautiful beyond expression; it is surrounded with mountains, and those mountains all bedropped and bespeckled with houses, gardens, and plantations of the rich Bourgeois, who have from thence a prospect of the city in the vale below on one hand, on the other the rich plains of the Lyonnois, with the rivers winding among them, and the Alps, with the mountains of Dauphiné, to bound the view. All yesterday morning we were busied in climbing up Mount Fourviere, where the ancient city stood perched at such a height, that nothing but the hopes of gain could certainly ever persuade their neighbours to pay them a visit. Here are the ruins of the emperor's palaces, that resided here, that is to say, Augustus and Severus; they consist in nothing but great masses of old wall, that have only their quality to make them respected. In a vineyard of the Minims are remains of a theatre; the fathers, whom they belong to, hold them in no esteem at all, and would have showed us their sacristy and chapel instead of them. The Ursuline nuns have in their garden some Roman baths, but we having the misfortune to be men, and heretics, they did not think proper to admit us. Hard by are eight arches of a most magnificent aqueduct, said to be erected by Antony, when his legions were quartered here. There are many other parts of it dispersed up and down the country, for it brought the water from a river many leagues off in La Forez. Here are remains too of Agrippa's seven great roads which met at Lyons; in some places they lie twelve feet deep in the ground. In short, a thousand matters that you shall not know, till you give me a description of the Païs de Tombridge, and the effect its waters have upon you.

XV.—Mr. GRAY to his MOTHER

Lyons, *Oct.* 13, *N.S.* 1739.

It is now almost five weeks since I left Dijon, one of the gayest and most agreeable little cities of France, for Lyons, its reverse in all these particulars. It is the second in the kingdom in bigness and rank, the streets excessively narrow and nasty; the houses immensely high and large (that, for instance where we are lodged, has twenty-five rooms on a floor, and that for five stories); it swarms with inhabitants like Paris itself, but chiefly a mercantile people, too much given up to commerce, to think of their own, much less of a stranger's diversions. We have no acquaintance in the town, but such English as happen to be passing through here, in their way to Italy and the south, which at present happen to be near thirty in number. It is a fortnight since we set out from hence upon a little excursion to Geneva. We took the longest road, which lies through Savoy, on purpose to see a famous monastery, called the grand Chartreuse, and had no reason to think our time lost. After having travelled seven days very slow (for we did not change horses, it being impossible for a chaise to go post in these roads) we arrived at a little village, among the mountains of Savoy, called Echelles; from thence we proceeded on horses, who are used to the way, to the mountain of the Chartreuse. It is six miles to the top; the road runs winding up it, commonly not six feet broad; on one hand is the rock, with woods of pine-trees hanging over head; on the other, a monstrous precipice, almost perpendicular, at the bottom of which rolls a torrent, that sometimes tumbling among the fragments of stone that have fallen from on high, and sometimes precipitating itself down vast descents with a noise like thunder, which is still made greater by the echo from the mountains on each side, concurs to form one of the most solemn, the most romantic, and the most astonishing scenes I ever beheld. Add to this the strange views made by the craggs and cliffs on the other hand; the cascades that in many places throw themselves from the very summit down into the vale, and the river below; and many other particulars impossible to describe; you will conclude we had no occasion to repent our pains. This place St. Bruno chose to retire to, and upon its very top founded the aforesaid convent, which is the superior of the whole order. When we

came there, the two fathers, who are commissioned to entertain
strangers (for the rest must neither speak one to another, nor
to any one else), received us very kindly; and set before us a
repast of dried fish, eggs, butter, and fruits, all excellent in their
kind, and extremely neat. They pressed us to spend the night
there, and to stay some days with them; but this we could
not do, so they led us about their house, which is, you must
think, like a little city; for there are 100 fathers, besides 300
servants, that make their clothes, grind their corn, press their
wine, and do everything among themselves. The whole is
quiet, orderly, and simple; nothing of finery, but the wonderful
decency, and the strange situation, more than supply the place
of it. In the evening we descended by the same way, passing
through many clouds that were then forming themselves on
the mountain's side. Next day we continued our journey by
Chamberry, which, though the chief city of the Dutchy, and
residence of the King of Sardinia, when he comes into this part
of his dominions, makes but a very mean and insignificant
appearance; we lay at Aix, once famous for its hot baths, and
the next night at Annecy; the day after, by noon, we got to
Geneva. I have not time to say anything about it, nor of our
solitary journey back again. . . .

XVI.—Mr. GRAY to his FATHER

LYONS, *Oct.* 25, *N.S.* 1739.

In my last I gave you the particulars of our little journey to
Geneva; I have only to add, that we stayed about a week, in
order to see Mr. Conway settled there. I do not wonder so
many English choose it for their residence; the city is very
small, neat, prettily built, and extremely populous; the Rhône
runs through the middle of it, and it is surrounded with new
fortifications, that give it a military, compact air; which, joined
to the happy, lively countenances of the inhabitants, and an
exact discipline always as strictly observed as in time of war,
makes the little republic appear a match for a much greater
power; though perhaps Geneva, and all that belongs to it, are
not of equal extent with Windsor and its two parks. To one
that has passed through Savoy, as we did, nothing can be more
striking than the contrast as soon as he approaches the town.
Near the gates of Geneva runs the torrent Arve, which separates
it from the King of Sardinia's dominions; on the other side of

it lies a country naturally, indeed, fine and fertile; but you meet with nothing in it but meagre, ragged, bare-footed peasants, with their children, in extreme misery and nastiness; and even of these no great numbers. You no sooner have crossed the stream I have mentioned but poverty is no more; not a beggar, hardly a discontented face to be seen; numerous and well-dressed people swarming on the ramparts; drums beating, soldiers, well clothed and armed, exercising; and folks, with business in their looks, hurrying to and fro; all contribute to make any person, who is not blind, sensible what a difference there is between the two governments, that are the causes of one view and the other. The beautiful lake, at one end of which the town is situated, its extent, the several states that border upon it, and all its pleasures, are too well known for me to mention them. We sailed upon it as far as the dominions of Geneva extend, that is, about two leagues and a half on each side, and landed at several of the little houses of pleasure, that the inhabitants have built all about it, who received us with much politeness. The same night we eat part of a trout taken in the lake, that weighed thirty-seven pounds; as great a monster as it appeared to us, it was esteemed there nothing extraordinary, and they assured us it was not uncommon to catch them of fifty pounds; they are dressed here and sent post to Paris upon some great occasions; nay, even to Madrid, as we were told. The road we returned through was not the same we came by. We crossed the Rhône at Seyssel, and passed for three days among the mountains of Bugey, without meeting with anything new. At last we came out into the plains of La Bresse, and so to Lyons again. Sir Robert has written to Mr. Walpole, to desire he would go to Italy; which he has resolved to do; so that all the scheme of spending the winter in the south of France is laid aside, and we are to pass it in a much finer country. You may imagine I am not sorry to have this opportunity of seeing the place in the world that best deserves it. Besides as the pope (who is eighty-eight, and has been lately at the point of death) cannot probably last a great while, perhaps we may have the fortune to be present at the election of a new one, when Rome will be in all its glory. Friday next we certainly begin our journey; in two days we shall come to the foot of the Alps, and six more we shall be in passing them. Even here the winter is begun; what then must it be among those vast snowy mountains where it is hardly ever summer? We are, however, as well armed as possible against the cold, with muffs, hoods, and masks of beaver, fur-boots, and bear skins. When we arrive at Turin, we shall rest after the fatigues of the journey. . .

XVII.—MR. GRAY TO HIS MOTHER

TURIN, *Nov. 7, N.S.* 1739.

I AM this night arrived here, and have just set down to rest me after eight days' tiresome journey. For the three first we had the same road we before passed through to go to Geneva; the fourth we turned out of it, and for that day and the next travelled rather among than upon the Alps; the way commonly running through a deep valley by the side of the river Arc, which works itself a passage, with great difficulty and a mighty noise, among vast quantities of rocks, that have rolled down from the mountain tops. The winter was so far advanced as in great measure to spoil the beauty of the prospect; however, there was still somewhat fine remaining amidst the savageness and horrour of the place. The sixth we began to go up several of these mountains; and as we were passing one, met with an odd accident enough. Mr. Walpole had a little fat black spaniel, that he was very fond of, which he sometimes used to set down, and let it run by the chaise side. We were at that time in a very rough road, not two yards broad at most; on one side was a great wood of pines, and on the other a vast precipice; it was noon-day, and the sun shone bright, when all of a sudden, from the wood-side (which was as steep upwards, as the other part was downwards) out rushed a great wolf, came close to the head of the horses, seized the dog by the throat, and rushed up the hill again with him in his mouth. This was done in less than a quarter of a minute; we all saw it, and yet the servants had not time to draw their pistols, or do anything to save the dog. If he had not been there, and the creature had thought fit to lay hold of one of the horses chaise, and we, and all must inevitably have tumbled above fifty fathoms perpendicular down the precipice. The seventh we came to Lanebourg, the last town in Savoy; it lies at the foot of the famous mount Cenis, which is so situated as to allow no room for any way but over the very top of it. Here the chaise was forced to be pulled to pieces, and the baggage and that to be carried by mules. We ourselves were wrapped up in our furs and seated upon a sort of matted chair without legs, which is carried upon poles in the manner of a bier, and so begun to ascend by the help of eight men. It was six miles to the top, where a plain opens itself about as many more in breadth, covered perpetually with very deep snow, and in the midst of that a great lake of unfathomable depth, from whence a river takes its rise, and tumbles over monstrous rocks quite down the other side of the mountain. The descent is six miles more, but infinitely more steep than the going up; and here the men perfectly fly down with you, stepping from stone to stone with incredible swiftness in places where none but they could go three paces without falling. The immensity of the precipices, the roaring of the river and torrents that run into it, the huge craggs covered with ice and snow, and the clouds below you and about you, are objects it is impossible to conceive without seeing them; and though we had heard many strange descriptions of the scene, none of them at all came up to it. We were but five hours in performing the whole, from which you may judge of the rapidity of the men's motion. We are now got into Piedmont, and stopped a little while at La Ferriere, a small village about three quarters of the way down, but still among the clouds, where we began to hear a new language spoken round about us; at last we got quite down, went through the Pas de Suse, a narrow road among the Alps, defended by two fortresses, and lay at Bossolens. Next evening through a fine avenue of nine miles in length, as straight as a line, we arrived at this city, which, as you know, is the capital of the Principality, and the residence of the King of Sardinia. . . .[1] We shall stay here, I believe, a fortnight, and proceed for Genoa, which is three or four days' journey to go post. —I am, etc.

XVIII.—MR. GRAY TO MR. WEST

TURIN, *Nov.* 16, N.S. 1739.

AFTER eight days' journey through Greenland, we arrived at Turin. You approach it by a handsome avenue of nine miles long, and quiet strait. The entrance is guarded by certain vigilant dragons, called Douâniers, who mumbled us for some time. The city is not large, as being a place of strength, and consequently confined within its fortifications; it has many

[1] That part of the letter here omitted contained only a description of the city, which, as Mr. Gray has given it to Mr. West in the following letter, and that in a more lively manner, I thought it unnecessary to insert; a liberty I have taken in other parts of this correspondence, in order to avoid repetitions.—*Mason*.

beauties and some faults; among the first are streets all laid out by the line, regular uniform buildings, fine walks that surround the whole, and in general a good lively clean appearance. But the houses are of brick plaistered, which is apt to want repairing; the windows of oiled paper, which is apt to be torn; and everything very slight, which is apt to tumble down. There is an excellent opera, but it is only in the carnival; balls every night, but only in the carnival; masquerades too, but only in the carnival. This carnival lasts only from Christmas to Lent; one half of the remaining part of the year is passed in remembering the last, the other in expecting the future carnival. We cannot well subsist upon such slender diet, no more than upon an execrable Italian comedy, and a puppet-show, called *Rappresentazione d'un' anima dannata*, which, I think, are all the present diversions of the place; except the Marquise de Cavaillac's Conversazione, where one goes to see people play at ombre and taroc, a game with seventy-two cards all painted with suns, and moons, and devils and monks. Mr. Walpole has been at court; the family are at present at a country palace, called La Venerie. The palace here in town is the very quintessence of gilding and looking-glass; inlaid floors, carved pannels, and painting, wherever they could stick a brush. I own I have not, as yet, anywhere met with those grand and simple works of art that are to amaze one, and whose sight one is to be the better for; but those of Nature have astonished me beyond expression. In our little journey up to the Grande Chartreuse, I do not remember to have gone ten paces without an exclamation, that there was no restraining: not a precipice, not a torrent, not a cliff, but is pregnant with religion and poetry. There are certain scenes that would awe an atheist into belief, without the help of other argument. One need not have a very fantastic imagination to see spirits there at noon-day. You have Death perpetually before your eyes, only so far removed as to compose the mind without frighting it. I am well persuaded St. Bruno was a man of no common genius to choose such a situation for his retirement, and perhaps should have been a disciple of his, had I been born in his time. You may believe Abelard and Heloïse were not forgot upon this occasion. If I do not mistake, I saw you too every now and then at a distance along the trees; *il me semble, que j'ai vu ce chien de visage là quelque part.* You seemed to call to me from the other side of the precipice, but the noise of the river below was so great, that I really could not distinguish what you said; it seemed to have a cadence like verse.

In your next you will be so good to let me know what it was.
The week we have since passed among the Alps has not equalled
the single day upon that mountain, because the winter was
rather too far advanced, and the weather a little foggy. However, it did not want its beauties; the savage rudeness of the
view is inconceivable without seeing it. I reckoned in one day
thirteen cascades, the least of which was, I dare say, one hundred
feet in height. I had Livy in the chaise with me, and beheld his
" *Nives cœlo propè immistæ, tecta informia imposita rupibus,
pecora jumentaque torrida frigore, homines intonsi and inculti,
animalia inanimaque omnia rigentia gelu; omnia confragosa,
præruptaque.*" [1] The creatures that inhabit them are, in all
respects, below humanity; and most of them, especially women,
have the *tumidum guttur*, which they call *goscia*. Mont Cenis,
I confess, carries the permission [2] mountains have of being
frightful rather too far; and its horrours were accompanied
with too much danger to give one time to reflect upon their
beauties. There is a family of the Alpine monsters I have
mentioned, upon its very top, that in the middle of winter
calmly lay in their stock of provisions and firing, and so are
buried in their hut for a month or two under the snow. When
we were down it, and got a little way into Piedmont, we began
to find " *Apricos quosdam colles, rivosque prope sylvas, and
jam humano cultu digniora loca.*" [3] I read Silius Italicus too,
for the first time; and wished for you, according to custom.
We set out for Genoa in two days' time.

XIX.—MR. GRAY TO MR. WEST

GENOA, *Nov.* 21, 1739.

HORRIDOS tractus, Boreæq; linquens
Regna Taurini fera, molliorem
Advehor brumam, Genuæq; amantes

Litora soles.

At least if they do not, they have a very ill taste; for I never
beheld anything more amiable. Only figure to yourself a vast
semicircular bason, full of fine blue sea, and vessels of all sorts
and sizes, some sailing out, some coming in, and others at anchor;

[1] See *Livii Hist.* lib. xxi. cap. xxxii. tom. iii. p. 421, ed. Drakenborch.
[2] A phrase borrowed from Madame De Sevigné, who quotes a *bon mot* on
Pelisson, " qu'il abusoit de la permission qu'ont les hommes, d'etre laids."
—*Mason.*
[3] See *Livii Hist.* lib. xxi. cap. xxxvii. p. 438.

and all round it palaces, and churches peeping over one another's heads, gardens, and marble terraces full of orange and cypress trees, fountains, and trellis-works covered with vines, which altogether compose the grandest of theatres. This is the first *coup d'œil*, and is almost all I am yet able to give you an account of, for we arrived late last night. To-day was, luckily, a great festival, and in the morning we resorted to the church of the Madonna delle Vigne, to put up our little orisons (I believe I forgot to tell you, that we have been some time converts to the holy Catholic Church); we found our Lady richly dressed out, with a crown of diamonds on her own head, another upon the child's, and a constellation of wax lights burning before them. Shortly after came the doge, in his robes of crimson damask, and a cap of the same, followed by the senate in black. Upon his approach began a fine concert of music, and among the rest two eunuchs' voices, that were a perfect feast to ears that had heard nothing but French operas for a year. We listened to this, and breathed nothing but incense for two hours. The doge is a very tall, lean, stately old figure, called Constantino Balbi; and the senate seem to have been made upon the same model. They said their prayers, and heard an absurd white friar preach, with equal devotion. After this we went to the Annonciata, a church built by the family Lomellini, and belonging to it; which is, indeed, a most stately structure, the inside wholly marble of various kinds, except where gold and painting take its place. From hence to the Palazzo Doria. I should make you sick of marble, if I told you how it was lavished here upon the porticoes, the balustrades, and terraces, the lowest of which extends quite to the sea. The inside is by no means answerable to the outward magnificence; the furniture seems to be as old as the founder of the family.[1] There great embossed silver tables tell you, in bas-relief, his victories at sea; how he entertained the Emperor Charles, and how he refused the sovereignty of the commonwealth when it was offered him; the rest is old-fashioned velvet chairs, and Gothic tapestry. The rest of the day has been spent, much to our hearts' content, in cursing French music and architecture, and in singing the praises of Italy. We find this place so very fine, that we are in fear of finding nothing finer. We are fallen in love with the Mediterranean Sea, and hold your lakes and your rivers in vast contempt. This is

" The happy country where huge lemons grow,"

[1] The famous Andrea Doria.

as Waller says; and I am sorry to think of leaving it in a week for Parma, although it be

> The happy country where huge cheeses grow.

XX.—Mr. GRAY to his MOTHER

BOLOGNA, *Dec.* 9, *N.S.* 1739.

OUR journey hither has taken up much less time than I expected. We left Genoa (a charming place, and one that deserved a longer stay) the week before last; crossed the mountains, and lay that night at Tortona, the next at St. Giovanni, and the morning after came to Piacenza. That city (though the capital of a dutchy) made so frippery an appearance, that instead of spending some days there, as had been intended, we only dined, and went on to Parma; stayed there all the following day, which was passed in visiting the famous works of Correggio in the Dome, and other churches. The fine gallery of pictures that once belonged to the dukes of Parma, is no more here; the King of Naples has carried it all thither, and the city had not merit enough to detain us any longer, so we proceeded through Reggio to Modena; this, though the residence of its duke, is an ill-built melancholy place, all of brick, as are most of the towns in this part of Lombardy. He himself lives in a private manner, with very little appearance of a court about him; he has one of the noblest collections of paintings in the world, which entertained us extremely well the rest of that day and a part of the next; and in the afternoon we came to Bologna. So now you may wish us joy of being in the dominions of his holiness. This is a populous city, and of great extent. All the streets have porticoes on both sides, such as surround a part of Covent Garden, a great relief in summer-time in such a climate; and from one of the principal gates to a church of the Virgin [where is a wonder-working picture, at three miles distance] runs a corridore of the same sort, lately finished, and, indeed, a most extraordinary performance. The churches here are more remarkable for their paintings than architecture, being mostly old structures of brick; but the palaces are numerous, and fine enough to supply us with somewhat worth seeing from morning till night. The country of Lombardy, hitherto, is one of the most beautiful imaginable; the roads broad, and exactly straight, and on either hand vast plantations of trees, chiefly mulberries and olives, and not a tree without a vine twining about it and spreading among its branches. This scene, indeed, which must be the most lovely in the world during the proper season, is at present all deformed by the winter, which here is rigorous enough for the time it lasts; but one still sees the skeleton of a charming place, and reaps the benefit of its product, for the fruits and provisions are admirable; in short you find everything, that luxury can desire, in perfection. We have now been here a week, and shall stay some little time longer. We are at the foot of the Appennine mountains; it will take up three days to cross them, and then we shall come to Florence, where we shall pass the Christmas. Till then we must remain in a state of ignorance as to what is doing in England, for our letters are to meet us there. If I do not find four or five from you alone, I shall wonder.

XXI.—MR. GRAY TO HIS MOTHER

FLORENCE, *Dec.* 19, *N.S.* 1739.

WE spent twelve days at Bologna, chiefly (as most travellers do) in seeing sights; for as we knew no mortal there, and as it is no easy matter to get admission into any Italian house, without very particular recommendations, we could see no company but in public places; and there are none in that city but the churches. We saw, therefore, churches, palaces, and pictures from morning to night; and the 15th of this month set out for Florence, and began to cross the Appennine mountains; we travelled among and upon them all that day, and, as it was but indifferent weather, were commonly in the middle of thick clouds, that utterly deprived us of a sight of their beauties; for this vast chain of hills has its beauties, and all the vallies are cultivated; even the mountains themselves are many of them so within a little of their very tops. They are not so horrid as the Alps, though pretty near as high; and the whole road is admirably well kept, and paved throughout, which is a length of fourscore miles, and more. We left the pope's dominions, and lay that night in those of the grand duke at Fiorenzuola, a paltry little town, at the foot of Mount Giogo, which is the highest of them all. Next morning we went up it; the post-house is upon its very top, and usually involved in clouds, or half buried in the snow. Indeed there was none of the last at the time we were there, but it was still a dismal habitation. The descent is most excessively

steep, and the turnings very short and frequent; however, we performed it without any danger, and in coming down could dimly
discover Florence, and the beautiful plain about it, through the
mists; but enough to convince us, it must be one of the noblest
prospects upon earth in summer. That afternoon we got
thither; and Mr. Mann, the resident, had sent his servant to
meet us at the gates, and conduct us to his house. He is the best
and most obliging person in the world. The next night we were
introduced at the Prince of Craon's assembly (he has the chief
power here in the grand duke's absence). The princess, and
he, were extremely civil to the name of Walpole, so we were asked
to stay supper, which is as much as to say, you may come
and sup here whenever you please; for after the first invitation
this is always understood. We have also been at the Countess
Suarez's, a favourite of the late duke, and one that gives the
first movement to everything gay that is going forward here.
The news is every day expected from Vienna of the great
duchess's delivery; if it be a boy, here will be all sorts of balls,
masquerades, operas, and illuminations; if not, we must wait
for the carnival, when all those things come of course. In the
meantime it is impossible to want entertainment; the famous
gallery, alone, is an amusement for months; we commonly pass
two or three hours every morning in it, and one has perfect
leisure to consider all its beauties. You know it contains many
hundred antique statues, such as the whole world cannot match,
besides the vast collection of paintings, medals, and precious
stones, such as no other prince was ever master of; in short, all
that the rich and powerful house of Medicis has in so many years
got together. And besides this city abounds with so many
palaces and churches, that you can hardly place yourself anywhere without having some fine one in view, or at least some
statue or fountain, magnificently adorned; these undoubtedly
are far more numerous than Genoa can pretend to; yet, in its
general appearance, I cannot think that Florence equals it in
beauty. Mr. Walpole is just come from being presented to the
electress palatine dowager; she is a sister of the late great
duke's; a stately old lady, that never goes out but to church,
and then she has guards, and eight horses to her coach. She
received him with much ceremony, standing under a huge black
canopy, and, after a few minutes talking, she assured him of her
good will, and dismissed him. She never sees anybody but thus
in form; and so she passes her life, poor woman! . . .

XXII.—Mr. GRAY to Mr. WHARTON

PROPOSALS FOR PRINTING BY SUBSCRIPTION, IN THIS LARGE
LETTER, THE TRAVELS OF T. G., GENT., WHICH WILL CONSIST
OF THE FOLLOWING PARTICULARS:

CHAP. I

THE author arrives at Dover; his conversation with the mayor
of that corporation. Sets out in the pacquet boat: grows very
sick; the author spews; a very minute account of all the circumstances thereof. His arrival at Calais; how the inhabitants
of that country speak French, and are said to be all Papishes;
the author's reflections thereupon.

II

How they feed him with soupe, and what soupe is. How he
meets with a capucin, and what a capucin is. How they shut
him up in a post-chaise and send him to Paris; he goes wondering along during six days; and how there are trees and houses
just as in England. Arrives at Paris without knowing it.

III

Full account of the river Seine, and of the various animals
and plants its borders produce. Description of the little
creature called an abbé, its parts, and their uses; with the
reasons why they will not live in England, and the methods
that have been used to propagate them there. A cut of the
inside of a nunnery; its structure wonderfully adapted to the
use of the animals that inhabit it; a short account of them, how
they propagate without the help of a male; and how they eat
up their own young ones, like cats and rabbits: supposed to
have both sexes in themselves like a snail. Dissection of a
dutchess, with copper-plates, very curious.

IV

Goes to the opera: grand orchestra of humstrums, bagpipes,
saltboxes, tabours, and pipes. Anatomy of a French ear, showing the formation of it to be entirely different from that of an

English one; and that sounds have a directly contrary effect upon one and the other. Farinelli, at Paris, said to have a fine manner, but no voice. Grand ballet, in which there is no seeing the dance for petticoats. Old women with flowers and jewels stuck in the curls of their grey hair. Red-heeled shoes and roll-ups innumerable; hoops and panniers immeasurable, paint unspeakable. Tables, wherein is calculated, with the utmost exactness, the several degrees of red, now in use, from the rising blushes of an advocate's wife, to the flaming crimson of a princess of the blood; done by a limner in great vogue.

V

The author takes unto him a taylour; his character. How he covers him with silk and fringe, and widens his figure with buckram, a yard on each side. Waistcoat and breeches so strait, he can neither breathe nor walk. How the barber curls him *en bequille*, and *à la negligèe*, and ties a vast solitaire about his neck. How the milliner lengthens his ruffles to his fingers' ends, and sticks his two arms into a muff. How he cannot stir; and how they cut him in proportion to his clothes.

VI

He is carried to Versailles, despises it infinitely. A dissertation upon taste. Goes to an installation in the Chapel Royal: enter the king and fifty fiddlers *solus*; kettle-drums and trumpet; queens and dauphins; princesses and cardinals; incense and the mass; old knights making curtsies; Holy Ghosts and fiery tongues.

VII

Goes into the country to Rheims, in Champagne, stays there three months; what he did there (he must beg the reader's pardon but) he has really forgot.

VIII

Proceeds to Lyons, vastness of that city. Can't see the streets for houses. How rich it is, and how much it stinks. Poem upon the confluence of the Rhone and the Sâone, by a friend of the author's; very pretty.

IX

Makes a journey into Savoy, and in his way visits the Grande
Chartreuse: he is set aside upon a mule's back, and begins to
climb up the mountains: rocks and torrents beneath, pine trees
and snows above: horrours and terrours on all sides. The
author dies of the fright.

X

He goes to Geneva. His mortal antipathy to a presbyterian
and the cure for it. Returns to Lyons; gets a surfeit with
eating ortolans and lampreys; is advised to go into Italy for
the benefit of the air.

XI

Sets out the latter end of November to cross the Alps. He
is devoured by a wolf; and how it is to be devoured by a wolf
the seventh day he comes to the foot of Mount Cenis. How he
is wrap'd up in bear-skins and beaver-skins; boots on his legs
caps on his head; muffs on his hands, and taffety over his eyes
He is placed on a bier, and is carried to heaven by the savage
blindfold. How he lights among a certain nation called Clouds
how they are always in a sweat, and never speak, but they
grunt; how they flock about him, and think him very odd for
not doing so too. He falls plump into Italy.

XII

Arrives at Turin: goes to Genoa, and from thence to Placentia
crosses the river Trebia. The ghost of Hannibal appears to
him, and what it and he say upon the occasion. Locked out o
Parma on a cold winter's night; the author, by an ingeniou
stratagem, gains admittance. Despises that city, and proceed
through Reggio to Modena. How the duke and dutchess li
over their own stables, and go every night to a vile Italia
comedy; despises them and it, and proceeds to Bologna.

XIII

Enters into the dominions of the Pope o'Rome. Meets th
devil, and what he says on the occasion. Very publick an
scandalous doings between the vine and the elm trees, and how

the olive trees are shocked thereupon. Author longs for Bologna sausages and hams, and how he grows as fat as an hog.

XIV

Observations on antiquities. The author proves that Bologna was the ancient Tarentum; that the battle of Salamis, contrary to the vulgar opinion, was fought by land, and that not far from Ravenna; that the Romans were a colony of the Jews; and that Eneas was the same with Ehud.

XV

Arrival at Florence. Is of opinion that the Venus of Medicis is a modern performance, and that a very indifferent one, and much inferior to the K. Charles at Charing-cross. Account of the city and manners of the inhabitants. A learned dissertation on the true situation of Gomorrah. . . .

And here will end the first part of these instructive and entertaining voyages. The subscribers are to pay twenty guineas, nineteen down, and the remainder upon delivery of the book. N.B. A few are printed on the softest royal brown paper, for the use of the curious.

My Dear, Dear Wharton,

(Which is a dear more than I give anybody else. It is very odd to begin with a parenthesis, but) You may think me a beast not having sooner wrote to you, and to be sure a beast I am. Now, when one owns it, I don't see what you have left to say. I take this opportunity to inform you (an opportunity I have had every week this twelvemonth) that I am arrived safe at Calais, and am at present at—Florence, a city in Italy, in I don't know how many degrees of N. latitude. Under the line I am sure it is not, for I am at this instant expiring with cold. You must know, that not being certain what circumstances of my history would particularly suit your curiosity, and knowing that all I had to say to you would overflow the narrow limits of many a good quire of paper, I have taken this method of laying before you the contents, that you may pitch upon what you please, and give me your orders accordingly to expatiate thereupon: for I conclude you will write to me: won't you? oh! yes, when you know that in a week I set out for Rome, and that the pope is dead, and that I shall be (I should say, God willing;

and if nothing extraordinary intervene; and if I am alive and well; and in all human probability) at the coronation of a new one. Now, as you have no other correspondent there, and as if you do not, I certainly shall not write again. (Observe my impudence.) I take it to be your interest to send me a vast letter, full of all sorts of news and politics, and such other ingredients, as to you shall seem convenient with all decent expedition, only do not be too severe upon the Pretender; and if you like my style, pray say so. This is *à la Françoise;* and if you think it a little too foolish, and impertinent, you shall be treated *alla Toscana* with a thousand *Signoria Illustrissimas,* in the mean time I have the honour to remain

Your lofing frind, tell deth,

T. GRAY.

FLORENCE, *March 12, N.S.* 1740.

P.S. This is *à l'Angloise.* I don't know where you are; if at Cambridge pray let me know all, how, and about it: and if my old friends, Thomson or Clarke, fall in your way, say I am extremely theirs. But if you are in town, I entreat you to make my best compliments to Mrs. Wharton. Adieu.

Yours, sincerely, a second time.

XXIII.—MR. GRAY TO HIS MOTHER

FLORENCE, *March* 19, 1740.

THE pope [1] is at last dead, and we are to set out for Rome on Monday next. The conclave is still sitting there, and likely to continue so some time longer, as the two French cardinals are but just arrived, and the German ones are still expected. It agrees mighty ill with those that remain inclosed: Ottoboni is already dead of an apoplexy; Alteiri and several others are said to be dying, or very bad: yet it is not expected to break up till after Easter. We shall lie at Sienna the first night, spend a day there, and in two more get to Rome. One begins to see in this country the first promises of an Italian spring, clear unclouded skies, and warm suns, such as are not often felt in England; yet, for your sake, I hope at present you have your proportion of them, and that all your frosts, and snows, and short breaths are, by this time, utterly vanished. I have nothing new or particular to inform you of; and, if you see things at home go on much in their old course, you must not imagine

<hr>

[1] Clement the Twelfth.

them more various abroad. The diversions of a Florentine Lent are composed of a sermon in the morning, full of hell and the devil; a dinner at noon, full of fish and meagre diet; and, in the evening, what is called a conversazione, a sort of assembly at the principal people's houses, full of I cannot tell what: besides this, there is twice a week a very grand concert. . . .

XXIV.—MR. GRAY TO HIS MOTHER

ROME, *April 2, N.S. 1740.*

THIS is the third day since we came to Rome, but the first hour I have had to write to you in. The journey from Florence cost us four days, one of which was spent at Sienna, an agreeable, clean, old city, of no great magnificence or extent; but in a fine situation, and good air. What it has most considerable is its cathedral, a huge pile of marble, black and white laid alternately, and laboured with a gothic niceness and delicacy in the old-fashioned way. Within too are some paintings and sculpture of considerable hands. The sight of this, and some collections that were shewed us in private houses, were a sufficient employment for the little time we were to pass there; and the next morning we set forward on our journey through a country very oddly composed; for some miles you have a continual scene of little mountains cultivated from top to bottom with rows of olive-trees, or else elms, each of which has its vine twining about it, and mixing with the branches; and corn sown between all the ranks. This diversified with numerous small houses and convents, makes the most agreeable prospect in the world: but, all of a sudden, it alters to black barren hills, as far as the eye can reach, that seem never to have been capable of culture, and are as ugly as useless. Such is the country for some time before one comes to Mount Radicofani, a terrible black hill, on the top of which we were to lodge that night. It is very high, and difficult of ascent; and at the foot of it we were much embarrassed by the fall of one of the poor horses that drew us. This accident obliged another chaise, which was coming down, to stop also; and out of it peeped a figure in a red cloak, with a handkerchief tied round its head, which, by its voice and mien, seemed a fat old woman; but, upon its getting out, appeared to be Senesino, who was returning from Naples to Sienna, the place of his birth and residence. On the highest part of the mountain is an old fortress, and near it a house built by one of the grand dukes for a hunting-seat, but now converted into an inn. It is the shell of a large fabrick, but such an inside, such chambers, and accommodations, that your cellar is a palace in comparison; and your cat sups and lies much better than we did; for, it being a saint's eve, there was nothing but eggs. We devoured our meagre fare; and, after stopping up the windows with the quilts, were obliged to lie upon the straw beds in our clothes. Such are the conveniences in a road, that is, as it were, the great thoroughfare of all the world. Just on the other side of this mountain, at Ponte-Centino, one enters the patrimony of the church; a most delicious country, but thinly inhabited. That night brought us to Viterbo, a city of a more lively appearance than any we had lately met with; the houses have glass windows, which is not very usual here; and most of the streets are terminated by a handsome fountain. Here we had the pleasure of breaking our fast on the leg of an old hare and some broiled crows. Next morning, in descending Mount Viterbo, we first discovered (though at near thirty miles distance) the cupola of St. Peter's, and a little after began to enter on an old Roman pavement, with now and then a ruined tower, or a sepulchre on each hand. We now had a clear view of the city, though not to the best advantage, as coming along a plain quite upon a level with it; however it appeared very vast, and surrounded with magnificent villas and gardens. We soon after crossed the Tiber, a river that ancient Rome made more considerable than any merit of its own could have done: however, it is not contemptibly small, but a good handsome stream; very deep, yet somewhat of a muddy complexion. The first entrance of Rome is prodigiously striking. It is by a noble gate, designed by Michael Angelo, and adorned with statues; this brings you into a large square, in the midst of which is a vast obelisk of granite, and in front you have at one view two churches of a handsome architecture, and so much alike that they are called the twins; with three streets, the middlemost of which is one of the longest in Rome. As high as my expectation was raised, I confess, the magnificence of this city infinitely surpasses it. You cannot pass along a street but you have views of some palace, or church, or square, or fountain, the most picturesque and noble one can imagine. We have not yet set about considering its beauties, ancient and modern, with attention; but have already taken a slight transient view of some of the most remarkable. St. Peter's I saw the day after we arrived, and was struck dumb with wonder. I there saw the Cardinal D'Auvergne, one of the French ones, who upon coming off his journey, immediately repaired hither to offer up his vows at the high altar, and went directly into the conclave; the doors of which we saw opened to him, and all the other immured cardinals came thither to receive him. Upon his entrance they were closed again directly. It is supposed they will not come to an agreement about a pope till after Easter, though the confinement is very disagreeable. I have hardly philosophy enough to see the infinity of fine things, that are here daily in the power of anybody that has money, without regretting the want of it; but custom has the power of making things easy to one. I have not yet seen his majesty of Great Britain, etc., though I have the two boys in the gardens of the Villa Borgese, where they go a-shooting almost every day; it was at a distance, indeed, for we did not choose to meet them, as you may imagine. This letter (like all those the English send, or receive) will pass through the hands of that family, before it comes to those it was intended for. They do it more honour than it deserves; and all they will learn from thence will be, that I desire you to give my duty to my father, and wherever else it is due, and that I am, etc.

XXV.—MR. GRAY TO HIS MOTHER

ROME, *April* 15, 1740. *Good-Friday.*

TO-DAY I am just come from paying my adoration at St. Peter's to three extraordinary relicks, which are exposed to public view only on these two days in the whole year, at which time all the confraternities in the city come in procession to see then. It was something extremely novel to see that vast church, and the most magnificent in the world, undoubtedly, illuminated (for it was night) by thousands of little crystal lamps, disposed in the figure of a huge cross at the high altar, and seeming to hang alone in the air. All the light proceeded from this, and had the most singular effect imaginable as one entered the great door. Soon after came one after another, I believe, thirty processions, all dressed in linen frocks, and girt with a cord, their heads covered with a cowl all over, only two holes to see through left. Some of them were all black, others red, others white, others party-coloured; these were continually coming and going with their tapers and crucifixes before them; and to each company, as they arrived and knelt before the great altar, were shewn from a balcony at a great height, the three wonders, which are, you must know, the head of the spear that wounded Christ; St. Veronica's handkerchief, with the miraculous impression of his face upon it; and a piece of the true cross, on the sight of which the people thump their breasts, and kiss the pavement with vast devotion. The tragical part of the ceremony is half a dozen wretched creatures, who with their faces covered, but naked to the waist, are in a side-chapel disciplining themselves with scourges full of iron prickles; but really in earnest, as our eyes can testify, which saw their backs and arms so raw we should have taken it for a red satin doublet torn, and shewing the skin through, had we not been convinced of the contrary by the blood which was plentifully sprinkled about them. It is late; I give you joy of Port-Bello, and many other things, which I hope are all true. . . .

XXVI.—Mr. GRAY to Mr. WEST

Tivoli, *May* 20, 1740.

This day being in the palace of his Highness the Duke of Modena, he laid his most serene commands upon me to write to Mr. West, and said he thought it for his glory, that I should draw up an inventory of all his most serene possessions for the said West's perusal.——*Imprimis*, a house, being in circumference a quarter of a mile, two feet and an inch; the said house containing the following particulars, to wit, a great room. Item, another great room; item, a bigger room; item, another room; item, a vast room; item, a sixth of the same; a seventh ditto; an eighth as before; a ninth as abovesaid; a tenth (see No. 1); item, ten more such, besides twenty besides, which, not to be too particular, we shall pass over. The said rooms contain nine chairs, two tables, five stools, and a cricket. From whence we shall proceed to the garden, containing two millions of superfine laurel hedges, a clump of cypress trees, and half the river Teverone, that pisses into two thousand several chamberpots. *Finis.*— Dame Nature desired me to put in a list of her little goods and chattels, and, as they were small, to be very minute about them. She has built here three or four little mountains, and laid them out in an irregular semi-circle; from certain others behind, at a greater distance, she has drawn a canal, into which she has put a little river of her's, called Anio; she has cut a huge cleft between the two innermost of her four hills, and there she has left it to its own disposal; which she has no sooner done, but, like a heedless chit, it tumbles headlong down a declivity fifty feet perpendicular, breaks itself all to shatters, and is converted into a shower of rain, where the sun forms many a bow, red, green, blue, and yellow. To get out of our metaphors without any further trouble, it is the most noble sight in the world. The weight of that quantity of waters, and the force they fall with, have worn the rocks they throw themselves among into a thousand irregular craggs, and to a vast depth. In this channel it goes boiling along with a mighty noise till it comes to another steep, where you see it a second time come roaring down (but first you must walk two miles farther) a greater height than before, but not with that quantity of waters; for by this time it has divided itself, being crossed and opposed by the rocks, into four several streams, each of which in emulation of the great one, will tumble down too; and it does tumble down, but not from an equally elevated place; so that you have at one view all these cascades intermixed with groves of olive and little woods, the mountains rising behind them, and on the top of one (that which forms the extremity of one of the half-circle's horns) is seated the town itself. At the very extremity of that extremity, on the brink of the precipice, stands the Sybils' temple, the remains of a little rotunda, surrounded with its portico, above half of whose beautiful Corinthian pillars are still standing and entire; all this on one hand. On the other, the open Campagna of Rome, here and there a little castle on a hillock, and the city itself on the very brink of the horizon, indistinctly seen (being eighteen miles off) except the dome of St. Peter's; which, if you look out of your window, wherever you are, I suppose, you can see. I did not tell you that a little below the first fall, on the side of the rock, and hanging over that torrent, are little ruins which they shew you for Horace's house, a curious situation to observe the

> " Præceps Anio, & Tiburni lucus, & uda
>   Mobilibus pomaria rivis."

Mæcenas did not care for such a noise, it seems, and built him a house (which they also carry one to see) so situated that it sees nothing at all of the matter, and for anything he knew there might be no such river in the world. Horace had another house on the other side of the Teverone, opposite to Mæcenas's; and they told us there was a bridge of communication, by which *" andava il detto Signor per trastullarsi coll istesso Orazio."* In coming hither we crossed the Aquæ Albulæ, a vile little brook that stinks like a fury, and they say it has stunk so these thousand years. I forgot the Piscina of Quintilius Varus, where he used to keep certain little fishes. This is very entire, and there is a piece of the aqueduct that supplied it too; in the garden below is old Rome, built in little, just as it was, they say. There are seven temples in it, and no houses at all: they say there were none.

May 21.

We have had the pleasure of going twelve miles out of our way to Palestrina. It has rained all day as if heaven and us were coming together. See my honesty, I do not mention a syllable of the temple of Fortune, because I really did not see it; which, I think, is pretty well for an old traveller. So we returned along the Via Prænestina, saw the Lacus Gabinus and Regillus, where, you know, Castor and Pollux appeared upon a certain occasion. And many a good old tomb we left on each hand, and many an aqueduct,

Dumb are whose fountains, and their channels dry.

There are, indeed, two whole modern ones, works of popes, that run about thirty miles a-piece in length; one of them conveys still the famous Aqua Virgo to Rome, and adds vast beauty to the prospect. So we came to Rome again, where waited for us a *splendidissimo regalo* of letters; in one of which came You, with your huge characters and wide intervals, staring. I would have you to know, I expect you should take a handsome crow-quill when you write to me, and not leave room for a pin's point in four sides of a sheet royal. Do you but find matter, I will find spectacles.

I have more time than I thought, and I will employ it in telling you about a ball that we were at the other evening. Figure to yourself a Roman villa; all its little apartments thrown open, and lighted up to the best advantage. At the upper end of the gallery, a fine concert, in which La Diamantina, a famous virtuosa, played on the violin divinely and sung angelically; Giovannino and Pasqualini (great names in musical story) also performed miraculously. On each side were ranged all the secular *grand monde* of Rome, the ambassadors, princesses, and all that. Among the rest *Il Serenissimo Pretendente* (as the Mantova gazette calls him) displayed his rueful length of person, with his two young ones, and all his ministry around him. " *Poi nacque un grazioso ballo,*" where the world danced, and I sat in a corner regaling myself with iced fruits, and other pleasant rinfrescatives.

XXVII.—Mr. GRAY to Mr. WEST

ROME, *May* 1740.

I AM to-day just returned from Alba, a good deal fatigued; for
you know the Appian [1] is somewhat tiresome.[2]   We dined at
Pompey's; he indeed was gone for a few days to his Tusculan,
but, by the care of his Villicus, we made an admirable meal.   We
had the dugs of a pregnant sow, a peacock, a dish of thrushes,
a noble scarus just fresh from the Tyrrhene, and some conchylia
of the lake with garum sauce.   For my part I never eat better
at Lucullus's table.   We drank half-a-dozen cyathi apiece of
ancient Alban to Pholoë's health; and, after bathing, and playing an hour at ball, we mounted our *essedum* again, and proceeded up the mount to the temple.   The priests there entertained us with an account of a wonderful shower of birds' eggs,
that had fallen two days before, which had no sooner touched
the ground, but they were converted into gudgeons; as also
that the night past, a dreadful voice had been heard out of the
Adytum, which spoke Greek during a full half-hour, but nobody
understood it.   But quitting my Romanities, to your great joy
and mine, let me tell you in plain English, that we come from
Albano.   The present town lies within the inclosure of Pompey's
villa in ruins.   The Appian way runs through it, by the side
of which, a little farther, is a large old tomb, with five pyramids
upon it, which the learned suppose to be the burying-place of
the family, because they do not know whose it can be else.   But
the vulgar assure you it is the sepulchre of the Curiatii, and by
that name (such is their power) it goes.   One drives to Castel
Gondolfo, a house of the pope's, situated on the top of one of the
Collinette, that forms a brim to the bason, commonly called the
Alban lake.   It is seven miles round; and directly opposite to
you, on the other side, rises the Mons Albanus, much taller than
the rest, along whose side are still discoverable (not to common
eyes) certain little ruins of the old Alba longa.   They had need
be very little, as having been nothing but ruins ever since the days

---

[1] " Appia *longarum* teritur regina viarum."—*Statii Silv.* ii. 2, 12.—
Mitford.

[2] However whimsical this humour may appear to some readers, I chose
to insert it, as it gives me an opportunity of remarking that Mr. Gray
was extremely skilled in the customs of the ancient Romans; and has
catalogued, in his commonplace book, their various eatables, wines,
perfumes, cloaths, medicines, etc., with great precision, referring under
every article to passages in the poets and historians where their names
are mentioned.—*Mason.*

of Tullus Hostilius. On its top is a house of the Constable Colonna's, where stood the temple of Jupiter Latialis. At the foot of the hill Gondolfo, are the famous outlets of the lake, built with hewn stone, a mile and a half underground. Livy, you know, amply informs us of the foolish occasion of this expense, and gives me this opportunity of displaying all my erudition, that I may appear considerable in your eyes. This is the prospect from one window of the palace. From another you have the whole Campagna, the city, Antium, and the Tyrrhene sea (twelve miles distant) so distinguishable, that you may see the vessels sailing upon it. All this is charming. Mr. Walpole says, our memory sees more than our eyes in this country. Which is extremely true; since, for realities, Windsor, or Richmond Hill, is infinitely preferable to Albano or Frescati. I am now at home, and going to the window to tell you it is the most beautiful of Italian nights, which, in truth, are but just begun (so backward has the spring been here, and everywhere else, they say). There is a moon! there are stars for you! Do not you hear the fountain? Do not you smell the orange flowers? That building yonder is the convent of S. Isidore; and that eminence, with the cypress trees and pines upon it, the top of M. Quirinal. This is all true, and yet my prospect is not two hundred yards in length. We send you some Roman inscriptions to entertain you. The first two are modern, transcribed from the Vatican library by Mr. Walpole.

> Pontifices olim quem fundavere priores,
>   Præcipuâ Sixtus perficit arte tholum; [1]
> Et Sixti tantum se gloria tollit in altum,
>   Quantum se Sixti nobile tollit opus:
> Magnus honos magni fundamina ponere templi,
>   Sed finem cæptis ponere major honos.
> Saxa agit Amphion, Thebana ut mænia condat:
>   Sixtus & immensæ pondera molis agit. [2]
> Saxa trahunt ambo longè diversa: sed arte
>   Hæc trahit Amphion; Sixtus & arte trahit.
> At tantum exsuperat Dircæum Amphiona Sixtus,
>   Quantum hic exsuperat cætera saxa lapis.

Mine is ancient, and I think not less curious. It is exactly transcribed from a sepulchral marble at the villa Giustiniani. I put stops to it, when I understand it.

> Dis Manibus
> Claudiæ, Pistes
> Primus Conjugi
> Optumae, Sanctae,
> Et Piae, Benemeritate.

[1] Sixtus V. built the dome of St. Peter's.
[2] He raised the obelisk in the great area.

Non æquos, Parcae, statuistis stamina vitæ.
Tam bene compositos potuistis sede tenere.
Amissa est conjux. cur ego & ipse moror?
Si · bella · esse · mî · iste · mea · vivere · debuit ·
Tristia contigerunt qui amissâ conjuge vivo.
Nil est tam miserum, quam totam perdere vitam.
Nec vita enasci dura peregistis crudelia pensa, sorores,
Ruptaque deficiunt in primo munere fusi.
O nimis injustæ ter denos dare munus in annos,
Deceptus · grautus · fatum · sic · pressit · egestas ·
Dum vitam tulero, Primus Pistes lugea conjugium.

XXVIII.—Mr. GRAY to his MOTHER

NAPLES, *June* 17, 1740.

OUR journey hither was through the most beautiful part of the finest country in the world; and every spot of it, on some account or other, famous for these three thousand years past. The season has hitherto been just as warm as one would wish it; no unwholesome airs, or violent heats, yet heard of. The people call it a backward year, and are in pain about their corn, wine, and oil; but we, who are neither corn, wine, nor oil, find it very agreeable. Our road was through Velletri, Cisterna, Terracina, Capua, and Aversa, and so to Naples. The minute one leaves his holiness's dominions, the face of things begins to change from wide uncultivated plains to olive groves and well-tilled fields of corn, intermixed with ranks of elms, every one of which has its vine twining about it, and hanging in festoons between the rows from one tree to another. The great old fig-trees, the oranges in full bloom, and myrtles in every hedge, make one of the delight-fullest scenes you can conceive; besides that, the roads are wide, well-kept, and full of passengers; a sight I have not beheld this long time. My wonder still increased upon entering the city, which I think, for number of people, outdoes both Paris and London. The streets are one continued market, and thronged with populace so much that a coach can hardly pass. The common sort are a jolly lively kind of animals, more industrious than Italians usually are; they work till evening; then take their lute or guitar (for they all play) and walk about the city, or upon the sea-shore with it, to enjoy the fresco. One sees their little brown children jumping about stark-naked, and the bigger ones dancing with castanets, while others play on the cymbal to them. Your maps will show you the situation of Naples; it is on the most lovely bay in the world, and one of the calmest seas. It has many other beauties besides those of nature. We have spent two days in visiting the remarkable places in the country round it, such as the bay of Baiæ, and its remains of antiquity; the lake Avernus, and the Solfatara, Charon's grotto, etc. We have been in the Sybil's cave and many other strange holes underground (I only name them, because you may consult Sandy's travels); but the strangest hole I ever was in, has been to-day at a place called Portici, where his Sicilian majesty has a country-seat. About a year ago, as they were digging, they discovered some parts of ancient buildings above thirty feet deep in the ground. Curiosity led them on, and they have been digging ever since; the passage they have made, with all its turnings and windings, is now more than a mile long. As you walk, you see parts of an amphitheatre, many houses adorned with marble columns, and incrusted with the same; the front of a temple, several arched vaults of rooms painted in fresco. Some pieces of painting have been taken out from hence, finer than anything of the kind before discovered, and with these the king has adorned his palace; also a number of statues, medals, and gems; and more are dug out every day. This is known to be a Roman town,[1] that in the emperor Titus's time was overwhelmed by a furious eruption of Mount Vesuvius, which is hard by. The wood and beams remain so perfect that you may see the grain; but burnt to a coal, and dropping into dust upon the least touch. We were to-day at the foot of that mountain, which at present smokes only a little, where we saw the materials that fed the stream of fire, which about four years since ran down its side. We have but a few days longer to stay here; too little in conscience for such a place. . . .

XXIX.—MR. GRAY TO HIS FATHER

FLORENCE, *July* 16, 1740.

AT my return to this city, the day before yesterday, I had the pleasure of finding yours dated June the 9th. The period of our voyages, at least towards the south, is come, as you wish. We have been at Naples, spent nine or ten days there, and returned to Rome, where finding no likelihood of a pope yet

---

[1] It should seem by the omission of its name, that it was not then discovered to be Herculaneum.—*Mason.* This was not the case, see a letter from Walpole to West on this subject (Walpole's *Works,* vol. iv. p. 448), dated Naples, June 14, 1740, where he calls the town by the name of Herculaneum.—*Mitford.*

these three months, and quite wearied with the formal assemblies, and little society of that great city, Mr. Walpole determined to return hither to spend the summer, where he imagines he shall pass his time more agreeably than in the tedious expectation of what, when it happens, will only be a great show. For my own part, I give up the thoughts of all that with but little regret; but the city itself I do not part with so easily, which alone has amusements for whole years. However, I have passed through all that most people do, both ancient and modern; what that is you may see, better than I can tell you, in a thousand books. The conclave we left in greater uncertainty than ever; the more than ordinary liberty they enjoy there, and the unusual coolness of the season, makes the confinement less disagreeable to them than common, and, consequently, maintains them in their irresolution. There have been very high words, one or two (it is said) have come even to blows; two more are dead within this last month, Cenci and Portia; the latter died distracted; and we left another (Altieri) at the extremity. Yet nobody dreams of an election till the latter end of September. All this gives great scandal to all good Catholics, and everybody talks very freely on the subject. The Pretender (whom you desire an account of) I have had frequent opportunities of seeing at church, at the corso, and other places; but more particularly, and that for a whole night, at a great ball given by Count Patrizii to the Prince and Princess Craon (who were come to Rome at that time, that he might receive from the hands of the emperor's minister there the order of the Golden Fleece), at which he and his two sons were present. They are good fine boys, especially the younger, who has the more spirit of the two, and both danced incessantly all night long. For him he is a thin ill-made man, extremely tall and awkward, of a most unpromising countenance, a good deal resembling King James the Second, and has extremely the air and look of an idiot, particularly when he laughs or prays. The first he does not often, the latter continually. He lives private enough with his little court about him, consisting of Lord Dunbar, who manages everything, and two or three of the Preston Scotch lords, who would be very glad to make their peace at home.

We happened to be at Naples on Corpus Christi Day, the greatest feast in the year, so had an opportunity of seeing their Sicilian majesties to advantage. The king walked in the grand procession, and the queen (being big with child) sat in a balcony. He followed the host to the church of St. Clara.

where high mass was celebrated to a glorious concert of music. They are as ugly a little pair as one can see: she a pale girl, marked with the small-pox; and he a brown boy with a thin face, a huge nose, and as ungain as possible.

We are settled here with Mr. Mann in a charming apartment; the river Arno runs under our windows, which we can fish out of. The sky is so serene, and the air so temperate, that one continues in the open air all night long in a slight nightgown without any danger; and the marble bridge is the resort of everybody, where they hear music, eat iced fruits, and sup by moonlight; though as yet (the season being extremely backward everywhere) these amusements are not begun. You see we are now coming northward again, though in no great haste; the Venetian and Milanese territories, and either Germany or the south of France (according to the turn the war may take) are all that remain for us, that we have not yet seen; as to Loretto, and that part of Italy, we have given over all thoughts of it.

XXX.—Mr. GRAY to Mr. WEST

Florence, *July* 16, 1740.

You do yourself and me justice, in imagining that you merit, and that I am capable of sincerity. I have not a thought, or even a weakness, I desire to conceal from you; and consequently on my side deserve to be treated with the same openness of heart. My vanity perhaps might make me more reserved towards you, if you were one of the heroic race, superior to all human failings; but as mutual wants are the ties of general society, so are mutual weaknesses of private friendships, supposing them mixt with some proportion of good qualities; for where one may not sometimes blame, one does not much care ever to praise. All this has the air of an introduction designed to soften a very harsh reproof that is to follow; but it is no such matter: I only meant to ask, Why did you change your lodging? Was the air bad, or the situation melancholy? If so, you are quite in the right. Only, is it not putting yourself a little out of the way of a people, with whom it seems necessary to keep up some sort of intercourse and conversation, though but little for your pleasure or entertainment (yet there are, I believe, such among them as might give you both), at least for your information in that study, which, when I left you, you thought of applying to? for that there is a certain study necessary to be followed, if we mean to be of any use in the world, I take for granted; disagreeable enough (as most necessities are), but, I am afraid, unavoidable. Into how many branches these studies are divided in England, everybody knows; and between that which you and I had pitched upon, and the other two, it was impossible to balance long. Examples shew one that it is not absolutely necessary to be a blockhead to succeed in this profession. The labour is long, and the elements dry and unentertaining; nor was ever anybody (especially those that afterwards made a figure in it) amused, or even not disgusted in the beginning; yet, upon a further acquaintance, there is surely matter for curiosity and reflection. It is strange if, among all that huge mass of words, there be not somewhat intermixed for thought. Laws have been the result of long deliberation, and that not of dull men, but the contrary; and have so close a connection with history, nay, with philosophy itself, that they must partake a little of what they are related to so nearly. Besides, tell me, have you ever made the attempt? Was not you frighted merely with the distant prospect? Had the Gothic character and bulkiness of those volumes (a tenth part of which perhaps it will be no further necessary to consult than as one does a dictionary) no ill effect upon your eye? Are you sure, if Coke had been printed by Elzevir, and bound in twenty neat pocket volumes, instead of one folio, you should never have taken him for an hour, as you would a Tully, or drank your tea over him? I know how great an obstacle ill spirits are to resolution. Do you really think, if you rid ten miles every morning, in a week's time you should not entertain much stronger hopes of the Chancellorship, and think it a much more probable thing than you do at present? The advantages you mention are not nothing; our inclinations are more than we imagine in our own power; reason and resolution determine them, and support under many difficulties. To me there hardly appears to be any medium between a public life and a private one; he who prefers the first, must put himself in a way of being serviceable to the rest of mankind, if he has a mind to be of any consequence among them: nay, he must not refuse being in a certain degree even dependent upon some men who are so already. If he has the good fortune to light on such as will make no ill use of his humility, there is no shame in this: if not, his ambition ought to give place to a reasonable pride, and he should apply to the cultivation of his own mind those abilities which he has not been permitted to use for others' service. Such a private happiness (supposing a small competence of fortune) is almost always in every one's power, and the proper enjoyment of age, as the other is the employment of youth. You are yet young, have some advantages and opportunities, and an undoubted capacity, which you have never yet put to the trial. Set apart a few hours, see how the first year will agree with you, at the end of it you are still the master; if you change your mind, you will only have got the knowledge of a little somewhat that can do no hurt, or give you cause of repentance. If your inclination be not fixed upon anything else, it is a symptom that you are not absolutely determined against this, and warns you not to mistake mere indolence for inability. I am sensible there is nothing stronger against what I would persuade you to, than my own practice; which may make you imagine I think not as I speak. Alas! is not so; but I do not act what I think, and I had rather be the object of your pity, than you should be that of mine; and, be assured, the advantage that I may receive from it, does not diminish my concern in hearing you want somebody to converse with freely, whose advice might be of more weight, and always at hand. We have some time since come to the southern period of our voyages; we spent about nine days at Naples. It is the largest and most populous city, as its environs are the most deliciously fertile country, of all Italy. We sailed in the bay of Baiæ, sweated in the Solfatara, and died in the grotto del Cane, as all strangers do; saw the Corpus Christi procession, and the king and the queen, and the city underground (which is a wonder I reserve to tell you of another time), and so returned to Rome for another fortnight; left it (left Rome!) and came hither for the summer. You have seen [1] an epistle to Mr. Ashton that seems to me full of spirit and thought, and a good deal of poetic fire. I would know your opinion. Now I talk of verses, Mr. Walpole and I have frequently wondered you should never mention a certain imitation of Spenser, published last year by a namesake [2] of yours, with which we are all enraptured and enmarvailed.

---

[1] The reader will find this in Dodsley's *Miscellany*, and also amongst Mr. Walpole's *Fugitive Pieces.—Mason.*

[2] Gilbert West, Esq. This poem " On the abuse of Travelling " is also in Dodsley's *Miscellany.—Mason.*

XXXI.—MR. GRAY TO MR. WEST [1]

THOUGH far unworthy to enter into so learned and political a correspondence, I am employed *pour barbouiller une page de sept pouces et demie en hauteur, et cinq en largeur ;* and to inform you that we are at Florence, a city of Italy, and the capital of Tuscany; the latitude I cannot justly tell, but it is governed by a prince called great duke; an excellent place to employ all one's animal sensations in, but utterly contrary to one's rational powers. I have struck a medal upon myself; the device is thus, O, and the motto *Nihilissimo*, which I take in the most concise manner to contain a full account of my person, sentiments, occupations, and late glorious successes. If you choose to be annihilated too, you cannot do better than undertake this journey. Here you shall get up at twelve o'clock, breakfast till three, dine till five, sleep till six, drink cooling liquors till eight, go to the bridge till ten, sup till two, and so sleep till twelve again.

> Lahore fessi venimus ad larem nostrum
> Desideratoque acquiescimus lecto:
> Hoc est, quod unum est, pro laboribus tantis.
> O quid solutis est beatius curis? [2]

We shall never come home again; a universal war is just upon the point of breaking out; all outlets will be shut up. I shall be secure in my nothingness, while you that will be so absurd as to exist, will envy me. You don't tell me what proficiency you make in the noble science of defence. Don't you start still at the sound of a gun? Have you learned to say Ha! ha! and is your neck clothed with thunder? Are your whiskers of a tolerable length? And have you got drunk yet with brandy and gunpowder? Adieu, noble captain!

T. GRAY.

XXXII.—MR. GRAY TO HIS MOTHER

FLORENCE, *Aug. 21, N.S.* 1740.

IT is some time since I have had the pleasure of writing to you, having been upon a little excursion cross the mountains to Bologna. We set out from hence at sunset, passed the Appen-

---

[1] The concluding part of a letter begun by Walpole and finished by Gray.
[2] See *Catulli Carm.* xxxi. v. 7. The order of the lines is somewhat transposed in the quotation in Gray's letter.—*Mitford.*

nines by moonlight, travelling incessantly till we came to Bologna at four in the afternoon next day. There we spent a week agreeably enough, and returned as we came. The day before yesterday arrived the news of a pope; and I have the mortification of being within four days' journey of Rome, and not seeing his coronation, the heats being violent, and the infectious air now at its height. We had an instance, the other day, that it is not only fancy. Two country fellows, strong men, and used to the country about Rome, having occasion to come from thence hither, and travelling on foot, as common with them, one died suddenly on the road; the other got hither, but extremely weak, and in a manner stupid; he was carried to the hospital, but died in two days. So, between fear and laziness, we remain here, and must be satisfied with the accounts other people give us of the matter. The new pope is called Benedict XIV., being created cardinal by Benedict XIII. the last pope but one. His name is Lambertini, a noble Bolognese, and archbishop of that city. When I was first there, I remember to have seen him two or three times; he is a short, fat man, about sixty-five years of age, of a hearty, merry countenance, and likely to live some years. He bears a good character for generosity, affability, and other virtues; and, they say, wants neither knowledge nor capacity. The worst side of him is, that he has a nephew or two; besides a certain young favourite, called Melara, who is said to have had, for some time, the arbitrary disposal of his purse and family. He is reported to have made a little speech to the cardinals in the conclave, while they were undetermined about an election, as follows: " Most eminent Lords, here are three Bolognese of different characters, but all equally proper for the popedom. If it be your pleasures, to pitch upon a Saint, there is Cardinal Gotti; if upon a Politician, there is Aldrovandi; if upon a Booby, here am I." The Italian is much more expressive, and, indeed, not to be translated; wherefore, if you meet with anybody that understands it, you may shew them what he said in the language he spoke it. " Emin^ssimi. Sigr^i. Ci siamo tré, diversi sì, mà tutti idonei al Papato. Si vi piace un Santo, c' è l'Gotti; se volete una testa scaltra, e Politica, c' è l'Aldrovandé; se un Coglione, ecco mi!" Cardinal Coscia is restored to his liberty, and, it is said, will be to all his benefices. Corsini (the late pope's nephew) as he has had no hand in this election, it is hoped, will be called to account for all his villainous practices. The Pretender, they say, has resigned all his pretensions to his eldest boy, and will accept of the grand chancellorship, which is thirty thousand crowns a year; the pension he has at present is only twenty thousand. I do not affirm the truth of this article; because, if he does, it is necessary he should take the ecclesiastical habit, and it will sound mighty odd to be called his Majesty the Chancellor.—So ends my gazette.

XXXIII.—MR. GRAY TO HIS FATHER

FLORENCE, *Oct.* 9, 1740.

THE beginning of next spring is the time determined for our return at furthest; possibly it may be before that time. How the interim will be employed, or what route we shall take is not so certain. If we remain friends with France, upon leaving this country we shall cross over to Venice, and so return through the cities north of the Po to Genoa; from thence take a felucca to Marseilles, and come back through Paris. If the contrary fall out, which seems not unlikely, we must take the Milanese, and those parts of Italy, in our way to Venice; from thence pass through the Tirol into Germany, and come home by the Low-Countries. As for Florence, it has been gayer than ordinary for this last month, being one round of balls and entertainments, occasioned by the arrival of a great Milanese lady; for the only thing the Italians shine in is their reception of strangers. At such times everything is magnificence: the more remarkable, as in their ordinary course of life they are parsimonious, even to a degree of nastiness. I saw in one of the vastest palaces in Rome (that of Prince Pamfilio) the apartment which he himself inhabited, a bed that most servants in England would disdain to lie in, and furniture much like that of a soph at Cambridge, for convenience and neatness. This man is worth £30,000 sterling a year. As for eating, there are not two cardinals in Rome that allow more than six paoli, which is three shillings a day for the expense of their table; and you may imagine they are still less extravagant here than there. But when they receive a visit from any friend, their houses and persons are set out to the greatest advantage, and appear in all their splendour; it is, indeed, from a motive of vanity, and with the hopes of having it repaid them with interest, whenever they have occasion to return the visit. I call visits going from one city of Italy to another; for it is not so among acquaintance of the same place on common occasions. The new pope has retrenched the charges of his own table to a sequin (ten shillings) a meal. The applause which all he says and does meets with, is enough to encourage him really to deserve fame. They say he is an able and honest man; he is reckoned a wit too. The other day, when the senator of Rome came to wait upon him, at the first compliments he made him, the pope pulled off his cap. His master of the ceremonies, who stood by his side, touched him softly, as to warn him that such a condescension was too great in him, and out of all manner of rule, upon which he turned to him and said, "Oh! I cry you mercy, good master, it is true, I am but a novice of a pope; I have not yet so much as learned ill-manners." . . .

XXXIV.—Mr. GRAY to M⸺ WEST

F⸺NCE, *April* 21, 1741.

I KNOW not what degree of satisfaction it will give you to be told that we shall set out from hence the 24th of this month, and not stop above a fortnight at any place in our way. This I feel, that you are the principal pleasure I have to hope for in my own country. Try at least to make me imagine myself not indifferent to you; for I must own I have the vanity of desiring to be esteemed by somebody, and would choose that somebody should be one whom I esteem as much as I do you. As I am recommending myself to your love, methinks I ought to send you my picture (for I am no more what I was, some circumstances excepted, which I hope I need not particularise to you); you must add then, to your former idea, two years of age, a reasonable quantity of dullness, a great deal of silence, and something that rather resembles, than is, thinking; a confused notion of many strange and fine things that have swum before my eyes for some time, a want of love for general society—indeed an inability to it. On the good side you may add a sensibility for what others feel, and indulgence for their faults and weaknesses, a love of truth, and detestation of everything else. Then you are to deduct a little impertinence, a little laughter, a great deal of pride, and some spirits. These are all the alterations I know of, you perhaps may find more. Think not that I have been obliged for this reformation of manners to reason or reflection, but to a severer schoolmistress, Experience. One has little

merit in learning her lessons, for one cannot well help it; but
they are more useful than others, and imprint themselves in
the very heart. I find I have been haranguing in the style of
the son of Sirach, so shall finish here, and tell you that our route
is settled as follows: First to Bologna for a few days, to hear the
viscontina sing; next to Reggio, where is a fair. Now, you
must know, a fair here is not a place where one eats gingerbread
or rides upon hobby-horses; here are no musical clocks, nor
tall Leicestershire women; one has nothing but masquing,
gaming, and singing. If you love operas, there will be the
most splendid in Italy, four tip-top voices, a new theatre, the duke
and dutchess in all their pomps and vanities. Does not this
sound magnificent? Yet is the city of Reggio but one step
above Old Brentford. Well; next to Venice by the 11th of
May, there to see the old doge wed the Adriatic whore. Then
to Verona, so to Milan, so to Marseilles, so to Lyons, so to Paris,
so to West, etc., in *sæcula sæculorum*. Amen.

Eleven months, at different times, have I passed at Florence;
and yet (God help me) know not either people or language.
Yet the place and the charming prospects demand a poetical
farewell, and here it is.

.   .   .   .

I will send you, too, a pretty little sonnet of a Sig^r. Abbate
Buondelmonte, with my imitation of it.

.   .   .   .

Here comes a letter from you.—I must defer giving my
opinion of Pausanias [1] till I can see the whole, and only have
said what I did in obedience to your commands. I have spoken
with such freedom on this head, that it seems but just you
should have your revenge; and therefore I send you the beginning
not of an epic poem, but of a metaphysic one. [2] Poems and
metaphysics (say you, with your spectacles on) are inconsistent
things. A metaphysical poem is a contradiction in terms. It
is true, but I will go on. It is Latin too to increase the absurdity.
It will, I suppose, put you in mind of the man who wrote a
treatise of canon law in hexameters. Pray help me to the
description of a mixt mode, and a little episode about space.

---

[1] Some part of a tragedy under that title, which Mr. West had begun;
but I do not find amongst Mr. Gray's papers either the sketch itself, or
Mr. Gray's free critique upon it, which he here mentions.—*Mason.*
[2] The beginning of the first book of a didactic poem, "De Principiis
Cogitandi." The fragment which he now sent contained the first fifty-
three lines.—*Mason.*

XXXV.—Mr. GRAY to Mr. WEST

London, *April, Thursday.*

You are the first who ever made a muse of a cough; to me it seems a much more easy task to versify in one's sleep (that indeed you were of old famous for) than for want of it. Not the wakeful nightingale (when she had a cough) ever sung so sweetly. I give you thanks for your warble, and wish you could sing yourself to rest. These wicked remains of your illness will sure give way to warm weather and gentle exercise; which I hope you will not omit as the season advances. Whatever low spirits and indolence, the effect of them, may advise to the contrary, I pray you add five steps to your walk daily for my sake; by the help of which, in a month's time I propose to set you on horseback.

I talked of the " Dunciad " as concluding you had seen it; if you have not, do you choose I should get and send it you? I have myself, upon your recommendation, been reading *Joseph Andrews.* The incidents are ill laid and without invention; but the characters have a great deal of nature, which always pleases even in her lowest shapes. Parson Adams is perfectly well; so is Mrs. Slipslop, and the story of Wilson; and throughout he shews himself well read in stage-coaches, country squires, inns, and inns of court. His reflections upon high people and low people, and misses and masters, are very good. However the exaltedness of some minds (or rather, as I shrewdly suspect, their insipidity and want of feeling or observation) may make them insensible to these light things (I mean such as characterise and paint nature), yet surely they are as weighty and much more useful than your grave discourses upon the mind, the passions, and what not. Now as the paradisaical pleasures of the Mahometans consist in playing upon the flute and lying with houris, be mine to read eternal new romances of Marivaux and Crebillon.

You are very good in giving yourself the trouble to read and find fault with my long harangues. Your freedom (as you call it) has so little need of apologies, that I would scarce excuse your treating me any otherwise; which, whatever compliment it might be to my vanity, would be making a very ill one to my understanding. As to matter of stile, I have this to say: The language of the age is never the language of poetry; except among the French, whose verse, where the thought or image does not support it, differs in nothing from prose. Our poetry, on the contrary, has a language peculiar to itself; to which

almost every one that has written has added something by
enriching it with foreign idioms and derivatives; nay sometimes
words of their own composition or invention. Shakespeare and
Milton have been great creators this way; and no one more
licentious than Pope or Dryden, who perpetually borrow expressions from the former. Let me give you some instances from
Dryden, whom everybody reckons a great master of our poetical
tongue.——Full of *museful mopeings*—unlike the *trim* of love—
a pleasant *beverage*—a *roundelay* of love—stood silent in his
mood—with knots and *knares* deformed—his *ireful mood*—in
proud *array*—his *boon* was granted—and *disarray* and shameful
rout—*wayward* but wise—*furbished* for the field—the *foiled
dodderd* oaks—*disherited*—*smouldering* flames—*retchless* of laws
—*crones* old and ugly—the *beldam* at his side—the *grandam-hag*
—*villanize* his father's fame.——But they are infinite; and our
language not being a settled thing (like the French) has an
undoubted right to words of an hundred years old, provided
antiquity have not rendered them unintelligible. In truth,
Shakespeare's language is one of his principal beauties; and he
has no less advantage over your Addisons and Rowes in this,
than in those other great excellences you mention. Every word
in him is a picture. Pray put me the following lines into the
tongue of our modern dramatics:

> But I, that am not shaped for sportive tricks,
> Nor made to court an amorous looking-glass:
> I, that am rudely stampt, and want love's majesty
> To strut before a wanton ambling nymph:
> I, that am curtail'd of this fair proportion,
> Cheated of feature by dissembling nature,
> Deform'd, unfinish'd, sent before my time
> Into this breathing world, scarce half made up—

And what follows. To me they appear untranslatable; and if
this be the case, our language is greatly degenerated. However,
the affectation of imitating Shakespeare may doubtless be
carried too far; and is no sort of excuse for sentiments ill-suited
or speeches ill-timed, which I believe is a little the case with me.
I guess the most faulty expressions may be these—*silken* son of
dalliance—*drowsier* pretensions—wrinkled *beldams*—*arched* the
hearer's brow and *riveted* his eyes in *fearful extasie*. These are
easily altered or omitted: and indeed if the thoughts be wrong
or superfluous, there is nothing easier than to leave out the whole.
The first ten or twelve lines are, I believe, the best;[1] and as for

---

[1] The lines which he means here are from—*thus ever grave and undisturb'd reflection*—to *Rubellius lives*. For the part of the scene, which he
sent in his former letter, began there.—*Mason.*

the rest, I was betrayed into a good deal of it by Tacitus; only
what he has said in five words, I imagine I have said in fifty
lines. Such is the misfortune of imitating the inimitable. Now,
if you are of my opinion, *una litura* may do the business better
than a dozen; and you need not fear unravelling my web. I
am a sort of spider; and have little else to do but spin it over
again, or creep to some other place and spin there. Alas! for
one who has nothing to do but amuse himself, I believe my
amusements are as little amusing as most folks. But no matter;
it makes the hours pass; and is better than ἐν ἀμαθίᾳ καὶ ἀμουσίᾳ
καταβιῶναι. Adieu.

XXXVI.—Mr. GRAY to Mr. WHARTON

My dear Wharton,

It is a long time since I ought to have returned you my thanks
for the pleasure of your letter, I should say, the prodigy of your
letter, for such a thing has not happened above twice within the
last age to mortal man, and no one here can conceive what it
may portend. Mr. Trollope, I suppose, has told you how I was
employed a part of the time; how, by my own indefatigable
application for these ten years past, and by the care and vigilance
of that worthy magistrate the Man-in-Blew [1] (who, I'll assure
you, has not spared his labour, nor could have done more for his
own son), I am got half way to the top of jurisprudence,[2] and
bid as fair as another body to open a case of impotency with all
decency and circumspection; you see my ambition: I do not
doubt, but some thirty years hence I shall convince the world
and you, that I am a very pretty young fellow, and may come
to shine in a profession, perhaps the noblest in the world, next
to man-midwifery. As for yours; if your distemper and you
can but agree about going to London, I may reasonably expect,
in a much shorter time, to see you, in your three-cornered villa,
doing the honours of a well-furnished table with as much dignity,
as rich a mien, and as capacious a belly as Dr. Mead. Methinks
I see Dr. Askew at the lower end of it, lost in admiration of your
goodly person and parts, cramming down his envy (for it will
rise) with the wing of a pheasant, and drowning it in neat

[1] Servant of the vice-chancellor's for the time being, usually known by
the name of Blue-coat, whose business it is to attend Acts for Degrees.—
Mason.
[2] *i.e.* Bachelor of Civil Law.—*Mason.*

Burgundy. But not to tempt your asthma too much with such a prospect, I should think you might be almost as happy as this, even in the country; but you know best, and I should be sorry to say anything that might stop you in the career of glory. Far be it from me to hamper the wheels of your gilded chariot. Go on Sir Thomas, and when you die (for even physicians must die) may the faculty in Warwick Lane erect your statue in Sir John Cutler's own niche.

As to Cambridge, it is, as it was, for all the world; and the people are, as they were, and Mr. Trollope is as he was, that is, half-ill, half-well; I wish with all my heart they were all better, but what can one do? There is no news, only I think I heard a whisper, as if the vice-chancellor should be with child (but I beg you not to mention this, for I may come into trouble about it). There is some suspicion that the professor of mathematicks had a hand in the thing. Dr. Dickens says the University will be obliged to keep it as it was got *in magistratu.*

I was going to tell you how sorry I am for your illness, but, I hope, it is too late to be sorry now; I can only say that I really *was* very sorry. May you live a hundred Christmases, and eat as many collars of brawn stuck with rosemary. Adieu.

I am sincerely yours,

T. GRAY.

Dec. 27, 1742, CAMBRIDGE.

Won't you come to the jubilee? Dr. Long is to dance a saraband and hornpipe of his own invention, without lifting either foot once from the ground.

XXXVII.—MR. GRAY TO MR. WHARTON

MY DEAR WHARTON,

This is only to entreat you would order *mes gens* to clean out the apartments, spread the carpets, air the beds, put up the tapestry, unpaper the frames, etc., fit to receive a great potentate, who comes down in the flying coach, drawn by green dragons, on Friday the 10th instant. As the ways are bad and the dragons a little out of repair (for they don't actually fly, but only go, like a lame ostrich, something between a hop and a trot), it will probably be late when he lands, so he would not chuse to be known, and desires there may be no bells nor bonfires; but as persons incog. love to be seen, he will slip into the coffee-house.

Is Mr. Trollope among you? good lack! he will pull off my head for never writing to him, oh Conscience, Conscience!

LONDON, *October* 8 [44 or 45].

XXXVIII.—MR. GRAY TO MR. WHARTON

I AM not lost; here am I at Stoke, whither I came on Tuesday, and shall be again in town on Saturday, and at Cambridge on Wednesday or Thursday, you may be anxious to know what has past. I wrote a note the night I came, and immediately received a very civil answer. I went the following evening to see the *party* (as Mrs. Foible says), was something abashed at his confidence: he came to meet me, kissed me on both sides with all the ease of one, who receives an acquaintance just come out of the country, squatted me into a *fauteuil*, began to talk of the town, and this and that and t'other, and continued with little interruption for three hours, when I took my leave very indifferently pleased, but treated with monstrous good-breeding, I supped with him next night (as he desired); Ashton was there, whose formalities tickled me inwardly, for he (I found) was to be angry about the letter I had wrote him. However in going home together our hackney-coach jumbled us into a sort of reconciliation: he hammered out somewhat like an excuse, and I received it very readily, because I cared not twopence, whether it were true or not, so we grew the best acquaintance imaginable, and I sate with him on Sunday some hours alone, when he informed me of abundance of anecdotes much to my satisfaction, and in short opened (I really believe) his heart to me, with that sincerity that I found I had still less reason to have a good opinion of him than (if possible) I ever had before. Next morning I breakfasted alone with Mr. Walpole; when we had all the *éclaircissement* I ever expected, and I left him far better satisfied than I have been hitherto. When I return I shall see him again.

Such is the epitome of my four days. Mr. and Mrs. Simms and Mad^{lle.} Nanny have done the honours of Leaden Hall to a miracle, and all join in a compliment to the doctor. Your brother is well, the books are in good condition. Mad^{me.} Chenevix has frighted me with *écritoires* she asks three guineas for, that are not worth three halfpence: I have been in several shops and found nothing pretty. I fear it must be bespoke at last.

The day after I went you received a little letter directed to me, that seems wrote with a skewer, please to open it, and you will find a receipt of Dan. Adcock for ten pound, which I will beg you to receive of Gillham for me. If the letter miscarried, pray take care the money is paid to no one else. I expect to have a letter from you when I come to town, at your lodgings.— Adieu, sir, I am sincerely yours,   T. G.

STOKE, *Thursday*, 16th *Nov.* [1744 or 1745].

XXXIX.—Mr. GRAY TO Mr. WALPOLE

CAMBRIDGE, *February* 3, 1746.

DEAR SIR,

You are so good to enquire after my usual time of coming to town: it is a season when even you, the perpetual friend of London, will, I fear, hardly be in it—the middle of June: and I commonly return hither in September; a month when I may more probably find you at home.

Our defeat to be sure is a rueful affair for the honour of the troops; but the duke is gone it seems with the rapidity of a cannon-bullet to undefeat us again. The common people in town at least know how to be afraid: but we are such uncommon people here as to have no more sense of danger than if the battle had been fought when and where the battle of Cannæ was.

The perception of these calamities, and of their consequences, that we are supposed to get from books, is so faintly impressed, that we talk of war, famine, and pestilence, with no more apprehension than of a broken head, or of a coach overturned between York and Edinburgh.

I heard three people, sensible middle-aged men (when the Scotch were said to be at Stamford, and actually were at Derby), talking of hiring a chaise to go to Caxton (a place in the high road) to see the Pretender and the Highlanders as they passed.

I can say no more for Mr. Pope (for what you keep in reserve may be worse than all the rest). It is natural to wish the finest writer, one of them, we ever had, should be an honest man. It is for the interest even of that virtue, whose friend he professed himself, and whose beauties he sung, that he should not be found a dirty animal. But however, this is Mr. Warburton's business, not mine, who may scribble his pen to the stumps and all in vain, if these facts are so. It is not from what he told me about himself that I thought well of him, but from a humanity, and goodness of heart, aye, and greatness of mind, that runs through his private correspondence, not less apparent than are a thousand little vanities and weaknesses mixed with those good qualities, for nobody ever took him for a philosopher. If you know anything of Mr. Mann's state of health and happiness, or the motions of Mr. Chute homewards, it will be a particular favour to inform me of them, as I have not heard this half-year from them.

I am sincerely yours,

T. GRAY.

XL.—MR. GRAY TO MR. WHARTON

YOU write so feelingly to little Mr. Brown, and represent your abandoned condition in terms so touching, that what gratitude could not effect in several months, compassion has brought out in a few days, and broke that strong attachment, or rather allegiance which I and all here owe to our sovereign lady and mistress, the president of presidents, and head of heads (if I may be permitted to pronounce her name, that ineffable Octogram-ιton), the power of *Laziness*. You must know she had been pleased to appoint me (in preference to so many old servants of hers, who had spent their whole lives in qualifying themselves for the office) grand picker of straws, and push-pin player in ordinary to her supinity (for that is her title), the first is much in the nature of lord president of the council, and the other, like the groom-porter, only without the profit; but as they are both things of very great honour in this country, I considered with myself the load of envy attending such great charges, and besides (between you and I) I found myself unable to support the fatigue of keeping up the appearance, that persons of such dignity must do, so I thought proper to decline it, and excused myself as well as I could; however as you see such an affair must take up a good deal of time, and it has always been the policy of this court to proceed slowly, like the imperial, and that of Spain, in the dispatch of business; so that you will the easier forgive me, if I have not answered your letter before.

You desire to know, it seems, what character the poem of your young friend [1] bears here. I wonder to hear you ask the opinion of a nation, where those who pretend to judge, don't

---

[1] "Pleasures of the Imagination." From the posthumous publication of Dr. Akenside's *Poems*, it should seem that the author had very much the same opinion afterwards of his own work, which Mr. Gray here expresses; since he undertook a reform of it which must have given him, had he concluded it, as much trouble as if he had written it entirely new.— *Mason*.

judge at all; and the rest (the wiser part) wait to catch the judgment of the world immediately above them, that is, Dick's coffeehouse, and the Rainbow; so that the readier way would be to ask Mrs. This and Mrs. T'other, that keeps the bar there. However to shew you I'm a judge, as well as my countrymen, though I have rather turned it over than read it (but no matter: no more have they), it seems to me above the middling, and now and then (but for a little while) rises even to the best, particularly in description. It is often obscure, and even unintelligible, and too much infected with the Hutcheson jargon; in short its great fault is that it was published at least nine years too early; and so methinks in a few words, *à la mode du temple*, I have very nearly dispatched what may perhaps for several years have employed a very ingenious man, worth fifty of myself. Here is a poem called the "Enthusiast," [1] which is all pure description, and as they tell me by the same hand. Is it so or not? Item a more bulky one upon "Health," [2] wrote by a physician: do you know him? Master Tommy Lucretius [3] (since you are so good to enquire after the child) is but a puleing chitt yet, not a bit grown to speak of; I believe, poor thing! it has got the worms, that will carry it off at last. Oh Lord! I forgot to tell you, that Mr. Trollope and I are under a course of tar water, he for his present, and I for my future distempers; if you think it will kill me, send away a man and horse directly, for I drink like a fish. I should be glad to know how your ———— goes on, and give you joy of it.

You are much in the right to have a taste for Socrates, he was a divine man. I must tell you, by way of the news of the place, that the other day, Mr. Traigneau (entering upon his professorship) made an apology for him an hour long in the schools, and all the world, except Trinity College, brought in Socrates guilty. Adieu, dear sir, and believe me your friend and servant, T. G.

CAMBRIDGE, *Thursday, April 26, 1746.*

XLI.—MR. GRAY TO MR. WHARTON

MY DEAR WHARTON,

I would make you an excuse (as indeed I ought) if they were a sort of thing I ever gave credit to myself in these cases, but I

[1] The "Enthusiast, or the Lover of Nature," written in 1740, by Joseph Warton.—*Mitford.*

[2] "The Art of Preserving Health," a didactic poem, 8vo, by John Armstrong, 1744.—*Mitford.*

[3] Master Tommy Lucretius seems to be the author's more familiar name for the poem "De Principiis Cogitandi."—*Mitford.*

know they are never true. Nothing so silly as indolence when it hopes to disguise itself, every one knows it by its saunter; as they do his majesty (God bless him) at a masquerade by the firmness of his tread, and the elevation of his chin. However, somewhat I had to say, that has a little shadow of reason in it. I have been in town (I suppose you know) flaunting about at public places of all kinds with my two Italianised friends. The world itself has some attractions in it to a solitary of six years' standing; and agreeable well-meaning people of sense (thank Heaven there are so few of them) are my peculiar magnet, it is no wonder then, if I felt some reluctance at parting with them so soon; or if my spirits when I returned back to my cell, should sink for a time, not indeed to storm or tempest, but a good deal below changeable. Besides Seneca says (and my pitch of philosophy does not pretend to be much above Seneca),[1] " *Nunquam mores quos extuli, refero, aliquid ex eo, quod composui, turbatur : aliquid ex his, quæ fugavi, redit :* " and it will happen to such as we, mere imps of science; well it may, when Wisdom herself is forced often—

> In sweet retired solitude
> To plume her feathers and let grow her wings
> That in the various bustle of resort,
> Were all too ruffled, and sometimes impaired.[2]

It is a foolish thing that one can't only not live as one pleases, but where and with whom one pleases, without money. Swift somewhere says, that money is liberty; and I fear money is friendship too, and society, and almost every external blessing. It is a great though ill-natured comfort to see most of those, who have it in plenty, without pleasure, without liberty, and without friends.

Mr. Brown (who I assure you holds up his head and his spirits very notably) will give you an account of your college proceedings if they may be so called, when nothing proceeds at all. Only the last week, Roger was so wise to declare *ex motu proprio*, that he took Mr. Delaval (who is now a fell. commoner) into his own tuition. This raised the dirty spirit of his friend Mr. May (now tutor in Francis's room) against him, and even gentle Mr. Peele (who never acts but in conjunction), together with Mr. Brown (who pretended to be mighty angry, though in reality heartily glad), and they all came to an *éclaircissement* in the parlour. They abused him pretty reasonably, and it ended in

---

[1] Vide *Senacæ Epistol.* vii. p. 17, ed. Gronovii, 8vo.—*Mitford.*
[2] See Milton's "Comus," v. 376.—*Mitford.*

threatening them as usual with a visitor. In short, they are all as rude as may be, leave him a table by himself, never go into the parlour till he comes out, or if he enters, when they are there, continue sitting even in his own magisterial chair. May bickers with him publickly about twenty paltry matters, and Roger t'other day told him, he was impertinent. What would you have more? you see they do as one would wish. If you were here, all would be right. I am surprised not to hear you mention when that will be. Pray give an account of yourself.

I am very sincerely yours,

T. G.

P.S. When I went to town, part of my errand was to sell a little stock I had, to pay off Birkett's old debt, due at Christmas. But it was so low, I should have lost near 12 per cent., and so it continues. If you think of being here near that time, and find it not inconvenient to you to lend me £40, you will save me the money I mention (as I remember you once offered). But if any inconvenience attend it, you must imagine I don't by any means desire it. And you need not be at the trouble of any excuse, as I well know, nothing but the not being able would hinder your doing it immediately. Let me know, because otherwise I have another journey to make to town.

Dec. 11 [1746], CAMBRIDGE.

XLII.—MR. GRAY TO MR. WHARTON

MY DEAR WHARTON,

I have received your bill, and am in confusion to hear you have got into debt yourself in order to bring me out of it; I did not think to be obliged to you so much, nor on such terms: but imagined you would be here, and might easily spare it. The money shall be repaid as soon as ever it is wanted, and sooner if the stock rise a little higher.

My note you will find at the end of my letter, which you ought to have, ἐάν τι κατὰ τὸ ἀνθρώπινον συμβαίνῃ. The rest of my acknowledgements are upon record where they ought to be, with the rest of your kindnesses. The bill was paid me here; I suppose there is no likelihood of its being stopped in town. It surprises me to hear you talk of so much business, and the uncertainty of your return; and what not? Sure you will find time to give me an account of your transactions, and your intentions. For your ears, don't let 'em think of marrying you! for I know if you marry at all, you will be *married*. I mean passively. And then (besides repenting of what you were not guilty of) you will never go abroad, never read anything more but farriery-books, and justice-books; and so either die of a consumption, or live on, and grow fat, which is worse. For me, and my retirement (for you are in the right to despise my dissipation *de quinze jours*), we are in the midst of Diog. Laertius and his philosophers, as a *procemium* to the series of their works, and those of all the poets and orators that lived before Philip of Macedon's death: and we have made a great chronological table [1] with our own hands, the wonder and amazement of Mr. Brown; not so much for public events, though these too have a column assigned them, but rather in a literary way, to compare the times of all great men, their writings and transactions: it begins at the 30th olympiad, and is already brought down to the 113th; that is 332 years. Our only modern assistants are Marsham, Dodwell, and Bentley. Tuthill continues quiet in his *læta paupertas*, and by this time (were not his friends of it) would have forgot there was any such place as Pembroke in the world. All things there are just *in statu quo ;* only the fellows, as I told you, are grown pretty rudish to their sovereign in general, for Francis is now departed. Poor dear Mr. Delaval indeed has had a little misfortune; intelligence was brought, that he had with him a certain gentlewoman, properly called Nell Burnet (but whose *nom de guerre* was Captain Hargraves), in an officer's habit, whom he had carried all about to see chapels and libraries, and make visits in the face of day. The master raised his *posse comitatus* in order to search his chambers, and declared they had certainly been there; which was very true, and the captain was then locked up in a cupboard there, while his lover stood below in order to convey him out at window, when all was over. However, they took care not to discover her, though the master affirmed—had he but caught her, he would soon have known whether it was a man or a woman. Upon this Mr. Delaval was desired to cut out his name, and did so: next day Dr. Long repented, and wrote a paper to testify he never knew any harm of him; which he brought to Dr. Whaley, who would have

[1] This laborious work was formed much in the manner of the President Heinault's *Histoire de France*. Every page consisted of nine columns; one for the olympiad, the next for the archons, the third for the public affairs of Greece, the three next for the philosophers, and the three last for poets, historians, and orators. I do not find it carried further than the date above-mentioned—*Mason*.

directly admitted him here, if Stuart had not absolutely refused.
He was offered about at several colleges, but in vain. Then
Dr. L. called two meetings to get him re-admitted there, but
every one was inexorable; and so he has lost his pupil, who
is gone, I suppose, to his aunt Price. Trollope continues in
Dev'reux-Court: all our hopes are now in the commencement.

Have you seen the works of two young authors, a Mr. Warton
and Mr. Collins, both writers of odes? it is odd enough, but each
is the half of a considerable man, and one the counterpart of the
other. The first has but little invention, very poetical choice of
expression, and a good ear. The second, a fine fancy, modelled
upon the antique, a bad ear, great variety of words and images,
with no choice at all. They both deserve to last some years, but
will not.

Adieu! dear sir, I am very sincerely yours,

T. G.

I was thirty years old yesterday. What is o'clock by you?
Dec. 27 [1746].

XLIII.—Mr. GRAY to Mr. WALPOLE

January 1747.

It is doubtless an encouragement to continue writing to you,
when you tell me you answer me with pleasure. I have another
reason which would make me very copious, had I anything to
say: it is, that I write to you with equal pleasure, though not
with equal spirits, nor with like plenty of materials. Please to
subtract then, so much for spirit, and so much for matter; and
you will find me, I hope, neither so slow, nor so short, as I might
otherwise seem. Besides, I had a mind to send you the remainder
of Agrippina, that was lost in a wilderness of papers. Certainly
you do her too much honour; she seemed to me to talk like an
old boy, all in figures and mere poetry, instead of nature and
the language of real passion. Do you remember "*Approchez vous,
Néron?*" [1] Who would not rather have thought of that half line
than all Mr. Rowe's flowers of eloquence? However, you will
find the remainder here at the end in an outrageous long speech.
It was begun above four years ago (it is a misfortune you know
my age, else I might have added), when I was very young.

[1] The speech of Agrippina in Racine's tragedy of "Britannicus,"
Act. IV. sc. ii. v. 1.

Poor West put a stop to that tragic torrent he saw breaking in upon him:—have a care, I warn you, not to set open the flood-gate again, lest it should drown you and me, and the bishop and all.

I am very sorry to hear you treat philosophy and her followers like a parcel of monks and hermits, and think myself obliged to vindicate a profession I honour, *bien que je n'en tienne pas boutique* (as Mad. Sevigné says). The first man that ever bore the name, if you remember, used to say that life was like the Olympic games (the greatest public assembly of his age and country), where some came to shew the strength and agility of their body, as the champions; others, as the musicians, orators, poets, and historians, to show their excellence in those arts; the traders to get money; and the better sort, to enjoy the spectacle, and judge of all these. They did not then run away from society for fear of its temptations; they passed their days in the midst of it; conversation was their business: they cultivated the arts of persuasion, on purpose to shew men it was their interest, as well as their duty, not to be foolish, and false, and unjust; and that too in many instances with success; which is not very strange, for they showed by their life, that their lessons were not impracticable; and that pleasures were no temptations, but to such as wanted a clear perception of the pains annexed to them. But I have done preaching *à la Grecque.* Mr. Ratcliffe [1] made a shift to behave very rationally without their instructions, at a season which they took a great deal of pains to fortify themselves and others against: one would not desire to lose one's head with a better grace. I am particularly satisfied with the humanity of that last embrace to all the people about him. Sure it must be somewhat embarrassing to die before so much good company!

You need not fear but posterity will be ever glad to know the absurdity of their ancestors. The foolish will be glad to know they were as foolish as they, and the wise will be glad to find themselves wiser. You will please all the world then, and if you recount miracles you will be believed so much the sooner. We are pleased when we wonder, and we believe because we are pleased. Folly and wisdom, and wonder and pleasure, join with me in desiring you would continue to entertain them: refuse us if you can.—Adieu, dear sir!   T. GRAY.

---

[1] Brother of the Earl of Derwentwater. He was executed at Tyburn, December 1746, for having been concerned in the Rebellion in Scotland. —*Mitford.*

XLIV.—Mr. GRAY to Mr. WALPOLE

CAMBRIDGE, 1747.

I HAD been absent from this place a few days, and at my return found Cibber's book upon my table. I return you my thanks for it, and have already run over a considerable part, for who could resist Mrs. Letitia Pilkington's recommendation? (by the way is there any such gentlewoman? or has somebody put on the style of a scribbling woman's panegyric to deceive and laugh at Colley?). He seems to me full as pert and as dull as usual. There are whole pages of common-place stuff, that for stupidity might have been wrote by Dr. Waterland, or any other grave divine, did not the flirting saucy phrase give them at a distance an air of youth and gaiety. It is very true, he is often in the right with regard to Tully's weaknesses; but was there any one that did not see them? Those, I imagine, that would find a man after God's own heart, are no more likely to trust the doctor's recommendation than the player's; and as to reason and truth, would they know their own faces, do you think, if they looked in the glass, and saw themselves so bedizened in tattered fringe and tarnished lace, in French jewels, and dirty furbelows, the frippery of a stroller's wardrobe?

Literature, to take it in its most comprehensive sense, and include everything that requires invention or judgment, or barely application and industry, seems indeed drawing apace to its dissolution, and remarkably since the beginning of the war. I remember to have read Mr. Spence's pretty book; though (as he then had not been at Rome for the last time) it must have increased greatly since that in bulk. If you ask me what I read, I protest I do not recollect one syllable; but only in general, that they were the best bred sort of men in the world, just the kind of *frinds* one would wish to meet in a fine summer's evening, if one wished to meet any at all. The heads and tails of the dialogues, published separate in 16mo, would make the sweetest reading in *natiur* for young gentlemen of family and fortune that are learning to dance. I rejoice to hear there is such a crowd of dramatical performances coming upon the stage. Agrippina can stay very well, she thanks you, and be damned at leisure. I hope in God you have not mentioned, or shewed to anybody that scene (for trusting in its badness, I forgot to caution you concerning it); but I heard the other day that I was writing a play, and was told the name of it, which nobody here could know,

I am sure. The employment you propose to me much better suits my inclination; but I much fear our joint-stock would hardly compose a small volume; what I have is less considerable than you would imagine, and of that little we should not be willing to publish all. . . .[1]

This is all I can anywhere find. You, I imagine, may have a good deal more. I should not care how unwise the ordinary run of readers might think my affection for him, provided those few, that ever loved anybody, or judged of anything rightly, might, from such little remains, be moved to consider what he would have been; and to wish that heaven had granted him a longer life and a mind more at ease.

I send you a few lines, though Latin, which you do not like, for the sake of the subject;[2] it makes part of a large design, and is the beginning of the fourth book, which was intended to treat of the passions. Excuse the three first verses; you know vanity, with the Romans, is a poetical licence.

XLV.—Mr. GRAY to Mr. WALPOLE

CAMBRIDGE, 1747.

I HAVE abundance of thanks to return you for the entertainment Mr. Spence's book has given me, which I have almost run over already; and I much fear (see what it is to make a figure) the breadth of the margin, and the neatness of the prints, which are better done than one could expect, have prevailed upon me to like it far better than I did in manuscript; for I think it is not the very genteel deportment of Polymetis, nor the lively wit of Mysagetes, that have at all corrupted me.

There is one fundamental fault, from whence most of the little faults throughout the whole arise. He professes to neglect the Greek writers, who could have given him more instruction on the very heads he professes to treat than all the others put together. Who does not know, that upon the Latin, the Sabine, and Hetruscan mythology (which probably might themselves, at a remoter period of time, owe their origin to Greece too) the Romans ingrafted almost the whole religion of Greece to make what is called their own? It would be hard to find any one circumstance that is properly of their invention. In the ruder

[1] What is here omitted was a short catalogue of Mr. West's poetry then in Mr. Gray's hands.—*Mason.*

[2] The admirable apostrophe to Mr. West, with which the fragment of the fourth book " De Principiis Cogitandi " opens.—*Mitford.*

days of the republic, the picturesque part of their religion
(which is the province he has chosen, and would be thought to
confine himself to) was probably borrowed entirely from the
Tuscans, who, as a wealthy and trading people, may be well
supposed, and indeed are known, to have had the arts flourishing in a considerable degree among them. What could inform
him here, but Dio. Halicarnassus (who expressly treats of those
times with great curiosity and industry) and the remains of the
first Roman writers? The former he has neglected as a Greek;
and the latter, he says, were but little acquainted with the arts,
and consequently are but of small authority. In the better
ages, when every temple and public building in Rome was
peopled with imported deities and heroes, and when all the
artists of reputation they made use of were Greeks, what wonder,
if their eyes grew familiarised to Grecian forms and habits
(especially in a matter of this kind, where so much depends
upon the imagination); and if those figures introduced with
them a belief of such fables, as first gave them being, and dressed
them out in their various attributes, it was natural then, and
(I should think) necessary, to go to the source itself, the Greek
accounts of their own religion; but to say the truth, I suspect
he was little conversant in those books and that language, for
he rarely quotes any but Lucian, an author that falls in everybody's way, and who lived at the very extremity of that period
he has set to his enquiries, later than any of the poets he has
meddled with, and for that reason ought to have been regarded
as but an indifferent authority; especially being a Syrian too.
His book (as he says himself) is, I think, rather a beginning than
a perfect work; but a beginning at the wrong end, for if anybody should finish it by enquiring into the Greek mythology, as
he proposes, it will be necessary to read it backward.

There are several little neglects that one might have told him
of, which I noted in reading it hastily; as page 311, a discourse
about orange-trees, occasioned by Virgil's "*inter odoratum
lauri nemus,*" where he fancies the Roman *laurus* to be our
laurel; though undoubtedly the bay-tree, which is *odoratum*,
and (I believe) still called *lauro*, or *alloro*, at Rome; and that the
"*Malum Medicum*" in the Georgick is the orange; though
Theophrastus, whence Virgil borrowed it, or even Pliny whom
he himself quotes, might convince him it is the *cedrato* which
he has often tasted at Florence. Page 144 is an account of
Domenichino's cardinal virtues, and a fling at the Jesuits, neither
of which belong to them. The painting is in a church of the

Barnabiti, dedicated to St. Carlo Borromeo, whose motto is *Humilitas*. Page 151, in a note, he says, the old Romans did not regard Fortune as a deity, tho' Servius Tullius (whom she was said to be in love with; nay, there was actually an affair between them) founded her temple in Foro Boario. By the way, her worship was Greek, and this king was educated in the family of Tarquinius Priscus, whose father was a Corinthian; so it is easy to conceive how early the religion of Rome might be mixed with that of Greece, etc. etc. etc.

Dr. Middleton has sent me to-day a book on the Roman senate, the substance of a dispute between Lord Hervey and him, though it never interrupted *their* friendship, he says, and I dare say not.

XLVI.—Mr. GRAY to Mr. WALPOLE

CAMBRIDGE, *March* 1, 1747.

As one ought to be particularly careful to avoid blunders in a compliment of condolence, it would be a sensible satisfaction to me (before I testify my sorrow, and the sincere part I take in your misfortune) to know for certain, who it is I lament. I knew Zara and Selima (Selima, was it? or Fatima?), or rather I knew them both together; for I cannot justly say which was which. Then as to your handsome cat, the name you distinguish her by, I am no less at a loss, as well knowing one's handsome cat is always the cat one likes best; or if one be alive and the other dead, it is usually the latter that is the handsomest. Besides, if the point were never so clear, I hope you do not think me so ill-bred or so imprudent as to forfeit all my interest in the survivor. Oh no! I would rather seem to mistake, and imagine to be sure it must be the tabby one that had met with this sad accident. Till this affair is a little better determined, you will excuse me if I do not begin to cry,

     " Tempus inane peto, requiem, spatiumque doloris."

Which interval is the more convenient, as it gives time to rejoice with you on your new honours.[1] This is only a beginning; I reckon next week we shall hear you are a Freemason, or a Gormogon [2] at least.—Heigh ho! I feel (as you to be sure have

---

[1] Mr. Walpole was about this time elected a Fellow of the Royal Society.
[2] See some account of the " Gormogons " in Nicholls's *Life of Hogarth*, p. 424. There is a print of Hogarth's with the title, " The Mystery of Masonry brought to light by the Gormogons." There is also a poem, by Harry Carey, called " The Moderator between the Freemasons and Gormogons."—*Mitford*.

done long since) that I have very little to say, at least in prose.
Somebody will be the better for it; I do not mean you, but your
cat, *feuë* Mademoiselle Selime, whom I am about to immortalise
for one week or fortnight, as follows. . . .

.   .   .   .

There's a poem for you, it is rather too long for an epitaph.

XLVII.—Mr. GRAY TO Mr. WHARTON

My dear Wharton,

You ask me, what I should answer in case any one should ask
me a certain question concerning you. In my conscience I
should say, yes; and the readier as I have had a revelation about
it. It was in a dream that told me you had taken a fancy to one
of the four last letters in the alphabet. I think it can't be X,
nor Z (for I know of no female Zeno, or Xenophon), it may be Y
perhaps, but I have somehow a secret partiality for W; am I near
it, or no? By this time I suppose 'tis almost a done thing. There
is no struggling with destiny, so I acquiesce. Thus far only I
should be glad to know with certainty, whether it be likely
[   ] should continue *in statu quo*, till the Commencement
(which I don't conceive), for [   ] I should think it rather
better for T. to give up his pretensions with a good grace, than to
wait the pleasure of those dirty cubs, who would infallibly prefer
the first that offers of their own people, but I submit this to your
judgment, you (as you first made him a competitor) ought to
determine at what time he may most decently withdraw. I
have some uneasiness too on Brown's account, who has sacrificed
all his interests with so much frankness, and is still so resolute to
do everything for us without reserve, that I should see him with
great concern under the paw of a fell visitor, and exposed to the
insolence of that old rascal, the master. Trollope (if you remember) would engage himself no longer than the end of this
year: 'tis true he has never said anything since, tending that
way, but he is not unlikely to remember it at a proper time.
And as to Smart,[1] he must necessarily be *abîmé* in a very short
time. His debts daily increase (you remember the state they
were in, when you left us). Addison, I know, wrote smartly to
him last week, but it has had no effect that signifies, only I
observe he takes hartshorn from morning to night lately. In

[1] Christopher Smart, the poet of " A Song to David."

the meantime he is amusing himself with a comedy of his own writing, which he makes all the boys of his acquaintance act, and intends to borrow the zodiack room, and have it performed publickly. Our friend Lawman, the mad attorney, is his copyist; and truly the author himself is to the full as mad as he. His piece, he says, is inimitable, true sterling wit, and humour, by God; and he can't hear the prologue without being ready to die with laughter. He acts five parts himself, and is only sorry he can't do all the rest. He has also advertised a collection of odes; and for his vanity and faculty of lying, they are come to their full maturity. All this, you see, must come to a jayl, or bedlam, and that without any help, almost without pity. By the way, now I talk of a jayl, please to let me know when and where you would have me pay my own debts.

Chapman, I suppose you know, is warm in his mastership; soon after his accession, I was to see him. There was a very brilliant (Cambridge) assembly, Middleton, Rutherforth, Heberden, Robinson, Coventry, and various others. He did the honours with a great deal of comical dignity, assisted by a bedmaker in greasy leather breeches, and a livery, and now he is gone to town to get preferment. But what you'll wonder at, and what delights me, Coventry is his particular confident (tho' very disagreeably to himself). He can't open his door, but he finds the master there, who comes to set with him at all hours, and brings his works with him, for he is writing a great book on the Roman constitution. Well, upon the strength of this, I too am grown very great with Coventry, and to say the truth (bating his nose, and another circumstance, which is nothing to me) he is the best sort of man in this place. Middleton has published a small octavo on the Roman senate, well enough, but nothing of very great consequence, and is now gone to be inducted into a sinecure (not £100 a year) that Sir J. Frederick gave him. What's worse, for the sake of this little nasty thing (I am told) he is determined to suppress a work that would have made a great noise, or publish it all mangled or disfigured, and this when he has (I am assured) near £700 a year of his own already, and might live independent, and easy, and speak his mind, in the face of the whole world clerical and laical, such a passion have some men to lick the dust, and be trampled upon. The fellow commoners (the bucks) are run mad, they set women upon their heads in the streets at noon-day, break open shops, game in the coffee-houses on Sundays, and in short act after my own heart.

My works are not so considerable as you imagine. I have read Pausanias and Athenæus all through, and Æschylus again. I am now in Pindar and Lysias; for I take verse and prose together like bread and cheese.

The chronology is growing daily. The most noble of my performances latterly is a pôme on the uncommon death of Mr. Walpole's cat, which being of a proper size and subject for a gentleman in your condition to peruse (besides that I flatter myself Miss —— will give her judgment upon it too), I herewith send you. It won't detain you long.

Adieu, my dear sir, I am ever yours,
T. G.

CAMBRIDGE, *March* [1747], *Tuesday Night.*

Trollope is in town, still at his lodgings, and has been very ill. Brown wrote a month ago to Hayes and Christopher; but has had no answer whether or no they shall be here at the commencement, can you tell? Morley is going to be married to a grave and stayed maiden of 30 years old with much pelf, and his own relation. Poor soul!

XLVIII.—MR. GRAY TO MR. WHARTON

MY DEAR WHARTON,

I rejoice to hear you are safe arrived, though drawn by *four wild horses,* like people one reads of in the book of martyrs, yet I cannot chuse but lament your condition, so cooped up in the Elvet House, with spirits and hobgoblins about you, and pleasure at one entrance quite shut out; you must so much the more set open all the other avenues to admit it, open your folios, open your De L'Isle, and take a prospect of that world, which the cruel architect has hid from your corporeal eyes, and confined them to the narrow contemplation of your own *backside,* and kitchen-garden.

Mr. Keene has been here, but is now gone to town for a little while, and returns to pass the winter with us. We are tolerably gracious, and he speaks mighty well of you; but when I look upon his countenance and his ways, I can never think of bestowing my poor Tuthill upon him (though it were never so advantageous, and they both had a mind to it), and so I have said nothing to either of them. I found, he had no hopes of your petition; and believe you are right in thinking no farther of it.

Your mention of Mr. Vane, reminds me of poor Smart (not that I, or any other mortal, pity him). About three weeks ago he was arrested here at the suit of a taylor in London for a debt of about £50 of three years standing. The college had about £28 due to him in their hands, the rest (to hinder him from going to the castle, for he could not raise a shilling) Brown, May, and Peele, lent him upon his note. Upon this he remained confined to his room, lest his creditors here should snap him; and the fellows went round to make out a list of his debts, which amount in Cambridge to above £350; that they might come the readier to some composition, he was advised to go off in the night, and lie hid somewhere or other. He has done so, and this has made the creditors agree to an assignment of £50 per annum out of his income, which is above £140, if he lives at Cambridge, not else. But I am apprehensive, if this come to the ears of Mr. Vane, he may take away the £40 hitherto allowed him by the Duke of Cleveland; for before all this (last summer) I know they talked of doing so, as Mr. Smart (they said) was now settled in the world. If you found an opportunity, possibly you might hinder this (which would totally ruin him now) by representing his absurdity in the best light it will bear; but at the same time they should make this a condition of its continuance, that he live in the college, soberly, and within bounds, for that upon any information to the contrary it shall be undoubtedly stopped. This would be doing a real service, though against the grain, yet I must own if you heard all his lies, impertinence, and ingratitude in this affair, it would perhaps quite set you against him, as it has his only friend (Mr. Addison) totally, and yet one would try to save him, for drunkenness is one great source of all this, and he may change it. I would not tell this matter in the north, were I you, till I found it was known by other means. We have had an opinion from the attorney-general in a manner directly contrary to the former. He does not seem to have been clear then; so that he may possibly not be so now. The King's Bench (he says) can take no cognisance of it; the visitor must do all, and he is the vice-chancellor by King James's charter, which is good. This is sad indeed, and the fellows, before they acquiesce in it, seem desirous of consulting Dr. Lee, who is well acquainted with college matters.

Have you seen Lyttleton's monody on his wife's death? there are parts of it too stiff and poetical, but others truly tender and elegiac, as one would wish. Dodsley is publishing three miscellaneous volumes; some new, many that have been

already printed. Lyttleton, Nugent, and G. West have given
him several things of theirs. Mr. Walpole has given him three
odes of mine (which you have seen before) and one of Mr. West's
(my friend who is dead) which in spite of the subject is excellent:
it is on the late queen's death. There is a Mr. Archibald Bower,[1]
a Scotchman bred in Italy, professor in three universities there,
and of the inquisition, he was employed by the Court of Rome
to write a history of the popes. As he searched into the
materials, his eyes were opened: he came to England, has
changed his religion, and continues his work in our language
under the patronage of Mr. Pitt, the Yorks, etc. The preface
is come out with the proposals, and promises exceeding well,
doubtless there is no part of history more curious, if it be well
performed.

My best wishes wait upon Mrs. Wharton, and ——. My
compliments to Miss Wharton, and to King Harry the 8th.
Brown will write; he's the . . . little man and always . . .

Adieu, I am ever yours,
T. G.

Novr. 30, CAMBRIDGE [1747].

P.S. I said something to Stonhewer, who (I believe) will do
what he can. He is now in London.

XLIX.—MR. GRAY TO MR. WHARTON

MY DEAR WHARTON,

Though I have been silent so long, do not imagine I am at all
less sensible to your kindness (which, to say the truth,) is of a
sort, that however obvious and natural it may seem, has never
once occurred to any of my good friends in town, where I have
been these seven weeks. Their methods of consolation were
indeed very extraordinary; they were all so sorry for my loss [2]
that I could not chuse but laugh. One offered me opera tickets,
insisted upon carrying me to the grand masquerade, desired me
to sit for my picture; others asked me to their concerts, or
dinners and suppers at their houses; or hoped I would drink

---

[1] A full account of Mr. Archibald Bower, and his history of the popes,
may be seen in the Biographical Dictionary. To the detection of his
forgeries and mistakes by Dr. Douglas, the late Bishop of Salisbury,
Goldsmith alludes in the " Retaliation."

> " New Lawders and Bowers the Tweed shall cross over,
> No countryman living their tricks to discover."—*Mitford.*

[2] The destruction of his house, in Cornhill, by fire.

chocolate with them while I stayed in town. All my gratitude
(or, if you please, my revenge), was to accept of everything they
offered me: if it had been but a shilling I would have taken it
Thank heaven, I was in good spirits, else I could not have done it
I profited all I was able of their civilities, and am returned into
the country loaded with their *bontés* and *politesses*, but richer
still in my own reflections, which I owe in great measure to them
too. Suffer a great master to tell them you, for me, in a better
manner.

> Aux sentimens de la Nature,
> Aux plaisirs de la Verité
> Preférant le goût frelaté
> Des plaisirs, qu'a fait l'Imposture
> Ou qu'inventa la Vanité,
> Voudrois-je partager ma vie
> Entre les jeux de la Folie,
> Et l'ennui de l'Oisiveté,
> Et trouver la Melancolie,
> Dans le sein de la Volupté? etc.[1]

Your friendship has interested itself in my affairs so naturally
that I cannot help troubling you with a little detail of them
The house I lost was insured for £500, and with the deduction
of three per cent. they paid me £485, with which I bought, when
stocks were lower, £525. The rebuilding will cost £590, and the
other expenses, that necessarily attend it, will mount that sum to
£650. I have an aunt that gives me £100, and another that I
hope will lend me what I shall want, but if (contrary to my
expectation) I should be forced to have recourse to your assistance, it cannot be for above £50, and that about Christmas
next, when the thing is to be finished: and now, my dear
Wharton, why must I tell you a thing so contrary to my own
wishes, and to yours, I believe? It is impossible for me to see
you in the north, or to enjoy any of those agreeable hours I had
flattered myself with. I must be in town several times during
the summer, in August particularly, when half the money is to
be paid: the relation that used to do things for me is, from illness, now quite incapable; and the good people here would
think me the most careless and ruinous of mortals, if I should
think of such a journey at this time. The only satisfaction I
can pretend to, is that of hearing from you; and particularly
about this time I was bid to expect good news.

Your opinion of Diodorus is doubtless right; but there are
things in him very curious, got out of better authors, now lost.

[1] These verses are extracted from the poem called " La Chartreuse,"
by Gresset. London edition, vol. i. p. 66.—*Mitford.*

Do you remember the " Egyptian History," and particularly the account of the gold-mines?[1] My own readings have been cruelly interrupted. What I have been highly pleased with, is the new comedy from Paris, by Gresset, " Le Méchant," one of the very best dramas I ever met with. If you have it not, buy his works altogether, in two little volumes. They are collected by the Dutch booksellers, and consequently there is some trash; but then there are the " Ver-vert," the epistle to P. Bougeant, the " Chartreuse," that to his sister, an ode on his country, and another on " Mediocrity," and the " Sidnei," another comedy, which have great beauties; there is a poem by Thomson, the " Castle of Indolence," with some good stanzas. Mr. Mason is my acquaintance. I liked that ode[2] very much, but have found no one else that did. He has much fancy, little judgement, and a good deal of modesty. I take him for a good and well-meaning creature; but then he is really in simplicity a child, and loves everybody he meets with. He reads little or nothing, writes abundance, and that with a design to make his fortune by it. There is now, I think, no hopes of the Pembroke business coming to anything. My poor Tuthill will be in a manner destitute (even of a curacy) by midsummer. I need not bid you think of him, if any probable means offer of doing him good. I fear he was not made to think much for himself. Pray let me hear from you soon; I am at Mrs. Roger's of Stoke, near Windsor, Bucks.

My thanks, and best compliments to Mrs. Wharton, and your family. Does that name include anybody that I am not yet acquainted with? Adieu! I am ever,

Truly yours,
T. GRAY.

June 5, 1748.

L.—MR. GRAY TO MR. WHARTON

April 25th, CAMBRIDGE [1749].

MY DEAR WHARTON,

I perceive that second parts are as bad to write as they can be to read. For this, which you ought to have had a week after the first, has been a full month in coming forth. The spirit of laziness (the spirit of the place) begins to possess even me, that have so long declaimed against it. Yet has it not so prevailed,

---

[1] This curious passage of Diodorus, to which Gray alludes, may be found in vol. i. lib. iii. cap. 12, p. 181, ed. Wesseling.—*Mitford.*

[2] " Ode to a Water Nymph."

but that I feel that discontent with myself, that *ennuy*, that ever accompanies it in its beginnings. Time will settle my conscience, time will reconcile my languid companion; we shall smoke, we shall tipple, we shall doze together, we shall have our little jokes, like other people, and our long stories. Brandy will finish what port begun; and a month after the time you will see in some corner of a London *Evening Post*—Yesterday, died the Rev. Mr. John Grey, Senior-Fellow of Clare-hall, a facetious companion, and well-respected by all that knew him. His death is supposed to have been occasioned by a fit of an apoplexy, being found fallen out of bed with his head in a chamber-pot.

I am half-ashamed to write university news to you, but as perhaps you retain some little leven of Pembroke Hall, your nursing mother, I am in hopes you will not be more than half-ashamed to read it. Pembroke then is all harmonious and delightful since the pacification; but I wish you would send them up some boys, for they are grown extremely thin from their late long indisposition. Keene's *Implications* have ended queerly, for contrary to all common-sense Peter Nourse and two others have joined Rogers, and brought in a shameful low creature by a majority. The master appeals to the visitor against their choice as of a person not qualified, he has received the appeal, and I suppose will put in Brocket (Dr. Keene's man) by main force. Chapman is at present in town in waiting; he has just married a Miss Barnwell, niece to one Dr. Barnwell who was minister of Trompington, with £2000, a plain woman, and about his own age. I hear that when he went to Leicester-house to know when the prince would be waited upon with the book of verses on the peace, the prince appointed no day at all; but ordered the verses to be sent, and left there. The design of receiving the university at Newcastle-house is said to be altered; the duke intending to come hither (I imagine) after the parliament is risen. Ross's *Epistles of Tully ad Familiares* will come out in about a week. It is in two handsome 8vo volumes, with an introduction and notes in English, but no translation, dedicated to Lord Gower. Now I am come to books, there is a new edition of Montesquieu's *Work* (which I mentioned to you before), publishing in 2 vols. 8vo. Have you seen old Crebillon's "Catilina," a tragedy which has had a prodigious run at Paris? Historical truth is too much perverted in it, which is ridiculous in a story so generally known, but if you can get over this, the sentiments and versification are fine, and most of the characters (particularly the principal one) painted with great spirit.

Observe, if you chuse to send for it, not to have Brindley's edition, which is all false prints, but Vaillant's. There is a work publishing in Denmark by subscription (four guineas), *Travels in Egypt* by Captain Norden. He was once in England (as tutor to a young Count Daniskiold, hereditary admiral of Denmark), and known to many persons as a man of sense, and that understood drawing extremely well; accordingly it is the plates that raise it to such a price, and are said to be excellent. The author himself is dead, and his papers are published by the academy at Copenhagen. Mr. Birch, the indefatigable, has just put out a thick 8vo of original papers of Queen Elizabeth's time. There are many curious things in it, particularly letters from Sir Robert Cecil (Salisbury) about his negotiations with Henry IVth of France; the Earl of Monmouth's odd account of Queen Elizabeth's death, several peculiarities of James Ist, and Prince Henry etc.; and above all an excellent account of the state of France, with characters of the king, his court, and ministry by Sir G. Carew, ambassador there. This, I think, is all new worth mentioning, that I have seen or heard of, except a natural history of Peru in Spanish, printed at London by Don —— something, a man of learning sent thither by that court on purpose.

I shall venture to accept of a part of that kind offer you once made me (for my finances are much disordered this year) by desiring you to lend me twenty guineas. The sooner you can do this, the more convenient it will be to me, and if you can find a method to pay it here, still more so. But if anything should happen that may defer it, or make this method troublesome, then I will desire you to make it payable in town after the first week in June, when I shall be obliged to go thither.

I want to hear from you, to know of your health and that of your family. My best compliments to Mrs. Wharton. Mr. Brown comes and throws in his *little compliments* too, and we are both very truly

Yours,
T. G.

LI.—MR. GRAY TO MR. WHARTON

MY DEAR WHARTON,

I promised Dr. Keene long since to give you an account of our magnificences here,[1] but the newspapers and he himself in person

---

[1] The Duke of Newcastle's installation as Chancellor of the University. —*Mason.*

have got the start of my indolence, so that by this time you are well acquainted with all the events that adorned that week of wonders. Thus much I may venture to tell you, because it is probable nobody else has done it, that our friend Chappy's zeal and eloquence surpassed all power of description. Vesuvio in an eruption was not more violent than his utterance, nor (since I am at my mountains) Pelion with all its pine trees in a storm of wind more impetuous than his action, and yet the senate-house still stands, and (I thank God) we are all safe and well at your service. I was ready to sink for him and scarce dared to look about me, when I was sure it was all over; but soon found I might have spared my confusion, for all people joined to applaud him: everything was quite right; and I dare swear, not three people here but think him a model of oratory. For all the duke's little court came with a resolution to be pleased; and when the tone was once given, the university, who ever wait for the judgement of their betters, struck into it with an admirable harmony. For the rest of the performances they were (as usual) very ordinary. Every one, while it lasted, was very gay and very busy in the morning, and very owlish and very tipsey at night. I make no exceptions from the Chancellour to Blew-coat. Mason's ode was the only entertainment that had any tolerable elegance, and for my own part I think it (with some little abatements) uncommonly well on such an occasion. Pray let me know your sentiments, for doubtless you have seen it. The author of it grows apace in my good graces: he is very ingenious, with great good-nature and simplicity. A little vain, but in so harmless and so comical a way, that it does not offend one at all; a little ambitious, but withal so ignorant in the world and its ways, that this does not hurt him in one's opinion. So sincere and undisguised, that no mind with a spark of generosity would ever think of hurting him, he lies so open to injury, but so indolent that if he cannot overcome this habit, all his good qualities will signify nothing at all. After all I like him so well, I could wish you knew him.

Tuthill who was here at the installation and in high spirits, will come to settle in Cambridge at Michaelmas, and I have hopes that these two, with Brown's assistance, may bring Pembroke into some esteem; but then there is no making bricks without straw. They have no boys at all, and unless you can send us a hamper or two out of the north to begin with, they will be like a few rats straggling about an old deserted mansion-house.

I should be glad (as you will see Keene often) if you could

throw in a word, as of your own head merely, about a fellow-ship for Stonhewer: he has several times mentioned it himself, as a thing he would try to bring about either at Queen's or Christ's, where he has interest: but I know not how, it has gone off again, and we have heard no more lately about it. I know it is not practicable here at Peter-house, because of his county; and though at Pembroke we might possibly get a majority, yet Roger is an animal that might play over again all his old game, and with a better appearance than before. You would therefore oblige me, if you would sound him upon this subject, for it is Stonhewer's wish, and (I think) would be an advantage to him, if he had a reason for continuing here some time longer: if you can get Keene to be explicit about it (but it must seem to be a thought entirely of your own) I will desire you to let me know the result. My best wishes, dear sir, ever attend on you and Mrs. Wharton.

I am most sincerely and unalterably yours,

T. G.

August 8th [1749], CAMBRIDGE.

LII.—MR. GRAY TO HIS MOTHER

CAMBRIDGE, *Nov.* 7, 1749.

THE unhappy news I have just received from you equally surprises and afflicts me.[1] I have lost a person I loved very much, and have been used to from my infancy; but am much more concerned for your loss, the circumstances of which I forbear to dwell upon, as you must be too sensible of them yourself; and will, I fear, more and more need a consolation that no one can give, except He who has preserved her to you so many years, and at last, when it was his pleasure, has taken her from us to himself: and perhaps, if we reflect upon what she felt in this life, we may look upon this as an instance of his goodness both to her, and to those that loved her. She might have languished many years before our eyes in a continual increase of pain, and totally helpless; she might have long wished to end her misery without being able to attain it; or perhaps even lost all sense, and yet continued to breathe; a sad spectacle to such as must have felt more for her than she could have done for herself. However you may deplore

[1] The death of his aunt, Mrs. Mary Antrobus, who died the 5th of November, and was buried in a vault in Stoke churchyard near the chancel door, in which also his mother and himself (according to the direction in his will) were afterwards buried.—*Mason.*

your own loss, yet think that she is at last easy and happy; and has now more occasion to pity us than we her. I hope, and beg, you will support yourself with that resignation we owe to Him, who gave us our being for our good, and who deprives us of it for the same reason. I would have come to you directly, but you do not say whether you desire I should or not; if you do, I beg I may know it, for there is nothing to hinder me, and I am in very good health.

LIII.—Mr. GRAY to Mr. WALPOLE

STOKE, *June 12,* 1750.

DEAR SIR,

As I live in a place, where even the ordinary tattle of the town arrives not till it is stale, and which produces no events of its own, you will not desire any excuse from me for writing so seldom, especially as of all people living I know you are the least a friend to letters spun out of one's own brains, with all the toil and constraint that accompanies sentimental productions. I have been here at Stoke a few days (where I shall continue good part of the summer); and having put an end to a thing,[1] whose beginning you have seen long ago, I immediately send it you. You will, I hope, look upon it in the light of a thing with an end to it: a merit that most of my writings have wanted, and are like to want, but which this epistle I am determined shall not want, when it tells you that I am ever

Yours,

T. GRAY.

Not that I have done yet; but who could avoid the temptation of finishing so roundly and so cleverly, in the manner of good Queen Anne's days? Now I have talked of writings, I have seen a book which is by this time in the press, against Middleton (though without naming him), by Asheton. As far as I can judge from a very hasty reading, there are things in it new and ingenious, but rather too prolix, and the style here and there savouring too strongly of sermon. I imagine it will do him credit. So much for other people, now to *self* again. You are desired to tell me your opinion, if you can take the pains, of these lines. I am once more,

Ever yours.

---

[1] This was the "Elegy in a Country Churchyard."—*Mitford.*

in more magazines than one. The chief errata[1] were *sacred bower* for *secret; hidden* for *kindred* (in spite of dukes and classicks); and *frowning* as in scorn for *smiling.* I humbly propose, for the benefit of Mr. Dodsley and his matrons, that take *awake*[2] for a verb, that they should read *asleep,* and all will be right. "Gil Blas" is the Lying Valet in five acts. The fine lady has half-a-dozen good lines dispersed in it. "Pompey" is the hasty production of a Mr. Coventry (cousin to him you knew), a young clergyman; I found it out by three characters, which once made part of a comedy that he shewed me of his own writing. Has that miracle of *tenderness and sensibility* (as she calls it) Lady Vane given you any amusement? Peregrine, whom she uses as a vehicle, is very poor indeed, with a few exceptions. In the last volume is a character of Mr. Lyttleton, under the name of Gosling Scrag, and a parody of part of his monody, under the notion of a pastoral on the death his grandmother.—I am ever yours,   T. GRAY.

LVII.—MR. GRAY TO MR. WALPOLE

YOUR pen was too rapid to mind the common form of a direction, and so, by omitting the words *near Windsor,* your letter has been diverting itself at another Stoke, near Ailesbury, and came not to my hands till to-day.

The true original chairs were all sold, when the Huntingdon's broke; there are nothing now but Halsey chairs, not adapted to the squareness of gothic dowager's rump. And by the way I do not see how the uneasiness and uncomfortableness of a coronation-chair can be any objection with you: every chair that is easy is modern, and unknown to our ancestors. As I remember there were certain low chairs, that looked like ebony, at Esher, and were old and pretty. Why should not Mr. Bentley improve upon them?—I do not wonder at Dodsley. You have talked to him of six *odes,* for so you are pleased to call everything I write, though it be but a receipt to make apple-dumplings. He has reason to gulp when he finds one of them only a long story. I don't know but I may send him very soon (by your hands) an ode to his own tooth, a high Pindaric upon

---

[1] Besides these errors of the text, in the *Magazine of Magazines,* the following occurred—"Their *harrow* oft the stubborn glebe has broke."—"And read their *destiny* in a nation's eyes."—"With uncouth rhymes and shapeless *culture* decked."—"Slow through the churchway *pass* we saw him borne,"—and many others of less consequence.—*Mitford.*

[2] "Awake and faithful to her wonted fires."

stilts, which one must be a better scholar than he is to understand a line of, and the very best scholars will understand but a little matter here and there.

It wants but seventeen lines of having an end, I don't say of being finished. As it is so unfortunate to come too late for Mr. Bentley, it may appear in the fourth volume of the *Miscellanies*, provided you don't think it execrable, and suppress it. Pray when the fine book [1] is to be printed, let me revise the press, for you know you can't; and there are a few trifles I could wish altered.

I know not what you mean by hours of love, and cherries, and pine-apples. I neither see nor hear anything here, and am of opinion that is the best way. My compliments to Mr. Bentley, if he be with you.—I am yours ever,   T. GRAY.

I desire you would not show that epigram I repeated to you, as mine. I have heard of it twice already as coming from you.

LVIII.—MR. GRAY TO MR. WALPOLE

I AM obliged to you for Mr. Dodsley's book, [2] and having pretty well looked it over, will (as you desire) tell you my opinion of it. He might, methinks, have spared the graces in his frontispiece, if he chose to be economical, and dressed his authors in a little more decent raiment—not in whited-brown paper, and distorted characters, like an old ballad. I am ashamed to see myself; but the company keeps me in countenance: so to begin with Mr. Tickell. This is not only a state-poem (my ancient aversion), but a state-poem on the peace of Utrecht. If Mr. Pope had wrote a panegyric on it, one could hardly have read him with patience: but this is only a poor short-winded imitator of Addison, who had himself not above three or four notes in poetry, sweet enough indeed, like those of a German flute, but such as soon tire and satiate the ear with their frequent return. Tickell has added to this a great poverty of sense, and a string of transitions that hardly become a school-boy. However I forgive him for the sake of his ballad, [3] which I always thought the prettiest in the world.

---

[1] The edition of his odes printed at Strawberry-hill.
[2] His collection of poems.
[3] " Colin and Lucy," beginning—

" Of Leinster fam'd for maidens fair."

All there is of M. Green here, has been printed before; there is a profusion of wit everywhere; reading would have formed his judgement, and harmonised his verse, for even his wood-notes often break out into strains of real poetry and music. "The School Mistress" is excellent in its kind and masterly; and (I am sorry to differ from you, but) "London" is to me one of those few imitations that have all the ease and all the spirit of an original. The same man's verses [1] on the opening of Garrick's theatre are far from bad. Mr. Dyer (here you will despise me highly) has more of poetry in his imagination than almost any of our number; but rough and injudicious. I should range Mr. Bramston only a step or two above Dr. King, who is as low in my estimation as in yours. Dr. Evans is a furious madman; and pre-existence is nonsense in all her altitudes. Mr. Lyttleton is a gentle elegiac person. Mr. Nugent [2] sure did not write his own ode. I like Mr. Whitehead's little poems, I mean the ode on a Tent, the verses to Garrick, and particularly those to Charles Townsend, better than anything I had seen before of him. I gladly pass over H. Browne and the rest, to come at you. You know I was of the publishing side, and thought your reasons against it none; for though, as Mr. Chute said extremely well, the *still small voice* of poetry was not made to be heard in a crowd; yet satire will be heard, for all the audience are by nature her friends; especially when she appears in the spirit of Dryden, with his strength, and often with his versification, such as you have caught in those lines on the Royal Unction, on the Papal Dominion, and Convents of both Sexes; on Henry VIII. and Charles II., for these are to me the shining parts of your "Epistle." [3] There are many lines I could wish corrected, and some blotted out, but beauties enough to atone for a thousand worse faults than these. The opinion of such as can at all judge, who saw it before in Dr. Middleton's hands, concurs nearly with mine. As to what any one says, since it came out; our people

---

[1] Johnson.

[2] The ode addressed to Mr. Pulteney, by Mr. Nugent (afterwards Earl Nugent), was distinguished for the following stanza, which has since received the honour of being quoted by Mr. Gibbon, in his character of Brutus:—

> "What! tho' the good, the brave, the wise,
> With adverse force undaunted rise
>   To break th' eternal doom;
> Though Cato liv'd, though Tully spoke,
> Though Brutus dealt the god-like stroke,
>   Yet perished fated Rome."—*Mitford.*

[3] Walpole's "Epistle to Thomas Asheton," from Florence.—*Mitford.*

(you must know) are slow of judgement; they wait till some bold body saves them the trouble, and then follow his opinion; or stay till they hear what is said in town, that is at some bishop's table, or some coffee-house about the Temple. When they are determined I will tell you faithfully their verdict. As for the beauties,[1] I am their most humble servant. What shall I say to Mr. Lowth, Mr. Ridley, Mr. Rolle, the Reverend Mr. Brown, Seward, etc.? If I say, "Messieurs! this is not the thing; write prose, write sermons, write nothing at all;" they will disdain me and my advice. What then would the sickly peer [2] have done, that spends so much time in admiring everything that has four legs, and fretting at his own misfortune in having but two; and cursing his own politic head and feeble constitution, that won't let him be such a beast as he would wish? Mr. S. Jenyns now and then can write a good line or two—such as these—

> Snatch us from all our little sorrows here,
> Calm every grief, and dry each childish tear, etc.

I like Mr. Aston Hervey's fable; and an ode (the last of all) by Mr. Mason, a new acquaintance of mine, whose " Musæus " too seems to carry with it a promise at least of something good to come. I was glad to see you distinguished who poor West was, before his charming ode,[3] and called it anything rather than a Pindaric. The town is an owl, if it don't like Lady Mary,[4] and I am surprised at it: we here are owls enough to think her eclogues very bad; but that I did not wonder at. Our present taste is Sir T. Fitz-Osborne's Letters.

I send you a bit of a thing for two reasons: first, because it is of one of your favourites, Mr. M. Green; and next, because I would do justice. The thought on which my second ode [5] turns is manifestly stole from hence; not that I knew it at the time, but having seen this many years before, to be sure it imprinted itself on my memory, and, forgetting the author, I took it for my own. The subject was the Queen's Hermitage.

.   .   .   .

> Tho' yet no palace grace the shore,
> To lodge the pair you [6] should adore,
> Nor abbeys great in ruins rise,
> Royal equivalents for vice;

[1] The " Epistle to Mr. Eckardt, the Painter." See Walpole's *Works*, vol. i. p. 19.—*Mitford*.
[2] Lord Hervey.—*Mitford*.
[3] Monody on the death of Queen Caroline.
[4] Lady Mary W. Montagu's poems.   [5] The " Ode to Spring."
[6] Speaking to the Thames.

Behold a grot in Delphic grove,
The Graces' and the Muses' love,
A temple from vainglory free;
Whose goddess is Philosophy;
Whose sides such licens'd idols [1] crown,
As Superstition would pull down:
The only pilgrimage I know,
That men of sense would choose to go.
Which sweet abode, her wisest choice,
Urania cheers with heavenly voice;
While all the Virtues gather round
To see her consecrate the ground.

If thou, the god with winged feet,
In council talk of this retreat;
And jealous gods resentment show
At altars rais'd to men below.
Tell those proud lords of heaven 'tis fit
Their house our heroes should admit.
While each exists (as poets sing)
A lazy, lewd, immortal thing;
They must, or grow in disrepute,
With earth's first commoners recruit.

Needless it is, in terms unskill'd,
To praise whatever Boyle shall build.
Needless it is the busts to name
Of men, monopolists of fame;
Four chiefs adorn the modest stone,
For virtue, as for learning known:
The thinking sculpture helps to raise
Deep thoughts, the genii of the place:
To the mind's ear, and inward sight,
There silence speaks, and shade gives light:
While insects from the threshold preach,
And minds dispos'd to musing teach;
Proud of strong limbs and painted hues,
They perish by the slightest bruise;
Or maladies begun within
Destroy more slow life's frail machine:
From maggot-youth, thro' change of state,
They feel like us the turns of fate:
Some born to creep have liv'd to fly,
And chang'd earth's cells for dwellings high:
And some that did their six wings keep,
Before they die, been forced to creep.

They politics, like ours, profess;
The greater prey upon the less.
Some strain on foot huge loads to bring,
Some toil incessant on the wing:
Nor from their vigorous schemes desist
Till death; and then they are never mist.
Some frolick, toil, marry, increase,
Are sick and well, have war and peace;
And broke with age in half a day,
Yield to successors, and away.

. . . . . .

    Adieu! I am ever yours,

        T. GRAY.

[1] The four Busts.

LIX.—Mr GRAY to Mr. WALPOLE

STOKE, *Jan.* 1753.

I AM at present at Stoke, to which place I came at half an hour's warning upon the news I received of my mother's illness, and did not expect to have found her alive; but when I arrived she was much better, and continues so. I shall therefore be very glad to make you a visit at Strawberry-hill, whenever you give me notice of a convenient time. I am surprised at the print,[1] which far surpasses my idea of London graving. The drawing itself was so finished, that I suppose it did not require all the art I had imagined to copy it tolerably. My aunts seeing me open your letter, took it to be a burying-ticket, and asked whether anybody had left me a ring; and so they still conceive it to be, even with all their spectacles on. Heaven forbid they should suspect it to belong to any verses of mine, they would burn me for a poet. On my own part I am satisfied, if this design of yours succeed so well as you intend it; and yet I know it will be accompanied with something not at all agreeable to me.— While I write this, I receive your second letter.—Sure, you are not out of your wits! This I know, if you suffer my head to be printed, you will infallibly put me out of mine. I conjure you immediately to put a stop to any such design. Who is at the expense of engraving it, I know not; but if it be Dodsley, I will make up the loss to him. The thing as it was, I know, will make me ridiculous enough; but to appear in proper person, at the head of my works, consisting of half a dozen ballads in thirty pages, would be worse than the pillory. I do assure you, if I had received such a book, with such a frontispiece, without any warning, I believe it would have given me a palsy. Therefore I rejoice to have received this notice, and shall not be easy till you tell me all thoughts of it are laid aside. I am extremely in earnest, and cannot bear even the idea.

I had written to Dodsley if I had not received yours, to tell

---

[1] A proof print of the Cul de Lampe, which Mr. Bentley designed for the "Elegy in a Country Churchyard," and which represents a village funeral; this occasioned the pleasant mistake of his two aunts. The remainder of the letter relates entirely to the projected publication of Mr. Bentley's designs, which were printed after by Dodsley, this same year. The latter part of it, where he so vehemently declares against having his head prefixt to that work, will appear highly characteristical to those readers who were personally acquainted with Mr. Gray. The print, which was taken from an original picture, painted by Echart, in Mr. Walpole's possession, was actually more than half engraved; but afterwards on this account suppressed.—*Mason.*

him how little I liked the title which he meant to prefix; but your letter has put all that out of my head. If you think it necessary to print these explanations for the use of people that have no eyes, I should be glad they were a little altered. I am to my shame in your debt for a long letter, but I cannot think of anything else, till you have set me at ease on this matter.

LX.—MR. GRAY TO MR. WHARTON

MY DEAR WHARTON,

I judge by this time you are in town: the reason that I thought would have deprived me of the pleasure of seeing you is now at an end. My poor mother, after a long and painful struggle for life, expired on Sunday morning: when I have seen her buried, I shall come to London; and it will be a particular satisfaction to me to find you there. If you can procure me a tolerable lodging near you, be so good (if you can conveniently) to let me know the night you receive this; if not, I shall go to my old landlord in Jermyn Street. I believe I shall come on Tuesday, and stay a few days, for I must return hither to pay my aunt her arrears, which she will demand with great exactness. Adieu, dear sir,

I am ever yours,
T. GRAY.

To me at Mrs. Rogers's of Stoke, near Windsor, Bucks.

March 15 [1753], STOKE.

LXI.—MR. GRAY TO MR. WHARTON

MY DEAR DOCTOR,

You may well suppose me no longer here, as I have neglected thus long to answer two very kind letters, and (which is more) to congratulate you on what most of your friends regard as a very happy event; but to me, I own, it has another face, as I have a much greater regard for you than for the young gentleman, whom I never saw; and foresee, that from this time you will never part with your bottle, which is properly the father of this boy. All my rhetorick will be thrown away, the gout may groan at you, and brandish its crutches, the stone rattle, and the palsy shake it's head unheeded. We shall be no match for claret if it can get an heir, as well as carry an election; now I talk of elections, we have a report here that your friend Mr. V. (I mean Lord Barnard) means to bring in his son-in-law at Durham. Is this true? H. Vane sets out for the north on Saturday, so I suppose the bishop's entry will be over next week: and next Monday fortnight I hope to set out myself with Stonehewer, who is going down to his father's, in a post-chaise. We shall not come very fast, as I propose to see Burleigh, Bevoir Castle, etc., by the way. But I shall write again before I come, to tell you exactly what day we shall be at York. If the time does not suit you, you will inform me as soon as possible. I did not run away from his grace, but followed your advice, had a very affectionate squeeze by the hand, and a fine compliment in a corner. Many people here have been curious to know what it was; but I have kept my own secret, for indeed I do not know myself; only I remember it felt warm, and sweated a little. Adieu! You will not fail to present my compliments to Mrs. Wharton. If she drank as much claret as you have done, we shall have the boy stand for the county, as soon as he can walk alone. Mr. Brown (I believe) will be engaged here with Plummer greatest part of the summer; he and Tuthill desire to be remembered to you both. I am ever,

Truly yours,
T. GRAY.

CAMB., *June 28th*, 1753. *Thursday.*

LXII.—MR. GRAY TO MR. WHARTON

CAMBRIDGE, *Saturday, July* 14, 1753.

MY DEAR DOCTOR,

This is only to tell you that we set out on Monday morning, and shall travel leisurely, not by the direct road, for we intend to see several houses and places as we go; on Thursday we see York, and next morning as early as we can (certainly before ten o'clock) shall hope to meet you at Studley. You will understand all this with Archbishop Potter's proviso; God willing, and provided nothing hinder, for if we are overturned and *tous fracassées*, or if the mob at Leeds cut us off as friends to turnpikes; or if the waters are out, and drown us; or (as Herodotus says) if we can go no further for *feathers*;[1] in all these cases, and

---

[1] This passage from the fourth book of *Herodotus* is humorously applied, by Swift, to the number of authors existing in England. "A happiness

many more, we may chance to fail you. My respects to Mrs. Wharton.

I am ever yours,

T. GRAY.

LXIII.—MR. GRAY TO MR. WHARTON

Oct. 18 [1753], STOKE.

MY DEAR DOCTOR,

You will wonder not to have heard sooner of me. The reason has been the instability of my own situation. As soon as I arrived at Cambridge, I found a letter informing me my aunt Rogers had had a stroke of the palsy, so that I stayed only a single day, and set out for this place. I found her recovered surprisingly from the greatest danger, her speech only is not yet quite restored; but it is easily intelligible to such as are used to her. Is not this something extraordinary at seventy-seven?

I met Mason at York, and passed that evening with him. —— has absolutely no support at present but his fellowship; yet he looks more like a hero than ever I knew him, like one that can stare poverty in the face without being frighted; and instead of growing little and humble before her, has fortified his spirit, and elevated his brow, to meet her like a man. In short if he can hold it, I shall admire him; for I always maintained, that nobody has occasion for pride, but the poor; and that everywhere else it is a sign of folly.

My journey was not so bad as usual in a stage-coach. There was a Lady Swinburne, a Roman Catholick, not young, that had been much abroad, seen a great deal, knew a great many people, very chatty and communicative, so that I passed my time very well; and on the third day left them at Stilton, and got to Cambridge that night. As I know and have heard mighty little to entertain you with, I can only tell you my observations on the face of the country, and the season, in my way hither, that you may compare them with what you see at Durham. Till I came to York, I thought the face of everything rather altered for the worse, certainly not better than that corner of the bishoprick about Darlington. At Topcliff I saw a large vine full of black

(he says) derived to us, with a great many others, from our Scythian ancestors, among whom the number of pens was so infinite, that the Grecian eloquence had no other way of expressing it than by saying— ' That in the regions far to the north it was hardly possible for a man to travel; the very air was so replete with feathers.' "—*Tale of a Tub*, sect. vii.

grapes, that seemed ripe. At Helperby met a flock of geese in *full song*: if their person had not betrayed them, one might have taken them for nightingales. At York walnuts ripe, twenty for a penny. From thence especially, south of Tadcaster, I thought the country extremely beautiful, broke into fine hills covered with noble woods (particularly towards the east), and everything as verdant almost as at midsummer: this continued to Doncaster, the hazle and white-thorn were turning yellow in the hedges, the sycamore, lime, and ash, where it was young or much exposed, are growing rusty, but far greener, than in your county. The old ash, the oak, and other timber, shewed no signs of winter: some few of the lands were even in stubble, but for the most part they were ploughed up, or covered with turnips. I find Mr. Evelyn in his book of forest trees, published in Queen Anne's time, takes notice—"That Shropshire, and several other counties, and rarely any beyond Stamford to Durham, have the vernacular (or French elm) growing for many miles together." I cannot say I saw any, but about Scrubey, in Nottinghamshire, and they were young ones newly planted, near a hedgerow. He also mentions the elm of a more scabrous leaf, harsh and very large, which becomes a huge tree; *mentioned in the* statute-books *under the name* [1] *of the* wych-hayle. For my part, I could find no sort but the last, at least of any size, or growing in a wild way, till I came into Northamptonshire. I thought the winter more advanced in Lincolnshire, and so on till I had passed Huntingdon, than it was in the West Riding of Yorkshire. In Northamptonshire I first observed the appearances of a long drought, which continued quite hither. The turf is everywhere brown and burnt up, as in Italy; even the low meadows want their usual verdure. At Cambridge the finest grapes I ever saw there. The lime-trees were only changing colour, but had dropped few of their leaves. In the smoke of London they had almost lost their old leaves, but made fresh shoots as green as in April; and here, before my window, are two young sycamores, which have done the same, but still retain all their old leaves too, without any change of colour. At Trompington the new rye was green in the fields, and three inches high: it is the same in this county. We are here upon a loam with a bed of gravel below, and rag-stone beneath that. The hay is usually all in by old midsummer, this year it was all cut by new midsummer, but a great deal of it lost for want

[1] These words in italics are supplied; the manuscript being imperfect —*Mitford*.

of rain, which likewise spoiled the tares and peas. In the beginning of August was rain for near three weeks, which saved the corn. Oats were in some places cut before the wheat, which was all got in by the 20th of August. Barley, beans, etc., by the 7th of September. I came hither the 6th of October, and they had then, within a mile of the Thames (where the soil is better than here), begun to sow wheat. For six weeks before my arrival it had been continued fine weather, and the air, till sunset, was like July. Never almost was such a year known for fruit. The nectarines and best peaches had been all gathered three weeks before. The grapes were then perfectly ripe, and still continue the best I ever eat in England. October 9th, it began to rain, and we have had showers every day since, with brisk winds in the S. and S.W.; to-day it is in the north, clear sunshine, but cold, and a little wintry: and so ends my Georgick in prose. Excuse me if I had nothing better to send you; it is partly from my own eyesight, and partly from the report of such as have no prejudice in favour of their county, because they hardly know there is any other. I write chiefly to draw on a letter from you, for I am impatient to know many things: but remember this election-time letters are apt to be opened at the offices. Pray make my sincere acknowledgements to my *kind hostess;* I trust she was not the worse for her journey. I hope you know that

I am ever yours,

T. G.

At Mrs. Rogers's, of Stoke,
  near Windsor, Bucks.

P.S. Everything resounds with the wood-lark and robin; and the voice of the sparrow is heard in our land. Remember me to all that remember there is such a person.

Adieu!

LXIV.—Mr. GRAY to Mr. MASON

Durham, *Dec.* 26, 1753.

A LITTLE while before I received your melancholy letter, I had been informed by Mr. Charles Avison of one of the sad events you mention.[1] I know what it is to lose persons that one's eyes and

---

[1] The death of my father, and of Dr. Marmaduke Pricket, a young physician of my own age, with whom I was brought up from infancy, who died of the same infectious fever.—*Mason.*

heart have long been used to; and I never desire to part with the remembrance of that loss, nor would wish you should. It is something that you had a little time to acquaint yourself with the idea beforehand; and that your father suffered but little pain, the only thing that makes death terrible. After I have said this, I cannot help expressing my surprise at the disposition he has made of his affairs. I must (if you will suffer me to say so) call it great weakness; and yet perhaps your affliction for him is heightened by that very weakness; for I know it is possible to feel an additional sorrow for the faults of those we have loved, even where that fault has been greatly injurious to ourselves.—Let me desire you not to expose yourself to any further danger in the midst of that scene of sickness and death; but withdraw as soon as possible to some place at a little distance in the country; for I do not, in the least, like the situation you are in. I do not attempt to console you on the situation your fortune is left in; if it were far worse, the good opinion I have of you tells me, you will never the sooner do anything mean or unworthy of yourself; and consequently I cannot pity you on this account, but I sincerely do on the new loss you have had of a good and friendly man, whose memory I honour. I have seen the scene you describe, and know how dreadful it is; I know too I am the better for it. We are all idle and thoughtless things, and have no sense, no use in the world any longer than that sad impression lasts; the deeper it is engraved the better.

LXV.—Mr. GRAY to Mr. WHARTON

STOKE, *Aug.* 13 [1754.]

MY DEAR SIR,

Having been some little time absent from hence, I missed of your letter, or I had answered it as soon as you desire me. The opportunity of a good house I hope you will not suffer to escape you, whether the rent be too high, you alone can properly judge. There is a great comfort to be sure in a good house. Some appearance of economy, I should think would give you credit, in that part of the town you are to be well with: they pride themselves in living much within their income;—upon the whole I seem to have a partiality for Mr. Crumpe, but be sure never to repent; if you think you shall, by all means settle yourself in the great house. Beside I do not know, but some great old doctor may come and squat himself down there at your elbow (for I suppose there may be some convenience in succeeding to a house of the same profession), and then you would be horridly out of humour. In short you see with your own eyes, you know the quarter, and must necessarily be best qualified to decide. Dr. Fothergill's invitation is very civil. As to the depth of science which you seem to dread, it always grows shallower as one comes nearer, though it makes a great noise at a distance. The design of the society at least is a good one; but if they are warm and professed enemies of the college, I should think the same reason that makes Heberden withdraw himself, should prevent your admission in it. It will be easy to delay it, however, on various pretences, without disobliging any one.

I am glad you agree with me in admiring Mr. Southcote's paradise, which whenever you see it again, will improve upon you. Do you know, you may have it for £20,000, but I am afraid the lands are not very improvable. You don't say enough of Esher, it is my other favourite place. It was a villa of Cardinal Wolsey's, of which nothing but the gateway remained. Mr. Kent supplied the rest, but I think with you, that he had not read the Gothic classics with taste or attention. He introduced a mixed style, which now goes by the name of the *Battey-Langley manner*. He is an architect, that has published a book of bad designs;—if you have seen Mr. Walpole's, pray let me hear your opinion, which I will not anticipate by saying anything about it. To be sure its extreme littleness will be the first thing that strikes you. By all means see Lord Radnor's again. He is a simple old Phobus, but nothing can spoil so glorious a situation, which surpasses everything round it. I take it ill you should say anything against the Mole; it is a reflection, I see, cast at the Thames. Do you think that rivers which have lived in London, and its neighbourhood, all their days, will run roaring and tumbling about, like your tramontane torrents in the north. No, they only glide and whisper. In your next expedition, you will see Claremont, and Lord Portman's, which joins my Lord Lincoln's, and above all Mr. Hamilton's, at Cobham, in Surrey, which all the world talks of, and I have seen seven years ago. The year indeed does not behave itself well, but think what it must be in the north. I suppose the roads are impassable with the deep snow still.

I could write abundance more, but am afraid of losing this post. Pray let me hear from you, as soon as you can, and make my compliments to Mrs. Wharton. Mason is by this time in town again. Tuthill, —— Brown, I believe, at Cambridge. Adieu!

I am ever yours,
T. G.

I am obliged to you for sending the tea, which is excellent.

LXVI.—Mr. GRAY to Mr. WHARTON

Stoke, *Sept.* 18, 1754.

Dear Sir,

I rejoice to find you at last settled to your heart's content, and delight to hear you talk of giving your house some *Gothic ornaments* already. If you project anything, I hope it will be entirely within doors, and don't let me (when I come gaping into Coleman-street) be directed to the gentleman's at the ten pinnacles, or with the church porch at his door. I am glad you enter into the spirit of Strawberry-castle;—it has a purity and propriety of Gothicism in it (with very few exceptions) that I have not seen elsewhere. The eating-room and library were not compleated when I was there, and I want to know what effect they have. My Lord Radnor's Vagaries (I see) did not keep you from doing justice to his situation, which far surpasses everything near it, and I do not know a more *laughing* scene than that about Twickenham and Richmond. Dr. Akenside (I perceive) is no conjuror in architecture, especially when he talks of the ruins of Persepolis, which are no more Gothic than they are Chinese. The Egyptian style (see Dr. Pococke, not his discourses, but his prints) was apparently the mother of the Greek, and there is such a similitude between the Egyptian and those Persian ruins, as gave room to Diodorus [1] to affirm that the old buildings of Persia were certainly performed by Egyptian artists. As to the other parts of his opinion, that the Gothic manner is the Saracen or Moorish, he has a great authority to support him, that of Sir Christopher Wren, and yet (I cannot help thinking) is un-doubtedly wrong. The palaces in Spain I never saw but in description, which gives us little or no idea of things; but the

---

[1] See *Diodori Hist.* ed. Wesseling, lib. i. c. 46, v. i. p. 55. Diodorus says that the royal palaces in Persepolis, in Susa, and those in Media, were built by Egyptian architects when Cambyses burnt the temples of Egypt, carried their riches into Asia, and transported their artificers there.—*Mitford.*

doge's palace at Venice I have seen (which is in the Arabesque manner), and the houses of Barbary you may see in Dr. Shaw's book, not to mention abundance of other eastern buildings in Turkey, Persia, etc., that we have views of, and they seem plainly to be corruptions of the Greek architecture, broke into little parts indeed, and covered with little ornaments, but in a taste very distinguishable from what we call Gothic. There is one thing that runs through the Moorish buildings, that an imitator would certainly have been first struck with, and would have tried to copy, and that is the cupolas, which cover every-thing, baths, apartments, and even kitchens—yet who ever saw a Gothic cupola; it is a thing plainly of Greek original. I do not see anything but the slender spires, that serve for steeples, which may perhaps be borrowed from the Saracen minarets or their mosques.

I was in Northamptonshire when I received your letter, but am now returned hither. I have been at Warwick, which is a place worth seeing. The town is on an eminence, surrounded every way with a fine cultivated valley, through which the Avon winds, and at the distance of five or six miles, a circle of hills well wooded, and with various objects crowning them, that close the prospect. Out of the town on one side of it rises a rock that might remind one of your rocks at Durham, but that it is not so savage or so lofty, and that the river which washes its foot is perfectly clear, and so gentle that its current is hardly visible. Upon it stands the castle, the noble old residence of the Beauchamps and Nevilles, and now of Earl Brooke. He has sashed the great apartment, that's to be sure (I can't help these things), and being since told that square sash windows were not Gothic, he has put certain whim-whams within side the glass, which appearing through, are to look like fretwork. Then he has scooped out a little burrough in the massy walls of the place, for his little self and his children, which is hung with paper, and printed linen, and carved chimney-pieces, in the exact manner of Berkley-square or Argyle-buildings. What in short can a lord do nowadays, that is lost in a great old solitary castle, but skulk about, and get into the first hole he finds, as a rat would do in like case. A pretty long old stone bridge leads you into the town, with a mill at the end of it, over which the rock rises with the castle upon it, with all its battlements, and queer-ruined towers, and on your left hand the Avon strays through the park, whose ancient elms seem to remember Sir Philip Sidney (who often walked under them), and talk of him to this day.   The Beauchamp earls of Warwick lie under stately monuments in the choir of the great church, and in our lady's chapel adjoining to it.   There also lie Ambrose Dudley, Earl of Warwick, and his brother, the famous Lord Leicester, with Lettice, his countess.   This chapel is preserved entire, though the body of the church was burnt down sixty years ago, and rebuilt by Sir C. Wren.   I had heard often of Guy-Cliff, two miles from the town, so I walked to see it; and of all improvers commend me to Mr. Greathead, its present owner.   He shewed it me himself, and is literally a fat young man, with a head and face much bigger than they are usually worn.   It was naturally a very agreeable rock, whose cliffs covered with large trees hung beetling over the Avon, which twists twenty ways in sight of it; there was the cell of Guy Earl of Warwick cut in the living stone, where he died a hermit (as you may see in a penny history, that hangs upon the rails in Moorfields); there were his fountains bubbling out of the cliff; —there was a chantry founded to his memory in Henry the VIth's time, but behold the trees are cut down to make room for flowering shrubs, the rock is cut up till it is as smooth and as sleek as satin; the river has a gravel-walk by its side; the cell is a grotto with cockle-shells and looking-glass; the fountains have an iron gate before them, and the chantry is a barn, or a little house.   Even the poorest bits of nature that remain are daily threatened; for he says (and I am sure, when the Great-heads are once set upon a thing, they will do it) he is determined it shall be *all new*.   These were his words, and they are fate.   I have also been at Stow, at Woburn (the Duke of Bedford's), and at Moxton (Duke of Guilford's), but I defer these chapters till we meet.   I shall only tell you for your comfort, that the parts of Northamptonshire where I have been, is in fruits, in flowers, and in corn, very near a fortnight behind this part of Buckinghamshire; that they have no nightingales, and that the other birds are almost as silent as at Durham.   It is rich land, but upon a clay, and in a very bleak, high, exposed situation. I hope you have had some warm weather since you last complained of the south.   I have thought of seeing you about Michaelmas, though I shall not stay long in town; I should have been at Cambridge before now if the Duke of Newcastle and his foundation-stone would have let me, but I want them to have done before I go.   I am sorry Mr. Brown should be the only one that has stood upon punctilios with me, and would not write first; pray tell him so.   Mason is (I believe) in town, or at

Chiswick. No news of Tuthill. I wrote a long letter to him in answer to one he wrote me, but no reply. Adieu!

I am ever yours,
T. G.

Brown called here this morning before I was up, and breakfasted with me.

LXVII.—Mr. GRAY to Dr. WHARTON

ODE IN THE GREEK MANNER

[THE ODE ON "THE PROGRESS OF POESY"]

IF this be as tedious to you as it is grown to me, I shall be sorry that I sent it you. I do not pretend to *deballate* [1] any one's pride, I love my own too well to attempt it. As to mortifying their vanity, it is too easy and too mean a task for me to delight in. You are very good in shewing so much sensibility on my account, but be assured my taste for praise is not like that of children for fruit; if there were nothing but medlars and blackberries in the world, I could be very well content to go without any at all. I dare say Mason (though some years younger than I) was as little elevated with the approbation of Lord D. and Lord M. as I am mortified by their silence. I desire you would by no means suffer this to be copied, nor even shew it, unless to very few, and especially not to mere scholars, that can scan all the measures in Pindar, and say the "Scholia" by heart. The oftener (and in spite of poor Trollope), the *more* you write to me, the happier I shall be. I envy your opera. Your politicks I don't understand, but I think matters can never continue long in the situation they now are. "Barbarossa" [2] I have read,

---

[1] *Humble* any one's pride.—*Mitford. Mason.*

[2] "Barbarossa." This play was written by Dr. Brown, the admirer and friend of Warburton, and author of the "Estimate," essay on satire. Garrick wrote the epilogue, the following line of which gave the greatest offence to the author:—

"Let the poor devil eat, allow him that," etc.

"A very indifferent new tragedy (says Mr. Walpole, in a letter to Mr. Bentley, p. 305) now making: the author unknown, but believed to be Garrick himself. There is not one word of Barbarossa's real story, but almost the individual history of Merope. Not one new thought, and which is the next material want, but one line of perfect nonsense.

'And rain down transports in the shape of sorrow.'

To complete it, the manners are so ill observed, that a Mahometan princess royal is at full liberty to visit her lover in Newgate, like the banker's daughter in George Barnwell."—*Mitford.*

but I did not cry; at a modern tragedy, it is sufficient not to laugh. I had rather the king's arms looked askew upon me than the mitre; it is enough to be well bred to both of them. You do not mention Lord Strathmore, so that I doubt if you received my little letter about him. Mason is still here: we are all mighty glad he is in orders, and no better than any of us. Pray inform me if Dr. Clarke is come to town, and where he is fixed, that I may write to him, angry as he is. My compliments to my friend Mrs. Wharton, to your mother, and all the little gentry. I am ever, dear doctor, most sincerely yours.

CAMB., *Dec.* 26, 1754.

LXVIII.—MR. GRAY TO DR. WHARTON

March 9, 1755, CAMBRIDGE.

MY DEAR DOCTOR,

According to my reckoning, Mrs. Wharton should have been brought to bed before this time; yet you say not a syllable of it. If you are so loth to publish *your productions*, you cannot wonder at the repugnance I feel to spreading abroad mine. But in truth, I am not so much against publishing as against publishing *this*[1] *alone*. I have two or three ideas more in my head; what is to come of them? must they too come out in the shape of little sixpenny flams, dropping one after another, till Mr. Dodsley thinks fit to collect them with Mr. this's song, and Mr. t'other's epigram, into a pretty volume! I am sure Mason must be sensible of this, and therefore can never mean what he says. To be sure, doctor, it must be owned, that physick, and indeed all professions, have a bad effect upon the mind. This it is my duty and interest to maintain. But I shall still be very ready to write a satire upon the clergy, and an epode against historiographers, whenever you are hard pressed: and (if you flatter me) may throw in a few lines with somewhat handsome, upon *Magnesia alba* and alicant-soap. As to humanity you know my aversion to it, which is barbarous and inhuman; but I cannot help it, God forgive me. I am not quite of your opinion with regard to strophe[2] and antistrophe, setting aside the diffi-

---

[1] His ode on the " Progress of Poetry."—*Mason.*

[2] He often made the same remark to me in conversation, which led me to form the last " Ode to Caractacus " in shorter stanzas. But we must not imagine that he thought the regular Pindaric method without its use, thought, as he justly says, when formed in long stanzas, it does not fully succeed in point of effect on the ear. For there was nothing which he

culties, methinks it has little or no effect upon the ear, which scarce perceives the regular return of metres, at so great a distance from one another. To make it succeed, I am persuaded the stanzas must not consist of above nine lines each at the most. Pindar has several such odes.

Lord Strathmore is come, and makes a tall genteel figure in our eyes. His tutors and he appear to like one another mighty well. When we know more of him than his outside, you and the historian shall hear of it. I am going to ask a favour of you, which I have no better pretence for doing than that I have long been used to give you trouble. It is that you would go to the London insurance office, in Birchin-lane, for me, and pay two insurances; one of my house at Wanstead (Policy No. 9675), the other of that in Cornhill (No. 23470), from Lady-day next to Lady-day 1756. The first is twenty shillings, the second, twelve shillings; and be pleased to enclose the two receipts (stamped) in a cover, and send them to me. The sooner the better, for I am always in a little apprehension, during this season of conflagrations. I know you will excuse me, and therefore will make no excuses. I cannot think of coming to town till some time in April myself.

I know you have wrote a very obliging letter to Tuthill, but as I have not seen it, and he is not in my way at present, I leave him to answer for himself. Adieu, dear sir, and make my compliments to your family.

I am ever yours,
T. G.

LXIX.—Mr. GRAY to Dr. WHARTON

Aug. 6, 1755, Stoke.

DEAR DOCTOR,

I was just arrived from my Hampshire [1] expedition, and going to enquire after your little family, and how they had

more disliked than that chain of irregular stanzas which Cowley introduced, and falsely called Pindaric; and which from the extreme facility of execution, produced a number of miserable imitators. Had the regular return of strophe, antistrophe, and epode no other merit than that of extreme difficulty, it ought on this very account to be valued; because we well know that "easy writing is no easy reading." It is also to be remarked, that Mr. Congreve, who (though without any lyrical powers) first introduced the regular Pindaric form into the English language, made use of the short stanzas which Mr. Gray here recommends. See his "Ode to the Queen," *Works*, vol. iii. p. 438, ed. Birm.—*Mason.*

[1] Mr. Gray went on the 15th of July to Mr. Chute's at the Vine, from thence he went to Portsmouth, and returned to Stoke on the 31st of July, as appears by a journal which he kept.—*Mitford.*

got over the measles, when I found a letter from Stonehewer, in which he says nothing on that head, whence I conclude they are out of danger, and you free from anxiety about them. But he tells me you expect me in town, for which I am at a loss to account, having said nothing to that purpose, at least, I am sure nothing with that meaning. I said I was to go to Twickenham, and am now expecting a letter from Mr. Walpole, to inform me when he shall be there. My stay will be at farthest a week with him, and at my return I shall let you know, and if the season be better than it now is, enquire, if you continue inclined to visit Windsor and its environs. I wished for you often on the southern coast, where I have been, and made much the same tour that Stonehewer did before me. Take notice that the oaks grow quite down to the beach, and that the sea forms a number of bays little and great, that appear glittering in the midst of thick groves of them. Add to this the fleet (for I was at Portsmouth two days before it sailed) and the number of vessels always passing along, or sailing up Southampton river (which is the largest of these bays I mention), and enters about ten miles into the land, and you will have a faint idea of the *South*. From Fareham to Southampton, where you are upon a level with the coast, you have a thousand such peeps and delightful openings; but would you see the whole at once, you must get upon Ports-down, five miles upon this side Portsmouth. It is the top of a ridge that forms a natural terrass three miles long, literally not three times broader than Windsor-terrass, with a gradual fall on both sides, and covered with a turf like Newmarket. To the north, opens Hampshire and Berkshire, covered with woods, and interspersed with numerous gentlemen's houses and villages, to the south, Portsmouth, Gosport, etc., just at your foot in appearance, the fleet, the sea winding and breaking in bays into the land, the deep shade of tall oaks in the enclosures, which become blue, as they go off to distance. Porchester-castle, Calshot-castle, and all the Isle of Wight, in which you plainly distinguish the fields, hedge rows, and woods, next the shore, and a background of hills behind them. I have not seen a more magnificent or more varied prospect. I have been also at Tichfield, at Netly-abbey (a most beautiful ruin in as beautiful a situation), at Southampton, at Bevis-mount, at Winchester, etc. My gout is gone, but I am not absolutely well yet. I heard Mason was expected on Monday last, but was not to speak of it, therefore you will say nothing till you see him. I do not understand this; nor what he means by coming, it

seems wrong to me. What did you think of the *morceau*[1] I
sent you. Pray speak your mind. My best compliments to
Mrs. Wharton. Adieu.   I am ever yours,

                                                    T. G.

LXX.—MR. GRAY TO DR. WHARTON

STOKE, *Aug.* 21, 1755.

DEAR DOCTOR,

Instead of going to Twickenham I was obliged to send my
excuses, and the same day Mr. Walpole sent a messenger to say
he was confined in town with a fever, and a rash. He has since
wrote me word that he is well again. But for me, I continue
much as I was, and have been but once out of the house to walk
since I returned from Hampshire. Being much inclined to
bleeding myself, I yet was fearful to venture, lest it should bring
on a regular fit of the gout, so I sent for advice at last, and
expected Dr. Hayes should tell me presently whether it were
gout or rheumatism; in his talk, he treated it rather as the
former, but his prescription appears to me to be meant for the
latter. You will judge, he took away ten or eleven ounces of
blood, and ordered these draughts night and morning: *Sal.
Absinth. Succ. Limon finitâ effervescentiâ add. Aqua. Alexit.
Simpl. Menth. Piperit, Magnes. alb., Tinct. G. Guiac. Spirituos.*
The quantities I can't read; only I think there is a drachm of
the tincture, and half a drachm of magnesia in each draught.
The blood had no sign of inflammation, but of a bright red;
the serum of a dark yellow with little transparency, not viscid
to the touch. The draughts (which I took over night only)
made me sweat almost immediately, and opened a little in the
morning, the consequence is, that I have still many slight
complaints, broken and unrefreshing sleeps, as before, less
feverish than I was in a morning. Instead of it a sensation of
weariness and soarness in both feet, which goes off in the day,
a frequent dizziness and lightness of head, easily fatigued with
motion. Sometimes a little pain in my breast, as I had in the
winter. These symptoms are all too slight to make an illness,
but they do not make perfect health, that is sure.

Though I allow abundance for your kindness and partiality
to me, I am much pleased with the good opinion you seem to

---

[1] A copy of the *first* part of the " Bard," but which, I am sorry to say,
is not preserved among Dr. Wharton's MSS.—*Mitford.*

have of the " Bard." You may alter that, " *Robed in* the sable, etc.*" almost in your own words, thus,

> With fury pale, and pale with woe,
> Secure of Fate, the Poet stood, etc.

Though *haggard*, which conveys to you the idea of a *witch*, is indeed only a metaphor taken from an unreclaimed hawk, which is called a *haggard*, and looks wild and *farouche*, and jealous of its liberty. I have sent now to Stonehewer a bit more of the " Prophecy," and desire him to shew it you immediately: it is very rough and unpolished at present. Adieu, dear sir,

I am ever truly yours,

T. G.

LXXI.—Mr. GRAY to Dr. WHARTON

Jan. 9, Cambridge, 1756.

Dear Doctor,

I am quite of Mr. Alderman's opinion; provided you have a very fair prospect of success (for I do not love repulses, though I believe in such cases, they are not attended with any disgrace) such an employment must necessarily give countenance and name to one in your profession, not to mention the use it must be of in refreshing and keeping alive the ideas of practice you have already got, and improving them by new observation. It cannot but lead to other business too, in a more natural way than perhaps any other, for whatever lucky chance may have introduced into the world, here and there, a physician of great vogue, the same chance may hardly befal another in an age; and the indirect and byways that doubtless have succeeded with many, are rather too dirty for you to tread. As to the time it would take up, so much the better. Whenever it interferes with more advantageous practice, it is in your power to quit it. In the meantime it will prepare you for that trouble and constant attendance which much business requires a much greater degree of. For you are not to dream of being your own master, till old age and a satiety of gain shall set you free. I tell you my notions of the matter, as I see it at a distance, which you, who stand nearer, may rectify at your pleasure.

I have continued the soap every other day from the time I left you, except an interval or two of a week or ten days at a time, which I allow in order to satisfy myself, whether the good effects of it were lasting, or only temporary. I think I may say, it has absolutely cured that complaint I used to mention to you; and (what is more) the ill-habit, which perhaps was the cause of that, and of the flying pains I have every now and then felt in my joints: whenever I use it, it much increases my appetite, and the heart-burn is quite banished, so I may venture to say, it does good to my stomach. When I shall speak of its bad effects, you are no longer to treat me as a whimsical body, for I am certain now that it disorders the head, and much disturbs one's sleep. This I now avoid by taking it immediately before dinner; and besides, these things are trifles compared with the good it has done me. In short, I am so well it would be folly to take any other medicine, therefore I reserve lime water, for some more pressing occasion. I should be glad to know the particulars of Lord Northumberland and the archbishop's illnesses, and how far it has eased them in the gout.

I am glad you admire Machiavel, and are entertained with Buffon, and edified with the divine Ashton. The first (they say) was a good man, as much as he has been abused; and we will hope the best of the two latter. Mr. [   ] who as [   ] sent me word, desired to be acquainted with me, called here, before I came down, and would pay a visit to my rooms. He made Dr. Long conduct him thither, left me a present of a book (not of his own writing) and a note with a very civil compliment. I wrote to him to thank him, and have received an answer, that fifteen years ago might have turned my head. I know [   ] will abuse him to you, but I insist he is a slanderer, and shall write a satire upon him, if he does not do justice to my new admirer. I have not added a line more to old "Caradoc." When I do, you will be sure to see it. You who give yourself the trouble to think of my health, will not think me very troublesome, if I beg you to bespeak me a rope-ladder (for my neighbours every day make a great progress in drunkenness, which gives me reason to look about me), it must be full thirty-six feet long, or a little more, but as light and manageable as may be, easy to unroll, and not likely to entangle. I never saw one, but I suppose it must have strong hooks, or something equivalent at top, to throw over an iron bar to be fixed withinside of my window. However you will chuse the properest form, and instruct me in the use of it. I see an Ephraim Hadden, near Hermitage-stairs, Wapping, that advertises them, but perhaps you may find a better artisan near you. This with a canister of tea, and another of snuff, which I left at your house, and a pound of soap from Mr. Field (for mine

is not so good here) will fill a box, which I beg the favour of you
to send me when you can conveniently.   My best compliments to
Mrs. Wharton.   I am ever yours,

T.G.

LXXII.—MR. GRAY TO DR. WHARTON

PEMB. HALL, March 25, 1756.

DEAR DOCTOR,

    Though I had no reasonable excuse for myself before I received
your last letter, yet since that time I have had a pretty good one;
having been taken up in quarrelling with Peter-House, [1] and in
removing myself from thence to Pembroke.   This may be looked
upon as a sort of æra in a life so barren of events as mine, yet I
shall treat it in Voltaire's manner, and only tell you that I left
my lodgings because the rooms were noisy, and the people of the
house *dirty:* [2] this is all I would chuse to have said about it; but
if you, in private, should be curious enough to enter into a
particular detail of facts and minute circumstances, Stonehewer,
who was witness to them, will probably satisfy you.   All I shall
say more is, that I am for the present extremely well lodged here,
and as quiet as in the Grande Chartreuse; and that everybody
(even the Dr. Longs and Dr. Mays) are as civil as they could be
to Mary of Valens [3] in person.   With regard to any advice I
can give as to the hospital, I freely own it ought to give way to
Dr. Heberden's counsels, who is a much better judge, and (I
should think) disinterested.   I love refusals no more than you
do.   But as to your effluvia, I maintain that one sick *rich* has
more of pestilence and putrefaction about him than a whole
ward of sick poor.

    You should have received Mason's present [4] as last Saturday
I desire you to tell me your critical opinion of the new ode
and also whether you have found out two lines, which he has

    [1] The reason of Mr. Gray's changing his college, which is here only
glanced at, was in few words this: Two or three young men of fortune
who lived in the same staircase, had for some time intentionally disturbe
him with their riots, and carried their ill-behaviour so far as frequently
to awaken him at midnight.   After having borne with their insults longe.
than might reasonably have been expected, even from a man of less
warmth of temper, Mr. Gray complained to the governing part of the
Society; and not thinking that his remonstrance was sufficiently attende
to, quitted the college.   The slight manner in which he mentions thi
affair, when writing to one of his most intimate friends, certainly doe.
honour to the placability of his disposition.—*Mason.*

    [2] Uncivil.—*Mason.*   [3] Foundress of the college.—*Mason.*
    [4] The four odes which I had just published separately.—*Mason.*

inserted in another of them, that are superlative.[1] We do not expect that the world, which is just going to be *invaded*, will bestow much attention on them; if you hear anything you will tell us.

The similitude between the Italian republicks and ancient Greece has often struck me, as it does you. I do not wonder that Sully's *Memoirs* have highly entertained you; but cannot agree with you, in thinking him or his master two of the *best* men in the world. The king was, indeed, one of the best-natured men that ever lived; but it was owing only to chance that his intended marriage with Mad. d'Estrées, or with the Marq^se. de Verneuil, did not involve him and the kingdom in the most inextricable confusion. And his design upon the Princess of Condé (in his old age) was worse still. As to the minister, his base application to Concini, after the murther of Henry, has quite ruined him in my esteem, and destroyed all the merit of that honest surly pride for which I honoured him before. Yet I own that as kings and ministers go, they were both extraordinary men. Pray look at the end of Birch's State Papers of Sir T. Edmondes, for the character of the French Court at that time, written by Sir George Carew.

Pray don't suspect me of any such *suspicions* as you mention. I would hardly believe you were tired of me, though you told me so yourself, sensible as I am, nevertheless, that you might have reason enough to be so. To prove what I say, I have thoughts of coming to you for three days in April; there is to be a *concerto spirituale*, in which M^e. Mingotti (who has just lain in) and Riccioralli will sing the *Stabat Mater* of Pergolesi. You and Mason and I are to be at it together; so pray make no excuses nor put-offs, saving to you however the liberty of saying whether you have a bed to spare (I mean for me, not for him) in your house. Adieu, dear sir,

I am ever faithfully yours,

T. G.

My best compliments to Mrs. Wharton. I give you joy of the divine Ashton; it is indeed a conquest you have made.

---

[1] I should leave the reader to guess (if he thought it worth his while) what this couplet was, which is here commended so much beyond its merit, did not the ode conclude with a compliment to Mr. Gray, in which part he might probably look for it, as those lines were written with the greater care. To secure, therefore, my friend from any imputation of vanity, whatever becomes of myself, I shall here insert the passage.

> While thro' the west, where sinks the crimson Day,
> Meek Twilight slowly sails, and waves her banners gray.—*Mason.*

LXXIII.—MR. GRAY TO MR. MASON

STOKE, *July* 25, 1756.

I FEEL a contrition for my long silence; and yet perhaps it is the last thing you trouble your head about. Nevertheless I will be as sorry as if you took it ill. I am sorry too to see you so punctilious as to stand upon answers, and never to come near me till I have regularly left my name at your door, like a mercer's wife, that imitates people who go a visiting. I would forgive you this, if you could possibly suspect I were doing anything that I liked better; for then your formality might look like being piqued at my negligence, which has somewhat in it like kindness. But you know I am at Stoke, hearing, seeing, doing absolutely nothing. Not such a nothing as you do at Tunbridge, chequered and diversified with a succession of fleeting colours; but heavy, lifeless, without form and void; sometimes almost as black as the moral of Voltaire's " Lisbon," [1] which angers you so. I have had no more muscular inflations, and am only troubled with this depression of mind. You will not expect therefore I should give you any account of my *verve*, which is at best (you know) of so delicate a constitution, and has such weak nerves, as not to stir out of its chamber above three days in a year. But I shall enquire after yours, and why it is off again? It has certainly worse nerves than mine, if your reviewers have frighted it. Sure I (not to mention a score of your other critics) am something a better judge than all the man-midwives and Presbyterian parsons [2] that ever were born. Pray give me leave to ask you, do you find yourself tickled with the commendations of such people? (for you have your share of these too). I dare say not; your vanity has certainly a better taste. And can then the censure of such critics move you? I own it is an impertinence in these gentry to talk of one at all, either in good or in bad; but this we must all swallow: I mean not only we that write, but all the *we's* that ever did anything to be talked of.

While I am writing I receive yours, and rejoice to find that the genial influences of this fine season, which produce nothing in me, have hatched high and unimaginable fantasies in you.[3]

[1] His poem, " Sur la Destruction de Lisbon," published about that time. —*Mason.*
[2] The reviewers, at the time, were supposed to be of these professions. —*Mason.*
[3] I had sent him my first idea of Caractacus, drawn out in a short argument.—*Mason.*

I see, methinks, as I sit on Snowdon, some glimpse of Mona and her haunted shades, and hope we shall be very good neighbours. Any druidical anecdotes that I can meet with, I will be sure to send you when I return to Cambridge; but I cannot pretend to be learned without books, or to know the Druids from modern bishops at this distance. I can only tell you not to go and take Mona for the Isle of Man: it is Anglesey, a tract of plain country, very fertile, but picturesque only from the view it has of Caernarvonshire, from which it is separated by the Menaï, a narrow arm of the sea. Forgive me for supposing in you such a want of erudition.

I congratulate you on our glorious successes in the Mediterranean. Shall we go in time, and hire a house together in Switzerland? It is a fine poetical country to look at, and nobody there will understand a word we say or write.

LXXIV.—Mr. GRAY to Mr. MASON

CAMBRIDGE, *May* 1757.

You are so forgetful of me that I should not forgive it, but that I suppose " Caractacus " may be the better for it. Yet I hear nothing from him neither, in spite of his promises: there is no faith in man, no not in a Welchman; and yet Mr. Parry [1] has been here, and scratched out such ravishing blind harmony, such tunes of a thousand years old, with names enough to choak you, as have set all this learned body a dancing, and inspired them with due reverence for my old Bard his countryman, whenever he shall appear. Mr. Parry, you must know, has put my ode in motion again, and has brought it at last to a conclusion. 'Tis to him, therefore, that you owe the treat which I send you inclosed; namely, the breast and merry-thought, and rump too of the chicken which I have been chewing so long, that I would give the world for neck-beef or cow-heel.

You will observe, in the beginning of this thing, some alterations of a few words, partly for improvement, and partly to avoid repetitions of like words and rhymes; yet I have not got rid of them all; the six last lines of the fifth stanza are new, tell me whether they will do. I am well aware of many weakly things towards the conclusion, but I hope the end itself will do;

[1] A capital performer on the Welch harp, and who was either born blind, or had been so from his infancy.—*Mason.* For an account of Parry, the son of this blind harper, see Northcote's *Life of Sir J. Reynolds*, p. 93.—*Mitford.*

give me your full and true opinion, and that not upon deliberation, but forthwith. Mr. Hurd himself allows that *Lyon port*
is not too bold for Queen Elizabeth.

I have got the old Scotch ballad on which "Douglas"[1] was
founded; it is divine, and as long as from hence to Aston.
Have you never seen it? Aristotle's best rules are observed in
it, in a manner that shews the author had never read Aristotle.
It begins in the fifth act of the play: you may read it two-thirds
through without guessing what it is about; and yet when you
come to the end, it is impossible not to understand the whole
story. I send you the two first stanzas.

.   .   .   .

LXXV.—Mr. GRAY to Mr. WALPOLE

STOKE, *July* 11, 1757.

I WILL not give you the trouble of sending your chaise for me.
I intend to be with you on Wednesday in the evening. If the
press stands still all this time for me, to be sure it is dead in
child-bed. I do not love notes, though you see I had resolved
to put two or three.[2] They are signs of weakness and obscurity.
If a thing cannot be understood without them, it had better be
not understood at all. If you will be vulgar, and pronounce it
Lunnun, instead of London,[3] I can't help it. Caradoc[4] I have
private reasons against; and besides it is in reality Carādoc,
and will not stand in the verse.

I rejoice you can fill all your *vuides ;* the Maintenon could
not, and that was her great misfortune. Seriously though, I
congratulate you on your happiness, and seem to understand it.
The receipt is obvious; it is only, Have something to do; but
how few can apply it. Adieu!—I am ever yours,

T. GRAY.

[1] He had a high opinion of this first drama of Mr. Home. In a letter
to another friend, dated August 16, this year, he says: "I am greatly
struck with the 'Tragedy of Douglas,' though it has infinite faults. The
author seems to me to have retrieved the true language of the stage, which
had been lost for these hundred years; and there is one scene (between
Matilda and the old peasant) so masterly, that it strikes me blind to all
the defects in the world." The ballad, which he here applauds, is to be
found in Mr. Percy's *Reliques of Antient Poetry*, vol. iii. p. 89, a work
published after the date of this letter.—*Mason.*

[2] To the "Bard."

[3] "Ye Towers of Julius, *London*'s lasting shame." "Bard," v. 87.

[4] Gray alludes to the line "Leave your despairing *Caradoc*, to mourn."
Which he afterwards altered to, "Leave me unblessed, unpitied here to
mourn."—*Mitford.*

LXXVI.—Mr. GRAY to Mr. WALPOLE

I AM so charmed with the two specimens of Erse poetry, that I cannot help giving you the trouble to enquire a little farther about them, and should wish to see a few lines of the original, that I may form some slight idea of the language, the measures, and the rhythm.

Is there anything known of the author or authors, and of what antiquity are they supposed to be? Is there any more to be had of equal beauty, or at all approaching to it? I have been often told that the poem called "Hardicanute" (which I always admired and still admire) was the work of somebody that lived a few years ago. This I do not at all believe, though it has evidently been retouched in places by some modern hand: but however, I am authorised by this report to ask whether the two poems in question are certainly antique and genuine. I make this enquiry in quality of an antiquary, and am not otherwise concerned about it: for, if I were sure that any one now living in Scotland had written them to divert himself, and laugh at the credulity of the world, I would undertake a journey into the Highlands only for the pleasure of seeing him.

LXXVII.—Mr. GRAY to Mr. WALPOLE

I HAVE been very ill this week with a great cold and a fever, and though now in a way to be well, am like to be confined some days longer: whatever you will send me that is new, or old, and long, will be received as a charity. Rousseau's people do not interest me; there is but one character and one style in them all, I do not know their faces asunder. I have no esteem for their persons or conduct, am not touched with their passions; and as to their story, I do not believe a word of it—not because it is improbable, but because it is absurd. If I had any little propensity, it was to Julie; but now she has gone and (so hand over head) married that Monsieur de Wolmar, I take her for a *vraie Suissesse*, and do not doubt but she had taken a cup too much like her lover. All this does not imply that I will not read it out, when you can spare the rest of it.

LXXVIII.—Mr. GRAY to Dr. WHARTON

Aug. 17, 1757, Stoke.

Dear Doctor,

It feels to me as if it were a long while since I heard from you. Not a word to flatter or to abash the vanity of an author! Suffer me then to tell you, that I hear we are not at all popular. The great objection is obscurity, nobody knows what we would be at. One man (a peer) I have been told of, that thinks the last stanza of the second ode relates to Charles the First and Oliver Cromwell, in short the συνετοι appear to be still fewer than even I expected.

You will imagine all this does not go very deep; but I have been almost ever since I was here exceedingly dispirited, besides being really ill in body. No gout, but something feverish that seems to come almost every morning, and disperses soon after I am up. The Cobhams are here, and as civil as usual. Garrick and his wife have been down with them some days, and are soon to come again. Except the little amusement they give me, and two volumes of the encyclopedia, now almost exhausted, I have nothing but my own thoughts to feed upon, and you know they are of the gloomy cast. Write to me then, for *sweet St. Charity*, and remember, that while I am my own,

I am most faithfully yours,

T. G.

My best services to Mrs. Wharton.

LXXIX.—Mr. GRAY to Mr. HURD [1]

Stoke, August 25, 1757.

I do not know why you should thank me for what you had a right and title to; [2] but attribute it to the excess of your politeness; and the more so, because almost no one else has made me the same compliment. As your acquaintance in the University (you say) do me the honour to *admire*, it would be ungenerous in me not to give them notice, that they are doing a very unfashionable thing; for all people of condition are agreed not to admire, nor even to understand. One very great man, writing to an acquaintance of his and mine, says that he had read them

---

[1] Bishop of Litchfield and Coventry.
[2] A present of his two Pindaric odes just then published.

seven or eight times; and that now, when he next sees him, he shall not have above *thirty questions* to ask. Another (a peer) believes that the last stanza of the second ode relates to King Charles the First and Oliver Cromwell. Even my friends tell me they do not *succeed*, and write me moving topics of consolation on that head. In short, I have heard of nobody but an actor and a doctor of divinity that profess their esteem for them. Oh yes, a lady of quality (a friend of Mason's), who is a great reader. She knew there was a compliment to Dryden, but never suspected there was anything said about Shakespeare or Milton, till it was explained to her; and wishes that there had been titles prefixed to tell what they were about.

From this mention of Mason's name you may think, perhaps, we are great correspondents. No such thing; I have not heard from him these two months. I will be sure to scold in my own name, as well as in yours. I rejoice to hear you are so ripe for the press, and so voluminous; not for my own sake only, whom you flatter with the hopes of seeing your labours both public and private, but for yours too; for to be employed is to be happy. This principle of mine (and I am convinced of its truth) has, as usual, no influence on my practice. I am alone, and *ennuyé* to the last degree, yet do nothing. Indeed I have one excuse; my health (which you have so kindly enquired after) is not extraordinary, ever since I came hither. It is no great malady, but several little ones, that seem brewing no good to me. It will be a particular pleasure to me to hear whether Content dwells in Leicestershire, and how she entertains herself there. Only do not be too happy, nor forget entirely the quiet ugliness of Cambridge.

LXXX.—Mr. GRAY to Dr. WHARTON

STOKE, *Sept.* 7, 1757.

DEAR DOCTOR,

I am greatly obliged to your care and kindness for considering, with more attention than it deserves, the article of my health; at present I am far better, and take long walks again, have better spirits, and am more capable of amusement. The offer you make me of your lodgings for a time I should gladly embrace, both for the sake of seeing you, and for variety, and because it will answer another end, by furnishing me with a reason for not going into the country to *a place where I am invited* (I think you understand me). But the truth is, I cannot afford to hurry

about from place to place; so I shall continue where I am, and
trust to *illness*, or some other cause, for an excuse, since to *that*
place, I am positive, I will not go.   It hurts me beyond measure
that I am forced to make these excuses, but go I cannot, and
something must be said.   These are cruel things!

The family you mention near me are full as civil as ever;
Miss Speed seems to understand; and to all such as do not,
she says—Φωνάντα συνετοῖσι—in so many words.   And this is
both my motto and comment.   I am afraid you mistake Mr.
Roper's complaisance for approbation.   Dr. Brown (I hear) says,
they are the best odes [1] in our language.   Mr. Garrick, the best
in our's, or *any other*.   I should not write this immodest panegy-
rick, did not you guess at the motive of their applause.   Lord
Lyttleton and Mr. Shenstone admire, but wish they were a little
clearer.   Lord Barrington's explanation, I think, I told you
before, so will not repeat it.   Mr. Fox thinks, if the bard sung
his song but once over, King Edward could not possibly understand him.   Indeed I am of his opinion, and am certain, if he
had sung it fifty times, it was impossible the king should know
a jot the more about Edward the III., and Queen Elizabeth, and
Spencer, and Milton, etc. . . .   Mr. Wood (Mr. Pitt's Wood) is
disappointed in his expectations.   Dr. Akenside criticises
opening a *source* [2] with a *key*.   The *Critical Review* you have seen
or may see.   He is in raptures (they say it is Professor Franklin)
but mistakes the Æolian lyre [3] for the *harp of Æolus*, and on this
mistake founds a compliment and a criticism.   This is, I think,
all I have heard, that signifies.

The encyclopedia, I own, may cloy one, if one sits down to
it.   But you will own, that out of one great good dinner, a
number of little good dinners may be made, that would not cloy
one at all.   There is a long article *sur le beau*, that for my life,
cannot understand.   Several of the geographical articles are
carelessly done, and some of the antiquities or ancient history.

My best compliments to Mrs. Wharton; I hope the operation

---

[1] From a note communicated to me by my friend Mr. Boswell, I find
that on the 29th June 1757, Gray received forty guineas for his two odes
—*Mitford.*

[2]   " Thine too these golden *keys*, immortal boy,
          This can *unlock* the gates of joy,
          Of horror that, and thrilling fears,
          Or *ope* the sacred *source* of sympathetic tears."

                              " Progress of Poetry," iii. 1, v. 91.

[3] See *Critical Review*, vol. vii. p. 31.

character and customs of the people. For example, I never heard in my days that midnight and the moon were sisters; that they carried rods of ebony and gold, or met to whisper on the top of a mountain: but now I could lay my life it is all true; and do not doubt it will be found so in some Pantheon of the Druids, that is to be discovered in the library at Herculaneum. The *Car of Destiny and Death* is a very noble invention of the same class, and, as far as that goes, is so fine, that it makes me more delicate than perhaps I should be, about the close of it. *Andraste sailing on the wings of Fame*, that snatches the wreaths from oblivion to hang them on her loftiest amaranth, though a clear and beautiful piece of *unknown* mythology, has too *Greek* an air to give me perfect satisfaction.

Now I proceed. The preparation to the chorus, though so much akin to that in the former act, is excellent. The remarks of Evelina and her suspicions of the brothers, mixed with a secret inclination to the younger of them (though, I think, her part throughout wants retouching), yet please me much, and the contrivance of the following scene much more. *Masters of wisdom, no*, etc., I always admired; as I do the rocking stone, and the distress of Elidurus. Evelina's examination of him is a well-invented scene, and will be, with a little pains, a very touching one; but the introduction of Arviragus is superlative. I am not sure whether those few lines of his short narrative, *My strength repair'd, it boots not, that I tell*, etc., do not please me as much as anything in the whole drama. The sullen bravery of Elidurus, the menaces of the chorus, that *Think not religion*, etc., the trumpet of the Druids, that *I'll follow him, tho' in my chains*, etc. *Hast thou a brother, no*, etc., the placability of the chorus, when they see the motives of Elidurus's obstinacy, give me great contentment: so do the reflections of the Druid on the necessity of lustration, and the reasons for Vellinus's easy escape; but I would not have him *seize on a spear*, nor *issue hasty through the cavern's mouth*. Why should he not steal away, unasked and unmissed, till the hurry of passions in those that should have guarded him was a little abated? But I chiefly admire the two speeches of Elidurus; *Ah, Vellinus, is this then*, etc., and *Ye do gaze on me, Fathers*, etc.; the manner in which the chorus reply to him is very fine; but the image at the end wants a little mending. The next scene is highly moving! it is so very good, that I must have it made yet better.

Now for the last act. I do not know what you would have, but to me the design and contrivance of it is at least equal to any part of the whole. The short-lived triumph of the Britons, the address of Caractacus to the Roman victims, Evelina's discovery of the ambush, the mistake of the Roman fires for the rising sun, the death of Arviragus, the interview between Didius and Caractacus, his mourning over his dead son, his parting speech (in which you have made all the use of Tacitus that your plan would admit), everything, in short, but that little dispute between Didius and him, *'Tis well, and therefore to encrease that reverence,* etc., down to, *Give me a moment* (which must be omitted or put in the mouth of the Druids), I approve in the highest degree. If I should find any fault with the last act, it could only be with trifles and little expressions. If you make any alterations, I fear it will never improve it; I mean as to the plan. I send you back the two last sheets, because you bid me. I reserve my nibblings and minutiæ for another day.

LXXXII.—Mr. GRAY to Dr. WHARTON

October 7, 1757.

DEAR DOCTOR,

I heartily rejoice with you, that your little family are out of danger, and all apprehensions of that kind over with them for life. Yet, I have heard, you were ill yourself, and kept your bed: as this was (I imagine) only by way of regimen, and not from necessity, I hope soon to be told you have no farther occasion for it; yet, take care of yourself, for there is a bad fever now, very frequent, it is among the boys at Eton; and (I am told) is much spread about London too. My notion is, that your violent quick pulse, and soapy diet, would not suit well with feverish disorders. Though our party at Slough turned out so ill, I could not help being sorry that you were not with us.

Have you read Mr. Hurd's (printed) letter to Mason, on the " Marks of Imitation?" You do not tell me your opinion of it. You bid me send you criticisms on myself, and even *compliments.* Did I tell you what the speaker says? The second ode, he says, is a good pretty tale, but nothing to the " Churchyard." Mr. Bedingfield, in a golden shower of panegyric, writes me word, that at York Races he overheard three people, whom, by their dress and manner, he takes for lords, say, that I was impenetrable and inexplicable, and they wished I had told them in prose what I meant in verse, and then they bought me (which was what most displeased him) and put me in their pocket. Dr. Warburton is come to town, and likes them extremely. He says, the world never passed so just an opinion upon anything as upon them; for that, in other things, they have affected to like or dislike, whereas here they own they do not understand, which he looks upon to be very true: but yet thinks they understand them as well as they do Milton or Shakespeare, whom they are obliged by fashion to admire. Mr. Garrick's compliment you have seen; I am told it was printed in the *Chronicle* of last Saturday. The review I have read, and admire it, particularly that observation, that the "Bard" is taken from *Pastor, cum traheret*. And the advice to be more an *original*, and, in order to be so, the way is (he says), to cultivate the native flowers of the soil, and not introduce the exotics of another climate.

I am greatly pleased with Mason's "Caractacus" in its present state. The contrivance and arrangement of events, the manners of the country, the characters and passions strike me wonderfully. The difficult part is now got over; nothing remains but to polish and retouch a little; yet only the beginning of the first chorus is done of the lyric part; have you seen it? Adieu, dear sir,

And believe me ever yours,

T. G.

I shall be in town probably sooner than you come to stay there.

LXXXIII.—Mr. GRAY to Dr. WHARTON

December 8, 1757.

Dear Doctor,

I have received the draught you were so good to send me, and the money is paid. You apprehend too much from my resolutions about writing. They are only made to be broken, and after all, it will be just as the maggot bites. You have a very mean opinion of the epic, if you think it consists only in laying out a plan. In four-and-twenty years, at a moderate computation, I may have finished twelve books, and nine years after I hope to publish. I shall then be seventy-four years old, and I shall get £500 for the copy, to make me easy for the remainder of my days. Somebody has directed a letter to the *Rev.* Mr. G. at Strawberry-Hill, which was sent me yesterday hither. It is anonymous, consists of above nine pages, all about the "Bard," and if I would hear as much more about his companion, I am to direct to the post house at Andover.[1] I do not know but I may have that curiosity, for his observations (whoever it is) are not nonsense. He takes the liberty of a person unknown, and treats me with abundance of freedom. I guess it to be some *reading* clergyman. Mr. Brown and I join in our best compliments to Mrs. Wharton, and I am, dear sir,

Most sincerely yours,

T. G.

LXXXIV.—MR. GRAY TO MR. MASON

CAMBRIDGE, *Dec.* 19, 1757.

A LIFE spent out of the world has its hours of despondence, its inconveniences, its sufferings, as numerous and as real, though not quite of the same sort, as a life spent in the midst of it. The power we have, when we will exert it over our own minds, joined to a little strength and consolation, nay, a little pride we catch from those that seem to love us, is our only support in either of these conditions. I am sensible I cannot return you more of this assistance than I have received from you; and can only tell you, that one who has far more reason than you, I hope, ever will have to look on life with something worse than indifference, is yet no enemy to it; but can look backward on many bitter moments, partly with satisfaction, and partly with patience; and forward too, on a scene not very promising, with some hope, and some expectations of a better day. The cause, however, which occasioned your reflection (though I can judge but very imperfectly of it) does not seem, at present, to be weighty enough to make you take any such resolution as you meditate. Use it in its season, as a relief from what is tiresome to you, but not as if it was in consequence of anything you take ill; on the contrary, if such a thing had happened at the time of your transmigration I would defer it merely to avoid that appearance.

[1] Gray's, then unknown, critic and correspondent, was, I believe, " Mr J. Butler, of Andover." In a MS. letter from Gray to Dodsley (which Mr. Bindley purchased at the sale of Mr. Isaac Reed's books), after he has mentioned how he wishes his poems to be printed, and added some notes, etc., he says: " When you have done, I shall desire you to present, in my name, a copy to Mr. Walpole, in Arlington Street; another to Mr. Daines Barrington (he is one of the Welch judges) in the Inner Temple; and a third, to *Mr. J. Butler at Andover*. Whether this latter gentleman is living or not, or in that neighbourhood, I am ignorant; but you will oblige me in making the enquiry. If you have no better means of knowing, a line directed to the postmistress at Andover will bring you information; after this, you may, if you please, bestow another copy or two on me.—I am, etc."—*Mitford.*

As to myself, I cannot boast, at present, either of my spirits, my situation, my employments, or fertility. The days and the nights pass, and I am never the nearer to anything, but that one to which we are all tending; yet I love people that leave some traces of their journey behind them, and have strength enough to advise you to do so while you can. I expect to see "Caractacus" completed, and therefore I send you the books you wanted. I do not know whether they will furnish you with any new matter; but they are well enough written, and easily read. I told you before, that (in a time of dearth) I would borrow from the "Edda," without entering too minutely on particulars: but, if I did so, I would make each image so clear, that it might be fully understood by itself; for in this obscure mythology we must not hint at things, as we do with the Greek fables, that everybody is supposed to know at school. However, on second thoughts, I think it would be still better to graft any wild picturesque fable, absolutely of one's own invention, on the Druid-stock; I mean on those half dozen of old fancies that are known to be a part of their system. This will give you more freedom and latitude, and will leave no hold for the critics to fasten on.

I send you back the elegy,[1] as you desired me to do. My advices are always at your service to take or to refuse, therefore you should not call them severe. You know I do not love, much less pique myself on criticism; and think even a bad verse as good a thing or better than the best observation that ever was made upon it. I like greatly the spirit and sentiment of it (much of which you perhaps owe to your present train of thinking); the disposition of the whole too is natural and elegiac; as to the expression, I would venture to say (did not you forbid me) that it is sometimes too easy. The last line I protest against (this, you will say, is worse than blotting out rhymes); the descriptive part is excellent.

Pray, when did I pretend to finish, or even insert passages into other people's works, as if it were equally easy to pick holes and to mend them? All I can say is, that your elegy must not end with the worst line in it.[2] It is flat; it is prose; whereas that, above all, ought to sparkle, or at least to shine. If the sentiment must stand, twirl it a little into an apophthegm; stick a flower in it; gild it with a costly expression; let it strike the fancy, the ear, or the heart, and I am satisfied.

[1] "Elegy in the Garden of a Friend."
[2] An attempt was accordingly made to improve it; how it stood when this criticism upon it was written, I cannot now recollect.—*Mason.*

The other particular expressions which I object to, I mark on the manuscript. Now, I desire you would neither think me severe, nor at all regard what I say, further than as it coincides with your own judgment; for the child deserves your partiality; it is a healthy well-made boy, with an ingenuous countenance, and promises to live long. I would only wash its face, dress it a little, make it walk upright and strong, and keep it from learning *paw* words.

I hope you couched my refusal [1] to Lord John Cavendish in as respectful terms as possible, and with all due acknowledgments to the duke. If you hear who it is to be given to, pray let me know; for I interest myself a little in the history of it, and rather wish somebody may accept it that will retrieve the credit of the thing, if it be retrievable, or ever had any credit. Rowe was, I think, the last man of character that had it; Eusden was a person of great hopes in his youth, though at last he turned out a drunken parson; Dryden was as disgraceful to the office, from his character, as the poorest scribbler could have been from his verses.

LXXXV.—Mr. GRAY to Dr. WHARTON

February 21, 1758.

DEAR DOCTOR,

I feel very ungrateful (which is the most uneasy of all feelings) in that I have never once enquired how you and your family enjoy the region of air and sunshine, into which you are removed, and with what contempt you look back on the perpetual fogs that hang over Mrs. Payne and Mrs. Paterson. Yet you certainly have not been the less in my mind. That at least has packed up with you, has helped Mrs. Wharton to arrange the mantlepiece, and drank tea next summer in the grotto. But I am much puzzled about the bishop and his fixtures, and do not stomach the loss of that money.

Would you know what I am doing? I doubt you have been told already, and hold my employment cheap enough; but every one must judge of his own *capabilities*, and cut his amusements according to his disposition. The drift of my present studies is to know, wherever I am, what lies within reach, that may be

[1] Of being poet laureat on the death of Cibber, which place the late Duke of Devonshire (then Lord Chamberlain) desired his brother to offer to Mr. Gray; and his lordship had commissioned me (then in town) to write to him concerning it.—*Mason.*

worth seeing; whether it be building, ruin, park, garden, prospect, picture, or monument. To whom it does, or has belonged, and what has been the characteristic and taste of different ages. You will say, this is the object of all antiquaries. But pray, what antiquary ever saw these objects in the same light, or desired to know them for a like reason? In short, say what you please, I am persuaded whenever my list [1] is finished, you will approve it, and think it of no small use. My spirits are very near the *freezing-point*; and for some hours of the day, this exercise, by its warmth and gentle motion, serves to raise them a few degrees higher. I hope the misfortune that has befallen Mrs. Cibber's canary-bird will not be the ruin of " Agis." It is probable you will have curiosity enough to see it, as it comes from the writer of " Douglas." I expect your opinion. I am told that Swift's *History of the Tory Administration* is in the press; and that Stuart's *Attica* [2] will be out this spring. Adieu! Dear sir,

                              I am ever yours,

                                             T. G.

Mr. Brown joins his compliments with mine to you and Mrs. Wharton.

LXXXVI.—Mr. GRAY TO Dr. WHARTON

Sunday, April 9, 1758.

MY DEAR SIR,

I am equally sensible of your affliction,[3] and of your kindness that made you think of me at such a moment. Would to God I could lessen the one, or requite the other with that consolation which I have often received from you, when I most wanted it: but your grief is too just, and the cause of it too fresh, to admit of any such endeavour. What indeed is all human consolation? Can it efface every little amiable word or action of an object we loved from our memory? Can it convince us that all the hopes we had entertained, the plans of future satisfaction we had

---

[1] A *Catalogue of the Antiquities, Houses, etc., in England and Wales*, which Gray drew up in the blank pages of Kitchen's English atlas: after his death, Mr. Mason printed a few copies, and distributed them among the friends of Gray; and, in 1787, a new edition was printed for sale.— *Mitford.*

[2] Gray was a subscriber to this book, as appears by a note in one of his pocket-journals.—*Mitford.*

[3] Occasioned by the death of his eldest (and at the time his only) son.— *Mason.*

formed, were ill-grounded and vain, only because we have lost
them? The only comfort (I am afraid) that belongs to our condition is to reflect (when time has given us leisure for reflection)
that others have suffered worse, or that we ourselves might have
suffered the same misfortune at times and in circumstances that
would probably have aggravated our sorrow. You might have
seen this poor child arrive at an age to fulfil all your hopes, to
attach you more strongly to him by long habit, by esteem, as
well as natural affection, and that towards the decline of your
life, when we most stand in need of support, and when he might
chance to have been your *only* support; and then by some
unforeseen and deplorable accident, or some painful lingering
distemper, you might have lost him. Such has been the fate of
many an unhappy father! I know there is a sort of tenderness
which infancy and innocence alone produce; but, I think, you
must own the other to be a stronger and more overwhelming
sorrow.

I am glad Mrs. Wharton has fortitude enough not to suffer
this misfortune to prevail over her, and add to the natural
weakness of her present condition. Mr. Brown sincerely sympathises with you, and begs to be kindly remembered to you
both. I have been . . . *and should have been* in town by this
time, had I not heard Mason was coming hither soon, and I was
unwilling to miss him. Adieu, my dear Wharton, and believe
me ever

Most sincerely yours,
T. G.

LXXXVII.—Mr. GRAY to Dr. WHARTON

DEAR DOCTOR,

I am much concerned to hear the account you give of yourself, and particularly for that dejection of spirits which inclines
you to see everything in the worst light possible, and throw a
sort of voluntary gloom not only over your present, but future
days, as if even your situation now were not preferable to that
of thousands round you, and as if your prospect hereafter might
not open as much of happiness to you as to any person you know.
The condition of our life perpetually instructs us to be rather
slow to hope, as well as to despair, and (I know you will forgive
me, if I tell you) you are often a little too hasty in both, perhaps

from constitution. It is sure we have great power over our own minds, when we chuse to exert it; and though it be difficult to resist the mechanic impulse and bias of our own temper, it is yet possible; and still more so, to delay those resolutions it inclines us to take, while we almost always have cause to repent.

You tell me nothing of Mrs. Wharton's or your own state of health. I will not talk to you more on this subject, till I hear you are both well, for that is the grand point, and without it we may as well not think at all. You flatter me in thinking that anything I can do [1] could at all alleviate the just concern your late loss has given you; but I cannot flatter myself so far, and know how little qualified I am at present to give any satisfaction to myself on this head, and in this way, much less to you. I by no means pretend to inspiration, but yet I affirm that the faculty in question is by no means voluntary. It is the result (I suppose) of a certain disposition of mind, which does not depend on one's self, and which I have not felt this long time. You that are a witness how seldom this spirit has moved me in my life, may easily give credit to what I say.

I am in hopes of seeing you very soon again in my way to Stoke. Mrs. Rogers has been very ill this spring, and my other aunt writes me word, that she herself has had something (which she takes for a paralytic stroke) which came as she walked in the garden, and is afraid she shall lose the use of one leg; so that it looks to me as if I should have perhaps some years to pass in a house with two poor bed-ridden women, a melancholy object, and one that in common humanity I cannot avoid. I shall be glad to know whether I can be in Gloucester Street for a week, ten or twelve days hence.

I had wrote to you sooner, but that I have been on a little expedition lately to see Ely, Peterborough, Crowland-Abbey, Thorney, Fotheringay, and many other old places, which has amused me a little.

Poor Mason is all alone at Aston (for his curate is gone to be tutor to somebody) with an inflammation in his eyes, and he could scarce see to write me a few lines. Adieu, dear sir,

I am ever yours,

T. G.

June 18, 1758.

[1] Dr. Wharton had requested him to write an epitaph on the child.— *Mason.*

*H 628

LXXXVIII.—Mr. GRAY to Dr. WHARTON

STOKE, *Aug.* 9, 1758.

DEAR DOCTOR,

I have been, since I saw you in town, pretty much on the wing, at Hampton, Twickenham, and elsewhere. I staid at the first of these places with the Cobhams two days, and should (I own) gladly have done so longer, but for the reason we talked about. The place, spite of the weather, is delightful: every little gleam of sunshine, every accident of light, opens some new beauty in the view, and I never saw in so small a spot so much variety and so many natural advantages, nor ever hardly wished more for your company to partake of them. We were also at Hampton-Court, Sion, and several places in the neighbourhood again, particularly at Lord Lincoln's, who (I think) is hurting his view by two plantations in front of his terrace, that regularly answer one another, and are of an oval form, with rustic buildings in the middle of them, a farm, dairies, etc. They stand on the opposite side of the water, and (as they prosper) will join their shade to that of the hills in the horizon, exclude all the intermediate scene of enclosures, meadows, and cattle feeding, and reduce that great distance to nothing. This seems to be the advice of some new gardener, or director of my lord's taste; his successor perhaps may cut all down again.

I shall beg the favour of you (as you were so kind to offer it) to buy us a lottery-ticket, if you find the market will not be much lower than at present, and (if you think it has no great hazard in it) enclose it to me here. I will take care to repay you as soon as I come to town, or (if you chuse it) directly. My best respects to Mrs. Wharton. Pray let me hear soon how you both are. Believe me,

Ever yours,

T. G.

LXXXIX.—Mr. GRAY to Mr. STONEHEWER

CAMBRIDGE, *Aug.* 18, 1758.

I AM as sorry as you seem to be, that our acquaintance harped so much on the subject of materialism when I saw him with you in town, because it was plain to which side of the long-debated question he inclined. That we are indeed mechanical and dependent beings, I need no other proof than my own feelings; and from the same feelings I learn, with equal conviction, that we are not *merely* such: that there is a power within that struggles against the force and bias of that mechanism, commands its motion, and, by frequent practice, reduces it to that ready obedience which we call *habit;* and all this in conformity to a preconceived opinion (no matter whether right or wrong) to that least material of all agents, a thought. I have known many in his case who, while they thought they were conquering an old prejudice, did not perceive they were under the influence of one far more dangerous; one that furnishes us with a ready apology for all our worst actions, and opens to us a full licence for doing whatever we please; and yet these very people were not at all the more indulgent to other men (as they naturally should have been); their indignation to such as offended them, their desire of revenge on anybody that hurt them was nothing mitigated: in short, the truth is, they wished to be persuaded of that opinion for the sake of its convenience, but were not so in their heart; and they would have been glad (as they ought in common prudence) that nobody else should think the same, for fear of the mischief that might ensue to themselves. His French author I never saw, but have read fifty in the same strain, and shall read no more. I can be wretched enough without them. They put me in mind of the Greek sophist that got immortal honour by discoursing so feelingly on the miseries of our condition, that fifty of his audience went home and hanged themselves; yet he lived himself (I suppose) many years after in very good plight.

You say you cannot conceive how Lord Shaftesbury came to be a philosopher in vogue; I will tell you. First, he was a lord; 2dly, he was as vain as any of his readers; 3dly, men are very prone to believe what they do not understand; 4thly, they will believe anything at all, provided they are under no obligation to believe it; 5thly, they love to take a new road, even when that road leads nowhere; 6thly, he was reckoned a fine writer, and seemed always to mean more than he said. Would you have any more reasons? An interval of above forty years has pretty well destroyed the charm. A dead lord ranks but with commoners: vanity is no longer interested in the matter, for the new road has become an old one. The mode of free-thinking is like that of ruffs and farthingales, and has given place to the mode of not thinking at all; once it was reckoned graceful half to discover and half conceal the mind, but now we have been long accustomed to see it quite naked: primness and affectation of style, like the good breeding of Queen Anne's court, has turned to hoydening and rude familiarity.

XC.—MR. GRAY TO DR. WHARTON

DEAR DOCTOR,

I ought to have informed you sooner, that I had received the ticket you were so good to buy for me, but I have been obliged to go every day almost to Stoke-House, where the Garricks have been all the last week. They are now gone, and I am not sorry for it, for I grow so old, that I own people in high spirits and gayety overpower me, and entirely take away mine. I can yet be diverted with their sallies, but if they appear to take notice of my dullness, it sinks me to nothing. I do not know whether you will blame me, but I found so good an opportunity given me of entering into the quarrel between Mason and him, that I could not help seizing it, and trying to shew him the folly of hearkening to half-witted friends and tale-bearers, and the greater folly of attempting to hurt, or merely to pique, so worthy and so estimable a man. If I did nothing else, I at least convinced him, that I spoke entirely from myself; and that I had the most entire good opinion, and most unalterable respect, as well as kindness, for Mason.

I congratulate you on our successes, and condole with you on our misfortunes. But do you think we draw the nearer to any happy conclusion of the war, or that we can bear so great a burden much longer? The K. of Prussia's situation embarrasses me; surrounded as he is, and reduced to the defence of his own little marquisate.

Your encyclopedia is the object of my envy. I am reduced to French plays and novels, Willis's *Mitred Abbies,* and the *History of Norfolk* in three volumes folio. These *latter* authors have I think the most wit; though the others know rather more of the world.

I wish the air of Hampstead were not so necessary to you all but am glad you always know where to find health, and that she lives so near you. I continue better than has been usual for me in the summer, though I neither walk, nor take anything: 'tis in mind only that I am weary and disagreeable. Mrs. Rogers is declining every day; her stomach gone; very weak; sometimes giddy; and subject to disorders in her bowels. Yet

I do not apprehend any immediate danger, but believe she will be reduced to keep her bed entirely. My best compliments to Mrs. Wharton; pray let me hear from you, as soon as you are in a humour for writing; though from hence I can requite your kindness with so little to amuse you.

I am ever truly yours,

T. G.

Stoke, *Aug.* 31, 1758.

XCI.—Mr. GRAY to Dr. WHARTON

Sept. 16, 1758.

Dear Doctor,

Having been for a considerable time without any news of you, I have taken it into my head that you are ill, or that Mrs. Wharton is so. You will not wonder if I grow a little super-stitious, when you know that I have not been a step out of the house for this fortnight or more past; for Mrs. Rogers has been at the point of death with a disorder in her stomach, accompanied with continual and laborious retchings, and a total loss of appetite, that has reduced her to the weakness of an infant, I mean her body, though her senses are still perfect, and (what I think remarkable) she has recovered the use of her speech (which for several years has been hardly intelligible), and pronounces almost as plain as ever she did. She is now, for three days past (such is the strength of her constitution), in a way of recovery. I do not mean that she will ever recover her strength again, but I think she may live a good while in this helpless state; however, it is very precarious, and Dr. Hayes believes her quite worn out. I certainly do not put on (to you) more tenderness than I really feel on this occasion, but the approaches of death are always a melancholy object, and common humanity must suffer something from such a spectacle.

It is an age since I heard anything from Mason; if I do not mistake, this should be his month of waiting, unless he has exchanged his turn with somebody. If he be in town you must probably have heard of him, and can give me some intelligence. My old new acquaintance Lady Denbigh is here at Stoke-house, but I do not believe I shall be able to get out, or have any oppor-tunity of seeing her, while she stays.

If my fancies (which I hope in God are mere fancies) should prove true, I hope you will let somebody tell me how you do.

If not, I shall beg you to tell me yourself as soon as possible, and set my understanding to rights.   Adieu, dear sir,

I am ever most sincerely yours,

T. G.

XCII.—Mr. GRAY to Dr. WHARTON

Nov. 1758, STOKE.

DEAR DOCTOR,

My judgment is, that if your picture possess but any one of the beauties you see and describe in it, it must be certainly worth eight or ten times as much as you gave for it.   I only wonder you should forget to say by what lucky chance you came by it. Old *Frank* was a Dutch master of some note; the history of that school I am very little acquainted with, but if I am not mistaken there was lately published a French account of their lives in two or more volumes 4to which I have seen at Nourse's, in which you may meet with better information.   I am agreeably employed here in dividing *nothing* with an *old harridan*, who is the spawn of Cerberus and the dragon of Wantley.   When I shall get to town I cannot divine, but doubtless it will be between this and Christmas.   You were so good to offer me house-room for some of my lumber: I am therefore packing up certain boxes and baskets which I believe you will be troubled with.   But I beg Mrs. Wharton to consider well first, whether it will be inconvenient to her.   If she assures me it will not, I shall inform you shortly of their shapes and numbers.   At present it seems to me, that there will be three or four large boxes, and five baskets of china; the last Madame Foster shall accommodate.

Ah! poor King of Prussia![1] what will become of him?   I am told here, that matters are much worse than is yet avowed. I also hear that seven generals have refused the command, which Hopson is now gone with, who has been before censured for ill-conduct, and is besides so infirm that he will not live the voyage. Adieu, dear sir,

I am ever yours,

T. G.

[1] Gray's lamentation was excited, I conclude, by the defeat of the King of Prussia at Hochkirchen, by the Austrians under Marshal Daun.   In this battle he lost 7000 men, his tents, and baggage; and the day was rendered memorable by the death of Marshal Keith, who was shot through the heart.—*Mitford.*

XCIII.—Mr. GRAY to Mr. MASON

Stoke, *Nov.* 9, 1758.

I SHOULD have told you that "Caradoc" came safe to hand;[1] but my critical faculties have been so taken up in dividing *nothing* with an old woman,[2] that they are not yet composed enough for a better and more tranquil employment: shortly, however, I will make them obey me. But am I to send this copy to Mr. Hurd, or return it to you? Methinks I do not love this travelling to and again of manuscripts by the post. While I am writing, your second packet is just arrived. I can only tell you in gross, that there seem to me certain passages altered which might as well have been let alone; and that I shall not be easily reconciled to Mador's own song.[3] I must not have my fancy raised to that agreeable pitch of heathenism and wild magical enthusiasm, and then have you let me drop into moral philosophy and cold good sense. I remember you insulted me when I saw you last, and affected to call that which delighted my imagination, *nonsense.* Now I insist that sense is nothing in poetry, but according to the dress she wears, and the scene she appears in. If you should lead me into a superb Gothic building with a thousand clustered pillars, each of them half a mile high, the walls all covered with fretwork, and the windows full of red and blue saints that had neither head nor tail; and I should find the Venus of Medici in person, perked up in a long niche over the high altar, do you think it would raise or damp my devotions? I say that Mador must be entirely a Briton; and that his pre-eminence among his companions must be shewn by superior wildness, more barbaric fancy, and a more striking and deeper harmony both of words and numbers: if British antiquity be too narrow, this is the place for invention; and if it be pure invention, so much the clearer must the expression be, and so much the stronger and richer the imagery. There's for you now!

[1] A second manuscript of "Caractacus" with the odes inserted. —*Mason.*
[2] Mrs. Rogers died about this time, and left Mr. Gray and Mrs. Olliffe, another of his aunts, her joint executors.—*Mason.*
[3] He means here the second ode, which was afterwards greatly altered. —*Mason.*

XCIV.—Mr. GRAY to Dr. WHARTON

Dear Doctor,

.   .   .   .   .   .

I am glad you are master of a "*pieta*." I could have said *pieta* myself, if I had not left off being a coxcomb or a connoisseur. Palma (that is the *old* one) was a good colourist, like most of the Venetians, but remarkable for bad drawing, particularly of hands and arms. What you say of Dr. Ak. I fully agree with you in, and have mentioned it to Mason. As soon as I can write to Mr. H., I shall repeat to him a *part* of your own words, which I think will prevail, besides I know he thinks himself obliged to you in Dr. Hn's affairs. I have seen no Rousseau, or anybody else: all I can tell you is, that I am to dine with my Lady Carlisle to-morrow, who is a melancholy dowager, reduced from Castle-Howard and ten thousand pounds a year to £1500, her jewels, plate, and a fine house in town excellently well furnished. She has just discovered too (I am told in confidence) that she has been long the object of calumny and scandal. What am I to say to comfort her?

I do not dislike the laureat at all, to me it is his best ode.[1] but I don't expect any one should find it out, for Otbert and Ateste are surely less known than Edward the Ist and Mount Snowdon; it is no imitation of me; but a good one of

Pastor, cum traheret, etc.

which was falsely laid to my charge. Adieu, dear sir, I am ever yours.

December 2, 1758.

XCV.—Mr. GRAY to Dr. WHARTON

Saturday, July 21, 1759.

Dear Doctor,

I have at last found rest for the sole of my gouty foot in your old dining-room,[2] and hope, in spite of the damnation denounced by the bishop's two chaplains, that you may find at least equal

[1] " Ode for his Majesty's Birthday," November 10, 1758. See Whitehead's *Poems*, vol. ii. p. 263.—*Mitford.*

[2] The house in Southampton Row, where Mr. Gray lodged, had been tenanted by Dr. Wharton; who, on account of his ill-health, left London the year before; and was removed to his paternal estate at Old Park, near Durham.—*Mason.*

satisfaction and repose at Old Park; if your bog prove as comfortable as my oven, I shall see no occasion to pity you; and only wish that you may *brew* no worse than I *bake*.

You totally mistake my talents, when you impute to me any magical skill in planting roses. I know I am no conjuror in these things; when they are done, I can find fault, and that is all. Now this is the very reverse of genius, and I feel my own littleness. Reasonable people know themselves better than is commonly imagined, and therefore (though I never saw any instance of it) I believe Mason, when he tells me he understands planting better than anything whatever. The *prophetic eye of taste* (as Mr. Pitt called it) sees all the beauties that a place is susceptible of, long before they are born; and when it plants a seedling, already sits under the shadow of it, and enjoys the effect it will have from every point of view that lies in prospect. You must, therefore, invoke Caractacus, and he will send his spirits from the top of Snowdon to Cross-Fell or Warden-Law.

The thermometer is in the passage-window (where the sun never comes) near the head of the back-stairs. Since you went I have never observed it lower than 68, most part of the day at 74, and yesterday at five in the afternoon it was at 79, the highest I have ever seen it. It now is prepared to correspond regularly with you, at the hours you mention. The weather, for this fortnight, has been broiling without interruption, one thunder-shower excepted, which did not cool the air at all. Rye (I am told) is begun to be cut near London. In Cambridgeshire, a fortnight ago, the promise of harvest was the finest I ever saw; but the farmers complain (I hear) that the ears do not fill for want of wet. The wheat was then turning yellow. Duke-cherries are over in London, three days ago they sold for half-a-crown a pound. Caroons and black-hearts, very large and fine, drive about the streets in wheel-barrows a penny a pound. Raspberries, a few are yet remaining, but in a manner over. Melons are ripe, and apricots and Orleans-plums are to be seen in the fruit-shops. Roses are (I think) over a week ago. The jessamine (at Mrs. Dod's, on a S.W. wall) was in full bloom (if you remember) long before you went from hence, and so it continues. That below in the garden, on a N.E. wall, has been all this week covered with flowers. My nosegays, from Covent-garden, consist of nothing but scarlet-martagons, everlasting-peas, double-stocks, pinks, and flowering-marjoram. As I have kept no exact account hitherto this year, I can say no more of July that now is. Therefore, I shall annex one for the year

1754, which I observed day by day at Stoke. Observe it had been then a cold rainy summer.

The heat was very moderate this month, and a great deal of rain fell. The sown hay was all got in by the first day; but the meadow-hay was not before the 23d. It was very good and in plenty, but sold at forty shillings a load in the field, on account of the scarcity the year preceding. Barley was in ear on the first day; grey and white peas in bloom. The bean flowers were going off. Duke-cherries in plenty on the 5th; hearts were also ripe. Green melons on the 6th, but watry and not sweet. Currants begun to ripen on the 8th; and red gooseberries had changed colour; tares were then in flower, and meadow-hay cutting. Lime-trees in full bloom on the 9th. Mushrooms in perfection on the 17th. Wheat and oats had changed colour; and buck-wheat was in bloom on the 19th. The vine had then opened its blossoms, and the end of the month grapes were near the size of small peas. Turnips appeared above ground on the 22nd; and potatoes were in flower. Barley had changed its hue, and rye was almost ripe on the 23d. The pineapple-strawberry was then in perfection. Black caroons were ripe, and some duke-cherries still remained on walls the 26th, but the hearts were then all spoiled by the rain. Gooseberries, red and white, were then ripe, and currants in abundance.

Haws turned red . .			Pyracantha in berry .	
Honey-suckles in full bloom	on the 1st.		Mountain-Ash . .	
Broomflower went off			White-Beam . .	11th.
			Orange flowering .	
Phlomis, or yellow-tree-sage . . .	2nd.		Winter Cherry .	
			Single Velvet Rose goes off	15th.
Virginia flowering Raspberry blew			Lavender and Marjoram blow . . .	22nd.
Shrub Cinque-foil .	3rd.		Damask, Red, Moss, and Double Velvet Roses go off . . .	26th.
Spiræa-frutex .				
Syringa went off .			Rosa-Mundi and Rose without Thorns go off	28th.
Balm of Gilead blowing .	7th.		White Rose goes off .	31st.
Common Jasmine blew .				
Moss-Provence Rose .	8th.		These were all the flowering shrubs observed by me.	
Yellow and Austrian Rose go off				
Yellow Jasmine blows .				
White and Gum-Cistus .			GARDEN FLOWERS	
Tamarisk in flower .			Convolvulus Minor blows	
Coccygria . .			Garden Poppy .	
Virginia-Sumach .	9th.		Single Rose-Campion .	
Tutsan or Park-leaves .			Double Larkspur . .	2nd.
Spanish-Broom .			Candy-Tuft . .	
Scarlet and Painted Geraniums . .			Common Marigold . .	
			Pansies continue blowing	

Lupines, blue and white, blow	.	.	} 2nd.	Double Rose-Campion . African Ragwort . .	} 19th.
Purple Toads-flax . .				Whole Carnations blow .	23d.
White and Blue Campanula				Double White Stock in bloom . . .	24th.

Double Scarlet Lychnis blows . . . — Tree Primrose . . — White Lilly . . — 9th. Willow-Bay . . — Scarlet-Bean . . — French Marigold . . —

In the Fields: Scabious, St. John's Wort, Trefoil, Yarrow, Bugloss, Purple Vetch, Wild-thyme, Pale Wood-Orchis, Betony, and white Clover flowering on the first. Large blue Cranes-bill the 9th; Ragwort, Moth-mullein, and Brambles, the 20th; Knapweed all the month. There was rain, more or less, 13 days out of the 31, this month; and 17 days out of 30, in June preceding.

Yellow Lupine blows .} Tree-Mallow . . } 11th. Amaranthus Cat's-tail .}

Striped Lilly blows . .} 19th. Fairchild's Mule . .}

I was too late for the post on Saturday, so I continue on Monday. It is now six in the afternoon, and the thermometer is mounted to 80, though the wind is a N.E. by N. The gay Lady Essex is dead of a fever during her lying in; and Mrs. Charles York last week, with one of her children, of the sore throat. Heberden and (I think) Taylor attended her; the latter had pronounced her out of danger, but Heberden doubted about her. The little boy was at Acton, and escaped the infection.

Everybody continues as quiet about the invasion as if a Frenchman, as soon as he set his foot on our coast, would die, like a toad in Ireland. Yet the king's tents and equipage are ordered to be ready at an hour's warning. Nobody knows positively what is the damage that Rodney [1] has done, whether much or little; he can only guess himself; and the French have kept their own secret, as yet. Of the twelve millions raised for the year, eight are gone already; and the old party assure us there is no more to be had for next year. You may easily guess at the source of my intelligence, and therefore will not talk of it. News is hourly expected of a battle in Westphalia, for P. Ferdinand was certainly preparing to fight the French, who have taken Minden by storm.

I have heard the D. of N. is much broke ever since his sister Castlecomer died, not that he cared for her, or saw her above once a year; but she was the last of the brood that was left;

[1] This alludes to the bombardment of Havre-de-grace, by Admiral Rodney, in the month of July in this year; the French having collected several large flat-bottomed boats there, for a threatened invasion on some part of the British territories.—*Mitford.*

and he now goes regularly to church, which he never did before.
Adieu! I am ever yours.

I hope Mrs. Wharton's native air will be more civil to her,
when they are better acquainted; my best compliments to her;
I am glad the children are well.

XCVI.—MR. GRAY TO DR. WHARTON

DEAR DOCTOR,

I cannot say anything to you about Mason, whose motions
I am entirely a stranger to, and have not once heard from him
since he left London, till (the 3d of this month) a letter came, in
which he tells me that Gaskarth is at Aston with him, and that
the latter end of the month, or the beginning of the next, he
shall be in town, as he goes into waiting the last fortnight in
October. Lord Holdernesse has sent him no less than four
expresses (literally so) with public news, good and bad, which
has made him of infinite importance in the eyes of that neighbourhood. I cannot pretend, therefore, to guess whether he
will be able to come to you. I am sorry to tell you that I try
in vain to execute your commission about tapestry. What is so
bad as wry-mouthed histories? and yet for this they ask me
at least double the price you talk of. I have seen nothing neither
that would please me at any price. Yet I allow tapestry (if at
all tolerable) to be a very proper furniture for your sort of house;
but doubt if any bargain of that kind is to be met with, except
at some old mansion-sale in the country, where people will disdain tapestry, because they hear that paper is all the fashion.
Stonehewer has been in Northamptonshire till now; as you told
me the subject of your letter, I did not send it thither to him,
besides that, he was every day expected in town. At last he is
come, and has it, but I have not yet seen him; he is gone to-day
(I believe) to Portsmouth to receive a Morocco ambassador, but
returns very shortly. There is one advantage in getting into
your abbey at Christmas time, that it will be at its worst, and if
you can bear it then, you need not fear for the rest of the year.
Mr. Walpole has lately made a new bed-chamber, which as it is
in the best taste of anything he has yet done, and in your own Gothic
way, I must describe a little. You enter by a peaked door at
one corner of the room (out of a narrow winding passage, you
may be sure) into an alcove, in which the bed is to stand, formed

by a screen of pierced work opening by one large arch in the middle to the rest of the chamber, which is lighted at the other end by a bow-window of three bays, whose tops are of rich painted glass in mosaic. The ceiling is covered and fretted in star and quatre-foil compartments, with roses at the intersections, all is *papier-mâché*. The chimney on your left is the high altar in the cathedral of Rouen (from whence the screen also is taken), consisting of a low surbased arch between two octagon towers, whose pinnacles almost reach the ceiling, all of nich-work; the chairs and dressing-table are real carved ebony, picked up at auctions. The hangings uniform, purple paper, hung all over with the court of Henry the VIII. copied after the Holbeins in the queen's closet at Kensington, in black and gold frames. The bed is to be either from Burleigh (for Lord Exeter is new-furnishing it, and means to sell some of his original household stuff) of the rich old tarnished embroidery; or if that is not to be had, and it must be new, it is to be a cut velvet with a dark purple pattern on a stone-colour satin ground, and deep mixed fringes and tassels. There's for you, but I want you to see it. In the meantime I live in the Musæum, and write volumes of antiquity. I have got (out of the original ledger-book of the signet) King Richard the Third's oath to Elizabeth, late *calling herself Queen of* England, to prevail upon her to come out of sanctuary with her five daughters. His grant to Lady Hastings and her son, dated six weeks after he had cut off her husband's head. A letter to his mother, another to his chancellor, to persuade his solicitor-general not to marry Jane Shore then in Ludgate by his command. Sir Thomas Wyat's defence at his trial, when accused by Bishop Bonner of high treason; Lady Purbeck and her son's remarkable case, and several more odd things unknown to our historians. When I come home I have a great heap of the Conway Papers (which is a secret) to read and make out. In short, I am up to the ears.

The fish you mention is so accurately described, that I know it at sight. It is the ink-fish, or *loligo* of the Romans. In Greek, τευθὸς; in Italian, *calamaio*; in French, *calmar*. You will find it ranged by Linnæus in the class of *Vermes*, the order of *Mollusca*, the genus of *Sepia*, No. 4, page 659. The smaller ones are eaten as a delicacy fried, with their own ink for sauce, by the Italians and others. You may see it in Aldrovandus.

I do not see much myself of the face of nature here, but I enquire. Wheat was cutting in Kent the 23d of July, the 25th at Enfield. The 27th, wheat, barley, and oats cutting all at once about Windsor; the forward peas all got in, ground ploughed and turnips sowed. 9th of August, harvest still continued in Buckinghamshire; the 27th, about Kennington, it was just over, being delayed for want of hands; in some places, fifty miles from London, it is but just over now for the same reason. The 3d of August, catharine-pears, muscle-plums, and small black cherries were sold in wheelbarrows. Filberds in plenty the 8th. Mulberries and fine greengage plums the 19th. Fine nectarines and peaches the 27th. The 4th of September, melons and perdrigon-plums. The 8th, walnuts twenty a penny. This is all I know about fruit. My weather is not very complete.

[Here follows a table of weather conditions and temperatures for a month.]

I go no farther than you do, but it is down in my book.

What do you say to all our victories? The night we rejoiced for Boscawen, [1] in the midst of squibs and bonfires arrived Lord G. Sackville. He sees company, and to-day has put out a short address to the public, saying he expects a court-martial (for no one abroad had authority to try him), and desires people to suspend their judgement. I fear it is a rueful case.

I believe I shall go on Monday to Stoke for a time, where Lady Cobham has been dying. My best respects to Mrs. Wharton. Believe me ever

Faithfully yours,

T. G.

Southampton Row, *Sept.* 18, 1759.

XCVII.—Mr. GRAY to Dr. WHARTON

Dear Doctor,

I know not what to say to you after so long a silence, but that I have been down to Stoke to see poor Lady Cobham, and after about three weeks passed there, she being obliged to come for advice (as they call it) to town, I returned with her, and have been ever since, till about ten days ago, by her desire in the house with her in Hanover-Square. She is dying (as it now plainly appears) of a dropsy, and the contemplation of lingering death is not apt to raise the spirits of any spectator. . . . I have had an enquiry from Mr. Jonathan about painted glass,

---

[1] Victory of Admiral Boscawen over the French fleet under M. de la Clue, in the Mediterranean.—*Mitford.*

and have given him such information as I could procure. The manufacture at York seems to be the thing for your purpose, but the name of the person I cannot learn. He at Worcester sells it for two shillings a pound (for it is sold by weight). I approve very well of the canopy-work border on the sides of each light descending to the bottom, provided it do not darken the window too much, and take up so much of the twenty inches space as to make the plain glass in the middle appear over narrow. But I have been more used to see the whole top of coloured glass (from where the arch begins to turn), the gloom above contributing much to the beauty of the clear view below. I cannot decide: the first is more Gothic and more uncommon; the latter more convenient and more cheerful. Green glass is not classical, nor ever seen in a real church-window, but where there is history painted, and there the green is remarkably bad. I propose the rich amethyst-purple instead of it. The mosaic pattern can hardly come amiss, only do not let too much yellow and scarlet come together. If I could describe the mosaic at Mr. Walpole's it would be of no use to you, because it is not merely made of squares put together, but painted in a pattern of Price, and shaded. It is as if little balaustines, or pomegranate flowers, were set four together and formed a lozenge. These are of a golden yellow, with a white pearl at the junctions, and the spaces inclosed by them are scarlet or blue. This repeated makes a diaper-work, and fills the whole top of the window. I am sorry any of your designs depend upon Virginia; I fear it will fail you. Stonehewer tells me you have a neighbouring scene superior to any banks of the Thames, where I am to live . . . clever, and forced from him by a nonsensical speech of Beckford's. The second was a studied and puerile declamation on funeral honours (on proposing a monument for Wolfe). In the course of it he wiped his eyes with one handkerchief, and Beckford (who seconded him) cried too, and wiped with two handkerchiefs at once, which was very moving. The third was about Gen. Amherst, and in commendation of the industry and ardour of our American commanders, very spirited and eloquent. This is a very critical time, an action being hourly expected between the two great fleets, but no news as yet. I don't know where my thermometer left off, but I do not find any observations till the 8th September.

[Here follows another table.]

My best respects to Mrs. Wharton. I am, dear sir, ever yours.
Nov. 28 [1759].

DEAR DOCTOR,

I am much obliged to you for your antique news. Froissard is a favourite book of mine (though I have not attentively read him, but only dipp'd here and there), and it is strange to me that people who would give thousands for a dozen portraits (originals of that time) to furnish a gallery, should never cast an eye on so many moving pictures of the life, actions, manners, and thoughts of their ancestors done on the spot, and in strong though simple colours. In the succeeding century Froissard (I find) was read with great satisfaction by everybody that could read, and on the same footing with King Arthur, Sir Tristram, and Archbishop Turpin; not because they thought him a fabulous writer, but because they took them all for true and authentic historians. To so little purpose was it in that age for a man to be at the pains of writing truth! Pray are you come to the four Irish kings, that went to school to K. Richard ye 2d's master of the ceremonies, and the man who informed Froissard of all he had seen in St. Patrick's Purgatory.

You ask after Quebec. Gen. Townsend says it is much like Richmond-Hill, and the river as fine (but bigger), and the vale as *riant*, as rich, and as well cultivated. No great matters are attributed to his conduct. The officer who brought over the news, when the Prince of Wales asked how long Gen. Townsend commanded in the action after Wolfe's death? answered, " A minute, sir." It is certain he was not at all well with Wolfe, who for some time had not cared to consult with him, or communicate any of his designs to him. He has brought home an Indian boy with him (designed for Lord G. Sackville, but he did not chuse to take him) who goes about in his own dress, and is brought into the room to divert his company. The general after dinner one day had been shewing them a box of scalps, and some Indian arms and utensils. When they were gone, the boy got the box, and found a scalp, which he knew by the hair belonged to one of his own nation. He grew into a sudden fury (though but eleven years old), and catching up one of the scalping-knives made at his master with intention to murther him, who in his surprise hardly knew how to avoid him; and by laying open his breast, making signs, and with a few words of French jargon that the boy understood, at last with much difficulty pacified him. The first rejoicing night he was terribly frighted, and thought the bonefire was made for him, and that they were going to torture and devour him. He is mighty fond of venison blood-raw; and once they caught him flourishing his knife over a dog that lay asleep by the fire, because (he said) it was *bon-manger*.

You have heard of the Irish disturbances (I reckon); never were two Houses of Parliament so . . . This is not a figure, but literally so. They placed an old woman on the throne, and called for pipes and tobacco; made my lord chief-justice administer an oath (which they dictated) to my lord chancellor; beat the Bishop of Killaloe black and blue; played at football with Chenevix, the old refugee Bishop of Waterford; rolled my Lord Farnham in the kennel; pulled Sir Thos. Prendergast by the nose (naturally large) till it was the size of a cauliflower, and would have hanged Rigby, if he had not got out of a window. All this time *the castle* remained in perfect tranquillity. At last the guard was obliged to move (with orders not to fire), but the mob threw dirt at them. Then the horse broke in upon them, cutting and slashing, and took seventeen prisoners: next morning they were all set at liberty, and said to be poor silly people that knew nothing of the matter. The same night there was a ball at the castle, and play till four in the morning. This tumult happened two days before the news of Hawke's victory got to Dublin; and there was another some time before, when first it was known that the Brest fleet had sailed. Warning was given (from the *best hands* in England) six weeks before that time, that there would be a *rising of the Papists* in Ireland; and the first person whom the mob insulted was a Mr. Rowley, a member, always in opposition to the court, but a *Presbyterian*. It is strange (but, I am assured, true) that the government have not yet received any account of the matter from thence, and all the Irish here are ready to fight a man that says there has been any riot at all at Dublin. The notion that had possessed the crowd was, that a union was to be voted between the two nations, and they should have no more Parliaments there.

Prince Ferdinand has done a strange thing in Germany. We have always studiously avoided doing anything to incur the ban of the empire. He has now (without waiting for commands from hence) detached 14,000 men, the flower of his flock, to assist the King of Prussia in Saxony against the empress-queen and the empire. The old gentleman does not know how to digest it after giving him £2000 a year on the Irish Establishment, and

£20,000 for the battle of Minden (not out of his own pocket, don't mistake; but out of your's, under the head of extra-ordinaries). A great fleet is preparing, and an expedition going forward; but nobody knows where to: some say Martinico, others Minorca. All thought of a congress is vanished, since the empress has shewed herself so cool to our proposal.

Mr. Pitt (not the great, but the little one, my acquaintance) is setting out on his travels. He goes with my Lord Kinnoul to Lisbon; then (by sea still) to Cales, then up the Guadal-quivir to Seville and Cordova, and so perhaps to Toledo, but certainly to Grenada; and after breathing the perfumed air of Andalusia, and contemplating the remains of Moorish magnifi-cence, re-embarks at Gibraltar or Malaga, and sails to Genoa. Sure an extraordinary good way of passing a few winter months, and better than dragging through Holland, Germany, and Switzerland, to the same place. Now we have been contriving to get my Ld Strathmore (for whose advantage it will be in several respects) to bear a part in this expedition, and to-day we have brought it about, and they will go in a fortnight; but this is a secret, and you must not tell, for fear my lady should be frighted at so much sea.

The attorney and solic^r general (to whom it was referred) have declared that Lord G. Sackville may be tried by a court-martial. Ld Holdernesse has wrote him a letter to inform him of this, and *desires* to know (these are the words) how his l^{dp} *would have* them proceed, as there is no *specific charge* against him. I am told he has answered, that he cannot pretend to prescribe how a court, that sits in judgement upon him, is to proceed against him; that he well knows nothing can justly be alledged against him; but doubts not, from Pr Ferdinand's treatment of him, that there was some charge against him, especially as he finds himself *dismissed from all his employ-ments*. I hear, too, that (whatever the lawyers have said) the general officers insist they will not have anything to do with his cause, as he is no longer of the army. So (I suppose) after a little bustle the matter will drop.

Here is a new farce of Macklin the player's, that delights the town much, "Love-à-la-Mode," a beau Jew, an English gentleman jockey, a Scotch baronet, and an Irish officer in the Prussian service, that make love to a merchant's niece. The Irishman is the hero, and the happy man, as he deserves; for Sir Reilichan O'Callaghan is a modest, brave, and generous soldier; yet with the manners, the brogue, and the understanding of an Irishman, which makes a new character. The king is so pleased with the Scotch character (which is no compliment to that nation) that he has sent for a copy of the piece, for it is not printed, to read.

I am sorry to hear you have reason to complain of Mr. Bell, because he seemed to have some taste in Gothic, and it may not be easy to find such another. It is for my sake, not from your own judgement, that you see the *affair* I mentioned to you in so good a light; I wish I could foresee any such consequences as you do; but fear it will be the very reverse, and so do others than I. The Museum goes on as usual; I have got the Earl of Huntingdon and Sᵣ. George Bowes's letters to Cecil about the rebellion in the north. Heberden has married Miss Woolaston, of Charterhouse-square, this week, whom he formerly courted, but could not then afford to have; for she has (they say) but £2000 fortune. I have not yet seen her. My best respects to Mrs. Wharton.

I am ever yours,
T. G.

XCIX.—Mr. GRAY to Dr. WHARTON

April 22nd, 1760, LONDON.

DEAR DOCTOR,

I am not sorry to hear you are exceeding busy, except as it has deprived me of the pleasure I should have in hearing often from you, and as it has been occasioned by a little vexation and disappointment. To find one's self business (I am persuaded) is the great art of life; and I am never so angry as when I hear my acquaintance wishing they had been bred to some poking profession, or employed in some office of drudgery, as if it were pleasanter to be at the command of other people than at one's own; and as if they could not go unless they were wound up; yet I know and feel what they mean by this complaint: it proves that some spirit, something of genius (more than common) is required to teach a man how to employ himself. I say *a man*, for women, commonly speaking, never feel this distemper; they have always something to do: time hangs not on their hands (unless they be fine ladies), a variety of small inventions and occupations fill up the void, and their eyes are never open in vain.

I thank you heartily for the sow, if you have no occasion for her, I have; and if his lᵈᵖ. will be so kind as to drive her up

to town, will gladly give him forty shillings and the chitterlings
into the bargain. I could repay you with the story of my
Lady F^{r.} but (I doubt) you know my sow already, especially
as you dwell near Raby. However I'll venture; it may be
you have not heard it. About two months ago Mr. Creswick
(the D. of Cleveland's managing man) received an anonymous
letter as from a lady, offering him (if he would bring about a
match between her and his lord) £3000 to be paid after marriage
out of the estate. If he came into the proposal, a place was
named where he might speak with the party. He carried the
letter directly to the old Lady Darlington, and they agreed he
should go to the place. He did so, and found there a man,
agent for the lady; but, refusing to treat with any but principals,
after a little difficulty was conducted to her in person, and
found it was my Lady F. (S^{r.} Ev. F.'s fine young widow).
What passed between them I know not; but that very night
she was at Lady Darl^{n.}'s assembly (as she had used to be) and
no notice taken. The next morning she received a card to
say Lady D. had not expected to see her after *what had passed;*
otherwise she would have ordered her porter not to let her in.
The whole affair was immediately told to everybody. Yet she
had continued going about all public places *tête levée,* and
solemnly denying the whole to her acquaintance. Since that
I hear she owns it, and says her children were unprovided for,
and desires to know which of her friends would not have done
the same? But as neither of these expedients succeed very well,
she has hired a small house, and is going into the country for
the summer.

Here has just been a duel between the Duke of Bolton and
Mr. Stewart (a candidate for the county of Hampshire at the
late election), what the quarrel was I do not know; but they
met near Mary-le-bone, and the D. in making a pass over-
reached himself, fell down and hurt his knee, the other bid him
get up, but he could not; then he bid him ask his life, but he
would not; so he let him alone, and that's all. Mr. Stewart
was slightly wounded.

The old Pundles that sat on Ld. G. Sackville (for they were
all such, but two, Gen. Cholmondeley and Ld. Albermarle) have
at last hammered out their sentence. He is declared disobedient
and unfit for all military command. It is said that nine (out
of the fifteen) were for death, but as two-thirds must be unani-
mous, some of them came over to the merciful side. I do not
affirm the truth of this. What he will do with himself, nobody

guesses. The poor old duke went into the country some time ago, and (they say) can hardly bear the sight of anybody. The unembarrassed countenance, the looks of sovereign contempt and superiority, that his l^{dp.} bestowed on his accusers during the trial, were the admiration of all: but his usual talents and art did not appear, in short his cause would not support him. Be that as it will, everybody blames *somebody*, who has been out of all temper and intractable during the whole time. Smith (the aid-de-camp, and principal witness for Ld. G.) had no sooner finished his evidence, but he was forbid to mount guard, and ordered to sell out. The court and the criminal went halves in the expence of the shorthand writer, so Ld. G. has already published the trial, before the authentic copy appears; and in it are all the foolish questions that were asked, and the absurdities of his judges, you may think perhaps that he intends to go abroad and hide his head: *au contraire*, all the world visits him on his condemnation. He says himself his situation is better than ever it was; the Scotch have all along affected to take him under their protection; his wife has been daily walking with Lady Augusta (during the trial) in Leicester Gardens, and Lord B.'s chariot stands at his door by the hour.

Ld. Ferrers has entertained the town for three days; I was not there, but Mason and Stonehewer were in the D. of Ancaster's gallery, and in the greatest danger (which I believe they do not yet know themselves), for the cell underneath them (to which the prisoner retires) was on fire during the trial, and the D. of Anc^{r.} with the workmen, by sawing away some timbers, and other assistance, contrived to put it out without any alarm given to the court: several now recollect they smelt burning, and heard a noise of sawing, but none guessed as to the cause. Miss Johnson, daughter to the murthered man, appeared so cool, and gave so gentle an evidence, that at first sight every one concluded she was bought off; but this could do him little good. The surgeon and his own servants laid open such a scene of barbarity and long-meditated malice, as left no room for his plea of lunacy, nor any thought of pity in the hearers. The oddest thing was this plea of temporary lunacy, and his producing two brothers of his to prove it, one a clergyman suspended for Methodism by the B^{p.} of London); the other a sort of squire, that goes in the country by the name of *Ragged and Dangerous*. He managed the cause himself with more cleverness than any of his counsel, and (when found guilty) asked pardon for his plea, and laid it upon the persuasions of his family. Mrs. Shirley (his mother), Lady Huntingdon, and others of the relations were at court yesterday with a petition for mercy; but on the 5th of May he is to be hanged at Tyburn.

The town are reading the K. of Prussia's poetry (" Le Philosophe sans souci "), and I have done like the town; they do not seem so sick of it as I am. It is all the scum of Voltaire and Bolingbroke, the *crambe recocta* of our worst Freethinkers, tossed up in German-French rhyme. *Tristram Shandy* is still a greater object of admiration, the man as well as the book. One is invited to dinner, where he dines, a fortnight beforehand. His portrait is done by Reynolds, and now engraving. Dodsley gives £700 for a second edition, and two new volumes not yet written; and to-morrow will come out two volumes of sermons by him. Your friend, Mr. Hall, has printed two lyric epistles, one to my Cousin Shandy on his coming to town, the other to the grown gentlewomen, the misses of York: they seem to me to be absolute madness. These are the best lines in them—

> I'll tell you a story of Elijah—
> Close by a mob of children stood,
> Commenting on his sober mood,
> And back'd them (their opinions) like such sort of folks,
> With a few stones and a few jokes:
> Till weary of their pelting and their prattle,
> He ordered out his bears to battle.
> It was delightful fun
> To see them run
> And eat up the young cattle.

The seventh volume of Buffon is come over: do you chuse to have it?

Poor Lady Cobham is at last delivered from a painful life. She has given Miss Speed above £30,000.

Mr. Brown is well: I heard from him yesterday, and think of visiting him soon. Mason and Stonehewer are both in town and (if they were here) would send their best compliments to you and Mrs. Wh^n. with mine. You see I have left no room for weather, yet I have observed the birth of the spring, which (though backward) is very beautiful at present. Mind, from this day the thermometer goes to its old place below in the yard, and so pray let its sister do. Mr. Stillingfleet (with whom I am grown acquainted) has convinced me it ought to do so. Adieu

C.—Mr. GRAY to Mr. STONEHEWER

LONDON, *June* 29, 1760.

THOUGH you have had but a melancholy employment, it is worthy of envy, and (I hope) will have all the success it deserves.[1] It was the best and most natural method of cure, and such as could not have been administered by any but your gentle hand. I thank you for communicating to me what must give you so much satisfaction.

I too was reading M. D'Alembert,[2] and (like you) am totally disappointed in his "Elements." I could only taste a little of the first course: it was dry as a stick, hard as a stone, and cold as a cucumber. But then the letter to Rousseau is like himself; and the discourses on Elocution, and on the Liberty of Music, are divine. He has added to his translations from Tacitus; and (what is remarkable) though that author's manner more nearly resembles the best French writers of the present age than anything, he totally fails in the attempt. Is it his fault, or that of the language?

I have received another Scotch packet with a third specimen, inferior in kind (because it is merely description), but yet full of nature and noble wild imagination. Five bards pass the night at the castle of a chief (himself a principal bard); each goes out in his turn to observe the face of things, and returns with an extempore picture of the changes he has seen; it is an October night, the (harvest-month of the Highlands). This is the whole plan; yet there is a contrivance, and a preparation of ideas, that you would not expect. The oddest thing is, that every one of them sees ghosts (more or less). The idea that struck and surprised me most, is the following. One of them (describing a storm of wind and rain) says—

> Ghosts ride on the tempest to-night.
> Sweet is their voice between the gusts of wind;
> *Their songs are of other worlds!*

Did you never observe (*while rocking winds are piping loud*) that pause, as the gust is recollecting itself, and rising upon the ear in a shrill and plaintive note, like the swell of an Æolian harp? I do assure you there is nothing in the world so like the voice of

[1] Mr. Stonehewer was now at Houghton-le-Spring, in the bishoprick of Durham, attending on his sick father, rector of that parish.—*Mason.*
[2] Two subsequent volumes of his *Melanges de Literature et Philosophie.*—*Mason.*

a spirit. Thomson had an ear sometimes: he was not deaf to this; and has described it gloriously, but given it another different turn, and of more horror. I cannot repeat the lines: it is in his "Winter." There is another very fine picture in one of them. It describes the breaking of the clouds after the storm before it is settled into a calm, and when the moon is seen by short intervals.

> The waves are tumbling on the lake,
> And lash the rocky sides.
> The boat is brim-full in the cove,
> The oars on the rocking tide.
> Sad sits a maid beneath a cliff,
> And eyes the rolling stream;
> Her Lover promised to come,
> She saw his boat (when it was evening) on the lake;
> *Are these his groans in the gale?*
> *Is this his broken boat on the shore?* [1]

CI.—Mr. GRAY to Dr. WHARTON

[*July*, 1760.]

Dear Doctor,

I heard yesterday from your old friend Mr. Field, that Mrs Wharton had brought you a son, and as I sincerely hope this may be some addition to your happiness, I heartily congratulate you both on the occasion. Another thing I rejoice in, is, to know that you not only grow reconciled to your scene, but discover beauties round you that once were deformities. I am persuaded the whole matter is, to have always something going forward. Happy they that can create a rose-tree, or erect a honeysuckle that can watch the brood of a hen, or see a fleet of their own ducklings launch into the water! It is with a sentiment of envy that I speak it, who never shall have even a thatched roof of my own, nor gather a strawberry, but in Covent Garden. I will not believe in the *vocality* of Old Park till next summer, when perhaps I may trust my own ears.

---

[1] The whole of this descriptive piece has been since published in a note to a poem, entitled "Croma" (See *Ossian's Poems*, vol. i. p. 350, 8vo). It is somewhat remarkable that the manuscript, in the translator's own hand, which I have in my possession, varies considerably from the printed copy. Some images are omitted, and others added. I will mention one which is not in the manuscript, *the spirit of the mountain shrieks*. In the tragedy of Douglas, published at least three years before, I always admired this fine line, *the angry spirit of the water shriek'd*.—Quere, Did Mr. Home take this sublime image from Ossian, or has the translator of Ossian since borrowed it from Mr. Home?—*Mason*.

I remain, bating some few little excursions that I have made, still in town, though for these three weeks I have been going into Oxfordshire with Madam Speed. But her affairs, as she says, or her vagaries, as I say, have obliged her to alter her mind ten times within that space. No wonder, for she has got at least £30,000, with a house in town, plate, jewels, china, and old japan infinite, so that indeed it would be ridiculous for her to know her own mind. I, who know mine, do intend to go to Cambridge, but that owl, Fobus, is going thither to the commencement; so that I am forced to stay till his nonsense is at an end. Chapman you see is dead at last, which signifies not much, I take it, to anybody; for his family (they say) are left in good circumstances. I am neither sorry nor glad, for Mason (I doubt) will scarce succeed to his prebend. The old creature is down at Aston, where my lord [1] has paid him a visit lately, as the town says in *a miff*, about the garter, and other *trumps* he has met with of late. I believe this at least is certain, that he has deserted his old attachments, and worships another idol, who receives his incense with a good deal of coldness and negligence.

I can tell you but little of St. Germain. He saw Monsieur D'Affray at the Hague (who in a day or two, on receiving a courier from his own court), asked the States leave to apprehend him,[2] but he was gone, and arrived safe in St. Mary Ax, where he had lodgings (I fancy) at his old friend La Cours, the Jew physician. After some days, a messenger took charge of him, and he was examined (I believe) before Mr. Pitt. They however dismissed him, but with orders to leave England directly. Yet I know care was taken that he should be furnished with proper passports to go safe through Holland, to Hamburgh; which gives some room to believe, what many at first imagined, that he was charged with some proposals from the French coast. He is a likely person enough to make them believe at Paris that he could somehow serve them on such an occasion.

We are in great alarms about Quebec; the force in the town was not 8000 men, sufficient to defend the place (naturally strong) against any attack of the French forces, unfurnished as they must be for a formal siege; but by no means to meet them

---

[1] Lord Holdernesse.

[2] Count de St. Germain, who commanded an army on the Rhine of 30,000 men against the allied forces; conceiving disgust at being obliged to serve under the Duke de Broglio, who was his junior in the service, relinquished his command; and it is, I conclude, to him that Gray alludes. Count d'Affray was the French ambassador at the Hague.—*Mitford.*

in the field. This however is what Murray has chosen to do, whether from rashness, or deceived by false intelligence, I cannot tell. The returns of our loss are undoubtedly false, for we have above 100 officers killed or taken. All depends upon the arrival of our garrison from Louïsberg, which was daily expected. But even that (unless they bring provisions with them) may increase the distress; for at the time when we were told of the plenty and cheapness of all things at Quebec, I am assured a piece of fresh meat could not be had for twenty guineas.

If you have seen Stonehewer, he has probably told you of my old Scotch (or rather Irish) poetry. I am gone mad about them. They are said to be translations (literal and in prose) from the *Erse* tongue, done by one Macpherson, a young clergyman in the Highlands. He means to publish a collection he has of these specimens of antiquity; but what plagues me is, I cannot come at any certainty on that head. I was so struck, so *extasié* with their infinite beauty, that I writ into Scotland to make a thousand enquiries. The letters I have in return are ill wrote, ill reasoned, unsatisfactory, calculated (one would imagine) to deceive one, and yet not cunning enough to do it cleverly. In short, the whole external evidence would make one believe these fragments (for so he calls them, though nothing can be more entire) counterfeit; but the internal is so strong on the other side, that I am resolved to believe them genuine, spite of the devil and the kirk. It is impossible to convince me that they were invented by the same man that writes me these letters. On the other hand, it is almost as hard to suppose, if they are original, that he should be able to translate them so admirably. What can one do? Since Stonehewer went, I have received another of a very different and inferior kind (being merely descriptive), much more modern than the former (he says), yet very old too. This too in its way is extremely fine. In short, this man is the very dæmon of poetry, or he has lighted on a treasure hid for ages. The Welch poets are also coming to light. I have seen a discourse in MS. about them (by one Mr. Evans, a clergyman) with specimens of their writings. This is in Latin, and though it don't approach the other, there are fine scraps among it.

You will think I am grown mighty poetical of a sudden; you would think so still more, if you knew there was a satire printed against me and Mason jointly; it is called "Two Odes:" the one is inscribed to Obscurity (that is me), the other to Oblivion.

It tells me what I never heard before; for (speaking of himself) the author says though he has

> Nor the pride, nor self-opinion,
> That possess the happy pair,
> Each of taste the fav'rite minion,
> Prancing thro' the desert air:
> Yet shall he mount, with classic housings grac'd,
> By help mechanick of equestrian block,
> And all unheedful of the Critic's mock,
> Spur his light courser o'er the bounds of Taste.

The writer is a Mr. Colman, who published the "Connoisseur," nephew to the late Lady Bath, and a friend of Garrick's. I believe his odes sell no more than mine did, for I saw a heap of them lie in a bookseller's window, who recommended them to me as a very pretty thing.

If I did not mention *Tristram* to you, it was because I thought I had done so before. There is much good fun in it, and humour sometimes hit, and sometimes missed. I agree with your opinion of it, and shall see the two future volumes with pleasure. Have you read his sermons (with his own comic figure at the head of them)? They are in the style, I think, most proper for the pulpit, and shew a very strong imagination and a sensible heart. But you see him often tottering on the verge of laughter, and ready to throw his perriwig in the face of his audience. Now for my season.

April 10. I observed the elm putting out.
12. That and the pear looked green. Therm. at 62.
13. Very fine; white poplar and willow put out.
15. Standard pear (sheltered) in full bloom.
18. Lime and hornbeam green.
19. Swallow flying.
20. Therm. at 60. Wind S.W. Skylark, chaffinch, thrush, mew, and robin singing. Horse-chesnut, wild-briar, bramble, and sallow had spread their leaves; hawthorn and lilac had formed their blossoms; blackthorn, double-flowered peach and pears in full bloom; double tonquils, hyacinths, anemones, single wall-flowers, and auriculas, in flower. In the fields—dog violets, daisies, dandelions, butter-cups, red-archangel, and shepherd's purse.
21. Almond out of bloom, and spreading its leaves.
26. Lilacs flowering.
May 1. Gentianella in flower.
2. Pear goes off; apple blows. Therm. at 63. Wind N.E.; still fair and dry.
3. Evening and all night hard rain.
4. Th. at 40. Wind N.E.; rain.
11. Very fine. Wind N.E. Horse-chesnut in full bloom; walnut and vine spread; lilacs, Persian jasmine, tulips, wall-flowers, pheasant-eye, lilly-in-the-valley, in flower. In the fields— furze, cowslips, hare-bells, and cow-parsnip.

May 13. Jasmine and acacia spread. Fine weather.
    18. Showery. Wind high.
    19. Same. Therm. at 56.
    20. Thunder, rain, 54.
    21. Rain, wind N.E., 52.
    31. Green peas 15*d.* a quart.
June 1. Therm. at 78.
    2. Scarlet strawberries, duke-cherries. Hay-making here.
    3. Wind S.S.E. Therm. at 84 (the highest I ever saw it), it was
       at noon; since which, till last week, we had hot dry weather;
       now it rains like mad. Cherries and strawberries in bushels.

I believe there is no fear of war with Spain.

[*July*, 1760.]

CII.—Mr. GRAY to Dr. CLARKE [1]

PEMBROKE HALL, *August* 12, 1760.

NOT knowing whether you are yet returned from your sea-water,
I write at random to you. For me, I am come to my resting-
place, and find it very necessary, after living for a month in a
house with three women that laughed from morning to night,
and would allow nothing to the sulkiness of my disposition.
Company and cards at home, parties by land and water abroad,
and (what they call) *doing something*, that is, racketting about
from morning to night, are occupations, I find, that wear out
my spirits, especially in a situation where one might sit still and
be alone with pleasure; for the place was a hill [2] like Clifden,
opening to a very extensive and diversified landscape, with the
Thames, which is navigable, running at its foot.

I would wish to continue here (in a very different scene, it must
be confessed) till Michaelmas; but I fear I must come to town
much sooner. Cambridge is a delight of a place, now there is
nobody in it. I do believe you would like it, if you knew what
it was without inhabitants. It is they, I assure you, that get it
an ill name and spoil all. Our friend Dr. —— [3] (one of its
nuisances) is not expected here again in a hurry. He is gone to
his grave with five fine mackerel (large and full of roe) in his
belly. He eat them all at one dinner; but his fate was a turbot
on Trinity Sunday, of which he left little for the company besides
bones. He had not been hearty all the week; but after this sixth
fish he never held up his head more, and a violent looseness
carried him off.—They say he made a very good end.

---

[1] Physician at Epsom. With this gentleman Mr. Gray commenced an
early acquaintance at college.—*Mason.*
[2] Near Henley.   [3] Vide Letter CIV.

Have you seen the Erse fragments since they were printed? I am more puzzled than ever about their antiquity, though I still incline (against everybody's opinion) to believe them old. Those you have already seen are the best; though there are some others that are excellent too.

CIII.—Mr. GRAY to Mr. MASON

CAMBRIDGE, *August 20, 1760.*

I HAVE sent "Musæus"[1] back as you desired me, scratched here and there. And with it also a bloody satire,[2] written against no less persons than *you and I* by name. I concluded at first it was Mr. ——, because he is your friend and my humble servant; but then I thought he knew the world too well to call us the favourite minions of taste and of fashion, especially as to odes. For to them his ridicule is confined; so it is not he, but Mr. Colman, nephew to Lady Bath, author of the "Connoisseur," a member of one of the inns of court, and a particular acquaintance of Mr. Garrick. What have you done to him? for I never heard his name before; he makes very tolerable fun with me where I understand him (which is not everywhere); but seems more angry with you. Lest people should not understand the humour of the thing (which indeed to do they must have our lyricisms at their finger ends), letters come out in *Lloyd's Evening Post* to tell them who and what it was that he meant, and says it is like to produce a great combustion in the literary world. So if you have any mind to *combustle* about it well and good; for me, I am neither so literary nor so combustible.[3] The *Monthly Review*, I see, just now has much stuff about us on this occasion. It says one of us at least has always borne his faculties meekly. I leave you to guess which of us that is; I think I know. You simpleton you! you must be meek, must you? and see what you get by it.

[1] I had desired Mr. Gray to revise my monody on Mr. Pope's death, in order that I might correct it for the edition I was then preparing of my poems.—*Mason.*

[2] The parodies in question, entitled "Odes to Obscurity and Oblivion," were written by Messrs. Lloyd and Colman, and have been reprinted since in Mr. Lloyd's Poems.—*Mason.*

[3] Had Mr. Pope disregarded the sarcasms of the many writers that endeavoured to eclipse his poetical fame, as much as Mr. Gray here appears to have done, the world would not have been possessed of a *Dunciad*; but it would have been impressed with a more amiable idea of its author's temper. It is for the sake of showing how Mr. Gray felt on such occasions that I publish this letter.—*Mason.*

I do not like your improvements at Aston, it looks so like settling; if I come I will set fire to it. I will never believe the B——s and the C——s are dead, though I smelt them; that sort of people always live to a good old age. I dare swear they are only gone to Ireland, and we shall soon hear they are bishops.

The Erse fragments have been published five weeks ago in Scotland, though I had them not (by a mistake) till the other day. As you tell me new things do not reach you soon at Aston, I inclose what I can; the rest shall follow, when you tell me whether you have not got the pamphlet already. I send the two to Mr. Wood which I had before, because he has not *the affectation of not admiring*.[1] I have another from Mr. Macpherson, which he has not printed; it is mere description, but excellent too in its kind. If you are good and will learn to admire, I will transcribe and send it.

As to their authenticity, I have made many enquiries, and have lately procured a letter from Mr. David Hume (the historian), which is more satisfactory than anything I have yet met with on that subject. He says—

" Certain it is that these poems are in everybody's mouth in the Highlands, have been handed down from father to son, and are of an age beyond all memory and tradition. Adam Smith, the celebrated professor in Glasgow, told me that the piper of the Argyleshire Militia repeated to him all those which Mr. Macpherson had translated, and many more of equal beauty. Major Mackay (Lord Rae's brother) told me that he remembers them perfectly well; as likewise did the Laird of Macfarlane (the greatest antiquarian we have in this country), and who insists strongly on the historical truth as well as the poetical beauty of these productions. I could add the Laird and Lady Macleod, with many more, that live in different parts of the Highlands, very remote from each other, and could only be acquainted with what had become (in a manner) national works.[2]

---

[1] It was rather a want of credulity than admiration that Mr. Gray should have laid to my charge. I suspected that, whether the fragments were genuine or not, they were by no means literally translated. I suspect so still; and a former note gives a sufficient cause for that suspicion. See p. 232.—*Mason.*

[2] All this external evidence, and much more, has since been collected and published by Dr. Blair (see his appendix to his *Critical Dissertation on the Works of Ossian*); and yet notwithstanding a later Irish writer has been hardy enough to assert, that the poems in question abound with the strangest anachronisms: for instance, that Cucullin lived in the first, and Fingal in the third century; two princes who are said to have made war with the Danes, a nation never heard of in Europe till the ninth; which war could not possibly have happened till 500 years after the death of

There is a country surgeon in Lochaber who has by heart the entire epic poem mentioned by Mr. Macpherson in his preface; and, as he is old, is perhaps the only person living that knows it all, and has never committed it to writing, we are in the more haste to recover a monument which will certainly be regarded as a curiosity in the republic of letters: we have, therefore, set about a subscription of a guinea or two guineas apiece, in order to enable Mr. Macpherson to undertake a mission into the High-lands to recover this poem, and other fragments of antiquity."

He adds, too, that the names of Fingal, Ossian, Oscar, etc., are still given in the Highlands to large mastiffs, as we give to ours the names of Cæsar, Pompey, Hector, etc.

CIV.—Mr. GRAY to Dr. WHARTON

London, *October* 21, 1760.

Dear Doctor,

Don't be afraid of me. I will not come till you tell me I may; though I long very much to see you. I hear you have let your hair grow, and visit none of your neighbouring gentry; two (I should think) capital crimes in that county, and indeed in all counties. I hear too (and rejoice) that you have recovered your hearing. I have nothing equally important to tell you of myself, but that I have not had the gout since I saw you; yet don't let me brag, the winter is but just begun.

I have passed a part of the summer on a charming hill near Henley,[1] with the Thames running at my feet; but in the company of a pack of women, that wore my spirits, though not their own. The rest of the season I was at Cambridge in a duller and more congenial situation. Did I tell you that our friend Chapman, a week before he died, eat five huge mackerel (fat and full of roe) at one dinner, which produced an indigestion; but on Trinity Sunday he finished himself with the best part of a large turbot, which he carried to his grave, poor man! he never held up his head after. From Cambridge I am come hither, yet am going into Kent for a fortnight or so. You astonish me in wondering that my Lady Cobham left me nothing. For my

the supposed poet who sings it. (See O'Halloran's introduction to the *Study of the History and Antiquities of Ireland*, quarto, 1772.) To what-ever side of the question truth may lean, it is of little moment to me; my doubts arising (as I have said in the former note) from internal evidence only, and a want of proof of the fidelity of the translation.—*Mason.*

[1] Park Place, the seat of the Honourable Henry Seymour Conway, the friend and correspondent of Walpole.—*Mitford.*

part, I wondered to find she had given me £20 for a ring, as much as she gave to several of her own nieces. The world said, before her death, that Mrs. Speed and I had shut ourselves up with her in order to make her will, and that afterwards we were to be married.

There is a second edition of the Scotch fragments, yet very few admire them, and almost all take them for fictions. I have a letter from D. Hume, the historian, that asserts them to be genuine, and cites the names of several people (that know both languages) who have heard them current in the mouths of pipers, and other illiterate persons in various and distant parts of the Highlands. There is a subscription for Mr. Macpherson, which will enable him to undertake a mission among the mountaineers, and pick up all the scattered remnants of old poetry. He is certainly an admirable judge, if his *learned* friends do not pervert or overrule his taste.

Mason is here in town, but so dissipated with his duties at Sion-Hill, or his attention to the *beaux-arts*, that I see but little of him. The last spring (for the first time) there was an exhibition in a public room of pictures, sculptures, engravings, etc., sent in by all the artists, in imitation of what has been long practised in Paris. Among the rest there is a Mr. Sandby, who excels in landscape, with figures, views of buildings, ruins, etc., and has been much employed by the duke, Lord Harcourt, Lord Scarborough, and others. Hitherto he has dealt in wash'd drawings and water-colours, but has of late only practised in oil. He (and Mason together) have cooked up a great picture of Mount Snowdon, in which the bard and Edward the First make their appearance; and this is to be his *Exhibition-picture* for next year, but (till then) it is a sort of secret.

The great expedition [1] takes up everybody's thoughts. There is such a train of artillery on board as never was seen before during this war. Some talk of Brest, others of Rochfort, if the wind (which is very high) does not blow it away. I do believe it will succeed, for the French seem in a miserable way.

The duke [2] is well recovered of his paralytic attack, though it is still visible in his face when he speaks. It has been occasioned by the long intermission of his usual violent exercises, for he cannot ride or walk much on account of a dropsy confined

---

[1] The strong armament destined for a secret expedition was collected at Portsmouth; but after being detained there the whole summer, the design was laid aside.—See Smollett's *History of England*, vol. v. p. 230.—*Mitford.*

[2] Duke of Cumberland.—*Mitford.*

to a *certain part*, and not dangerous in itself. Yet he appears at Newmarket, but in his chaise.

Mason and Mr. Brown send their best services. Dr. Heberden enquires *kindly* after you, and has his good dinners as usual. Adieu, dear sir, and present my compliments to Mrs. Wharton. I am ever

Truly yours,

T. G.

CV.—Mr. GRAY to Dr. WHARTON

Pemb. Coll., *Jan.* 1761.

Dear Doctor,

The best piece of news I have to send you is, that Mason is Residentiary of York, which is worth near £200 a year. He owes it to our friend Mr. F. Montagu, who is brother-in-law to Dean Fountayne. The precentorship (worth as much more) being vacant at the same time, Lord Holdernesse has obtained that too for him. But for this, he must come and kiss hands; and as the ceremony is not yet over, we do not proclaim it aloud for the present. He now, I think, may wait for Mr. Hutton's exit with great patience; and shut his insatiable repining mouth. I hope to see him here in his way to town.

I pity your brother, and have little hope left of his wife's recovery; though I have been told that Dr. Lowth's, after she had continued for some years in that condition, was perfectly restored. It may be worth while to enquire in what method she was treated. The papers were to have been sent to Boswell Court, the week after I left London, to be seen, before they were packed up. Mr. Jonathan is perhaps unable to attend to it, but doubtless you have ordered somebody to hasten Bromwick, and see that the sets are right. I shall not be in London till the middle of March. My old friend Miss Speed has done what the world calls a very foolish thing. She has married the Baron de la Peyriere, son to the Sardinian minister, the Comte de Viry. He is about twenty-eight years old (ten years younger than herself), but looks nearer forty. This is not the effect of debauchery, for he is a very sober man, good-natured, and honest, and no conjurer. The estate of the family is about £4000 a year. The Castle of Viry is in Savoy, a few miles from Geneva, commanding a fine veiw of the lake. What she has done with her money I know not, but (I suspect) kept it to herself. Her religion she need not change; but she must never expect to be well received at that court till she does: and I do not think she will make quite a *Julie* in the country.

The " Heloïse " cruelly disappointed me, but it has its partisans, among which we see Mason and Mr. Hurd. For me, I admire nothing but " Fingal " [1] (I conclude you have read it, if not Stonehewer can lend it you), yet I remain still in doubt about the authenticity of those poems, though inclining rather to believe them genuine in spite of the world. Whether they are the inventions of antiquity, or of a modern Scotchman, either case to me is alike unaccountable. *Je m'y perd.*

I take no joy in the Spanish war, being too old to privateer, and too poor to buy stock: nor do I hope for a good end of any war as it will be now probably conducted. Oh! that foolishest [2]

---

[1] In a letter to another friend, informing him that he had sent Fingal down to him, he says: " For my part I will stick to my credulity, and if I am cheated, think it is worse for him (the translator) than for me. The epic poem is foolishly so called, yet there is a sort of plan and unity in it very strange for a barbarous age; yet what I more admire are some of the detached pieces—the rest I leave to the discussion of antiquarians and historians; yet my curiosity is much interested in their decision." No man surely ever took more pains with himself to believe anything, than Mr. Gray seems to have done on this occasion.—*Mason.*

[2] Mr. Pitt. " As I cannot put Mr. Pitt to death (says Mr. Walpole in a letter to Mr. Conway) at least I have buried him. Here is his epitaph:

> ' Admire his eloquence.—It mounted higher
>   Than Attic purity, or Roman fire.
>   Adore his services—our lions view,
>   Ranging where Roman eagles never flew;
>   Copy his soul supreme o'er Lucre's sphere
>   —But oh! beware Three Thousand Pounds a year.' "—

> Walpole's *Works*, vol. v. p. 85. See also p. 559,
>   in a letter to the Countess of Ailesbury.

" Pitt insisted on a war with Spain, was resisted, and last Monday resigned. The city breathed vengeance on his opposers, the Council quaked, and the Lord knows what would have happened. But yesterday, which was only Friday, as this giant was stalking to seize the Tower of London, he stumbled over a silver penny, picked it up, carried it home to Lady Esther, and they are now as quiet good sort of people as my Lord and Lady Bath, who lived in the vinegar-bottle.—In fact, madam, this immaculate man, has accepted the Barony of Chatham for his wife, with a pension of £3000 a year for three lives: and though he has not quitted the House of Commons, I think my Lord A—— would be now as formidable there. The pension he has left *us* is a war for 3000 lives, perhaps for twenty times three thousand lives! But

> Does this become a soldier? *this* become
>   Whom armies followed, and a people loved?

" What! to sneak out of the scrape, prevent peace and avoid the war! blast one's character, and all for the sake of a paltry annuity, a long-necked peeress, and a couple of Grenvilles! "—*Mitford.*

of great men that sold his inestimable diamond for a paltry peerage and pension: the very night it happened was I swearing it was a damned lie, and never could be. But it was for want of reading Thomas à Kempis, who knew mankind so much better than I.

Young Pitt (whom I believe you have heard me mention) is returned to England. From him I hope to get much information concerning Spain which nobody has seen. He is no bad observer. I saw a man yesterday who has been a-top of Mount Ætna, and seen the ruins of a temple at Agrigentum, whose columns (when standing) were 96 feet in height. A moderate man might hide himself in one of the flutings. By the way, there is a Mr. Phelps (now gone secretary to the embassy to Turin) who has been all over Sicily, and means to give us an account of its remains. There are two more volumes of Buffon (the 9th and 10th) arrived in England, and the two last maps of D'Anville's Europe. One Mr. Needham, tutor to a Lord Gormanstown, now on his travels, has made a strange discovery. He saw a figure of Isis at Turin, on whose back was a pilaster of antique characters, not hieroglyphics, but such as are sometimes seen on Egyptian statues. When he came to Rome, in the Vatican Library he was shewed a glossary of the ancient Chinese tongue. He was struck with the similitude of the characters, and on comparing them with an exact copy he had of the inscription, found that he could read it, and that it signified— (" This statue of Isis is copied from another, in such a city; the original is so many measures in height, and so many in breadth ").—If this be true, it may open many new things to us. Deguignes some time ago wrote a dissertation to prove that China was peopled from Egypt.

I still flatter myself with the notion of seeing you in summer; but God knows how it will be. I am persuading Mr. Brown to make a visit to Lady Strathmore (who has often invited him), and then you will see him too. He is at present not very well, having something of the sciatica, which hangs about him. Present my best services to Mrs. Wharton.

I am ever truly yours,

T. G.

P.S. The queen is said here to be ill, and to spit blood. She is not with child, I am afraid.

CVI.—Mr. GRAY to Dr. WHARTON

LONDON, *Jan.* 31, 1761.

MY DEAR DOCTOR,

You seem to forget me; if it were for any other reason than that you are very busy, that is, very happy, I should not so easily pass it over. I send you a Swedish and English calendar; the first column is by Berger, a disciple of Linnæus; the second, by Mr. Stillingfleet; the third (very imperfect indeed), by me. You are to observe, as you tend your plantations, and take your walks, how the spring advances in the north, and whether Old Park most resembles Upsal or Stratton. This latter has on one side a barren black heath, on the other a light sandy loam; all the country about it is a dead flat. You see it is necessary you should know the situation (I do not mean any reflection upon anybody's place), and this is Mr. Stillingfleet's description of his friend Mr. Marsham's seat, to which in summer he retires and botanises. I have lately made an acquaintance with this philosopher,[1] who lives in a garret here in the winter, that he may support some near relations who depend upon him. He is always employed, and always cheerful, and seems to me a very worthy honest man. His present scheme is to send some persons properly qualified to reside a year or two in Attica, to make themselves acquainted with the climate, productions, and natural history of the country, that we may understand Aristotle and Theophrastus, etc., who have been heathen Greek to us for so many ages. This he has got proposed to Lord Bute, who is no unlikely person to put it in execution, being himself a botanist, and having now in the press a new system of botany of his own writing, in several volumes; the profits of which he gives to Dr. Hill (the inspector), who has got the place of master gardener at Kensington, reckoned worth near £2000 a year: there is an odd thing for you!

One hears nothing of the king but what gives one the best opinion of him imaginable. I hope it may hold. The royal family run loose about the world, and people do not know how to treat them, nor they how to be treated. They visit and are visited. Some come to the street-door to receive them, and that they say is too much; others to the head of the stairs, and

---

[1] See an account of Mr. Stillingfleet in the Life prefixed to his *Works* by the Rev. William Coxe, 3 vols. 8vo. A sonnet by him is published in Todd's edition of Milton, vol. v. p. 446.

that they think is too little. Nobody sits down with them, not even in their own houses, unless at a card table, so the world are likely to grow very weary of the honour. None but the Duke of York enjoy themselves (you know he always did), but the world seems weary of this honour too, for a different reason. I have just heard no bad story of him. When he was at Southampton in the summer, there was a clergyman in the neighbourhood with two very handsome daughters. He had soon wind of them, and dropped in for some reason or other, came again and again, and grew familiar enough to eat a bone of their mutton. At last he said to the father, " Miss —— leads a mighty confined life here, always at home; why can't you let one of them go and take an airing now and then with me in my chaise? " " Ah! sir," (says the parson), " do but look at them, a couple of hale fresh-coloured hearty wenches! They need no airing, they are well enough; but there is their mother, poor woman, has been in a declining way many years. If your royal highness would give her an airing now and then, it would be doing us a great kindness indeed! "

You see old Wortley Montagu is dead at last at eighty-three. It was not mere avarice and its companion abstinence that kept him alive so long. He every day drank (I think it was) half a pint of tokay, which he imported himself from Hungary in greater quantity than he could use, and sold the overplus for any price he chose to set upon it. He has left better than half a million of money. To Lady Mary £1200 a year, in case she gives up her pretensions to dowry, and if not it comes to his son. To the same son £1000 per annum for life only, and after him to his daughter Lady Bute (now this son is about £80,000 in debt). To all Lady Bute's children, which are eleven, £2000 apiece. *All the remainder* to Lady Bute, and after her to her second son, who takes the name of Wortley, and (if he fail) to the next in order. And after all these and their children, to Lord Sandwich, to whom *in present* he leaves some old manuscripts. Now I must tell you a story of Lady Mary: as she was on her travels, she had occasion to go somewhere by sea, and (to save charges) got a passage on board a man-of-war. The ship was (I think) Commodore Barnet's. When he had landed her, she told him she knew she was not to offer to pay for her passage; but in consideration of his many civilities, intreated him to wear a ring for her sake, and pressed him to accept it, which he did. It was an emerald of remarkable size and beauty. Some time after, as he wore it, some friend was admiring it, and asking how he came by it. When he heard from whence it came he laughed, and desired him to shew it to a jeweller whom he knew. The man was sent for. He unset it: it was a paste, not worth forty shillings.

The ministry are much out of joint. Mr. Pitt much out of humour, his popularity tottering, chiefly occasioned by a pamphlet against the German war, written by that *squeaking* acquaintance of ours, Mr. Manduit: it has had a vast run. The Irish are very intractable, even the Lord J.'s themselves: great difficulties about who shall be sent over to tame them; my Lord H^sse. again named, but (I am told) has refused it; everybody waits for a new Parliament to settle their ideas.

I have had no gout since you went; I will not brag, lest it return with redoubled violence. I am very foolish, and do nothing to mark that I ever was. I am going to Cambridge to take the *fresh air* this fine winter, for a month or so; we have had snow one day this winter, but it did not lie, it was several months ago. The 18th of January I took a walk to *Kentish Town*, wind N.W. bright and frosty. Thermometer at noon was at 42. The grass remarkably green and flourishing. I observed on dry banks facing the south that chickweed, dandelion, groundsel, red archangel, and shepherd's purse were beginning to flower. This is all I know of the country.

My best compliments to Mrs. Wharton. I hear her butter is the best in the bishoprick; and that even Deborah has learned to spin. I rejoice you are all in health; but why are you deaf, and blind too, or you could not vote for F. V. I have abundance more to say, but my paper won't hear of it. Adieu!

1755.

UPSAL IN SWEDEN.[1] Lat. 59° 51¾".		STRATTON IN NORFOLK. Lat. 52° 45".		CAMBRIDGE.
Hasel begins to f.	12 April	23 Jan.		——
Snow-drop F.	13 April	26 Jan.		4 Feb.
(White Wagtail appears)	13 April	12 Feb.		3 Feb.
Violets F.	3 May	28 Mar.		28 Mar.
Snow-drop goes off				——
Apricot f.		1 April		——
Elm F.	8 May	1 April		——
(Swallow returns)	9 May	6 April		——

[1] This is only an extract from the two calendars of A. M. Berger at Upsal and Mr. Stillingfleet at Stratton. See Stillingfleet's *Tracts*, p. 260-316. At p. 321 of the same interesting work, is given the calendar of flora, by Theophrastus at Athens, lat. 37° 25". I am not aware of any other works of this description published in England, "except the comparative view of the two calendars kept by the Rev. Gilbert White at

	UPSAL IN SWEDEN. Lat. 59° 51½".	STRATTON IN NORFOLK. Lat. 52° 45".	CAMBRIDGE.
(Cuckoo heard)	12 May	17 April	——
(Nightingale sings)	15 May	9 April	——
Birch L.	13 May	1 April	——
Alder L.	14 May	7 April	——
Bramble L.	7 May	3 April	——
Elm L.	15 May	10 April	16 April.
Hawthorn L.	15 May		10 April.
Acacia L.	15 May	12 April	——
Lime L.	21 May	12 April	16 April.
Aspen L.	20 May	26 April	——
Sycamore L.		13 April	——
White Poplar L.		17 April	——
Beech L.		21 April	——
Chesnut and Maple L.		18 April	——
Oak L.	20 May	18 April	18 April.
Ash L.	21 May	22 April	——
Fig L.		21 April	24 April.
Horse Chesnut F.		12 May	12 May.
Mulberry L.		14 May	——
Crab and Apple f.		23 April	22 April.
Cherry f.		18 April	17 April.
Lilac f.		27 April	24 April.
Hawthorn f.		10 May	12 May.
Plumb tree f.		16 April	——
Lilly o' the Valley f.		3 May	——
Broom F.		24 April	——
Mulberry L.		14 May	——
Elder f.	29 June	25 April	——
Lady Smock f.	28 May	18 April	——
Pea and Bean f.		29 April	——
Strawberries ripe	26 June	9 July	16 June.
Cherries	7 July	. (on walls)	25 June.
Currants	9 July	30 June	4 July.
Hay cut	7 July	{ near London at Stoke }	18 May.
Rye	4 Aug.		19 June.
Wheat		21 Aug. (latest)	15 Sept.
Barley	16 Aug.	3 Aug.	4 Sept.
(Cuckoo silent)	15 July	End of July	——
(Swallow gone)	17 Sept.	21 Sept.	28 Sept.
Birch, Elm, Sycamore, Lime, change colour }	22 Sept.	14 Sept.	——
Ash drops its leaves	6 Oct.	9 Oct.	5 Oct.
Elm stripped	7 Oct.		——
Lime falls	12 Oct.		——
Hasel stripped	17 Oct.		——

N.B. l. stands for opening its leaves; L. for in full leaf; f. for beginning to flower; F. for full bloom.

Selborne; and by William Markwick, Esq., at Catsfield, near Battle."
This is a work of great exactness, and the result of as much, and as patient observation as perhaps was ever brought to the subject. It is formed upon an attentive comparison of the seasons, from 1768 to 1793. See White's *Selborne*, 8vo, vol. ii. p. 121-156. It would be extremely useful to the lover of nature to have these four calendars (all of them kept in different latitudes) reprinted in one volume.—*Mitford.*

The summer flowers, especially such as blow about the solstice, I take no notice of, as they blow at the same time in Sweden and in England; at least the difference is only a day or two.

Observe, from this calendar it appears that there is a wonderful difference between the earlier phænomena of the spring in Sweden and in England, no less than seventy-eight days in the following of the snowdrop, sixty-one days in the appearance of the wagtail, sixty-two days in the bloom of the lilac, forty-three days in the leafing of the oak, forty days in the blooming of the cherry-tree, thirty-six days in the singing of the nightingale, thirty-three days in the return of the swallow, twenty-five in that of the cuckoo, and so on. Yet the summer flowers nearly keep time alike in both climates. The harvest differs not a fortnight; some of the fruits only nine days. Nay, strawberries come earlier there by thirteen days than with us. The swallow stays with us only four days longer than with them. And the ash-tree begins to lose its leaves within three days of the same time. These differences and these uniformities I know not how to account for.

Mr. Stillingfleet's calender goes no farther than October 26. But I observed that on December 2 many of our rose-trees had put out new leaves, and the lauristine, polyanthus, single yellow and bloody wallflowers, cytisus, and scarlet geraniums were still in flower.

January 15, 1756. The honeysuckles were in leaf, and single hepatica and snowdrop in flower.

As to the noise of birds, Mr. Stillingfleet marks their times thus in Norfolk—

4 Feb.	Woodlark singing.
12 Ditto.	Rooks pair.
16 Ditto.	Thrush sings.
— Ditto.	Chaffinch sings.
22 Ditto.	Partridges pair.
2 March.	Rooks build.
5 Ditto.	Ring Dove cooes.
14 April.	Bittern bumps.
16 Ditto.	Redstart returns.
28 Ditto.	Blackcap sings.
Ditto.	Whitethroat seen.
5 June.	Goatsucker (or Fern-Owl), heard in the evening. After the end of June, most birds are silent for a time, probably the moulting season; only the Goldfinch, Yellow Hammer, and Crested Wren are heard to chirp.
7 Aug.	Nuthatch chatters.
14 Ditto.	Stone Curlew whistles at night.
15 Ditto.	Young Owls heard in the evening.
17 Ditto.	Goatsucker no longer heard.
26 Ditto.	Robins singing.

6 Sept.   Chaffinch chirping.
5 Ditto.   Woodlark sings, and Fieldfares arrive
7 Ditto.   Blackbird sings.
9 Aug.   Thrush sings.
2 Oct.   Royston Crow comes.
0 Ditto.   Woodlark in full song.
  Ditto.   Ringdove cooes.
2 Ditto.   Woodcock returns.
4 Ditto.   Skylark sings.

I add the order of several fruits ripening at Stoke that year—

Hautboy-Strawberry	. 25 June.	Filberd . . .	18 Aug.
Wall Duke Cherry	. Ditto.	Nectarine . .	} 4 Sept.
Early Apricot .	. Ditto.	Newingt. Peach .	} 4 Sept.
Black-heart Cherry	. 2 July.	Morella Cherry .	
Raspberry .	. 4 Ditto.	Mulbery . .	} 18 Sept.
Gooseberry .	. 15 Ditto.	Walnut . .	} 18 Sept.
Muscadine Apricot	. Ditto.	Melon . .	
Black Fig . .	. 30 Ditto.	Burgamot Pear .	} 25 Ditto.
Muscle . .	)	Black Muscad. Grape	} 25 Ditto.
Orleans . .	} 18 Aug.	Nectarine over .	Ditto.
Green Gage . .	)	White Muscad. Grape	12 Oct.

CVII.—MR. GRAY TO MR. MASON

August 1761.

Be assured your York canon never will die; so the better the
thing is in value, the worse for you.[1] The true way to immortality is to get you nominated one's successor. Age and
diseases vanish at your name; fevers turn to radical heat, and
fistulas to issues: it is a judgement that waits on your insatiable
avarice. You could not let the poor old man die at his ease,
when he was about it; and all his family (I suppose) are cursing
you for it.

I wrote to Lord —— on his recovery; and he answers me
very cheerfully, as if his illness had been but slight, and the
pleurisy were no more than a hole in one's stocking. He got
it (he says) not by scampering, racketing, and riding post, as
I had supposed; but by going with ladies to Vauxhall. He is
the picture (and pray so tell him, if you see him) of an old alderman that I knew, who, after living forty years on the fat of the
land (not milk and honey, but arrack punch and venison), and
losing his great toe with a mortification, said to the last that he
owed it to two grapes, which he ate one day after dinner. He
felt them lie cold at his stomach the minute they were down.

[1] This was written at a time, when, by the favour of Dr. Fountayne,
Dean of York, I expected to be made a residentiary in his cathedral.—
Mason.

Mr. Montagu (as I guess, at your instigation) has earnestly
desired me to write some lines to be put on a monument which
he means to erect at Bellisle.   It is a task I do not love, knowing
Sir William Williams so slightly as I did: but he is so friendly a
person, and his affliction seemed to me so real, that I could not
refuse him.   I have sent him the following verses, which I neither
like myself, nor will he, I doubt: however, I have shewed him that
I wished to oblige him.   Tell me your real opinion.

CVIII.—Mr. GRAY to Mr. WALPOLE

Sunday, Feb. 28, 1762.

I RETURN you my best thanks for the copy of your book,[1] which
you sent me, and have not at all lessened my opinion of it since
I read it in print, though the press has generally a bad effect on
the complexion of one's works.   The engravings look, as you
say, better than I had expected, yet not altogether so well as I
could wish.   I rejoice in the good dispositions of our court, and
in the propriety of their application to you: the work is a thing
so much to be wished; has so near a connection with the turn of
your studies and of your curiosity; and might find such ample
materials among your hoards and in your head, that it will be a
sin if you let it drop and come to nothing, or worse than nothing,
for want of your assistance.[2]   The historical part should be in the
manner of Henault, a mere abridgement; a series of facts selected
with judgement that may serve as a clue to lead the mind along
in the midst of those ruins and scattered monuments of art that
time has spared.   This would be sufficient, and better than
Montfaucon's more diffuse narrative.   Such a work (I have
heard) Mr. Burke is now employed about, which, though not
intended for this purpose, might be applied perhaps to this use.
Then, at the end of each reign, should come a dissertation explanatory of the plates, and pointing out the turn of thought,
the customs, ceremonials, arms, dresses, luxury, and private
life, with the improvement or decline of the arts during that
period.   This you must do yourself, beside taking upon you the
superintendence, direction, and choice of materials.   As to the

---

[1] *The Anecdotes of Painting.*
[2] See a note from Lord Bute in the letters to and from ministers (Walpole's *Works*, vol. ii. p. 378), inviting Mr. Walpole to turn his thoughts
to a work of this kind; and Mr. Walpole's answer, offering to point out
and collect materials, and take any trouble in aiding, supervising, and
directing the whole plan.—*Mitford.*

expense, that must be the king's own entirely, and he must give
the book to foreign ministers and people of note; for it is
obvious no private man can undertake such a thing without a
subscription, and no gentleman will care for such an expedient;
and a gentleman it should be, because he must have easy access
to archives, cabinets, and collections of all sorts. I protest I
do not think it impossible but they may give into such a scheme;
they approve the design, they wish to encourage the arts, and
to be magnificent, and they have no Versailles or Herculaneum.

I hope to see you toward the end of March. If you bestow a
line on me, pray tell me whether the Baronne de la Peyriere is
gone to her Castle of Viry, and whether "Fingal" be discovered
or shrewdly suspected to be a forgery. Adieu!—I am yours ever,

T. GRAY.

CIX.—MR. GRAY TO DR. WHARTON

DEAR DOCTOR,

I feel very ungrateful every day that I continue silent, and
yet I do not write to you; but now the pen is in my hand, and
I am in for it. When I left you, in spite of the rain, I went out
of my way to Richmond, and made a shift to see the castle, and
look down upon the valley, through which the Swale winds, that
was all the weather would permit. At Rippon I visited the
church, which we had neglected before, with some pleasure, and
saw the Ure full to its brink, and very inclinable to overflow.
Some faint gleams of sunshine gave me an opportunity of walking over Studley, and descending into the ruins of Fountain's
Abbey, which I examined with attention. I passed over the
ugly moor of Harrowgate, made a bow to the Queen's Head,
and got late at night to Leeds; here the rain was so perverse I
could scarce see the town, much less go to Kirkstall Abbey,
which was my intention, so I proceeded to Wakefield and
Wentworth Castle. Here the sun again indulged me, and
opened as beautiful a scene of rich and cultivated country as
(I am told) Yorkshire affords. The water is all artificial, but
with an air of nature, much wood, a very good house in the
Queen Anne style, which is now new-fronting in a far better
taste by the present earl; many pictures not worth a farthing,
and a castle built only for a plaything on the top of the hill as a
point of view, and to command a noble prospect. I went on to
Sheffield, liked the situation in a valley by a pretty river's side,

surrounded with charming hills; saw the handsome parish
church, with the chapel, and monuments of the Talbots. Then
I entered the Peak, a country beyond comparison uglier than
any other I have seen in England, black, tedious, barren, and
not mountainous enough to please one with its horrors. This
is mitigated, since you were there, by a wood like a bowling
green, which soon brought me to Chatsworth. The house has
the air of a palace, the hills rising on three of its sides, shut out
the view of its dreary neighbourhood, and are covered with
wood to their tops; the front opens to the Derwent winding
through the valley, which by the art of Mr. Brown is now always
visible and full to its brim; for heretofore it could not well be
seen (but in rainy seasons) from the windows. A handsome
bridge is lately thrown over it, and the stables taken away,
which stood full in view between the house and the river. The
prospect opens here to a wider tract of country, terminated by
more distant hills; this scene is yet in its infancy, the objects
are thinly scattered, and the clumps and plantations lately
made, but it promises well in time. Within doors the furniture
corresponds to the stateliness of the apartments, fine tapestry,
marble door cases with fruit, flowers, and foliage, excellently
done by old Cibber's father; windows of plate glass in gilded
frames, and such a profusion of Gibbon's best carving in wood,
viz. dead game, fish, shells, flowers, etc., as I never saw any
where. The ceilings and staircases all painted by Verrio or
Laguerre, in their usual sprawling way,[1] and no other pictures
but in one room eight or ten portraits, some of them very good,
of James and Charles the First's time. The gardens are small,
and in the French style, with waterworks, particularly a grand
cascade of steps, and a *temple d'eaux* at the head of it.

From thence I went to Hardwicke.[2] One would think Mary
Queen of Scots was but just walked down into the park with her
guard for half-an-hour. Her gallery, her room of audience, her
anti-chamber with the very canopies, chair of state, footstool,
lit-de-repos, oratory, carpets, and hangings, just as she left them.
A little tattered indeed, but the more venerable, and all preserved with religious care, and papered up in winter. The park
and country are just like Hertfordshire. I went by Chesterfield
and Mansfield to revisit my old friend the Trent at Nottingham,
where I passed two or three days, and from thence took stage
coach to London.

[1] " Where sprawl the saints of Verrio and La Guerre."—*Pope*.
[2] Seat of the Duke of Devonshire in Nottinghamshire.—*Mason*.

When I arrived there, I found Professor Turner [1] had been dead above a fortnight, and being cockered and spirited up by some friends (though it was rather of the latest), I got my name suggested to Lord Bute, you may easily imagine who undertook it,[2] and indeed he did it with zeal. I received my answer very soon, which was what you may easily imagine, but joined with great professions of his *desire to serve me* on any future occasion, and many more fine words that I pass over, not out of modesty, but for another reason. So you see I have made my fortune, like Sir Fr. Wronghead. This *nothing* is a profound secret, and no one here suspects it even now; to-day I hear that Delaval [3] has got it, but we are not yet certain; next to myself I wished for him.

You see we have made a peace. I shall be silent about it, because if I say anything anti-ministerial, you will tell me you know the reason; and if I approve it, you will tell me I have expectations still: all I know is, that the D. of Newcastle and Lord Hardwicke both say it is an excellent peace, and only Mr. Pitt calls it inglorious and insidious.

I had a little gout twice while I was in town, which confined me some time; yet I bespoke your chairs. They are what is called *rout-chairs*, but as they are to be a little better in shape and materials than ordinary, will come to about 6s. 9d. a chair. I desired your brother to judge how he performed, and the first chat was made was to be sent to him to see.

My best respects to Mrs. Wharton, who I suppose receives them in bed. How does she do? My compliments to miss.—I am ever truly yours.

CAMBRIDGE, *Dec.* 4, 1762.

Mason is in Yorkshire now, but I missed of him.

CX.—Mr. GRAY to Mr. BROWN [4]

February 17, 1763.

You will make my best acknowledgements to Mr. Howe; who, not content to rank me in the number of his friends, is so polite as to make excuses for having done me that honour.

---

[1] Professor of Modern Languages in the University of Cambridge.—*Mason*.
[2] This person was the late Sir Henry Erskine. As this was the only application Mr. Gray ever made to ministry, I thought it necessary to insert his own account of it. The place in question was given to the tutor of Sir James Lowther.—*Mason*.
[3] Fellow of Pembroke Hall, and of the Royal Society.—*Mason*.
[4] Now Master of Pembroke Hall.—*Mason*.

I *was not born so far from the sun* as to be ignorant of Count Algarotti's name and reputation; nor am I so far advanced in years, or in philosophy, as not to feel the warmth of his approbation. The odes in question, as their motto shews, were meant to be *vocal to the intelligent alone.* How few *they* were in my own country, Mr. Howe can testify; and yet my ambition was terminated by that small circle. I have good reason to be proud, if my voice has reached the ear and apprehension of a stranger, distinguished as one of the best judges in Europe.

I am equally pleased with the just applause he bestows on Mr. Mason; and particularly on his " Caractacus," which is the work of a man: whereas " Elfrida " is only that of a boy, a promising boy indeed, and of no common genius: yet this is the popular performance, and the other little known in comparison.

Neither Count Algarotti nor Mr. Howe (I believe) have heard of Ossian, the son of Fingal. If Mr. Howe were not upon the wing, and on his way homewards, I would send it to him in Italy. He would there see that Imagination dwelt many hundred years ago, in all her pomp, on the cold and barren mountains of Scotland. The truth (I believe) is, that without any respect of climates, she reigns in all nascent societies of men, where the necessities of life force every one to think and act much for himself. Adieu!

CXI.—Mr. GRAY to Dr. WHARTON

Dear Doctor,

You may well wonder at my long taciturnity: I wonder too, and know not what cause to assign, for it is certain I think of you daily. I believe it is owing to the nothingness of my history, for except six weeks that I passed in town towards the end of spring, and a little jaunt to Epsom and Box-hill, I have been here time out of mind, in a place where no events grow, though we preserve those of former days by way of *hortus siccus* in our libraries. My slumbers were disturbed the other day by an unexpected visit from Mr. Walpole, who dined with me, seemed mighty happy for the time he stayed, and said he could like to live here; but hurried home in the evening to his new gallery, which is all gothicism and gold, and crimson, and looking-glass. He has purchased, at an auction in Suffolk, ebony chairs and old moveables, enough to load a waggon.

Mason and I have received letters from Count Algarotti, Chambellan de sa Majesté le Roi de Prusse, with observations (that is panegyrics) on our tragedies and our odes, and a present of certain Italian dissertations, which he has lately published, on the state of painting and musick: one of them is dedicated to Mr. Pitt, whom he styles—*Uomo immortale e Restitutore d'Inghilterra Amico del gran Frederico.*

I was in town when Mr. Middleton died, and immediately got all the information I could (first from Stonehewer, and then from your brother) of the dispositions he had made. I suppose they are as good as you expected, and though the prospect is but small that you should enjoy the benefit of them in your own person, yet that is not impossible; and your son (I think) stands a very good chance, which cannot chuse but open an agreeable prospect to you, in which I take a part, and congratulate you both upon it. I doubt you have not read Rousseau's *Emile* : [1] everybody that has children should read it more than once, for though it abounds with his usual glorious absurdity, though his general scheme of education be an impracticable chimera; yet there are a thousand lights struck out, a thousand important truths better expressed than ever they were before, that may be of service to the wisest man; particularly, I think, he has observed children with more attention, and knows their meaning and the working of their little passions better than any other writer. As to his religious discussions, which have alarmed the world, and engaged their thoughts more than any other part of his book, I set them all at nought, and wish they had been omitted. Mrs. Jonathan told me you begun your evening prayer as soon as I was gone, and that it had a great effect upon the congregation: I hope you have not grown weary of it, nor lay it aside when company

[1] That I may put together the rest of Mr. Gray's sentiments concerning this singular writer, I insert here an extract from a letter of a later date, written to myself. " I have not read the *Philosophic Dictionary*. I can now stay with great patience for anything that comes from Voltaire. They tell me it is flippery, and blasphemy, and wit. I could have forgiven myself if I had not read Rousseau's *Lettres de la Montagne*. Always excepting the contract social, it is the dullest performance he ever published. It is a weak attempt to separate the miracles from the morality of the gospel. The latter (he would have you think) he believes was sent from God; and the former he very explicitly takes for an imposture: this is in order to prove the cruelty and injustice of the State of Geneva in burning his *Emile*. The latter part of his book is to show the abuses that have crept into the constitution of his country, which point, if you are concerned about it, he makes out very well; and his intention in this is plainly to raise a tumult in the city, and to be revenged on the *Petit Conseil*, who condemned his writings to the flames."—*Mason.*

comes.   Poor Mrs. Bonfoy (who taught me to pray) is dead
she struggled near a week against the iliac passion (I fear) in
great torture, with all her senses about her, and with much
resolution took leave of her physician some days before she
expired, and would suffer no one to see her afterwards but
common servants.

You describe Winston *con tanto amore*, that I take it amiss
was not suffered to see it, and want to be buried there too
But enough of death! I have forgot to tell you that Dr. Long has
had an audience of the king and queen, an hour long, at Bucking
ham House.   His errand was to present them with a lyricore
(such a one!) of his own making, and a glass sphere: he had long
been soliciting this honour, which Lord Bute at last procured
him, and he is very happy.   The king told him he bid fair for a
century of life at least; asked him whether he preached; why
he did not write verses in the Cambridge collection; and what
not!   The Q. spoke French to him, and asked how he liked
Handel.   And I ask you how you like the present times;
whether you had not rather be a printer's devil than a secretary
of state?   You are to expect (I hear) a new ministry, composed
of the Earl of Shelburne, Mr. Rigby, Duke and Dutchess of
Bedford, Earl Gower, etc., which doubtless will give universal
satisfaction.   The great Lord Holland, who is at Paris, being
lately asked by a young man, who was returning home, whether
he had any commands in England, made no reply but by
shrugging up his shoulders and fetching a deep sigh.

I kept an exact account of heat and cold here in the spring
the sum and substance of which is, that (at nine in the morning
on the 18th of January the therm. was at 31; and the small
birds were so tame you might take them up with your hand
this was the greatest cold.   On the 15th of April it was at 58
and the same afternoon at 65, which was the greatest heat from
Jan. to May 1st.

Feb.   3. Snowdrops flowered.
       12. Crocus and hepatica fl. the snow then lieing, and therm. at 45
       18. Chaffinch sings.   Bees appear.
       21. White butterfly abroad.
       25. Gnats fly, and large flies.   Mezereon fl.
       27. Honeysuckle and gooseberry unfold their leaves.
March   1. Violet flowers (in the garden).   Rose opens its leaf.
        3. Daffodil and single hyacinth fl.   Spider spins.
        5. Thrush singing.
        6. Elder in leaf.   Currant and weeping willow in leaf.
        8. Apricot blows.   Skylark singing.
       11. Wind very high at S.E. which continued with hard frost.
       16. Frost gone.

March 18. Apricot in full bloom.
19. Almond flowers. Lilac, barberry, and guelder-rose in leaf.
April 2. Standard apricot, and wall-pears flower. Quince, apple, and sweet-briar in leaf. Currant flowers. Dutch elm opens its leaf.
4. Plumb in leaf.
5. Crown imperial fl.
6. Plumb flowers; hawthorn, horse-chesnut, mountain-ash in leaf.
9. Lime-tree in leaf; jonquil and single anemone flower. Lady-birds seen.
11. Cowslip flowers, and auriculas. Swallows appear. Young rooks caw in the nest.
14. Red-start appears. Cherries in full bloom.
15. Frontignac vine in leaf; double wall-flower blows.
16. Nigthingale sings. Apple blossoms.
April 19. Chaffinch and red-start sit on their eggs.
20. Elm, willow, and ash in flower (with the blackthorn), haw-thorn in full leaf.
21. Sycamore quite green. Oak puts out.

Pray present my respects to Mrs. and Miss Wharton.—I am ver sincerely yours.

PEMBROKE, *August 5th*, 1763.

We have nothing but rain and thunder of late.

CXII.—MR. GRAY TO COUNT ALGAROTTI

CAMBRIDGE, *Sep. 9th*, 1763.

SIR,

I received some time since the unexpected honour of a letter from you and the promise of a pleasure which till of late I had not the opportunity of enjoying. Forgive me if I make my acknowledgements in my native tongue, as I see it is perfectly familiar to you, and I (though not unacquainted with the writings of Italy) should from disuse speak its language with an ill grace, and with still more constraint to one who possesses it in all its strength and purity.

I see with great satisfaction your efforts to reunite the congenial arts of poetry, music, and the dance, which with the assistance of painting and architecture, regulated by taste, and supported by magnificence and power, might form the noblest scene, and bestow the sublimest pleasure, that the imagination can conceive. But who shall realise these delightful visions? There is, I own, one prince in Europe that wants neither the will, the spirit, nor the ability: but can he call up Milton from his grave? can he re-animate Marcello, or bid the Barbeuna or the Sallé move again? can he (as much a king as he is) govern

an Italian *virtuosa*, destroy her caprice and impertinence
without hurting her talents, or command those unmeaning
graces and tricks of voice to be silent that have gained th
adoration of her own country?

One cause that so long has hindered, and (I fear) will hinde
that happy union, which you propose, seems to be this: tha
poetry (which, as you allow, must lead the way, and direct th
operation of the subordinate arts) implies at least a libera
education, a degree of literature, and various knowledge, wherea
the others (with a few exceptions) are in the hands of slaves an
mercenaries, I mean of people without education, who, thoug
neither destitute of genius, nor insensible to fame, must yet mak
gain their principal end, and subject themselves to the prevailin
taste of those whose fortune only distinguishes them from th
multitude.

I cannot help telling you, that eight or ten years ago I was
witness to the power of your comic music.—There was a littl
troop of buffi that exhibited a burletta in London, not in th
Opera House, where the audience is chiefly of the better sor
but on one of the common theatres full of all kinds of peopl
and (I believe) the fuller from that natural aversion we bear t
foreigners; their looks and their noise made it evident they di
not come thither to hear; and on similar occasions I have know
candles lighted, broken bottles, and penknives flung on th
stage, the benches torn up, the scenes hurried into the stree
and set on fire. The curtain drew up, the music was of Cocch
with a few airs of Pergolesi interspersed. The singers were (a
usual) deplorable, but there was one girl (she called herself th
Niccolina) with little voice and less beauty; but with the utmos
justness of ear, the strongest expression of countenance, th
most speaking eyes, the greatest vivacity and variety of gestur
Her first appearance instantly fixed their attention; the tumu
sunk at once, or if any murmur rose, it was hushed by a genera
cry for silence. Her first air ravished everybody; they forgo
their prejudices, they forgot that they did not understand
word of the language; they entered into all the humour of th
part; made her repeat all her songs, and continued their tran
sports, their laughter, and applause to the end of the piec
Within these three last years the Paganini and Amici have me
with almost the same applause once a week from a polit
audience on the opera stage. The truth is, the opera itsel
though supported here at a great expense for so many year
has rather maintained itself by the admiration bestowed on

ew particular voices, on the borrowed taste of a few men of condition, that have learned in Italy how to admire, than by any genuine love we bear to the best Italian music: nor have we yet got any style of our own, and this I attribute in great measure to the language, which in spite of its energy, plenty, and the crowd of excellent writers this nation has produced, does yet (I am sorry to say it) retain too much of its barbarous original to adapt itself to musical composition. I by no means wish to have been born anything but an Englishman; yet I should rejoice to exchange tongues with Italy. Why this nation has made no advances hitherto in painting and sculpture it is hard to say. The fact is undeniable, and we have the vanity to apologise for ourselves, as Virgil did for the Romans, *Excudent alii, etc.* It is sure that architecture had introduced itself in the reign of the unfortunate Charles I., and Inigo Jones has left us some few monuments of his skill, that shew him capable of greater things. Charles had not only a love for the beautiful arts, but some taste in them. The confusion that soon followed swept away his magnificent collection; the artists were dispersed, or ruined, and the arts disregarded till very lately. The young monarch now on the throne is said to esteem and understand them. I wish he may have the leisure to cultivate and the skill to encourage them with due regard to merit; otherwise it is better to neglect them. You, sir, have pointed out the true sources and the best examples to your countrymen; they have nothing to do but to be what they once were: and yet perhaps it is more difficult to restore good taste to a nation, that has degenerated, than to introduce it in one, where as yet it has never flourished. You are generous enough to wish, and sanguine enough to foresee, that it shall one day flourish in England. I too must wish, but can hardly extend my hopes so far. It is well for us that you do not see our public exhibitions.—But our artists are yet in their infancy, and therefore I will not absolutely despair.

I owe to Mr. How the honour I have of conversing with Count Algarotti, and it seems as if I meant to indulge myself in the opportunity: but I have done. Sir, I will only add that I am proud of your approbation, having no relish for any other fame than what is conferred by the few real judges, that are so thinly scattered over the face of the earth.

I am, sir, with great respect,
Your most obliged humble servant,
T. GRAY.

CXIII.—Mr. GRAY to Dr. WHARTON

CAMBRIDGE, *July* 10, 1764.

Dear Doctor,

I do remember, and shall ever remember, as I ought, you extreme kindness in offering to be present, and to assist me i the *perilous hour*. When I received your letter I was please to find I had done everything almost that you advised. Th fault lay in deferring matters too long.

.   .   .   .

Nine or ten strokes of the lancet, and the application of caustic, with fomentations innumerable, I suffered manfully indeed the pain in idea is much greater than in reality, and no I am glad I know it. It is certain, I am better at present tha I had been in at least a year before the operation. I shoul tell you, that for some days before I submitted to it, I ha taken soap in large quantities, and for aught I know, the i flammation might be rather increased by it. Dr. Whytt remember) speaking of the use of lime-water and soap, say that if the patient be subject to the piles, he must omit th latter. Towards the end of my confinement, during which (yo may believe) I lived on nothing, came the gout in one foot, b *so tame you might have stroked it ;* [1] such a *minikin*, you migl have played with it; in three or four days it disappeared.

It was true, as Stonehewer told you, that I had a gre tendency towards Old Park and Hart-le-pool; but on prude consideration I find I cannot well afford it, and must defer th pleasure to another summer. The minikin and I act upon t same principles: she cannot be a river, nor I a traveller, witho money. If we had but a *head*, we should, both of us, make figure in the world.

Mason does not seem very impatient, for he writes word th he is busy in modelling antique vases in clay; and in reading course of ecclesiastical history, when I expected *consummatio* and was praying heaven to give him a good and gentle governes

[1] George Montagu said of our last earthquake " that it was so tame y might have stroked it." Walpole's *Letters*, v. 491. I have mention several coincidences of thought and expression of this kind in the lette of Gray and Walpole, which I conceived to be a kind of common propert the reader indeed will recognise much of that species of humour whi distinguishes Gray's correspondence in the letters of Walpole, inferior think, in its comic force; sometimes deviating too far from propriety search of subjects for the display of its talent, and not altogether free fro affectation.—*Mitford.*

o man wants such a thing more, in all senses; but his greatest
vants do not make him move a foot the faster, nor has he,
roperly speaking, anything one can call a passion about him,
xcept a little malice and revenge.

Our election is in Westminster Hall; but it is not likely that
ny great matter can be done in it till Michaelmas term next.
n the meantime Lord Sandwich and his friends do what they
an to keep up an interest and a bustle. Here is a poor scribbler
hat he hires to write a weekly paper called the *Scrutator*, who
y abuse of characters does all in his power to provoke people;
ut cannot so much as get himself answered. I could not find
ny one in town that ever heard of it (though the subject is
vell known there), and if anybody saw its name in the advertise-
1ents, I believe they only took it for a *scrutoire* to be sold.
'he nation is in the same hands as the university, and really
oes not make so manful a resistance. Grumble indeed every
ne does, but since Wilkes's affair, they fall off their metal, and
eem to shrink under the brazen hand of Norton and his
olleagues.

I hear there will be no parliament till after Christmas. If
he French should be so unwise as to suffer the Spanish Court
o go on in their present measures (for they refuse to pay the
ansom of Manilla, and have driven away our logwood cutters
lready), down go their friends in the ministry, and all the
chemes of right divine, and prerogative; and this is perhaps
1e best chance we have. Are you not struck with the great
imilarity there is between the first years of Charles I. and the
resent times? who would have thought it possible five years
go?

The old rogue Lord Bath is dead at last. I understood the
ontest for his spoils lay between your noble friend at Raby,
nd Mr. Colman, the comic poet, but whether they are fallen to
ther of them I have not heard as yet. Pray, what is the policy
f that castle? the elder brother lives more than usual in the
ountry, as if he were not in the best humour with his friends at
ourt; and the younger has been at times an orator in the
pposition. Have they been disobliged, or do they fear to
isoblige their former friends who may come into play again?

Two more volumes of Buffon are come over; I mention
1em in case you choose to have them. I know of nothing else,
xcept half a dozen new works of that inexhaustible, eternal,
itertaining scribbler Voltaire, who at last (I fear) will go to
eaven, for to him entirely it is owing that the king of France

and his council have received and set aside the decision of th
parliament of Thoulouse in the affair of Calas. The poor man
'tis true, has been broke on the wheel long ago; but his widow
and wretched family may have some reparation, and his
murtherers may smart a little for it.   You see a scribbler may
be of some use in the world.

If you see Stonehewer at his return from Buxton, be so good
to tell him that there will be only 200 [1] copies of Lord Herbert's
Life printed, half of which are for Lord Powis, and the rest will
be given away only.   If I happen to have two (which I do not
expect) he shall have one of them.

Ah! poor James Lyon!—how do the family bear it?   My
best respects to the lady of Old Park (the duchess I should say),
and Lady Mary, etc., I hope they are all well.   Are Mr. and Mrs
Jonathan with you?   Do you say your prayers o'nights? Adieu

I am ever yours,

T. G.

Mr. Brown, who is quite well, presents his humble service
He would wish to come to-morrow, only he thinks it impossible
and does not believe anybody did ever really go so far.

CXIV.—Mr. GRAY to Mr. NICHOLLS

I, RECEIVED your letter at Southampton; and as I would wish
to treat everybody according to their own rule and measure of
good breeding, have, against my inclination, waited till now
before I answered it, purely out of fear and respect, and an
ingenuous diffidence of my own abilities.   If you will not take
this as an excuse, accept it at least as a well-turned period,
which is always my principal concern.

So I proceed to tell you that my health is much improved
by the sea, not that I drank it, or bathed in it, as the common
people do: no!   I only walked by it, and looked upon it.   The
climate is remarkably mild, even in October and November;
no snow has been seen to lie there for these thirty years past,
the myrtles grow in the ground against the houses, and Guernsey
lilies bloom in every window;   the town, clean and well-built
surrounded by its old stone-walls, with their towers and gate

---

[1] The *Life of Lord Herbert of Cherbury*, for the first time printed at the
Strawberry Hill Press, in small 4to in 1764.   200 copies.   See Walpole
Works, ii. p. 515.—*Mitford.*

vays, stands at the point of a peninsula, and opens full south
o an arm of the sea, which, having formed two beautiful bays
on each hand of it, stretches away in direct view, till it joins
he British Channel; it is skirted on either side with gently-
ising grounds, cloathed with thick wood, and directly cross its
mouth rise the high lands of the Isle of Wight at distance, but
distinctly seen. In the bosom of the woods (concealed from
profane eyes) lie hid the ruins of Netley Abbey; there may be
icher and greater houses of religion, but the abbot is content
with his situation. See there, at the top of that hanging
meadow, under the shade of those old trees that bend into a
half circle about it, he is walking slowly (good man!) and
bidding his beads for the souls of his benefactors, interred in
hat venerable pile that lies beneath him. Beyond it (the
meadow still descending) nods a thicket of oaks that mask the
building, and have excluded a view too garish and luxuriant
or a holy eye; only on either hand they leave an opening to
he blue glittering sea. Did you not observe how, as that
white sail shot by and was lost, he turned and crossed himself
o drive the tempter from him that had thrown that distraction
in his way? I should tell you that the ferryman who rowed
me, a lusty young fellow, told me that he would not for all the
world pass a night at the abbey (there were such things seen
near it) though there was a power of money hid there. From
hence I went to Salisbury, Wilton, and Stonehenge; but of
hese I say no more, they will be published at the university
press.

P.S. I must not close my letter without giving you one
principal event of my history; which was, that (in the course
of my late tour) I set out one morning before five o'clock, the
moon shining through a dark and misty autumnal air, and got
o the seacoast time enough to be at the sun's levee. I saw
he clouds and dark vapours open gradually to right and left,
rolling over one another in great smoky wreaths, and the tide
as it flowed gently in upon the sands) first whitening, then
slightly tinged with gold and blue; and all at once a little line
of insufferable brightness that (before I can write these five
words) was grown to half an orb, and now to a whole one, too
glorious to be distinctly seen. It is very odd it makes no figure
on paper; yet I shall remember it as long as the sun, or at least
as long as I endure. I wonder whether anybody ever saw it
before? I hardly believe it.

CXV.—Mr. GRAY to Mr. WALPOLE

Sunday, Dec. 30, 1764.

I HAVE received the " Castle of Otranto," and return you m
thanks for it.   It engages our attention here,[1] makes some c
us cry a little, and all in general afraid to go to bed o' night
We take it for a translation, and should believe it to be a tru
story, if it were not for St. Nicholas.

When your pen was in your hand you might have been
little more communicative, for though disposed enough t
believe the opposition rather consumptive, I am entirel
ignorant of all the symptoms.   Your canonical book I have bee
reading with great satisfaction.   He speaketh as one havin
authority.   If Englishmen have any feeling left, methinks the
must feel now; and if the ministry have any feeling (whom
nobody will suspect of insensibility) they must cut off th
author's ears, for it is in all the forms a most wicked libel.   I
the old man and the lawyer put on, or is it real? or has som
real lawyer furnished a good part of the materials, and anothe
person employed them?   This I guess; for there is an uncouth
ness of diction in the beginning which is not supported through
out, though it now and then occurs again, as if the writer [2] wa
weary of supporting the character he had assumed, when th
subject had warmed him, beyond dissimulation.

Rousseau's *Letters* I am reading heavily, heavily!   H
justifies himself, till he convinces me that he deserved to b
burnt, at least that his book did.   I am not got through hin
and you never will.   Voltaire I detest, and have not seen hi
book: I shall in good time.   You surprise me, when you tal
of going in [3] February.   Pray, does all the minority go too
I hope you have a reason.   *Desperare de republica* is a deadl
sin in politics.

Adieu! I will not take my leave of you; for (you perceiv
this letter means to beg another, when you can spare a little.

---

[1] At Cambridge.
[2] Mr. Gray may probably allude to a pamphlet called " A Letter concern
ing Libels, Warrants, Seizure of Papers, and Security for the Peace c
Behaviour, with a View to some late Proceedings, and the Defence of ther
by the Majority: "—supposed to have been written by William Greave
Esq., a master in Chancery, under the inspection of the late Lord Camder
—Ed. of Walpole's *Works*.   [3] To Paris.

CXVII.—Mr. GRAY to Dr. WHARTON

Dear Doctor,

I deferred writing to you till I had seen a little more of this country than you yourself had seen, and now being just returned from an excursion, which I and the major have been making into the Highlands, I sit down to tell you about it: but first I must return to my journey hither, on which I shall be very short, partly because you know the way as far as Edinburgh, and partly that there was not a great deal worth remarking. The first night we passed at Tweedmouth (77 miles), the next at Edinburgh (53 miles), where Lord Strathmore left the major and me, to go to Lenox-love (Ld. Blantyre's) where his aunt lives. So that afternoon and all next day I had leisure to visit the castle, Holy-Rood-House, Heriot's Hospital, Arthur's Seat, etc., and am not sorry to have seen that most picturesque (at a distance) and nastiest (when near) of all capital cities.

I supped with Dr. Robertson and other literati, and the next morning Lord S. came for us. We crossed the Queen's Ferry in a four-oared yawl, without a sail, and were tossed about rather more than I should wish to hazard again. Lay at Perth, a large *Scotch* town, with much wood about it, on the banks of the Tay, a very noble river: next morning ferried over it, and came by dinner time to Glamis, being (from Edinburgh) 67 miles; which makes in all from Hetton, 197 miles. The castle stands in Strathmore (that is the great valley), which winds about from Stonehaven on the east coast of Kincairdinshire, obliquely as far as Stirling, near 100 miles in length, and from 7 to 10 miles in breadth, cultivated everywhere to the foot of the hills on either hand with oats or bere-barley, except where the soil is mere peat earth (black as a coal), or barren sand covered only with broom and heath, or a short grass fit for sheep. Here and there appear, just above ground, the huts of the inhabitants, which they call towns, built of and covered with turf; and among them, at great distances, the gentlemen's houses, with inclosures and a few trees round them. Amidst these our castle distinguishes itself, the middle part of it rising proudly out of what seems a thick wood of tall trees, with a cluster of hanging towers at the top. You descend to it gradually from the south, through a double and triple avenue of Scotch firs, 60 or 70 feet high, under three gateways. This approach is a full mile long, and when you have passed the second gate, the firs change to limes, and another oblique avenue goes off on either hand toward the offices; these as well as all the enclosures that surround the house, are bordered with three or four ranks of sycamores, ashes, and white poplars of the noblest height, and from 70 to 100 years old. Other alleys there are that go off at right angles with the long one, small groves and walled gardens of Earl Patrick's planting, full of broad leaved elms, oaks, birch, black cherry trees, laburnums, etc., all of great stature and size, which have not till this week begun to show the least sense of morning frosts. The third gate delivers you into a court with a broad pavement and grass plats, adorned with statues of the four Stuart kings, bordered with old silver firs and yew trees alternately, and opening with an iron palisade on either side to two square old-fashioned parterres, surrounded by stone fruit walls. The house from the height of it, the greatness of its mass, the many towers atop, the spread of its wings, has really a very singular and striking appearance, like nothing I ever saw. You will comprehend something of its shape from the plan of the second floor, which I enclose; the wings are about 50 feet high, the body (which is the old castle with walls 10 feet thick) is near 100 from the leads. I see to the south of me (just at the end of the avenue) the little town of Glames, the houses built of stone and slated; with a neat kirk and small square tower (a rarity in this region), just beyond it rises a beautiful round hill, and another ridge of a larger form adjacent to it, both covered with woods of tall fir: beyond them peep over the black hills of *Sid-law*, over which winds the road to Dundee. To the north, within about seven miles of me begin to rise the Grampians, hill above hill, on whose tops three weeks ago I could plainly see some traces of the snow that fell in May last. To the east winds away the *Strath* such as I have before described it, among the hills which sink lower and lower as they approach the sea. To the west, the same valley (no plain, but broken, unequal ground) runs on far above twenty miles in view. There I see the crags above Dunkeld; there *Beni-gloe* and *Beni-more* rise above the clouds, and there is that *She-Khallian* that spires into a cone above them all, and lies at least forty-five miles (in a direct line) from this place. L^{d.} S who is the greatest farmer in this neighbourhood, is from break of day to dark night among his husbandmen and labourers; he has near 2000 acres of lands in his own hand, and is at present employed in building a low wall of four miles long; and in widening the bed of the little river *Deane*, which runs to S. and

S.E. of the house, from about twenty to fifty feet wide, both to prevent inundations and to drain the lake of Forfar. This work will be two years more in completing; and must be three miles in length. All the Highlanders that can be got are employed in it; many of them know no English, and I hear them singing Erse-songs all day long. The price of labour is eightpence a day; but to such as will join together and engage to perform a certain portion in a limited time, two shillings. I must say that all our labours seem to prosper, and my L^d. has casually found in digging such quantities of shell-marle, as not only to fertilise his own grounds, but are disposed of at a good price to all his neighbours. In his nurseries are thousands of oaks, beech, larches, horse-chesnuts, spruce-fir, etc., thick as they can stand, and whose only fault is, that they are grown tall and vigorous before he has determined where to plant them out. The most advantageous spot we have for beauty lies west of the house, where (when the stone walls of the meadows are taken away) the grounds (naturally unequal) will have a very park-like appearance, they are already full of trees, which need only thinning here and there to break the regularity of their lines, and through them winds the *Burn of Glames*, a clear and rapid trout-stream, which joins the R. Deane hard by. Pursuing the course of this brook upwards, you come to a narrow sequestered valley, sheltered from all winds, through which it runs murmuring among great stones; on one hand the ground gently rises into a hill, on the other are the rocky banks of the rivulet almost perpendicular, yet covered with sycamore, ash, and fir, that (though it seems to have no place or soil to grow in, yet) has risen to a good height, and forms a thick shade. You may continue along this gill, and passing by one end of the village and its church for half a mile, it leads to an opening between the two hills covered with fir-woods that I mentioned above, through which the stream makes its way, and forms a cascade of ten or twelve feet over broken rocks. A very little art is necessary to make all this a beautiful scene. The weather till the last week has been in general very fine and warm: we have had no fires till now, and often have sat with the windows open an hour after sunset. Now and then a shower has come, and sometimes sudden gusts of wind descend from the mountains that finish as suddenly as they arose: but to-day it blows a hurricane. Upon the whole I have been exceedingly lucky in my weather, and particularly in my highland expedition of five days.

We set out then the 11th of September, and continuing along the Strath to the west passed through *Megill* (where is the tomb of *Queen Wanders, that was riven to dethe by staned-horses for nae gude that she did.* So the women there told me, I am sure), through Cowper of Angus, over the river Ila, then over a wide and dismal heath fit for an assembly of witches, till we came to a string of four small lakes in a valley, whose deep blue waters, and green margin, with a gentleman's house or two seated on them in little groves, contrasted with the black desert in which they were enclosed. The ground now grew unequal; the hills more rocky seemed to close in upon us, till the road came to the brow of a steep descent, and (the sun then setting) between two woods of oak we saw far below us the river Tay come sweeping along at the bottom of a precipice, at least 150 feet deep, clear as glass, full to the brim, and very rapid in its course. It seemed to issue out of woods thick and tall, that rose on either hand, and were overhung by broken rocky crags of vast height; above them to the west, the tops of higher mountains appeared, on which the evening clouds reposed. Down by the side of the river, under the thickest shades is seated the town of Dunkeld; in the midst of it stands a round cathedral, the towers and shell of the building still entire; a little beyond it a large house of the Duke of Athol with its offices and gardens extends a mile beyond the town; and as his grounds were interrupted by the streets and roads, he has flung arches of communication across them, that add to the scenery of the place, which of itself is built of good white stone, and handsomely slated, so that no one would take it for a Scotch town till they came into it; here we passed the night. If I told you how, you would bless yourself. Next day we set forward to Taymouth twenty-seven miles farther west; the road winding through beautiful woods, with the Tay almost always in full view to the right, being here from three to four hundred feet over. The Strath-Tay, from a mile to three miles or more wide, covered with corn, and spotted with groups of people, then in the midst of their harvest; on either hand a vast chain of rocky mountains, that changed their face, and opened something new every hundred yards, as the way turned, or the clouds passed. In short, altogether it was one of the most pleasing days I have passed these many years, and at every step I wished for you. At the close of the day we came to *Balloch*,[1] so the place was called, but now for decency

---

[1] Mr. Pennant, in his tour in Scotland, explains this word " the Mouth of the Loch."—*Mason.*

Taymouth; improperly enough, for here it is that the river issues out of Loch Tay (a glorious lake fifteen miles long, and one and a half broad), surrounded with prodigious mountains. There on its north-eastern brink impending over it, is the vast hill of Lawers; to the east is that monstrous creation of God, *She-khallian* (*i.e.* the Maiden's Pap), spiring above the clouds. Directly west (beyond the end of the lake) *Beni-more* (the great mountain) rises to a most awful height, and looks down on the tomb of Fingal. Lord Braidalbane's *policy* (so they call here all such ground as is laid out for pleasure) takes in about 2000 acres, of which his house, offices, and a deer-park about three miles round, occupy the plain or bottom, which is little above a mile in breadth; through it winds the Tay, which by means of a bridge I found here to be 156 feet over. His plantations and woods rise with the ground on either side of the vale, to the very summit of the enormous crags that overhang it; along them on the mountain's side runs a terrass one mile and a half long, that overlooks the course of the river. From several seats and temples perched on particular rocky eminences you command the lake for many miles in length, which turns like some huge river, and loses itself among the mountains that surround it. At its eastern extremity where the river issues out of it, on a peninsula, my lord has built a neat little town, and church, with a high square tower, and just before it lies a small round island in the lake covered with trees, amongst which are the ruins of some little religious house. Trees (by the way) grow here to great size and beauty. I saw four old chesnuts in the road, as you enter the park, of vast bulk and height. One beech tree I measured that was sixteen feet seven inches in the girth and (I guessed) near eighty feet in height. The gardener presented us with peaches, nectarines, and plums from the stone walls of the kitchen garden (for there are no brick nor hot walls); the peaches were good, the rest well tasted but scarce ripe. We had also golden-pippins from an espalier (not ripe), and a melon very well flavoured and fit to cut. Of the house I have little to say, it is a very good nobleman's house, handsomely furnished, and well kept, very comfortable to inhabit, but not worth going far to see. Of the earl's taste I have not much more to say, it is one of those noble situations that man cannot spoil; it is, however, certain that he has built an inn and a town just where his principal walks should have been, and in the most wonderful spot of ground that perhaps belongs to him. In this inn however we lay, and next day returning down the river four miles, we passed it over a fine bridge, built at the expense of the government, and continued our way to Loije-Rait, just below which, in a most charming scene, the *Tummell*, which is here the larger river of the two, falls into the Tay. We ferried over the Tummell, in order to get into Marshal Wade's road (which leads from Dunkeld to Inverness), and continued our way along it toward the north. The road is excellent, but dangerous enough in conscience, the river often running directly under us at the bottom of a precipice 200 feet deep, sometimes masqued indeed by wood, that finds means to grow where I could not stand; but very often quite naked and without any defence: in such places we walked for miles together, partly for fear, and partly to admire the beauty of the country; which the beauty of the weather set off to the greatest advantage. As evening came on, we approached the Pass of Gillikrankie, where in the year 1745 the Hessians with their prince at their head stopped short and refused to march a foot farther.

> " Vestibulum ante ipsum primisq; in faucibus Orci,"

stands the solitary mansion of Mr. Robinson of Faseley. Close by it rises a hill covered with oak, with grotesque masses of rock staring from among their trunks, like the sullen countenances of Fingal and all his family frowning on the little mortals of modern days. From between this hill and the adjacent mountains, pent in a narrow channel, comes roaring out the river Tummell, and falls headlong down, enclosed in white foam, which rises into a mist all round it.—But my paper is deficient, and I must say nothing of the pass itself, the black river Garry, the Blair of Athol, Mount Beni-gloe, my return (by another road) to Dunkeld the Hermitage, the *Stra-Brann*, and the rumbling Brigg. In short, since I saw the Alps I have seen nothing sublime till now. In about a week I shall set forward by the Stirling road on my return all alone. Pray for me till I see you, for I dread Edinburgh and the itch; and expect to find very little in my way worth the perils I am to endure. My best compliments to Mrs Wharton and the young ladies (including herself), and to Mr and Mrs. Jonathan, if they are with you. Adieu!

I am ever yours,

T. G.

[GLAMES, *Sept.* 1765.]

CXVIII.—Mr. GRAY to Mr. BEATTIE [1]

GLAMES CASTLE, *Sept.* 8, 1765.

A LITTLE journey I have been making to Arbroath has been the cause that I did not answer your very obliging letter so soon as I ought to have done. A man of merit, that honours me with his esteem, and has the frankness to tell me so, doubtless can need no excuses: his apology is made, and we are already acquainted, however distant from each other.

I fear I cannot (as I would wish) do myself the pleasure of waiting on you at Aberdeen, being under an engagement to go to-morrow to Taymouth, and, if the weather will allow it, to the Blair of Athol: this will take up four or five days, and at my return the approach of winter will scarce permit me to think of any further expeditions northwards. My stay here will, however, be a fortnight or three weeks longer; and if in that time any business or invitation should call you this way, Lord Strathmore gives me commission to say he shall be extremely glad to see you at Glames; and doubt not it will be a particular satisfaction to me to receive and thank you in person for the favourable sentiments you have entertained of me, and the civilities with which you have honoured me.

CXIX.—Mr. GRAY to Mr. BEATTIE

GLAMES CASTLE, *Oct.* 2, 1765.

I MUST beg you would present my most grateful acknowledgments to your society for the public mark of their esteem, which you say they are disposed to confer on me.[2] I embrace, with so deep and just a sense of their goodness, the substance of that honour they do me, that I hope it may plead my pardon with them if I do not accept the form. I have been, sir, for several years a member of the University of Cambridge, and formerly (when I had some thoughts of the profession) took a Bachelor of Laws' degree there; since that time, though long qualified by my standing, I have always neglected to finish my course, and claim my doctor's degree: judge, therefore, whether it will

[1] Professor of Moral Philosophy and Logic in the Marischal College, Aberdeen.—*Mason.*

[2] The Marischal College of Aberdeen had desired to know whether it would be agreeable to Mr. Gray to receive from them the degree of Doctor of Laws. Mr. Beattie wrote to him on the subject, and this is the answer. —*Mason.*

not look like a slight, and some sort of contempt, if I receive
the same degree from a sister university. I certainly would
avoid giving any offence to a set of men among whom I have
passed so many easy, and I may say, happy hours of my life;
yet shall ever retain in my memory the obligations you have
laid me under, and be proud of my connection with the University of Aberdeen.

It is a pleasure to me to find that you are not offended with
the liberties I took when you were at Glames; you took me too
literally, if you thought I meant in the least to discourage you
in your pursuit of poetry: all I intended to say was, that if
either vanity (that is, a general and undistinguishing desire of
applause), or interest, or ambition has any place in the breast
of a poet, he stands a great chance in these our days of being
severely disappointed; and yet, after all these passions are
suppressed, there may remain in the mind of one, "*ingenti
perculsus amore*" (and such I take you to be), incitements of a
better sort, strong enough to make him write verse all his life,
both for his own pleasure and that of all posterity.

I am sorry for the trouble you have had to gratify my curiosity
and love of superstition;[1] yet I heartily thank you. On Monday,
sir, I set forward on my way to England; where if I can be of
any little use to you, or should ever have the good fortune to
see you, it will be a particular satisfaction to me. Lord Strathmore and the family here desire me to make their compliments
to you.

P.S. Remember Dryden, and be blind to all his faults.[2]

CXX.—Mr. GRAY to Mr. NICHOLLS

It is long since that I heard you were gone in haste into Yorkshire
on account of your mother's illness, and the same letter informed
me that she was recovered, otherwise I had then wrote to you
only to beg you would take care of her, and to inform you that I

---

[1] Mr. Gray, when in Scotland, had been very inquisitive after the popular
superstitions of the country; his correspondent sent him two books on
this subject, foolish ones indeed, as might be expected, but the best that
could be had; a *History of Second-sight*, and a *History of Witches.—Mason.*

[2] Mr. Beattie, it seems, in their late interview, had expressed himself
with less admiration of Dryden than Mr. Gray thought his due. He told
him in reply, "that if there was any excellence in his own numbers, he had
learned it wholly from that great poet. And pressed him with great
earnestness to study him, as his choice of words and versification were
singularly happy and harmonious."—*Mason.*

had discovered a thing very little known, which is, that in one's whole life one can never have any more than a single mother. You may think this is obvious, and (what you call) a trite observation. You are a green gosling! I was at the same age (very near) as wise as you, and yet I never discovered this (with full evidence and conviction I mean) till it was too late. It is thirteen years ago, and seems but as yesterday, and every day I live it sinks deeper into my heart.[1] Many a corollary could I draw from this axiom for your use (not for my own), but I will leave you the merit of doing it for yourself. Pray tell me how your health is: I conclude it perfect, as I hear you offered yourself as a guide to Mr. Palgrave into the Sierra-Morena of Yorkshire. For me, I passed the end of May and all June in Kent, not disagreeably. In the west part of it, from every eminence, the eye catches some long reach of the Thames or Medway, with all their shipping; in the east the sea breaks in upon you, and mixes its white transient sails and glittering blue expanse with the deeper and brighter greens of the woods and corn. This sentence is so fine I am quite ashamed; but no matter! you must translate it into prose. Palgrave, if he heard it, would cover his face with his pudding sleeve. I do not tell you of the great and small beasts, and creeping things innumerable, that I met with, because you do not suspect that this world is inhabited by anything but men, and women, and clergy, and such two-legged cattle. Now I am here again very disconsolate, and all alone, for Mr. Brown is gone, and the cares of this world are coming thick upon me: you, I hope, are better off, riding and walking in the woods of Studley, etc., etc. I must not wish for you here; besides I am going to town at Michaelmas, by no means for amusement.

CXXI.—Mr. GRAY to Mr. WALPOLE

Cambridge, *Dec.* 13, 1765.

AM very much obliged to you for the detail you enter into on the subject of your own health, in this you cannot be too circumstantial for me, who had received no account of you, but at second hand: such as, that you were dangerously ill, and therefore went to France; that you meant to try a better climate, and

[1] He seldom mentioned his mother without a sigh. After his death her gowns and wearing apparel were found in a trunk in his apartments just as she had left them; it seemed as if he could never take the resolution to open it, in order to distribute them to his female relations, to whom, by his will, he bequeathed them.—*Mason.*

therefore staid at Paris; that you had relapsed, and were confined to your bed, and extremely in vogue, and supped in the best company, and were at all public diversions. I rejoiced to find (improbable as it seemed) that all the wonderful part of this is strictly true, and that the serious part has been a little exaggerated. This latter I conclude, not so much from your own account of yourself, as from the spirits in which I see you write: and long may they continue to support you! I mean in a reasonable degree of elevation; but if (take notice) they are so volatile, so flippant, as to suggest any of those doctrines of health which you preach with all the zeal of a French atheist—at least, if they really do influence your practice—I utterly renounce them and all their works. They are *evil spirits*, and will lead you to destruction. You have long built your hopes on temperance, you say, and hardiness. On the first point we are agreed. The second has totally disappointed you, and *therefore* you will persist in it, by all means. But then be sure to persist too in being young, in stopping the course of time, and making the shadow return back upon your sundial. If you find this not so easy, acquiesce with a good grace in my anilities, put on your under-stockings of yarn, or woollen, even in the night time. Don't provoke me! or I shall order you two night caps (which by the way would do your eyes good), and put a little of any French liqueur into your water, they are nothing but brandy and sugar, and among their various flavours, some of them may surely be palatable enough. The pain in your feet I *can bear*; but I shudder at the sickness in your stomach, and the weakness that still continues. I conjure you, as you love yourself—I conjure you by Strawberry—not to trifle with these edge-tools. There is no cure for the gout, when in the stomach, but to throw it into the limbs. There is no relief for the gout in the limbs, but in gentle warmth and gradual perspiration.

I was much entertained with your account of our neighbours. As an Englishman and an Antigallican, I rejoice at their dulness and their nastiness, though I fear we shall come to imitate them in both. Their atheism is a little too much, too shocking to rejoice at. I have been long sick at it in their authors, and hated them for it; but I pity their poor innocent people of fashion. They were bad enough when they believed everything!

I have searched where you directed me, which I could not do sooner, as I was at London when I received your letter, and could not easily find her grace's [1] works. Here they abound in every

<hr>

[1] Duchess of Newcastle.

library. The print you ask after is the frontispiece to *Nature's pictures drawn by Fancy's pencil*. But lest there should be any mistake, I must tell you the family are not at dinner, but sitting round a rousing fire and telling stories. The room is just such a one as we lived in at Rheims, I mean as to the glazing and ceiling. The chimney is supported by cariatides; over the mantel-piece the arms of the family. The duke and duchess are crowned with laurel. A servant stands behind him, holding a hat and feather. Another is shutting a window. Diepenbecke delin. and (I think) S. Clouwe sculps. It is a very pretty and curious print, and I thank you for the sight of it. If it ever was a picture, what a picture to have! I must tell you, that upon cleaning an old picture here at St. John's Lodge, which I always took for a Holbein, on a ring which the figure wears, they have found H. H. It has been always called B. V. Fisher; but is plainly a layman, and probably Sir Anthony Denny, who was a benefactor to the college.

What is come of your Sevigné curiosity? I should be glad of a line now and then, when you have leisure. I wish you well,— And am ever yours, T. GRAY.

CXXII.—MR. GRAY TO DR. WHARTON

March 5, 1766, PEMB. C.

DEAR DOCTOR,

I am amazed at myself when I think I have never wrote to you; to be sure it is the sin of witchcraft, or something worse. Something indeed might be said for it, had I been married like Mason, who (for the first time since that great event) has just thought fit to tell me that he never passed so happy a winter as the last, and this in spite of his anxieties, which perhaps (he says) might even make a part of his happiness, for his wife is by no means in health. She has a constant cough, yet he is assured her lungs are not affected, and that it is nothing of the consumptive kind. What say you to this case? May I flatter him that breeding will be a cure for this disorder? If so, I hear she is in a fair way to be well. As to me, I have been neither happy nor miserable, but in a gentle stupefaction of mind, and very tolerable health of body, hitherto: if they last, I shall not much complain. The accounts one has lately had from all parts make me suppose you buried under the snow, like the old Queen of Denmark. As soon as you are dug out, I should rejoice to hear your voice from the battlements of Old Park. The greatest cold we have felt here was Jan. 2; thermom. (in the garden) at four in the afternoon standing at $30\frac{1}{2}$ deg., and next day fell a little snow, which did not lie: it was the first we had had during the winter. Again, Feb. 5, toward night, therm. was down at 30 deg. with a clear sky. The snowdrops then beginning to blow in the garden. Next day was a little snow, but on the 11th and 12th fell a deep snow (the weather not very cold), which however was melted on the 15th, and made a flood in the river. Next day the thrush was singing, and the rooks building. At and about London, instead of snow, they had heavy rains. On the 19th the red hepatica blew, and next day the primrose. The crocus is now in full bloom. So ends my chronicle.

My oracle [1] of state (who now and then utters a little, as far as he may with discretion) is a very slave and pack-horse, that never breathes any air better than that of London; except like an apprentice on Sundays with his Master and Co.: however he is in health, and a very good boy. It is strange the turn that things have taken:—that the late ministry should negociate a reconciliation with Lord Bute, and that Lord Temple should join them; that they should, after making their (bad) apologies, be received with a gracious kind of contempt, and told that his lordship could enter into no political connections with them; that on the first division on the American business that happened in the House of Lords, they should however all join to carry a point against the ministry, by a majority indeed of four only, but the Duke of York present, and making one; that when the ministers expostulated in a proper place, they should be seriously assured the king would support them; that on a division, on an insignificant point to try their strength, in the House of Commons, they should again lose it by 12 majority; that they should persist nevertheless that Mr. Pitt should appear *tanquam e Machinâ*, speak for three hours and a half, and assert the rights of the colonies in their greatest latitude; that the minister should profess himself ready to act with, and even serve under him; that he should receive such a compliment with coldness, and a sort of derision; that Norton should move to send him to the Tower; that when the great questions came on, the ministry should always carry their point at one, two, three in the morning by majorities of 110 and 170 (Mr. Pitt entirely concurring with them, and the Tories, people of the Court, and many placemen

[1] I believe Gray alludes to Mr. Stonehewer, the friend and secretary of the Duke of Grafton.—*Mitford*

even Lord G. Sackville, constantly voting against them); all these events are unaccountable on any principles of common sense. I attribute much of the singular part to the interposition of *women* as rash as they are foolish. On Monday (I do not doubt, though as yet I do not certainly know it) the Bill to repeal the Stamp Act went through that House, and to-day it is before the Lords, who surely will not venture to throw it out. Oh, that they would!—but after this important business is well over, there must be an *éclaircissement*. Some amends must be made, and some gracious condescensions insisted on, or else who would go on that really means to serve his country! The D. of Bedford and Lord Temple were gone down to their villas, and I believe are not likely to come back. Lord Chesterfield, who had not been for many years at the House, came the other day to qualify himself, in order to have a proxy that should vote with the ministry. Somebody (I thought) made no bad application of those lines in Virgil, lib. 6, v. 489,[1]

"At Danaûm proceres, Agamemnoniæq Phalanges," etc.

to Mr. Pitt's first appearance (for no one expected him) in the House. Turn to the place. Everything is politics. There are no literary productions worth your notice, at least of our country. The French have finished their great encyclopædia in 17 volumes, but there are many flimsy articles very hastily treated, and great incorrectness of the press. There are now 13 volumes of Buffon's *Natural History*, and he has not come to the monkies yet, who are a very numerous people. The life of Petrarch[2] has entertained me; it is not well written, but very curious, and laid together from his own letters and the original writings of the fourteenth century. So that it takes in much of the history of

---

[1] At Danaûm proceres, Agamemnoniæq phalanges,
    Ut vidêre virum, fulgentiaque arma per umbras,
    Ingenti trepidare metu; pars vertere terga,
    Ceu quondam petiere ratis: pars tollere vocem,
    Exiguam: inceptus clamor frustratur hiantis.

[2] *Memoires pour la Vie de François Petrarque, tirés de ses Œuvres, et des Auteurs Contemporains*, par L'Abbé de Sade, 3 tom. 4to, 1764. The essay on the "Life and Character of Petrarch," by F. Tytler, Lord Woodhouslee, is directed against the hypothesis of the Abbé de Sade, that the Laura of Petrarch was *Laura de Noves*, who married *Hugh de Sade*. In a note to the sixth volume of his *Roman History* (p. 567), Gibbon sketches the character of this work—"The *Memoires sur la Vie de Petrarque* (he says) form a copious, original, and entertaining work, a labour of love, composed from the accurate study of Petrarch and his contemporaries. But the hero is too often lost in the general history of the age, and the author too often languishes in the affectation of politeness and gallantry."—*Mitford*.

those obscure times, and the characters of many remarkable persons. There are 2 vols. 4to, and another (unpublished yet) that will complete it.

Mr. Walpole writes me now and then a long and lively letter from Paris, to which place he went the last summer, with the gout upon him; sometimes in his limbs, often in his stomach and head. He has got somehow well (not by means of the climate, one would think), goes to all public places, sees all the best company, and is very much in fashion. He says he sunk, like Queen Eleanor, at Charing Cross, and has risen again at Paris. He returns again in April; but his health is certainly in a deplorable state. Mad. de la Perriere is come over from the Hague to be ministress at London: her father-in-law Viry is now first minister at Turin. I sat a morning with her before I left London. She is a prodigious fine lady, and a Catholick (though she did not expressly own it to me), not fatter than she was. She had a cage of foreign birds, and a piping bullfinch at her elbow, two little dogs on a cushion in her lap, a cockatoo on her shoulder, and a strong suspicion of rouge on her cheeks: they were all exceeding glad to see me, and I them.

Pray tell me the history of your winter, and present my respects to Mrs. Wharton. I hope Miss Wharton and Miss Peggy, with the assistance of sister Betty, make a great progress in natural history. Recommend me to all their good graces, and believe me ever—Truly yours.

If you chance to see or send to Mr. and Mrs. Leighton, I will trouble you to make my compliments. I have never received the box of shells, though possibly it may wait for me at Mr. Jonathan's in town, where I shall be in April. Mr. Brown is well, and desires to be remembered to you and Mrs. Wharton. I have just heard there are like to be warm debates in the House of Lords, but that the ministry will undoubtedly carry it in spite of them all. They say Lord Camden will soon be chancellor.

CXXIII.—Mr. GRAY to Dr. WHARTON

Dear Doctor,

Whatever my pen may do, I am sure my thoughts expatiate nowhere oftener, or with more pleasure, than to Old Park. I hope you have made my peace with Miss Deborah. It is certain, whether her name were in my letter or not, she was as present to my memory as the rest of the little family; and I desire you would present her with two kisses in my name, and one apiece to all the others; for I shall take the liberty to kiss them all (great and small) as you are to be my proxy.

In spite of the rain, which I think continued with very short intervals till the beginning of this month, and quite effaced the summer from the year, I made a shift to pass May and June, not disagreeably, in Kent. I was surprised at the beauty of the road to Canterbury, which (I know not why) had not struck me in the same manner before. The whole country is a rich and well cultivated garden; orchards, cherry grounds, hop grounds, intermixed with corn and frequent villages, gentle risings covered with wood, and everywhere the Thames and Medway breaking in upon the landscape, with all their navigation. It was indeed owing to the bad weather that the whole scene was dressed in that tender emerald green, which one usually sees only for a fortnight in the opening of spring; and this continued till I left the country. My residence was eight miles east of Canterbury, in a little quiet valley on the skirts of Barham Down.[1] In these parts the whole soil is chalk, and whenever it holds up, in half an hour it is dry enough to walk out. I took the opportunity of three or four days fine weather to go into the Isle of Thanet, saw Margate (which is Bartholomew Fair by the seaside), Ramsgate, and other places there; and so come by Sandwich, Deal, Dover, Folkestone, and Hythe, back again. The coast is not like Hartlepool, there are no rocks, but only chalky cliffs, of no great height, till you come to Dover. There indeed they are noble and picturesque, and the opposite coasts of France begin to bound your view, which was left before to range unlimited by anything but the horizon; yet it is by no means a *shipless* sea, but everywhere peopled with white sails and vessels of all sizes in motion; and take notice (except in the isle which is all cornfields, and has very little enclosure) there are in all places hedge rows and tall trees even within a few yards of the beach, particularly Hythe stands on an eminence covered with wood. I shall confess we had fires of a night (aye and a day too) several times even in June, but don't go and take advantage of this, for it was the most untoward year that ever I remember.

Your friend Rousseau (I doubt) grows tired of Mr. Davenport and Derbyshire; he has picked a quarrel with David Hume,

---

[1] At Denton, where his friend the Rev. William Robinson, brother to Matthew Robinson, Esq., late member for Canterbury, then resided.— *Mason.*

and writes him letters of fourteen pages folio, upbraiding him with all his *noirceurs ;* take one only as a specimen. He says, that at Calais they chanced to sleep in the same room together, and that he overheard David talking in his sleep, and saying, "*Ah! je le tiens, ce Jean Jacques là.*" In short (I fear), for want of persecution and admiration (for these are his real complaints), he will go back to the Continent.

What shall I say to you about the ministry? I am as angry as a common council man of London about my Lord Chatham; but a little more patient, and will hold my tongue till the end of the year. In the meantime I do mutter in secret, and to you, that to quit the House of Commons, his natural strength, to sap his own popularity and grandeur (which no one but himself could have done) by assuming a foolish title; and to hope that he could win by it, and attach to him a court that hate him, and will dismiss him as soon as ever they dare, was the weakest thing that ever was done by so great a man. Had it not been for this, I should have rejoiced at the breach between him and Lord Temple, and at the union between him and the Duke of Grafton and Mr. Conway: but patience! we shall see! Stonehewer perhaps is in the country (for he hoped for a month's leave of absence), and if you see him you will learn more than I can tell you.

Mason is at Aston; he is no longer so anxious about his wife's health, as he was, though I find she still has a cough, and moreover I find she is not with child; but he made such a bragging, how could one chuse but believe him.

When I was in town I marked in my pocket-book the utmost limits and divisions of the two columns in your thermometer, and asked Mr. Ayscough, the instrument maker on Ludgate Hill, what scales they were. He immediately assured me that one was Fahrenheit's, and showed me one exactly so divided; the other he took for Reaumur's, but, as he said, there were different scales of his contrivance, he could not exactly tell which of them it was. Your brother told me you wanted to know who wrote Duke Wharton's life in the *Biographia.* I think it is chiefly borrowed from a silly book enough called *Memoirs of that Duke*, but who put it together there no one can inform me. The only person certainly known to write in that vile collection (I mean these latter volumes) is Dr. Nicholls, who was expelled here for stealing books. Have you read the *New Bath Guide?* It is the only thing in fashion, and is a new and original kind of humour. Miss Prue's Conversion I doubt you will paste down, as Sir W. St. Quintyn did before he carried it to his daughter; yet I remember you all read *Crazy Tales* without pasting. Buffon's first collection of monkeys are come out (it makes the fourteenth volume), something, but not much, to my edification, for he is pretty well acquainted with their persons, but not with their manners.

I shall be glad to hear how far Mrs. E—— has succeeded, and when you see an end to her troubles. My best regards to Mrs. Wharton, and compliments to all your family: I will not name them lest I should affront anybody. Adieu, dear sir,

I am most sincerely yours,

T. G.

Pembroke College, *August* 26, 1766.

Mr. Brown is gone to see his brother, near Margate. When is Ld. Str. to be married? If Mr. and Mrs. Jonathan are with you I desire my compliments.

CXXIV.—Mr. GRAY to Mr. MASON

March 28, 1767.

I break in upon you at a moment when we least of all are permitted to disturb our friends, only to say, that you are daily and hourly present to my thoughts. If the worst be not yet past, you will neglect and pardon me, but if the last struggle be over—if the poor object of your long anxieties be no longer sensible to your kindness, or to her own sufferings—allow me (at least in idea, for what could I do, were I present, more than this?) to sit by you in silence, and pity from my heart not her, who is at rest, but you, who lose her. May He who made us, the Master of our pleasures and of our pains, preserve and support you! Adieu.

I have long understood how little you had to hope.

CXXV.—Mr. GRAY to Dr. WHARTON

Sunday, 21 *June*, 1767, Aston.

Dear Doctor,

Here we are, Mr. Brown and I, in a wilderness of sweets, an elysium among the coal-pits, a terrestrial heaven; mind, it is not I, but Mason, that says all this, and bids me tell it you. To-morrow we visit Dovedale and the wonders of the Peak, the

Monday following we go to York to reside, and two or three days after set out for Old Park, where I shall remain upon your hands; and Mr. Brown about the time of Durham races must go on to Gibside, and for aught I know to Glamis. Mason remains tied down to his minster for half a year. He and Mr. Brown desire their best compliments to you and Mrs. Wharton. Adieu!

I am ever yours,

T. Gray.

Mr. Brown owns the pleasantest day he ever past was yesterday at Roche Abbey; it is indeed divine.

CXXVI.—Mr. GRAY to Mr. BEATTIE

Old Park, near Darlington, Durham,
August 12, 1767.

I received from Mr. Williamson that very obliging mark you were pleased to give me of your remembrance. Had I not entertained some slight hopes of revisiting Scotland this summer, and consequently of seeing you at Aberdeen, I had sooner acknowledged, by letter, the favour you have done me. Those hopes are now at an end, but I do not therefore despair of seeing again a country that has given me so much pleasure, nor of telling you, in person, how much I esteem you and (as you choose to call them) your amusements. The specimen of them, which you were so good as to send me, I think excellent; the sentiments are such as a melancholy imagination naturally suggests in solitude and silence, and that (though light and business may suspend or banish them at times) return with but so much the greater force upon a feeling heart; the diction is elegant and unconstrained, not loaded with epithets and figures, nor flagging into prose; the versification is easy and harmonious. My only objection is . . .[1]

You see, sir, I take the liberty you indulged me in, when I first saw you; and therefore I make no excuses for it, but desire you would take your revenge on me in kind.

I have read over (but too hastily) Mr. Ferguson's book. There are uncommon strains of eloquence in it, and I was surprised to find not one single idiom of his country (I think) in the whole work. He has not the fault you mention: his

---

[1] A paragraph is here omitted, as it contained merely a few particular criticisms; a liberty of the same kind I have before taken in some of the preceding letters. The poem in question contained many touching reflections on mortality: it is to be hoped Dr. Beattie will one day give it to the public.—*Mason.*

application to the heart is frequent, and often successful. His love of Montesquieu and Tacitus has led him into a manner of writing too short-winded and sententious, which those great men, had they lived in better times and under a better government, would have avoided.

I know no pretence that I have to the honour Lord Gray is pleased to do me,[1] but if his lordship chooses to own me it certainly is not my business to deny it. I say not this merely on account of his quality, but because he is a very worthy and accomplished person. I am truly sorry for the great loss he has had since I left Scotland. If you should chance to see him, I will beg you to present my respectful humble service to his lordship.

I gave Mr. Williamson all the information I was able in the short time he staid with me. He seemed to answer well the character you gave me of him, but what I chiefly envied in him was his ability of walking all the way from Aberdeen to Cambridge, and back again; which if I possessed, you would soon see your obliged, etc.

CXXVII.—Mr. GRAY to Mr. BEATTIE

PEMBROKE HALL, *Dec.* 24, 1767.

SINCE I had the pleasure of receiving your last letter, which did not reach me till I had left the north, and was come to London, I have been confined to my room with a fit of the gout. Now I am recovered and in quiet at Cambridge, I take up my pen to thank you for your very friendly offers, which have so much the air of frankness and real good meaning, that were my body as tractable and easy of conveyance as my mind, you would see me to-morrow in the chamber you have so hospitably laid out for me at Aberdeen. But, alas! I am a summer-bird, and can only sit drooping till the sun returns: even then too my wings may chance to be clipped, and little in plight for so distant an excursion.

The proposal you make me, about printing at Glasgow what little I have ever written, does me honour. I leave my reputation in that part of the kingdom to your care; and only desire you would not let your partiality to me and mine mislead you. If you persist in your design, Mr. Foulis certainly ought to be acquainted with what I am now going to tell you. When I was

---

[1] Lord Gray had said that our author was related to his family.—*Mason.*

in London the last spring, Dodsley, the bookseller, asked my leave to reprint, in a smaller form, all I ever published, to which I consented, and added, that I would send him a few explanatory notes; and if he would omit entirely the "Long Story" (which was never meant for the public, and only suffered to appear in that pompous edition because of Mr. Bentley's designs which were not intelligible without it), I promised to send him something else to print instead of it, lest the bulk of so small a volume should be reduced to nothing at all. Now it is very certain that I had rather see them printed at Glasgow (especially as you will condescend to revise the press) than at London, but I know not how to retract my promise to Dodsley. By the way, you perhaps may imagine that I have some kind of interest in this publication, but the truth is, I have none whatever. The expense is his, and so is the profit, if there be any. I therefore told him the other day, in general terms, that I heard there would be an edition put out in Scotland by a friend of mine, whom I could not refuse, and that, if so, I would send thither a copy of the same notes and additions that I had promised to send to him. This did not seem at all to cool his courage; Mr. Foulis must therefore judge for himself, whether he thinks it worth while to print what is going to be printed also at London. If he does I will send him (in a packet to you) the same things I shall send to Dodsley. They are imitations of two pieces of old Norwegian poetry, in which there was a wild spirit that struck me; but for my paraphrases I cannot say much; you will judge. the rest are nothing but a few parallel passages, and small notes just to explain what people said at the time was wrapped in total darkness. You will please to tell me, as soon as you can conveniently, what Mr. Foulis says on this head, that (if he drops the design) I may save myself and you the trouble of this packet. I ask your pardon for talking so long about it; a little more, and my letter would be as big as all my works.

I have read, with much pleasure, an ode of yours (in which you have done me the honour to adopt a measure that I have used) on Lord Hay's birthday. Though I do not love panegyric, I cannot but applaud this, for there is nothing mean in it. The diction is easy and noble, the texture of the thoughts lyric, and the versification harmonious. The few expressions I object to are . . . [1] These, indeed, are minutiæ; but they weigh for something, as half a grain makes a difference in the value of a diamond.

[1] Another paragraph of particular criticism is here omitted.—*Mason.*

CXXVIII.—Mr. GRAY to Dr. WHARTON

Dear Doctor,

Many and various maladies have I laboured under since I left the north, but none of them (thanks to my summer expedition) *jusqu'à mourir*. The gout came regularly while I was in town, first in one, then in the other foot, but so tame you might have stroked it. Since I got hither, *another* of my troublesome companions for life has confined me to my room, but abstinence has (I believe) got the better of that too, and to-morrow I go abroad again. I sent to your brother, before I left London, the *maps* you wanted, the *Decouvertes des Russes*, *Voyage de Gmelin en Siberie*, Mr. Clerke of Chichester on the *Saxon coins*, Lee's *Linnæan Dictionary*, *Verrall's Cookery*, and something else that I have forgot; as to Hudson's *Flora Anglica*, it is not to be had, being out of print; a new and more correct edition is soon expected. Willoughby's book of *fishes* was never published in English, so would not answer your end. That of the *birds* is indeed in English, but not to be had in the shops, and sells at auctions from 30 to 40 shillings, so I did not buy it without farther orders. I hope this cargo is safe arrived. And another little one, that I sent to Miss Wharton and Miss Peggy, directed to the former, to be left at Mr. Tho. Wilkinson's, in Durham. This went by the Newcastle waggon about 6th of December, and contained twelve flower roots; viz. three Soleil d'or narcissus; two white Italian ditto (N.B. of the double white and yellow Italian there are none to be had this year); two Pileus cardinalis, red; one kroonvogel; one degeraad, double white; one Bella grisdelin; one hermaphrodite; and one incomparable, double blue, hyacinth. For these you must get glasses from Newcastle; in the same box was a pocket lens, which Miss Wharton (if she pleased) was to give to Aunt Middleton, who wanted such a thing.

I desire to know what you thought of Mason's plans for your ground (which makes so pretty a figure on paper); and whether *Summers* came to Old Park to advise about planting. He is a very intelligent modest young man, and might be of great use there. Has Miss Wharton served her time yet as bridemaid? I hope it may prove a good omen to her! Does Miss Peggy rival Claude Lorraine yet, and when does she go to York? Do Debo and Betty tend their chrysalises and their samplers? Is Kee's mouth as pretty as ever? Does Robin read like a doctor, dance like a fairy, and bow like a courtier? Does Dicky kick up his heels and study geography? Please to answer me as to all these particulars. My thermometer presents her compliments to her country sister, and proposes now to open a correspondence with her. She lives against a pale in the garden, with her back to the east at 9 o'clock in the morning precisely; at any other hour she is not visible, unless upon some great occasion. I was in London from 3d November to 14th December, during which time the weather was commonly open, damp, and mild, with the wind in the west, veering either to north or south. On the last-mentioned day I found some brambles and fever-few yet flowering in the hedges; and in gardens the double chrysanthemum, double chamomile, borage, stocks, and single wall-flowers. These were all cut off on the 24th by an east wind and hard frost. Thermometer at 31. Next day and to-day it was at 30. On the 26th a little snow fell, which still lies and freezes.

Our ministry has taken in some odd coadjutors not much to its credit or strength; it appeared from the first day that the parliament met that the opposition were all to pieces among themselves, and soon after, the Duke of Bedford civilly declared to Mr. Grenville that he had the highest opinion of his abilities, but as it was contrary to his principles to keep up a constant opposition to the king's measures, he must not wonder if his friends should drop the plan they had for some time been pursuing, accordingly he made his terms: four or five of them were directly to be provided for; the rest were to wait till there was room. Lord Shelburne (the secretary), and Mr. Cook (joint paymaster) were to have gone out, but Lord Chatham insisted on their staying in (it is said) and prevailed; Mr. Conway retires, and is to have the army when Lord Ligonier dies; this is voluntary, I imagine. Lord Northington goes off with his pension. Lord Weymouth and Earl Gower supply their places. Mr. Thynne is master of the household. Lord Sandwich, joint paymaster (Lord Hillsborough being created Secretary of State for America). Rigby is the other that must come in (to what place I know not), and conduct, I suppose, the House of Commons. How much better and nobler would it have been to have left all these beggars in the lurch! Indeed what could be said against it, as all that could oppose the ministry were already broke into three parts, and one of them had declared publicly against the other two? I conclude the Rockingham party will at last prevail, as they have some character and credit with the people still left.

Adieu! my dear sir, you have had, I hope, no return of your asthma since you lay in your own bed. My best respects to Mrs. Wharton, and love to all the family.

I am ever yours,

T. G.

Dec. 28, 1767, PEMB. COLL.

Shall I write out and send you what Leland says of your neighbourhood. It is nothing but short notes taken in his journey. But that journey was towards the end of Henry Eighth's reign, just after the dissolution of monasteries, which makes it valuable.

SPECIMEN

From St. Andre's Akeland to Raby Castle 5 miles part by arable, but more by pastures. And moorish hilly ground, baren of wood. Raby is the largest castel of Logginges in al the north cuntery, and is of a strong building; but not set ether on hil, or very strong ground. As I entered by a causey into it, there was a litle stayre on the right hand, and in the first area were but two towres, one at eche end, as entres, and no other builded; yn the second area, as an entring, was a great gate of iren with a tour, and 2 or 3 mo on the right hand, then were al the chief toures of the third court, as in the hart of the castel. The haul, and al the houses of offices be large and stately; and in the haul I saw an incredible great beame of an hart. The great chaumber was exceeding large, but now it is false-rofid, and devided into 2 or 3 partes. I saw there a little chaumber, wherein was in windows of colored glass al the petigre of ye Nevilles, etc.

CXXIX.—MR. GRAY TO MR. HOW

CAMBRIDGE, PEMB. COLL., *Jan.* 12, 1768.

SIR,

You perceive by Mr. Brown's letter that I passed all the summer in the north of England, went from thence to London, and did not arrive here till the middle of December, where I found your parcel. Since that time I have been generally confined to my room; and besides I was willing to go through the eight volumes before I returned you an answer. This must be my excuse to you, for only doing now what in mere civility I ought to have done long ago.

First, I must condole with you, that so neat an edition should swarm in almost every page with errors of the press, not only in notes and citations from Greek, French, and English authors but in the Italian text itself, greatly to the disreputation of the Leghorn publishers. This is the only reason, I think, that could make an edition in England necessary; but I doubt you would not find the matter much mended here; our presses as they improve in beauty, declining daily in accuracy; besides, you would find the expense very considerable, and the sale in no proportion to it, as in reality, it is but few people in England that read currently and with pleasure the Italian tongue, and the fine old editions of their capital writers are sold in London for a lower price than they bear in Italy. An English translation I can by no means advise; the justness of thought and good sense might remain, but the graces of elocution (which make a great part of Algarotti's merit) would be entirely lost, and that merely from the very different genius and complexion of the two languages.

I rather think these volumes should be handsomely bound before they are put into the library; they bind very neatly here; and if you approve it, Mr. Brown will order it to be done. Doubtless there can be no impropriety in making the same present to the university, nor need you at all to fear for the reputation of your friend: he has merit enough to recommend him in any country. A tincture of various sorts of knowledge, an acquaintance with all the beautiful arts, an easy command, a precision, warmth, and richness of expression, and a judgment that is rarely mistaken on any subject to which he applies it. Of the dialogues I have formerly told you my thoughts. The essays and letter (many of them entirely new to me) *on the arts*, are curious and entertaining; those on other subjects (even where the thoughts are not new, but borrowed from his various reading and conversation) often better put and better expressed than in the originals. I rejoice when I see Machiavel defended or illustrated, who to me appears one of the wisest men that any nation in any age has produced. Most of the other discourses, military or political, are well worth reading, though that on "Kouli-Khan" was a mere *jeu-d'esprit*, a sort of historical exercise. The letters from Russia I have read before with pleasure, particularly the narrative of Munich's and Lascy's campaigns. The detached thoughts are often new and just; but there should have been a revisal of them, as they are frequently to be found in his letters repeated in the very same words. Some too of the familiar letters might have been spared.

The " Congress of Cythera " I had seen and liked before, the
" Giudicio d'Amore " is an addition rather inferior to it.   The
verses are not equal to the prose, but they are above mediocrity.

I shall be glad to hear your health is improved, and that you
have thoughts of favouring us with your company here.   I am, sir,

Your most obedient humble servant,

THOS. GRAY.

CXXX.—MR. GRAY TO MR. BEATTIE

PEMBROKE HALL, *Feb.* 1, 1768.

I AM almost sorry to have raised any degree of impatience in
you, because I can by no means satisfy it.   The sole reason I
have to publish these few additions now, is to make up (in both)
for the omission of that " Long Story; " and as to the notes, I
do it out of spite, because the public did not understand the two
odes (which I have called Pindaric); though the first was not
very dark, and the second alluded to a few common facts to be
found in any sixpenny history of England, by way of question
and answer, for the use of children.   The parallel passages I
insert out of justice to those writers from whom I happened to
take the hint of any line, as far as I can recollect.

I rejoice to be in the hands of Mr. Foulis, who has the laudable
ambition of surpassing his predecessors, the *Etiennes* and the
Elzevirs, as well in literature, as in the proper art of his profession: he surprises me in mentioning a lady, after whom I have
been enquiring these fourteen years in vain.   When the two
odes were first published, I sent them to her; but as I was forced
to direct them very much at random, probably they never came
to her hands.   When the present edition comes out, I beg of Mr.
Foulis to offer her a copy, in my name, with my respects and
grateful remembrances;   he will send another to you, sir, and a
third to Lord Gray, if he will do me the honour of accepting it.
These are all the presents I pretend to make (for I would have it
considered only as a new edition of an old book); after this if he
pleases to send me one or two, I shall think myself obliged to him.
I cannot advise him to print a great number; especially as
Dodsley has it in his power to print as many as he pleases,
though I desire him not to do so.

You are very good to me in taking this trouble upon you:
all I can say is, that I shall be happy to return it in kind, whenever you will give me the opportunity.

CXXXI.—Mr. GRAY to Mr. WALPOLE

Feb. 14, 1768, PEMB. COLLEGE.

I RECEIVED the book [1] you were so good to send me, and have read it again (indeed I could hardly be said to have read it before) with attention and with pleasure. Your second edition is so rapid in its progress that it will now hardly answer any purpose to tell you either my own objections, or those of other people. Certain it is, that you are universally read here; but what *we* think is not so easy to come at. We stay as usual to see the success, to learn the judgement of the town, to be directed in our opinions by those of more competent judges. If they like you, we shall; if any one of name write against you, we give you up; for we are modest and diffident of ourselves, and not without reason. History in particular is not our *fort;* for (the truth is) we read only modern books and pamphlets of the day. I have heard it objected, that you raise doubts and difficulties, and do not satisfy them by telling us what is really the case. I have heard you charged with disrespect to the King of Prussia; and above all to King William, and the Revolution. These are seriously the most sensible things I have heard said, and all that I recollect. If you please to justify yourself, you may.

My own objections are little more essential: they relate chiefly to inaccuracies of style, which either debase the expression or obscure the meaning. I could point out several small particulars of this kind, and will do so, if you think it can serve any purpose after publication. When I hear you read, they often escape me, partly because I am attending to the subject, and partly because from habit I understand you where a stranger might often be at a loss.

As to your arguments, most of the principal parts are made out with a clearness and evidence that no one would expect, where materials are so scarce. Yet I still suspect Richard of the murder of Henry VI. The chronicler of Croyland charges it full on him, though without a name or any mention of circumstances. The interests of Edward were the interests of Richard too, though the throne were not then in view; and that Henry still stood in their way, they might well imagine, because, though deposed and imprisoned once before, he had regained his liberty and his crown; and was still adored by the people. I should think, from the word *tyranni,* the passage was written after

[1] Walpole's *Historic Doubts.*

have copies), a bit of something from the Welch, and certain little notes, partly from justice (to acknowledge the debt, where I had borrowed anything), partly from ill temper, just to tell the gentle reader that Edward I. was not Oliver Cromwell, nor Queen Elizabeth the Witch of Endor. This is literally all; and with all this, I shall be but a shrimp of an author. I gave leave also to print the same thing at Glasgow; but I doubt my packet has miscarried, for I hear nothing of its arrival as yet. To what you say to me so civilly, that I ought to write more, I reply in your own words (like the pamphleteer, who is going to confute you out of your own mouth), What has one to do when *turned of fifty* but really to think of finishing? However, I will be candid (for you seem to be so with me), and avow to you, that till four-score-and-ten, whenever the humour takes me, I will write, because I like it; and because I like myself better when I do so. If I do not write much, it is because I cannot. As you have not this last plea, I see no reason why you should not continue as long as it is agreeable to yourself, and to all such as have any curiosity or judgement in the subject you choose to treat. By the way let me tell you (while it is fresh) that Lord Sandwich, who was lately dining at Cambridge, speaking (as I am told) handsomely of your book, said it was a pity you did not know that his cousin Manchester had a genealogy of the kings, which came down no lower than to Richard III., and at the end of it were two portraits of Richard and his son, in which that king appeared to be a handsome man. I tell you it as I heard it: perhaps you may think it worth enquiring into.

I have looked into Speed and Leslie. It appears very odd that Speed in the speech he makes for P. Warbeck, addressed to James IV. of Scotland, should three times cite the *manuscript proclamation* of Perkin, then in the hands of Sir Robert Cotton: and yet when he gives us the proclamation afterwards (on occasion of the insurrection in Cornwall) he does not cite any such manuscript. In Casley's *Catalogue of the Cotton Library* you may see whether this manuscript proclamation still exists or not: if it does, it may be found at the Museum. Leslie will give you no satisfaction at all: though no subject of England, he could not write freely on this matter, as the title of Mary (his mistress) to the crown of England was derived from that of Henry VII. Accordingly he everywhere treats Perkin as an impostor; yet drops several little expressions inconsistent with that supposition. He has preserved no proclamation: he only puts a short speech into Perkin's mouth, the substance of which is taken by Speed, and translated in the end of his, which is a good deal longer: the whole matter is treated by Leslie very concisely and superficially. I can easily transcribe it, if you please; but I do not see that it could answer any purpose.

Mr. Boswell's book I was going to recommend to you, when I received your letter: it has pleased and moved me strangely, all (I mean) that relates to Paoli. He is a man born two thousand years after his time! The pamphlet proves what I have always maintained, that any fool may write a most valuable book by chance, if he will only tell us what he heard and saw with veracity. Of Mr. Boswell's truth I have not the least suspicion, because I am sure he could invent nothing of this kind. The true title of this part of his work is, a " Dialogue between a Green-goose and a Hero."

I had been told of a manuscript in Benet Library: the inscription of it is " Itinerarium Fratris Simeonis et Hugon' illuminatoris, 1322." Would not one think this should promise something? They were two Franciscan friars that came from Ireland, and passed through Wales to London, to Canterbury, to Dover, and so to France in their way to Jerusalem. All that relates to our own country has been transcribed for me, and (sorry am I to say) signifies not a halfpenny: only this little bit might be inserted in your next edition of the *Painters*: " Ad aliud caput civitatis (Londoniæ) est monasterium nigrorum monachorum nomine Westmonasterium, in quo constanter et communiter omnes reges Angliæ sepeliuntur—et eidem monasterio quasi immediatè conjungitur illud famosissimum palatium regis, in quo est illa vulgata camera, in cujus parietibus sunt omnes historiæ bellicæ totius Bibliæ ineffabiliter depictæ, atque in Gallico completissimè et perfectissimè conscriptæ, in non modicâ intuentium admiratione et maximâ regali magnificentiâ."

I have had certain observations on your *Royal and Noble Authors* given me to send you perhaps about three years ago: last week I found them in a drawer, and (my conscience being troubled) now enclose them to you. I have even forgot whose they are.

I have been also told of a passage in Ph. de Comines, which (if you know) ought not to have been passed over. The book is not at hand at present, and I must conclude my letter. Adieu! —I am ever yours,   T. GRAY.

CXXXV.—MR. GRAY TO DR. WHARTON

JERMYN STREET, *Aug.* 1 (AT MR. ROBERTS'S), 1768.

DEAR DOCTOR,

I have been remiss in answering your last letter, which was sent me to Ramsgate from Cambridge, for I have passed a good part of the summer in different parts of Kent, much to my satisfaction. Could I have advised anything essential in poor Mrs. —— case, I had certainly replied immediately, but we seem of one mind in it. There was nothing left but to appeal to delegates (let the trouble and expense be what they will almost), and to punish, if it be practicable, that old villain who upon the bench of justice dared to set at nought all common-sense and humanity.

I write to you now chiefly to tell you (and I think you will be pleased, nay I expect the whole family will be pleased with it) that on Sunday se'nnight Brocket died by a fall from his horse, being (as I hear) drunk, and some say, returning from Hinchinbroke. That on the Wednesday following I received a letter from the D. of Grafton, saying he had the king's commands to *offer* me the vacant professorship, that, etc. (but I shall not write all he says), and he adds at the end, *that from private as well as public considerations, he must take the warmest part in approving so well judged a measure, as he hopes I do not doubt of the real regard and esteem with which he has the honor to be*, etc., there's for you, so on Thursday the king signed the warrant, and next day at his levee I kissed his hand. He made me several gracious speeches, which I shall not report, because everybody who goes to court does so. By the way, I desire you would say that all the cabinet council in words of great favour approved the nomination of your humble servant; and this I am bid to say, and was told to leave my name at their several doors. I have told you the outside of the matter, and all the manner. For the inside you know enough easily to guess it, and you will guess right. As to his grace I have not seen him before or since.

I shall continue here perhaps a fortnight longer, perishing with heat; I have no thermometer with me, but I feel it as I did at Naples. Next summer (if it be as much in my power as it is in my wishes) I meet you at the foot of Skiddaw. My respects to Mrs. Wharton and the young ladies great and small. Love to Robin and Richard. Adieu!—I am truly yours.

CXXXVI.—Mr. GRAY to Mr. NICHOLLS.[1]

JERMYN STREET, *Aug.* 3, 1768.

THAT Mr. Brockett has broken his neck, by a fall from his horse
you will have seen in the newspapers, and also that I, your
humble servant, have kissed the King's hand for his succession.
They are both true, but the manner how you know not; only I
can assure you that I had no hand at all in his fall, and almost as
little in the second event.   He died on the Sunday; on Wednesday following his grace the Duke of Grafton wrote me a very
polite letter to say that his majesty had commanded him to
offer me the vacant professorship, not only as a reward of, etc.,
but as a credit to, etc., with much more too high for me to transcribe.   So on Thursday the king signed the warrant, and next
day, at his levee, I kissed his hand.   He made me several gracious
speeches, which I shall not repeat, because everybody that goes
to court does so: besides, the day was so hot, and the ceremony
so embarrassing to me, that I hardly knew what he said.

Adieu.   I am to perish here with heat this fortnight yet, and
then to Cambridge; to be sure my dignity is a little the worse
for wear, but mended and washed, it will do for me.

CXXXVII.—Mr. GRAY to Mr. BEATTIE

PEMBROKE HALL, *Oct.* 31, 1768.

IT is some time since I received from Mr. Foulis two copies of
my poems, one by the hands of Mr. T. Pitt, the other by Mr.
Merrill, a bookseller of this town.   It is indeed a most beautiful
edition, and must certainly do credit both to him and to me;
but I fear it will be of no other advantage to him, as Dodsley has
contrived to glut the town already with two editions beforehand,
one of 1500, and the other of 750, both indeed far inferior to that
of Glasgow, but sold at half the price.   I must repeat my thanks,
sir, for the trouble you have been pleased to give yourself on my
account; and through you I must desire leave to convey my
acknowledgements to Mr. Foulis, for the pains and expense he
has been at in this publication.

[1] Rector of Lounde and Bradwell in Suffolk.   His acquaintance with
Mr. Gray commenced a few years before the date of this, when he was a
student of Trinity Hall, Cambridge.—*Mason.*

We live at so great a distance, that, perhaps, you may not yet have learned, what, I flatter myself, you will not be displeased to hear. The middle of last summer his majesty was pleased to appoint me Regius Professor of Modern History in this University. It is the best thing the Crown has to bestow (on a layman) here; the salary is £400 per ann., but what enhances the value of it to me is, that it was bestowed without being asked. The person who held it before me died on the Sunday; and on Wednesday following the Duke of Grafton wrote me a letter to say, that the king offered me this office, with many additional expressions of kindness on his grace's part, to whom I am but little known, and whom I have not seen either before or since he did me this favour. Instances of a benefit so nobly conferred, I believe, are rare; and therefore I tell you of it as a thing that does honour, not only to me, but to the minister.

As I lived here before from choice, I shall now continue to do so from obligation: if business or curiosity should call you southwards, you will find few friends that will see you with more cordial satisfaction, than, dear sir, etc.

CXXXVIII.—Mr. GRAY to Dr. WHARTON

LONDON, *April 20*, 1769.

DEAR DOCTOR,

You have reason to call me negligent, nor have I anything to allege in my own defence, but two successive fits of the gout, which though weakly and not severe, were at least dispiriting, and lasted a long time. I rejoiced to hear your alarms for Robin and Kitty ended so happily, and with them (I hope) are fled a great part of your future inquietudes on this account. In the summer, I flatter myself, we may all meet in health once more at Old Park, and a part of us, perhaps, at the foot of Skiddaw. I am to call on Mason in my way, and bring him with me to visit his own works. Mr. Brown admitted your nephew according to your orders, and will provide him with a room against October.

I do not guess what intelligence Stonehewer gave you about my employments, but the worst employment I have had, has been to write something for musick against the Duke of Grafton comes to Cambridge. I must comfort myself with the intention, for I know it will bring abuse enough on me;[1] however it is done, and given to the vice-chancellor, and there is an end. I am come to town for a fortnight and find everything in extreme confusion, as you may guess from your newspapers. Nothing but force threatened on both sides, and the law (as usual) watching the event, and ready to side with the strongest. The only good thing I hear is that France is on the brink of a general bankruptcy, and their fleet (the only thing they have laid out money on of late) in no condition of service.

The spring is come in all its beauty, and for two or three days I am going to meet it at Windsor. Adieu! and let us pray it may continue till July. Remember me to Mrs. Wharton, and all the family.

I am ever yours,
T. G.

Mason has left us, and is gone to Aston.

CXXXIX.—Mr. GRAY to Mr. NICHOLLS

I was absent from college, and did not receive your melancholy letter till my return hither yesterday, so you must not attribute this delay to me but to accident. To sympathise with you in such a loss[2] is an easy task for me, but to comfort you not so easy; can I wish to see you unaffected with the sad scene now before your eyes, or with the loss of a person that, through a great part of your life, has proved himself so kind a friend to you? He who best knows our nature (for He made us what we are) by such afflictions recalls us from our wandering thoughts and idle merriment; from the insolence of youth and prosperity, to serious reflection, to our duty, and to Himself; nor need we

---

[1] When the late Duke of Grafton (says Mr. Mathias, in his *Observations on Gray*, p. 53) was elected Chancellor of the University of Cambridge, it is known that Mr. Gray, from an impulse of what he looked on as a species of duty, spontaneously offered to write the ode for his grace's installation. He considered it nevertheless as a sort of task, as a set composition; and a considerable time passed before he could prevail upon himself, or rather before he actually felt the power to begin it. But one morning after breakfast, Mr. Nicholls called on him, and knocking at his chamber door, Mr. Gray got up hastily and threw it open himself, and running up to him in a hurried voice and tone, exclaimed, " Hence, avaunt! 'tis holy ground!" Mr. Nicholls was so astonished that he thought his senses were deranged, but Mr. Gray in a moment after resumed his usual pleasant manner, and repeating several verses at the beginning of that inimitable composition, said, " Well, I have begun the ode, and now I shall finish it."—*Mitford.*

[2] The death of his uncle, Governor Floyer.

hasten to get rid of these impressions; time (by appointment of the same power) will cure the smart, and in some hearts soon blot out all the traces of sorrow; but such as preserve them longest (for it is partly left in our own power) do perhaps best acquiesce in the will of the chastiser.

For the consequences of this sudden loss, I see them well, and I think, in a like situation, could fortify my mind, so as to support them with cheerfulness and good hopes, though not naturally inclined to see things in their best aspect. When you have time to turn yourself round, you must think seriously of your profession; you know I would have wished to see you wear the livery of it long ago: but I will not dwell on this subject at present. To be obliged to those we love and esteem is a pleasure; but to serve and oblige them is a still greater; and this, with independence (no vulgar blessing), are what a profession at your age may reasonably promise: without it they are hardly attainable. Remember I speak from experience.

In the meantime while your present situation lasts, which I hope will not be long, continue your kindness and confidence in me, by trusting me with the whole of it; and surely you hazard nothing by so doing: that situation does not appear so new to me as it does to you. You well know the tenour of my conversation (urged at times perhaps a little farther than you liked) has been intended to prepare you for this event, and to familiarise your mind with this spectre, which you call by its worst name: but remember that " *Honesta res est læta paupertas.*" I see it with respect, and so will every one, whose poverty is not seated in their mind. There is but one real evil in it (take my word who know it well), and that is, that you have less the power of assisting others, who have not the same resources to support them. You have youth; you have many kind well-intentioned people belonging to you; many acquaintance of your own, or families that will wish to serve you. Consider how many have had the same, or greater cause for dejection, with none of these resources before their eyes. Adieu. I sincerely wish your happiness.

P.S. I have just heard that a friend of mine is struck with a paralytick disorder, in which state it is likely he may live incapable of assisting himself, in the hands of servants or relations that only gape after his spoils, perhaps for years to come: think how many things may befal a man far worse than poverty or death.

CXL.—MR. GRAY TO MR. NICHOLLS

PEMBROKE COLLEGE, *June* 24, 1769.

AND so you have a garden of your own, and you plant and transplant, and are dirty and amused! Are not you ashamed of yourself? Why, I have no such thing, you monster, nor ever shall be either dirty or amused as long as I live. My gardens are in the windows like those of a lodger up three pair of stairs in Petticoat Lane, or Camomile Street, and they go to bed regularly under the same roof that I do. Dear, how charming it must be to walk out in one's own *garding*, and sit on a bench in the open air, with a fountain and leaden statue, and a rolling stone, and an arbour: have a care of sore throats though, and the *agoe*.

However, be it known to you, though I have no garden, I have sold my estate and got a thousand guineas,[1] and fourscore pounds a year for my old aunt, and a twenty pound prize in the lottery, and Lord knows what arrears in the treasury, and am a rich fellow enough, go to; and [2] a fellow that hath had losses, and one that hath two gowns, and everything handsome about him, and in a few days shall have new window curtains. Are you avized of that? Ay, and a new mattress to lie upon.

My ode has been rehearsed again and again,[3] and the scholars have got scraps by heart. I expect to see it torn piece-meal in the *North Briton* before it is born. If you will come you shall see it, and sing in it amidst a chorus from Salisbury and Gloucester music meeting, great names there, and all well versed in " Judas Maccabæus." I wish it were once over, for then I immediately go for a few days to London, and so with Mr. Brown to Aston, though I fear it will rain the whole summer, and Skiddaw will be invisible and inaccessible to mortals.

[1] Consisting of houses on the west side of Hand Alley, London. Mrs. Olliffe was the aunt here mentioned, who had a share in this estate, and for whom he procured this annuity. She died in 1771, a few months before her nephew.—*Mason.*

[2] Mr. Mason has not remarked that these are the words of Dogberry, in " Much Ado about Nothing," which Gray uses. " I am a wise fellow, and which is more an officer, and which is more an householder, and which is more as pretty a piece of flesh as any in Messina; and one that knows the law, *go to, and a rich fellow enough, go to ; and a fellow that hath had losses, and one that hath two gowns, and everything handsome about him ,* bring him away. Oh! that I had been writ down an ass! "—*Mitford.*

[3] " Ode for Music " on the Duke of Grafton's installation. His reason for writing it is given in the next letter.—*Mason.*

I have got De la Landes' *Voyage through Italy*, in eight volumes; he is a member of the academy of sciences, and pretty good to read. I have read too an octavo volume of Shenstone's *Letters*. Poor man! he was always wishing for money, for fame, and other distinctions; and his whole philosophy consisted in living against his will in retirement, and in a place which his taste had adorned; but which he only enjoyed when people of note came to see and commend it. His correspondence is about nothing else but this place and his own writings, with two or three neighbouring clergymen who wrote verses too.

I have just found the beginning of a letter, which somebody had dropped: I should rather call it first thoughts for the beginning of a letter; for there are many scratches and corrections. As I cannot use it myself (having got a beginning already of my own) I send it for your use on some great occasion.

DEAR SIR,

" After so long silence, the hopes of pardon, and prospect of forgiveness might seem entirely extinct, or at least very remote, was I not truly sensible of your goodness and candour, which is the only asylum that my negligence can fly to, since every apology would prove insufficient to counter-balance it, or alleviate my fault. How then shall my deficiency presume to make so bold an attempt, or be able to suffer the hardships of so rough a campaign?" etc., etc., etc.

CXLI.—MR. GRAY TO MR. BEATTIE

CAMBRIDGE, *July* 16, 1769.

THE late ceremony of the Duke of Grafton's installation has hindered me from acknowledging sooner the satisfaction your friendly compliment gave me. I thought myself bound in gratitude to his grace, unasked, to take upon me the task of writing those verses which are usually set to music on this occasion.[1] I do not think them worth sending you, because they are by nature doomed to live but a single day; or, if their

---

[1] In a short note which he wrote to Mr. Stonehewer, June 12, when, at his request, he sent him the ode in manuscript, for his grace's perusal, he expresses this motive more fully. " I did not intend the duke should have heard me till he could not help it. You are desired to make the best excuses you can to his grace for the liberty I have taken of praising him to his face; but as somebody was necessarily to do this, I did not see why Gratitude should sit silent and leave it to Expectation to sing, who certainly would have sung, and that *à gorge deployée* upon such an occasion."—*Mason.*

existence is prolonged beyond that date, it is only by means of newspaper parodies, and witless criticisms. This sort of abuse I had reason to expect, but did not think it worth while to avoid.

Mr. Foulis is magnificent in his gratitude:[1] I cannot figure to myself how it can be worth his while to offer me such a present. You can judge better of it than I; if he does not hurt himself by it, I would accept his Homer with many thanks. I have not got or even seen it.

I could wish to subscribe to his new edition of Milton, and desire to be set down for two copies of the large paper; but you must inform me where and when I may pay the money.

You have taught me to long for a second letter, and particularly for what you say will make the contents of it. I have nothing to requite it with, but plain and friendly truth; and that you shall have joined to a zeal for your fame, and a pleasure in your success.

I am now setting forward on a journey towards the north of England; but it will not reach so far as I could wish. I must return hither before Michaelmas, and shall barely have time to visit a few places, and a few friends.

CXLII.—MR. GRAY TO MR. BONSTETTEN

CAMBRIDGE, 1770, *April 12th.*

NEVER did I feel, my dear Bonstetten,[2] to what a tedious length the few short moments of our life may be extended by impatience and expectation, till you had left me: nor ever knew before with

---

[1] When the Glasgow edition of Mr. Gray's poems was sold off (which it was in a short time), Mr. Foulis finding himself a considerable gainer, mentioned to Mr. Beattie that he wished to make Mr. Gray a present either of his *Homer*, in 4 vols. folio, or the *Greek Historians*, printed likewise at his press, in 29 vols. duodecimo.—*Mason.*

[2] These three letters are taken from Miss Plumtree's translation of Matthison's *Letters*, p. 533. Bonstetten, in his youth, resided some time at Cambridge, during which he enjoyed an almost daily intercourse with Gray, who attached himself to him with great ardour, and became soon his warmest and most confidential friend. Charles Von Bonstetten was Baillie of Nion, in the canton of Berne, author of letters on the pastoral parts of Switzerland, etc., and some other works. Mr. Mason (it appears) applied to him for leave to publish these letters, which he refused; afterwards permitting them to be printed by his friend Matthison, in the notes to some stanzas on the "Leman Lake," in which Gray is introduced:

" Where Agathon, the Muses', Graces' pride,
　　The palace's delight, the peasant's stay;
　E'en hence to distant Jura's shaggy side,
　　In warmest friendship clasped me as his Gray."—*Mitford.*

so strong a conviction how much this frail body sympathises with the inquietude of the mind. I am grown old in the compass of less than three weeks, like the sultan [1] in the Turkish tales, that did but plunge his head into a vessel of water, and take it out again, as the standers by affirmed, at the command of a Dervise, and found he had passed many years in captivity and begot a large family of children. The strength and spirits that now enable me to write to you, are only owing to your last letter, a temporary gleam of sunshine. Heaven knows when it may shine again. I did not conceive till now, I own, what it was to lose you, nor felt the solitude and insipidity of my own condition before I possessed the happiness of your friendship. I must cite another Greek writer to you, because it is much to my purpose. He is describing the character of a genius truly inclined to philosophy. " It includes," he says, " qualifications rarely united in one single mind, quickness of apprehension and a retentive memory, vivacity and application, gentleness and magnanimity; to these he adds an invincible love of truth, and consequently of probity and justice. Such a soul," continues he, " will be little inclined to sensual pleasures, and consequently temperate, a stranger to illiberality and avarice; being accustomed to the most extensive views of things and sublimest contemplations, it will contract an habitual greatness, will look down with a kind of disregard on human life, and on death; consequently, will possess the truest fortitude. Such," says he, " is the mind born to govern the rest of mankind." But these very endowments, so necessary to a soul formed for philosophy, are often its ruin, especially when joined to the external advantages of wealth, nobility, strength, and beauty; that is, if it light on a bad soil, and want its proper nurture, which nothing but an excellent education can bestow. In this case, he is depraved by the public example, the assemblies of the people, the courts of justice, the theatres, that inspire it with false opinions, terrify it with false infamy, or elevate it with false applause; and remember, that extraordinary vices, and extraordinary virtues, are equally the produce of a vigorous mind; little souls are alike incapable of the one and the other.

If you have ever met with the portrait sketched out by Plato, you will know it again; for my part, to my sorrow I have had

---

[1] Lady B—— M—— is the individual woman she was—she seems to have been gone three years, like the sultan in the Persian tales, who popped his head into a tub of water, pulled it up again, and fancied he had been a dozen years in bondage in the interim.—Walpole's *Letters*, v. 452.

that happiness. I see the principal features, and I foresee the dangers with a trembling anxiety. But enough of this, I return to your letter. It proves at least, that in the midst of your new gaieties, I still hold some place in your memory; and, what pleases me above all, it has an air of undissembled sincerity. Go on, my best and amiable friend, to shew me your heart simply, and without the shadow of disguise, and leave me to weep over it, as I now do, no matter whether from joy or sorrow.

CXLIII.—Mr. GRAY to Dr. WHARTON

18 *April*, 1770.

My dear Sir,

I have been sincerely anxious for Miss Wharton, whose illness must have been indeed severe. If she is only now recovering, let us hope everything from the spring; which begins (though slowly) to give new life to all things; and pray give my best respects to her, and thanks for remembering me and my Dictionary, at a time when she well may be excused for thinking of nothing but herself.

I have utterly forgot where my journal left off, but (I think) it was after the account of *Gordale*, near Settle. If so, there was little more worth your notice; the principal things were *Whorldale*, in the way from Skipton to Ottley, and *Kirkstall* Abbey, three miles from Leeds. The first is the valley formed by the River Wharf, well cultivated, well inhabited, well wooded. But with high rocky crags at distance, that border the green country on either hand. Through the midst of it was the river, in long windings, deep, clear, and full to the brink, and of no inconsiderable breadth. How it comes to be so fine and copious a stream here, and at Tadcaster (so much lower) should have nothing but a wide stony channel, with little or no water, I cannot tell you; *Kirkstall* is a noble ruin in the semi-Saxon style of building, as old as K. Stephen, toward the end of his reign, 1152; the whole church is still standing (the roof excepted) seated in a delicious quiet valley, on the banks of the River *Are*, and preserved with religious reverence by the Duke of Montagu. Adjoining to the church, between that and the river, are variety of chapels, and remnants of the abbey, shattered by the encroachments of the ivy, and surmounted by many a sturdy tree, whose twisted roots break through the fret of the vaulting, and hang streaming from the roofs. The gloom of these ancient cells, the shade and verdure of the landscape, the glittering and murmur of the stream, the lofty towers, and long perspectives of the church, in the midst of a clear bright day, detained me for many hours, and were the truest subjects for my glass I have yet met with anywhere; as I lay at that smoky, ugly, large town of Leeds, I dropt all farther thoughts of my journal; and after passing two days at Mason's (though he was absent), pursued my way by Nottingham, Leicester, Harborough, Kettering, Thrapston, and Huntingdon, to Cambridge, where I arrived 22 October, having met with no rain to signify, till this last day of my journey. There's luck for you.

I do think of seeing Wales this summer, having never found my spirits lower than at present, and feeling that motion and change of the scene is absolutely necessary to me. I will make Aston in my way to Chester, and shall rejoice to meet you there, the *last week in May*. Mason writes me word that he wishes it, and though his old house is down, and his new one not up, proposes to receive us like princes in grain. Adieu! my dear sir, and believe me,

Most faithfully yours,

T. G.

My best compliments to Mrs. Wharton and the family. Our weather till Christmas continued mild and open; 28 Dec. some snow fell, but did not lie. The 4th of January was stormy and snowy, which was often repeated during that month. And yet the latter half of it was warm and gentle. 18th Feb. was snow again, the rest of it mostly fine. Snow again on 15 March; from 20th to 30th of March was cold and dry, wind east, or north-east; on the 31st rain, from thence till within a week past, wind north-west, or north-east, with much hail and sleet; and on 4th April, a thunderstorm. It is now fine spring weather.

1 March.	First Violet appeared. Frogs abroad.
4 —	Almond blowed; and Gooseberry spread its leaves.
8 —	Apricot blowed.
1 April.	Violets in full bloom, and double Daffodils.
5 —	Wren singing. Double Jonquils.

CXLIV.—MR. GRAY TO MR. BONSTETTEN

April 19, 1770.

ALAS! how do I every moment feel the truth of what I have somewhere read, " *Ce n'est pas le voir, que de s'en souvenir ;* " and yet that remembrance is the only satisfaction I have left.

My life now is but a conversation with your shadow—the known sound of your voice still rings in my ears—there, on the corner of the fender, you are standing, or tinkling on the pianoforte, or stretched at length on the sofa. Do you reflect, my dearest friend, that it is a week or eight days before I can receive a letter from you, and as much more before you can have my answer; that all that time I am employed, with more than Herculean toil, in pushing the tedious hours along, and wishing to annihilate them; the more I strive, the heavier they move, and the longer they grow. I cannot bear this place, where I have spent many tedious years within less than a month since you left me. I am going for a few days to see poor Nicholls, invited by a letter, wherein he mentions you in such terms as add to my regard for him, and express my own sentiments better than I can do myself, "I am concerned," says he, "that I cannot pass my life with him. I never met with any one who pleased and suited me so well. The miracle to me is, how he comes to be so little spoiled, and the miracle of miracles will be, if he continues so in the midst of every danger and seduction, and without any advantages but from his own excellent nature and understanding. I own I am very anxious for him on this account, and perhaps your inquietude may have proceeded from the same cause. I hope I am to hear when he has passed that cursed sea, or will he forget me thus *in insulam relegatum* ? If he should it is out of my power to retaliate."

Surely you have written to him, my dear Bonstetten, or surely you will! he has moved me with these gentle and sensible expressions of his kindness for you; are you untouched by them?

You do me the credit, and false or true it goes to my heart, of ascribing to me your love for many virtues of the highest rank. Would to heaven it were so! but they are indeed the fruits of your own noble and generous understanding, which has hitherto struggled against the stream of custom, passion, ill company, even when you were but a child; and will you now give way to that stream when your strength is increased? Shall the jargon of French sophists, the allurements of painted women *comme il faut*, or the vulgar caresses of prostitute beauty, the property of all who can afford to purchase it, induce you to give up a mind and body by nature distinguished from all others, to folly, idleness, disease, and vain remorse. Have a care, my ever amiable friend, of loving what you do not approve. Know me for your most faithful and most humble despote.

CXLV.—Mr. GRAY to Mr. BONSTETTEN

May 9th, 1770.

I AM returned, my dear Bonstetten, from the little journey I made into Suffolk, without answering the end proposed. The thought that you might have been with me there, has embittered all my hours. Your letter has made me happy, as happy as so gloomy, so solitary a being as I am, is capable of being made. I know, and have too often felt, the disadvantages I lay myself under; how much I hurt the little interest I have in you, by this air of sadness so contrary to your nature and present enjoyments: but sure you will forgive, though you cannot sympathise with me. It is impossible for me to dissemble with you; such as I am I expose my heart to your view, nor wish to conceal a single thought from your penetrating eyes. All that you say to me, especially on the subject of Switzerland, is infinitely acceptable. It feels too pleasing ever to be fulfilled, and as often as I read over your truly kind letter, written long since from London, I stop at these words: " *La mort qui peut glacer nos bras avant qu'ils soient entrelacées.*"

CXLVI.—Mr. GRAY to Mr. BEATTIE

Pembroke Hall, July 2, 1770.

I REJOICE to hear that you are restored to better state of health, to your books, and to your muse once again. That forced dissipation and exercise we are obliged to fly to as a remedy, when this frail machine goes wrong, is often almost as bad as the distemper we would cure; yet I too have been constrained of late to pursue a like regimen, on account of certain pains in the head (a sensation unknown to me before), and of great dejection of spirits. This, sir, is the only excuse I have to make you for my long silence, and not (as perhaps you may have figured to yourself) any secret reluctance I had to tell you my mind concerning the specimen you so kindly sent me of your new poem.[1] On the contrary, if I had seen anything of importance to disapprove, I should have hastened to inform you, and never

[1] This letter was written in answer to one that inclosed only a part of the first book of the *Minstrel* in manuscript, and I believe a sketch of Mr. Beattie's plan for the whole.—*Mason.*

doubted of being forgiven. The truth is, I greatly like all I have seen, and wish to see more. The design is simple, and pregnant with poetical ideas of various kinds, yet seems somehow imperfect at the end. Why may not young Edwin, when necessity has driven him to take up the harp, and assume the profession of a minstrel, do some great and singular service to his country? (what service I must leave to your invention) such as no general, no statesman, no moralist could do without the aid of music, inspiration, and poetry. This will not appear an improbability in those early times and in a character then held sacred, and respected by all nations. Besides, it will be a full answer to all the Hermit has said, when he dissuaded him from cultivating these pleasing arts; it will show their use, and make the best panegyric of our favourite and celestial science. And lastly (what weighs most with me), it will throw more of action, pathos, and interest into your design, which already abounds in reflection and sentiment. As to description, I have always thought that it made the most graceful ornament of poetry, but never ought to make the subject. Your ideas are new, and borrowed from a mountainous country, the only one that can furnish truly picturesque scenery. Some trifles in the language or versification you will permit me to remark. . . .[1] (See Forbes's *Life of Beattie*, vol. i. p. 197, let. xlv. 4to.)

I will not enter at present into the merits of your *Essay on Truth*, because I have not yet given it all the attention it deserves, though I have read it through with pleasure; besides I am partial, for I have always thought David Hume a pernicious writer, and believe he has done as much mischief here as he has in his own country. A turbid and shallow stream often appears to our apprehensions very deep. A professed sceptic can be guided by nothing but his present passions (if he has any) and interests; and to be masters of his philosophy we need not his books or advice, for every child is capable of the same thing, without any study at all. Is not that *naiveté* and good humour, which his admirers celebrate in him, owing to this, that he has continued all his days an infant, but one that has unhappily been taught to read and write? That childish nation, the French, have given him vogue and fashion, and we, as usual, have learned from them to admire him at second hand.

[1] A few paragraphs of particular criticism are here omitted. Published in Beattie's *Life*, by Forbes.

CXLVII.—Mr. GRAY TO Dr. WHARTON

My dear Doctor,

It happened that I was in London at the time when Stone-hewer received your letter relating to Mr. L.'s request; as my name was mentioned in it, I ought to make my excuses to you as well as he, which it is indeed easy to do, as I could by no means ask anything but through him, and (though this had been in my power) it would have been a very bad plea to say, 'My L^{d.} you have done me a very unexpected favour not long since; and therefore I must beg you to do another, at my desire, for a friend of mine." But the truth is, at this time our application could not have had any success, as our principal would certainly never apply to three different persons, with whom he has no connection; nor care to be refused, or even obliged by them. The inside of things cannot be well explained by letters; but if you saw it, you would immediately see in its full light the impracticability of the thing.

I am lately returned from a six weeks ramble through Worcestershire, Gloucestershire, Monmouthshire, Herefordshire, and Shropshire, five of the most beautiful counties in the kingdom. The very light and principal feature in my journey was the river Wye, which I descended in a boat for near forty miles, from Ross to Chepstow. Its banks are a succession of nameless wonders! one out of many you may see not ill described by Mr. Whateley, in his *Observations on Gardening*,[1] under the name of the *New Weir*; he has also touched upon two others, *Tinterne Abbey*, and *Persfield* (Mr. Norris's), both of them famous scenes, and both on the Wye. Monmouth, a town I never heard mentioned, lies on the same river in a vale, that is the delight of my eyes, and the very seat of pleasure. The vale of Abergavenny, Ragland, and Chepstow Castles, Ludlow, Malvern Hills, Hampton Court near Lemster, the Leasowes, Hagley, the three cities and their cathedrals, and lastly Oxford (where I past two days in my return with great satisfaction), are the rest of my acquisitions, and no bad harvest to my thinking. I have a journal written by the companion [2] of my travels, that serves to recall and fix the fading images of these things.

[1] See Whateley's " Observations on the New Weir on the Wye," p. 111; description of Tintern Abbey, p. 136; of Persfield, p. 241.—*Mitford*.

[2] Mr. Norton Nicholls: of this gentleman see a full account in Mr. Mathias's edition of Gray's *Works*, vol i. p. 516. In the same year (says Mr. Gilpin in his preface to his *Observations on the River Wye*, p. iii.) in

I desire to hear of your health and that of your family. Ar
Miss Wh^{n.} and Miss Peggy quite recovered? My respects t
Mrs. Wharton and them.

I am ever yours,

T. G.

Pembroke College, *August* 24, 1770.

CXLVIII.—Mr. GRAY to Mr. NICHOLLS

Pembroke Hall, *Jan.* 26, 1771.

I REJOICE you have met with Froissart, he is the Herodotus of a
barbarous age; had he but had the luck of writing in as good a
language, he might have been immortal! His locomotive disposition (for then there was no other way of learning things),
his simple curiosity, his religious credulity, were much like those
of the old Grecian. When you have *tant chevauché*, as to get to
the end of him, there is Monstrelet waits to take you up, and will
set you down at Philip de Comines; but previous to all these,
you should have read Villehardouin and Joinville. I do not
think myself bound to defend the character of even the best of
kings: pray slash them all and spare not.

It would be strange too if I should blame your Greek studies,
or find fault with you for reading Isocrates; I did so myself
twenty years ago, and in an edition at least as bad as yours.
The " Panegyric," the " de Pace," " Areopagitic," and " Advice
to Philip," are by far the noblest remains we have of this writer,
and equal to most things extant in the Greek tongue; but it
depends on your judgment to distinguish between his real and
occasional opinion of things, as he directly contradicts in one
place what he has advanced in another: for example, in the
" Panathenaic " and the " de Pace," etc., on the naval power of

which this little journey was made, Mr. Gray made it likewise; and
hearing that I had put on paper a few remarks on the scenes, which he
had so lately visited, he desired a sight of them. They were then only in
a rude state; but the handsome things he said of them to a friend of his,
who obligingly repeated them to me, gave them, I own, some little degree
of credit in my own opinion; and made me somewhat less apprehensive
in risking them before the public. If this work afforded any amusement
to Mr. Gray, it was the amusement of a very late period of his life. He
saw it in London, about the beginning of June 1771; and he died, you
know, at the end of the July following. Had he lived, it is possible he
might have been induced to have assisted me with a few of his own remarks
on scenes which he had so accurately examined; the slightest touches of
such a master would have had their effect. No man was a greater admirer
of nature than Mr. Gray, nor admired it with better taste.—*Mitford.*

Athens; the latter of the two is undoubtedly his own undisguised sentiment.

I would by all means wish you to comply with your friend's
request, and write the letter he desires. I trust to the cause
and to the warmth of your own kindness for inspiration. Write
eloquently, that is from your heart, in such expressions as that
will furnish. Men sometimes catch that feeling from a stranger
which should have originally sprung from their own heart.

CXLIX.—Mr. GRAY to Dr. WHARTON

Feb. 2, PEMBROKE COLL., 1771.

It never rains but it pours, my dear Doctor, you will be glad to
hear that Mr. Brown has added to his mastership (which is better
than £150 a year) a living hard by Cambridge, Streatham in the
Isle of Ely, worth, as it was let above forty years ago, at least £240
more. It was in the gift of the crown during the vacancy of the
See of Ely, and that its value is really more than I have said,
you will hardly doubt when you hear it was carried against an
earl, a baron, and a bishop, the latter of the three so strenuous
a suitor, that he still persisted above a week after I had seen the
presentation signed to Mr. Brown by the king's own hand, nay,
he still persisted a day after the king had publicly declared in
the drawing-room that he had given it to Mr. Brown by name.
And who was this bishop? no other than your friend, who
wanted it for a nephew of his, a poor *unfortunate* nephew, that
had been so imprudent many a year ago to marry a farmer's
daughter, where he boarded when curate; and continued ever
since under a cloud, because his uncle would give him nothing.
As to us, we had a duke, an earl, a viscount, and a bishop on our
side, and carried it so swimmingly you would stare again. There
was a prologue, and an exegesis, and a peripeteia, and all the
parts of a regular drama; and the hero is gone to London, was
instituted yesterday, and to-day is gone to Lambeth, for the
archbishop too spoke a good word for us, and at a very critical
time. The old lodge has got rid of all its harpsichords, and
begins to brighten up: its inhabitant is lost like a mouse in an
old cheese. He has received your generous offer of a bene-
faction to the common good, but it is too much to tax yourself:
however, we all intend to bring in our mites, and shew the way
to the high and mighty; when a fund is once on foot they will
bestir themselves.

I am sincerely concerned to find Miss Wharton is still a invalid. I believe you must send her into the milder region of the south, where the sun dispels all maladies. We ourselve have had an untoward season enough: vast quantities of rai instead of winter, the thermometer never below 40 degrees often above 50, before Christmas; unusual high winds (whic still continue), particularly the 19th of Dec. at night it blew a dreadful storm. The first grain of snow was seen on Christ mas day, of which we have had a good deal since, but neve deep or lasting. The second week in January was really severe cold at London, and the Thames frozen over: one mornin that week the glass stood here (at eight in the morning) a 16 degrees, which is the lowest I ever knew it at Cambridge At London it never has been observed lower than 13 (under stand me right, I mean 13 above zero of Fahrenheit), and that was 5th Jan. 1739; now it is very mild again, but with very high winds at N.W.

I give you joy of our awkward peace with Spain. Mason is in town taking his swing, like a boy in breaking-up time. Remember me kindly to Mrs. Wharton, and all the good family. Did I tell you of my breaking-up, in summer, in the midland counties; and so far as Abergavenny one way, and Ludlow the other? I have another journal for you in several volumes. I have had a cough for above three months upon me which is incurable. Adieu!

> I am ever yours,
> T. G.

CL.—Mr. GRAY TO Dr. WHARTON

DEAR DOCTOR,

I was really far from well in health when I received your last letter: since that I am come to town and find myself considerably better. Mason has passed all the winter here with Stonehewer in Curzon-street, Mayfair, but thinks of returning homeward in a week or ten days, he had your letter (which had gone round by Aston) and was applying to Mr. Fraser and others for proper recommendations in case poor —— should be obliged to make use of them: but now you have given us some hopes that these expedients may not be necessary. I for my own part do heartily wish you may not be deceived, and that so cool a tyrant as her husband seems to be may willingly give up the houghts of exercising that tyranny, when it is most in his ower; but I own, it seems to me very unlikely: however, I ould not have you instrumental (but at her most earnest ntreaty) in placing her out of his reach. No persuasion or dvice on this head should come from you: it should be abso-tely her own firm resolution (before sure witnesses), for that the only thing that can authorise you to assist her. It must ave been her own fault (at least her weakness) that such a ecision as that of these delegates could find any grounds to go pon. I do not wonder that such an event has discomposed you: discomposed me to think of the trouble and expense it has rought upon you!

My summer was intended to have been passed in Switzerland, ut I have dropped the thought of it, and believe my expeditions ill terminate in Old Park: for travel I must, or cease to exist. ill this year I hardly knew what (mechanical) low spirits were: ut now I even tremble at an east wind; it is here the height of ummer, but with all the bloom and tender verdure of spring. t Cambridge the laurustinus and arbutus killed totally; pricots, almonds, and figs lost all their young shoots. Stone-ewer has had a melancholy journey: to-morrow we expect him ere. Adieu!

I am ever yours,

T. G.

At Frisby's, in Jermyn Street, St. James's, *May* 24, 1771.

APPENDIX

I.—Mr. BROWN to Dr. WHARTON

Pembroke Hall, *July 24, 1771.*

Dear Sir,

Here is Mr. Gray wishing to be well enough to take his journe
to Old Park, but in truth he knows not when he shall be so happy
Though he does not give over the hopes of it, yet he thinks it i
so uncertain when he can set about it, that he wishes not to alte
any plan you may have formed for passing away any part o
your summer. Some complaints of the gout he hath had; som
feverish disorder which hath frequently returned and left hir
low and dispirited, and another complaint added to it whic
renders travelling very inconvenient. He has been for six o
seven weeks in London, and almost all the time out of order
he came hither the beginning of this week; he had entertaine
great hopes that he should have been with you before this tim
I hope your nephew came safe into the north and that he i
well; we much esteem him here.

The weather is very fine at this time with us. I doubt not
is so with you, and I hope your daughters reap great benef
from it, and that they forget the severities of last winter.
join with Mr. Gray in sending to you and Mrs. Wharton, to you
sons and daughters, our best respects and heartiest wishes fo
their health and yours. Don't forget my compliments to you
nephew.

> I am, dear sir, affectionately yours,
> J. Brown.

II.—Mr. BROWN to Dr. WHARTON

Poor Mr. Gray! My dear sir, I am afraid his friends at Ol
Park will see him no more. Professor Plumptre and Dr. Gly
give us no hopes of his recovery, they both attend him, an
come together three or four times a day; they say it is the gou

the stomach, and they cannot get the better of it. Stephen,
is old servant, is very diligent and handy in his attendance
pon him, and Mr. Gray is well satisfied with it. He has very
equently convulsion fits. The physicians last night did not
xpect to find him alive this morning; and this morning they did
ot think he would live till the evening. They don't find him
orse this evening than he was in the morning, yet they say
nough he may have strength enough to last a few days, they
hink he has not strength enough to recover. He does not
lways talk coherently, and then recovers his thoughts again.
sent a special messenger yesterday to Mr. Stonehewer, who
ould probably find him ten or twelve hours before the post.
dieu! and accept of my best good wishes for yourself, Mrs.
Vharton and your family.

I am affectionately yours,

J. BROWN.

Monday Night, July 29, 1771.

III.—MR. BROWN TO DR. WHARTON

DEAR SIR,

Dr. Gisburn and Mr. Stonehewer came here last night, were
present at three or four consultations, and are gone away this
evening to London, without the least hopes of seeing our poor
riend again. He told me, if I understood him right, where a will
vould be found, but I shall not look so long as he is alive. I
ave been told that you have had a will in your custody; if it
pe so, it is too probable it will be wanted, and if one be found here,
t must be seen which of the two is the last. My best respects
ttend you and Mrs. Wharton and your family.

I am, dear sir, affectionately yours,

J. BROWN.

Tuesday Evening, July 30, 1771.

I think him dying, and that he has been sensible of his approaching death, nor hath he expressed any concern at the
houghts of leaving this world.

He is still alive—9 o'clock.

IV.—Mr. BROWN to Dr. WHARTON

DEAR SIR,

You must expect what will give you great concern; Mr. Gray
died about eleven last night; there is nothing to be added about
his death, but that the whole was peaceable and calm, so long as
he was himself; nor was there anything violent afterwards: but
we think that for some hours before he died, though he appeared
convulsed to us, yet that he himself felt no pain. This was the
opinion of the physicians. I found a will in the place of which
he had told me, dated 1st July 1770. I was concerned that
Mrs. Foster's name is totally omitted. £500 in the stocks is left
to her daughter Lady Goring. Mr. Williamson of Calcutta, a
relation on his father's side, is a legatee to the same value. To
Mr. Mason he has left all his books and all his papers, to be
destroyed or preserved at his direction. He hath joined me
with Mr. Mason in the executorship. To Mr. Stonehewer and
Dr. Wharton each £500 reduced bank annuities, and to each one
of his diamond rings. He has desired to be buried near his
mother at Stoke, near Windsor, and that one of his executors
would see him laid in the grave. A melancholy task which must
come to my share, for Mr. Mason is not here, and it will be necessary to proceed in a very few days. This morning at eight,
nine, ten, he was but little altered. You have my best wishes,
you and your family. I know they will grieve every one of them
for the loss of Mr. Gray.

I am, dear sir, very affectionately yours,

JAMES BROWN.

PEMBROKE HALL, *Wednesday, July 31, 1771.*

I shall return as soon as I can.

V.—Mr. BROWN to Dr. WHARTON

PEMBROKE HALL, *Aug. 17, 1771.*

DEAR SIR,

Everything is now dark and melancholy in Mr. Gray's room,
not a trace of him remains there; it looks as if it had been for
some time uninhabited, and the room bespoke for another
inhabitant. The papers are in good hands, Mr. Mason carried

them with him to York; and his furniture he bequeathed to his relations here. The thoughts I have of him will last, and will be useful to me the few years I can expect to live. He never spoke out, but I believe from some little expressions I now remember to have dropt from him, that for some time past he thought himself nearer his end than those about him apprehended. I shall rejoice in the happiness of your family, and desire my best respects to Mrs. Wharton, and your sons and your daughters.

I am affectionately yours,

J. BROWN.

Remember me to your nephew; the bill you sent is in the hands of Mr. May. Adieu!

VI.—MR. MASON TO DR. WHARTON

YORK, *Aug.* 18, 1771.

DEAR SIR,

The best apology I can make to you for not writing to you sooner, will be to give you an account how I have been employed since the sad event happened, which now occasions my writing.

I received the melancholy news at Bridlington Key, full ten days after it had happened; I crossed the Humber immediately, and got to Cambridge the day after, in order to assist and relieve Mr. Brown as soon and as much as I was able. He returned not from Stoke and London till the Saturday. On Sunday I set out with him for London, to prove the will, and having done so, returned on Monday. This was a great and an unnecessary loss of time. But nothing would satisfy his cautious temper but our doing it personally. On Tuesday and Wednesday we delivered up the furniture of the rooms to the Antrobuses, and in the meanwhile the books were packed up and sent to the lodge; so that by this dispatch he will have nothing to take charge of but what remains to the executorship. The papers I brought all with me here yesterday. My first business shall be to sort the letters, which are numerous. I shall seal up those of the living correspondents, and return them when convenient. I find a good many of yours, which I shall return you with all fidelity.

You will perhaps wonder why I staid so little a while with him. The time of my residence here began the very day after

I reached Cambridge. Mr. Cayley's servants and goods were gone to his parsonage. He stayed the Sunday over, and that was all he could possibly do, so that it was impossible for me to prolong my stay another day. However, the great burthen, *i.e.* the care of little matters, is now off his hands. You who know his attention to little matters, know how much he will be relieved by what is already done. You know, too, he could never have attended to other things till these had been done, and he would have been months of doing without me, what I trust has been now done as effectually in three days. I purpose to return to him in November, to transfer the stock bequeathed, and to give up the title deeds of the house in Cornhill. In the meantime, my dear Doctor Wharton, shall not I assure myself of seeing you at York? Come, I beseech you, and condole with me on our mutual, our irreparable loss. The great charge, which his dear friendship has laid upon me, I feel myself unable to execute without the advice and assistance of his best friends; you are among the first of these: and the first, too, whose counsel I could take on the occasion. As soon as the foolish hurry of this idle week is over, my house will be empty and my time my own. Come when it suits you, I shall take care to have a bed for you at the deanery, if these rooms be too small. Mrs. Wharton, perhaps, will accompany you, and take this opportunity of seeing her sister. My best compliments to her and the young ladies.

> Believe me, most cordially yours,
> W. MASON.

Excuse great haste and much confusion of mind, for I have been hurried and concerned beyond expression.

VII.—MR. WALPOLE TO MR. COLE

PARIS, *August*

DEAR SIR,

I am excessively shocked at reading in the papers that Mr. Gray is dead! I wish to God you may be able to tell me it is not true! yet in this painful uncertainty I must rest some days! None of my acquaintance are in London. I do not know to whom to apply but to you. Alas! I fear in vain! Too many circumstances speak it true. The detail is exact: a second paper arrived by the same post, and does not contradict it:—and what is worse, I saw him but four or five days before I came hither; he had been to Kensington for the air, complained of gout flying about him; of sensations of it in his stomach; and indeed I thought him changed, and that he looked ill. Still I had not the least idea of his being in danger. I started up from my chair when I read the paragraph.—A cannon-ball could not have surprised me more! The shock but ceased to give way to my concern; and my hopes are too ill founded to mitigate it. If nobody has the charity to write to me, my anxiety must continue till the end of the month; for I shall set out on my return on the 26th; and unless you receive this time enough for your answer to leave London on the 20th in the evening, I cannot meet it till I find it in Arlington-street, whither I beg you to direct it. If the event is but too true, pray add to this melancholy service that of telling me any circumstances you know of his death. Our long, very long friendship and his genius must endear to me everything that relates to him. What writings has he left? Who are his executors? I should earnestly wish, if he has destined anything to the public, to print it at my press. It would do me honour, and would give me an opportunity of expressing what I feel for him. Methinks, as we grow old, our only business here is to adorn the graves of our friends, or to dig our own.

Dear sir, yours ever,

HOR. WALPOLE.

P.S. I heard this unhappy news last night, and have just been told that Lord Edward Bentinck goes in haste to-morrow to England, so that you will receive this much sooner than I expected: still, I must desire you to direct to Arlington-street, as being the surest conveyance to me.

Mr. Cole, in his answer to this letter, says, " that Gray died worth about £6000, having sold his paternal property in houses, not being made for tenants and repairs, and placed the money in the funds, with a part of which, as I am informed, he purchased an annuity, in order to have a fuller income.

" He went off pretty easily, considering the nature of his complaint, the gout in his stomach, which occasioned a sickness and loss of appetite, neither would anything rest on his stomach. . . . It was not till Friday before he died that he had any convulsions, when he was seized with the first, and had them, occasionally, till his death on Tuesday night following, though not to any great degree: the master being with him till half an hour before his decease. As it was warm weather, and the distance considerable, it was impossible to comply with that part of his will relating to his coffin, which was wrapped in lead. . . . He retained his senses to the last, but gave proof of their decay a day or two before his death, which he expected, as he told one of his cousins, saying—'Molly, I shall die.' The decay I mentioned was this: seeing the master sit by him, he said—'Oh, sir! let Dr. Halifax or Dr. Heberden be sent to.'—He certainly meant for physical assistance:—now Dr. Halifax, the Regius Professor of Law, his acquaintance, was a divine, and no physician." . . .

METRUM

OBSERVATIONS ON ENGLISH METRE

THOUGH I would not with Mr. Urry,[1] the editor of Chaucer, insert words and syllables, unauthorised by the oldest manuscripts, to help out what seems lame and defective in the measure of our ancient writers, yet as I see those manuscripts, and the first[2] printed editions, so extremely inconstant in their manner of spelling one and the same word as to vary continually, and often in the compass of two lines, and seem to have no fixed orthography, I cannot help thinking it probable, that many great inequalities in the metre are owing to the neglect of transcribers, or that the manner of reading made up for the defects which appear in the writing. Thus the *y* which we often see prefixed to participles passive, *y*cleped, *y*hewe, etc., is not a mere arbitrary insertion to fill up the verse, but is the old Anglo-Saxon augment, always prefixed formerly to such participles, as *ge*lufod (loved) from lufian (to love), *ge*ræd, from ædan (to read), etc., which augment, as early as Edward the Confessor's time, began to be written with a *y*, or an *i*, as *i*lufod, *i*seld, for *ge*lufod, *ge*seld (loved, sold), as Dr. Hickes[3]

[1] See the preface to Urry's *Chaucer.* Fol.
[2] This inconstancy of the manner of spelling one and the same word is not confined to the first printed copies, but is found equally in the MSS. themselves. This is no wonder, for the Italians themselves, contemporary with Chaucer, writing in an age when literature began to flourish, and in a language more regular and grammatical than that of any neighbouring country, had yet no fixed orthography, as appears from the original manuscripts of Francesco Barberino, Boccaccio, and Petrarch, which are still preserved. See *Crescimbeni Comentarj,* l. 6.
[3] And see Somner's *Saxon Dictionary* in Le. Chaucer seems to have been well aware of the injustice that his copyists might chance to do to him: he says, towards the end of his " Troilus,"

> " And for there is so great diversite,
> In English, and in writing of our tong;
> So pray I to God, that none miswrite thee,
> Ne thee mis-metre for defaut of tong
> And redde where so thou be, or else song,
> That thou be understond', God I beseech—"

et in another place he says,

> " But for the rime is light and lewde,
> Yet make it somewhat agreable
> Though some verse fayle in a syllable."
>
> 3rd B. of " Fame."

informs us in his *Anglo-Saxon Grammar*, c. 22, p. 136. This
syllable, though (I suppose) then out of use in common speech,
our poets inserted, where it suited them, in verse. The same
did they by the final syllable of verbs, as bren*nin*, correc*tin*,
dron*kin*, etc. (to burn, correct, drink), which was also Saxon,
all the infinitives in that tongue ending with an *an*, or *eon*, as
*bebyrige*an, to bury, *mag*an, to be able, *gefe*on, to rejoice, and
most of the participles passive, and the plural persons terminat-
ing with the same letter, as, *gefund*en, found, *beswung*en, beaten,
etc.; and *we, ge, hi, miht*on (we, he, they, might), we *wold*on, we
would; we *sceold*on, we should; we *ar*on, we are, etc. This
termination began to be omitted after the Danes were settled
among us; for in the Cimbrick tongue the verbs usually finished
in *a*, as grei*p*a, to gripe, hab*a*, to have, which in the Saxon were
grei*p*an, hab*an*; the transition is very apparent thence to the
English, which we now speak. As then our writers [1] inserted
these initial and final letters, or omitted them; and, where we
see them written, we do not doubt that they were meant to fill
up the measure; it follows, that these poets had an ear no

And so says Lydgate of himself:

> " Because I know the verse therein is wrong,
>   As being some too short, and some loo long."
>   *Chronicle of Troye*, p. 316.

[1] The same thing is observable in the MSS. and first editions of the
Italian poets. Even in Dante's and in Petrarch's time, as,

> " Nello stato primaio non si rinselva."
>   " Purgatorio," c. 14, v. 66.

And,

> " Ecco Cin da Pistoia, Guitton d'Arezzo."
>   " Trionfo dell' Amore," capit. 4, v. 32.

In both which verses there is a syllable too much, on which Crescimbeni
observes, " Costumavano gli antichi rimatori, ogni volta che in fin d' una
voce s' incontrava la vocale *i* tra due altri vocali, troncar la voce, e pro-
nunziarla fino alla sillaba accentuata acutamente, benchè la voce a
arbitrio la scrivessero or tronca con l'apostrofe, ed ora intera." (*Istor.
della Volg. Poesia*, l. 1, p. 9.) And one would think that they occasionally practised the same thing in syllables not consisting of a vowel only,
by that verse of an ancient poet, which he cites,

> " Tu sei quel arma*tura*, per cui vencimmo,"

where in reading they probably sunk the last syllable of *armatura*, because
the accent did not fall upon it. This might less offend them, because
their ears were so used to the Provençal dialect, in which abundance of
words are the same with the Italian, were not the last syllable cut off, as
pie*tat* for pie*tate*, seq*uent* for seguente, pode*ruz* for pode*roso*, *fach* for fatto,
etc., and doubtless from that language the Italians borrowed their custom
of sinking the vowel in the end of many words at pleasure, when the next
begins with a consonant, which they now do in prose, as well as in verse

insensible to defects in metre; and where the verse seems to halt, it is very probably occasioned by the transcriber's neglect, who, seeing a word spelt differently from the manner then customary, changed or omitted a few letters without reflecting on the injury done to the measure. The case is the same with the genitive case singular and the nominative plural of many nouns, which by the Saxon inflection had an additional syllable, as *word*, aword, *wordis*, of a word: *smith*, a smith, *smithis*, of a smith, *smithas*, smith, which, as Hickes observes, is the origin of the formation of those cases in our present tongue; but we now have reduced them, by our pronunciation, to an equal number of syllables with their nominative singular. This was commonly done too, I imagine, in Chaucer's and Lydgate's time; but, in verse, they took the liberty either to follow the old language in pronouncing the final syllable, or to sink the vowel and abridge it, as was usual, according to the necessity of their versification. For example, they would read either vĭŏlēttĕs with four syllables, or violets with three; ban*kis*, or banks; triŭmphys, or triŭmphs, indifferently. I have mentioned (in some remarks on the verses of Lydgate) the *e* mute, and their use of it in words derived from the French, and I imagine that they did the same in many words of true English origin, which the Danes had before robbed of their final consonant, writing *bute* for the Saxon *butan* (without), *bifora* for *biforan* (before), *ondrede* for *ondreadan* (to dread), *gebringe* for *gebringan* (to bring), *doeme* for *deman* (to deem), and abundance of other words. Here we may easily conceive, that though the *n* was taken away, yet the *e* continued to be pronounced faintly, and though in time it was quite dropped in conversation, yet when the poet thought fit to make a syllable of it, it no more offended their ears than it now offends those of a Frenchman to hear it so pronounced, in verse.

Puttenham, in his *Art of Poetry*, addressed to Queen Elizabeth in 1587, tells us, l. 2. c. 4, that " Chaucer, Lydgate, and others used *cesures* either very seldom, or not at all, or else very licentiously; and many times made their meetres (they called them *riding ryme*) of such unshapely words as would allow no convenient cesure; and therefore did let their rymes run out at length, and never staid till they came to the end; which manner, though it were not to be misliked in some sort of meetre, yet in every long verse the cesure ought to be kept precisely, if it were but to serve as a law to correct the licentious-ness of rymers. Besides that, it pleaseth the eare better, and

sheweth more cunning in the maker by following the rule of his
restraint, for a rymer that will be tied by no rules at all, but
range as he list, may utter what he will; but such maner of
poesy is called in our vulgar,[1] ' *ryme dogrell*,' with which rebuke
we will that in no case our Maker shall be touched."

Then Puttenham gives rules for the cæsura, which he tells us,
" In a verse of twelve syllables should always divide it exactly
in the middle; in one of ten, it should fall on the fourth, in one
of eight on the same, in one of seven on the same, or on none
at all," etc. I mention no [2] more than these, as they are now
the only measures admitted into our serious poetry, and I shall
consider how his rules hold in modern practice.

Alexandrines,[3] or verses of twelve syllables, it is true,
though Spenser sometimes does otherwise, must, if they

---

[1] It appears from Alderman Fabian's prologue to the second volume of his
Chronicle, written in Henry the Seventh's reign, that the free verse, where
no exact number of syllables was observed, was then called *doggrell*. Thus.

> " Now would I fayne
> In wordes plaine
> Some honour sayne,
>   And bring to mynde
> Of that aunciente citye,
> That so goodly is to se,
> And full trewe ever hath be,
>   And also full kynde, etc.
> For though I shuld all day tell,
> Or that with my *ryme dogerell*
> Myght I not yet halfe do spell
>   This townes great honour, etc.

> To the reader.

> Whoso hym liketh these versys to rede,
> Wyth favour I pray he wyll theym spell,
> Let not the rudeness of them hym lede
> For to desprave this *ryme dogerell*," etc.

[2] Lines of six, five, or four syllables are intermixed in lyric compositions,
but, as Puttenham says, " they need no censure, because the breath
asketh no relief."

[3] Puttenham says, " The Alexandrine is with our modern rhymers most
usual, with the auncyent makers it was not so. For before Sir Thomas
Wyatt's time they were not used in our vulgar: they be for grave and
stately matters fitter, than for any other ditty of pleasure. If the cesure
be just in the middle, and that ye suffer the verse to run at full length,
and do not (as common rimers do, or their printer, for sparing of paper)
cut them off in the middest, wherein they make in two verses but halfe
rime, they do very wel." (" Art of Poesie," l. ii. c. 3.) The poets of
Henry the Eighth's time mixed it with the line of fourteen syllables alternately, which is so tiresome, that we have long since quite banished it.
Thus many things of Wyatt's and Lord Surrey's are written, and those of
Queen Elizabeth on the Queen of Scots.

would strike the ear agreeably, have their pause in the middle,
as—

> And after toilsome days | a soft repose at night.

Or—

> He both her warlike Lords | outshined in Helen's eyes

And this uniformity in the cæsura is just the reason why we no
longer use them but just to finish a lyric stanza: they are also
sometimes interspersed arbitrarily among verses of ten syllables.
This is an odd custom, but it is confirmed by the sanction which
Dryden and Pope have given to it, for they soon tire the ear
with this sameness of sound; and the French seemed to have
judged ill in making them their heroic [1] measure.

Verses of *eight* syllables are so far from being obliged to have
their cæsura on the fourth, that Milton, the best example of an
exquisite ear that I can produce, varies it continually, as—

To live with her, | and live with thee	.	On the 4th.
In unreproved | pleasures free	. .	——— 5th.
To hear the lark | begin his flight	. .	——— 4th.
And singing | startle the dŭll night	.	—— 3d.
Whĕre thĕ grēat sŭn | bĕgīns hĭs stāte	.	——— 4th.
The clouds | in thousand liveries dight	.	——— 2d.
With masque | and antique pageantry	.	——— 2d

The more we attend to the composition of Milton's harmony,
the more we shall be sensible how he loved to vary [2] his pauses,
his measures, and his feet, which gives that enchanting air of
freedom and wildness to his versification, unconfined by any
rules but those which his own feeling and the nature of his

---

[1] They were not so till towards the end of the sixteenth century. " Quant
aux vers de *douze* syllabes, que nous appellons Alexandrins, combien
qu'ils proviennent d'une longue anciennetè, toutefois nous en avions
perdu l'usage. Car, lorsque Marot insere quelques uns dedans ses Epi-
grammes ou Tombeaux, c'est avec cette suscription, Vers Alexandrins;
comme si c'étoit chose nouvelle et inaccoustumée d'en user.—Le premier
des nôtres, qui les mit en credit, fut Baïf en ses Amours de Francine,
suivy depuis par Du Bellay au livre de ses Regrets, et par Ronsard en ses
Hymnes, et finalement par Du Bartas, qui semble vouloir renvier sur tous
les autres en ses deux Semaines." (See Pasquier, l. vii. c. 8 and 11.) Yet
Ronsard, in his " Art of Poetry," continues to call the decasyllabic
measure only *heroic verse*, and uses it in his " Franciade " and other long
compositions.

[2] Lord Surrey (who was Puttenham's example for sweetness and proportion of metre) generally, though not always, makes his cæsura on the
fourth; as,

> " True wisdom join'd | with simpleness,
> The night | discharged of all care,   . On the 2d.
> Where wine the wit | may not oppresse
> The faithful wife | without debate,
> Such slepes | as may beguile the night,
> Content thyself | with thine estate,
> Ne wish for death, | ne feare his might."

subject demanded. Thus he mixes the line of eight syllables
with that of seven, the trochee and the spondee with the iambic
foot, and the single rhyme with the double. He changes the
cæsura as frequently in the heptasyllabic measure, as,

Oft ŏn ă plăt | of rising ground . (Octosyll.)
I hear | the far-off curfew sound, (Oct:—) On the 2d.
Ovĕr sŏme | wide-water'd shore . . . —— 3d.
Swinging slow | with sullen roar: . . . —— 3d.
Or if the air | will not permit, etc. (Oct:—) —— 4th.
Far from all resort | of mirth . . . —— 4th.
Save the cricket | on the hearth . . . —— 4th.
Or the bellman's | drowsy charm . . . —— 4th.

But the greatest confinement which Puttenham would lay
on our verse is that of making the cæsura constantly fall on the
fourth syllable of our decasyllabic measure, which is now become
our only heroic [1] metre for all poems of any length. This
restraint Wyatt and Lord Surrey submitted to, though here
and there you find an instance of their breaking through it,
though rarely. So,

From these hye hilles | as when a spring doth falle,
It trilleth down | with still and subtle course,
Of this and that | it gathers aye, and shall
Till it have just | downe flowed to stream and force:
So fareth Love, | when he hath ta'en a course;
Rage is his raine; | resistance 'vaileth none;
The first eschue | is remedy alone.   Wyatt.

And these verses of Surrey:

In active games | of nimbleness and strength
Where we did strain, | trained with swarms of youth,
Our tender limbs, | which yet shot up in length:
The secret groves, | which oft we made resound
Of plesaunt plaint, | and of our Lady's praise,
Recording oft, | what grace each one had found,
What hope of speed, | what dread of long delays;

[1] We probably took it from the Italians. Their heroic measure has
indeed eleven syllables, because of the rhyme, which is double; but as
our language requires single rhyme, the verse was reduced to ten syllables;
the run of it is the same to the ear. The Italians borrowed it from the
Provençals, there being verses extant still of this kind by Arnauld Daniel,
who died in 1189, and is celebrated by Petrarch, under the title of " Gran
Maestro d'amor," and of Arnauld de Merveille, who flourished about
1190, as

      " Fazes auzir vostras castas preguieras
      Tant doussament, qu'a pietat sia moguda
      De s'inclinar a ma justa demanda," etc.
            Crescimbeni Istor. della Volg. Poesia, l. i. p. 6.

Dante judges it the best adapted of any metre to noble subjects. " Quorum
omnium Endecasyllabum videtur esse superbius, tam temporis occupa-
tione quam capacitate sententiæ, constructionis, et vocabulorum, etc.—
et omnes hoc Doctores perpendisse videntur, Cantiones illustres principi-
antes ab illo." " De Vulgari Eloquentiâ," l. ii. c. 5.

> The wild forèst, | the clothed holts with green,
> With reines availed, | and swift-ybreathed horse,
> With cry of hound, | and merry blasts between,
> Where we did chase | the fearful hart of force, etc.

But our poets have long since got loose from these fetters. Spenser judiciously shook them off; Milton, in his "Paradise Lost," is ever changing and mingling his pauses, and the greatest writers after him have made it their study to avoid what Puttenham regarded as a rule of perfect versification.

These reflections may serve to shew us, that Puttenham, though he lived within about one hundred and fifty years of Chaucer's time, must have been mistaken with regard to what the old writers called their *riding rhyme;* for the *Canterbury Tales,* which he gives as an example of it, are as exact in their measure and in their pause as in the "Troilus and Cresseide," where he says, "*the metre is very grave and stately;*" and this not only in the "Knight's Tale," but in the comic introduction and characters; as,

> A monke ther was | fair for the maistery,
> An outrider | that loved venery,[1]
> A manly man, | to ben an abbot able,
> Many a dainty horse | had he in stable;   (On the 6th.)
> And when he rode, | men might his bridle heare,
> Gingiling in a whistling wind, | as cleare   (On the 8th.)
> And eke as loud, as doth the chapell-bell, etc.

I conclude, that he was misled by the change which words had undergone in their accents since the days of Chaucer, and by the seeming defects of measure which frequently occur in the printed copies. I cannot pretend to say what it was they called *riding rhyme,* but perhaps it might be such as we see in the northern "Tale of Sir Thopas" in Chaucer.

> Sir Thopas was | a doughty swaine,
> White was his face, | as pain[2] de maine,[2]
> His lippis red as rose, |
> His rudd[4] is like | scarlet in graine,
> And I you tell | in gode certaine
> He had a seemly nose. | Etc.

But nothing can be more regular than this sort of stanza, the pause always falling just in the middle of those verses which are

---

[1] Venerie, **Fr.** hunting.

[2] " When thou beholdest before thy Lord *peyne-mayne:*
  A baker chosen, and waged well forthe,
  That only he should that businesse applye," etc.
      Alexander Barclay's *Eclogues,*
      Written in the beginning of Henry ye 8's reign.

[3] The whitest bread.   [4] *Rudu,* Sax. colour of the cheek.

of eight syllables, and at the end of those of six. I imagine that it was this very regularity which seemed so tedious to *mine host of the Tabbarde*, as to make him interrupt Chaucer in the middle of his story, with

> " No more of this for Goddis dignitè—
> Mine earès akin of thy draftie [1] speeche,
> Now such a rime the Devil I beteeche,[2]
> This may well be clepe *Rime Dogrell*, quoth he," etc.

Hence too we see that Puttenham is mistaken in the sense of *rhyme dogrell*, for so far was it *from being tied to no rule at all*, that it was consistent with the greatest exactness in the cæsura and in the measure; but as he himself has said very well in another place (b. ii. ch. ix.), " the over busie and too speedie returne of one manner of tune doth too much annoy and, as it were, glut the eare, unless it be in small and popular musickes, sung by these Cantabanqui [3] upon benches and barrels-heads, where they have none other audience than boys and country fellows, that pass by them in the street; or else by blind harpers or such like tavern-minstrels, that give a fit of mirth for a groat;

---

[1] *Tedious*, from *drof*, Sax. dirty, filthy.

[2] *Beteacan*, Sax. to give, or commit to.

[3] Doubtless the degenerate successors of those ancient *Jongleurs* in Provence, Italy, and other countries described by Crescimbeni, where he is speaking of the old romances. " Or questi Romanzi non v' ha dubbio che si cantavano, e forse non s'ingannò colui, che fu di parere, che i Romanzatori in panca vendessero l' opere loro cantando, imperocchè fioriva anticamente in Francia un' arte detta de' Giuglari, i quali erano faceti e spiritosi uomini, che solevano andar cantando i loro versi per le corte alle mense de' grandi, colla viuola, o' coll' arpa, o' con altro stromento.— Molti de' poeti Provenzali de' primi tempi questa stessa esercitarono ed anco de' nostri Italiani, che in quella lingua poetarono." (*Comentarj del Crescimbeni*, l. v. c. 5, p. 333.) And he cites on this occasion these verses in a romance composed about the year 1230:

> " Quand les tables ostées furent
> Cil Jugleur en pies esturent,
> S' ont Vielles et Harpes prises;
> Chansons, sons, vers, et reprises,
> Et de Gestes chanté nos ont," etc.

These verses are in the *Tournoyement d' Antichrist*, by Huon de Mari, a monk of St. Germain. Fauchet, l. i. ch. 8.

And Huon de Villeneuve, a writer of the same age, addresses himself to the company whom he is going to entertain in these words:

> " Gardez, qu' il n'i ait noise, ne tabor, ne criée,
> Il est ensinc coustume en la vostre contrée.
> Quant uns Chanterres vient entre gent honorée
> Et il a en droit soi la Vielle attrempée;
> Ja tant n'aura mantel, ne cotte desramée,
> Que sa premiere [1] laisse ne soit bien escoutée:
> Puis font chanter avant, se de riens lor agrée,
> Ou tost sans vilenie puet recoillir s'estrée," etc.

[1] *Couple*, ou Entrée.

and their matters being for the most part stories of old time, as the 'Tale of Sir Thopas,' the 'Reportes of Bevis [1] of Southampton,' 'Adam Bell,' and 'Clymme of the Clough,' and such other old romances and historical rhymes, made on purpose for the recreation of the common people at Christmas dinners and bride-ales in taverns and ale-houses, and such other places of base resort," etc. This was before *dogrell*, whose frequent return of rhyme and similarity of sound easily imprinted it in the memory of the vulgar; and, by being applied of old to the meanest uses of poetry, it was grown distasteful to the ears of the better sort.

But the *riding rhyme* I rather take to be that which is confined to one measure, whatever that measure may be, but not to one rhythm; having sometimes more, sometimes fewer syllables, and the pause hardly distinguishable, such as the "Prologue and History of Beryn," found in some MSS. of Chaucer, and the Cook's "Tale of Gamelyn," where the verses have twelve, thirteen, or fourteen syllables, and the cæsura on the sixth, seventh, or eighth, as it happens. This having an air of rusticity, Spenser has very well adapted it to pastoral poetry, and in his hands it has an admirable effect, as in the eclogue called "March," which is in the same metre as Chaucer's "Tale of Sir Thopas"; and in "February" and "May," where the two fables of the Oak and Bryer, and the Fox and Kid, for humour and expression are equal to anything in our language. The measure, like our usual verse of eight syllables, is dimeter-iambic, but admits of a trochee, spondee, amphybrachys, anapæst, etc., in almost every place. Thus,

Sēēst hŏw brăg yon bullock bears . . .	Trochee in the 1st.
So smirk, so smooth, his pricked ears? . .	Pure Iambic.
His horns bēen ăs brăde, as rainbow bent, .	Anapæst in the 2d.
His dĕwlăp ăs līthe, as Lass of Kent! .	The same.
Seē hŏw hĕ vĕntĕth intŏ thĕ wind . .	Anapæst in the last.
Wēenĕst, ŏf lŏve is not ĭn his mind? etc. .	Trochee in the 1st.

---

[1] The English romance, so called, is in rude verse, seemingly of great antiquity. The Italians have one which is named *Buovo d' Antona*, probably on the same story, mentioned by Gio. Villani, who died in 1348. See *Crescimbeni Comentarj*, l. v. c. 6.

This English romance is in free octasyllabic rhyme, written, as Mr. Thomas Warton observes (in his *Observations on the Fairy Queen*, Lond. 1754, 8vo) in that short measure which was frequently sung to the harp in Queen Elizabeth's days, a custom which descended from the ancient bards (p. 36). Bevis is supposed to have been Earl of Southampton about the time of the Norman Invasion; his residence was at Duncton in Wiltshire; his sword, called *Morglay*, is kept as a relic in Arundel Castle, not equalling in length that of Edward the Third at Westminster. See Selden's notes on Drayton's *Polyolbion*, canto iii.

And,

Though marked him, with melting eyes,	Pure Iambic.
A thrilling throb frŏm hĕr heărt dĭd rise,	Anapæst in the 4th.
And ĭntĕrrŭptĕd ăll hĕr ŏthĕr speech	{ Amphibrachys in the 2d. Tribrachys in the 3d.
Wĭth sŏme ōld sŏrrŏw, thăt māde ă nĕw breăch,	
Seemĕd shĕ saw ĭn hĕr yŏungling's fāce	{ Trochee in the 1st. Anapæst in the 3d.
The' ōld līnĕămĕnts ŏf hĭs Fāther's grace	{ Anapæst in 2d and 3d.

In these last six lines, the first has eight syllables, and the second
nine, the third and fourth ten, the fifth nine, and the last ten:
and this is the only English measure which has such a liberty
of choice allowed in its feet, of which Milton has taken some
little advantage, in using here and there a trochee in his octosyllabics, and in the first foot only of his heroic verses. There
are a very few instances of his going farther for the sake of some
particular expression, as in that line,

Bŭrnt āftĕr thĕm tŏ thĕ bŏttŏmlĕss pĭt,

where there is a spondee in the first place, a pyrrhic in the third,
and a trochee in the fourth, and that line,

Wĭth ĭmpĕtŭoŭs recoil and jarring sound,

with an anapæst in the first place, etc.

Spenser has also given an instance [1] of the decasyllabic
measure with an unusual liberty in its feet, in the beginning of
his pastoral called "August," thus,

Thĕn lŏ, Pĕrīgŏt, thĕ plĕdge whĭch I plĭght,
Ă māzĕr ywroŭght ŏf thĕ māplĕ wāre,
Whĕreĭn ĭs ĕnchāsĕd mānў ă faĭr sĭght
Of beărs ănd tўgĕrs, thăt mākĕn fiĕrce wăr, etc.

where there are trochees, etc., in every foot but the last. I do
not doubt that he had some ancient examples of this rhythm in
his memory, when he wrote it. Bishop Douglas, in his Prologue
to the Eighth *Æneid*, written about eighty years before Spenser's
Calendar, has something of the same kind.

I make no mention of the hexameter, sapphic, and other
measures which Sir Philip Sidney and his friends [2] attempted

---

[1] And after him Dr. Donne (in his satires) observes no regularity in the
pause, or in the feet of his verse, only the number of syllables is equal
throughout. I suppose he thought this rough uncouth measure suited
the plain familiar style of satirical poetry.

[2] We see from Spenser's *Letters*, that he himself, his friend Mr. Harvey,
and Mr. Dyer, one of his patrons, approved of this method and practised
it. Mr. Drant (he says) had derived the rules and principles of the art,

to introduce in Queen Elizabeth's reign, because they soon dropped into oblivion. The same thing had happened in France a little before, where, in 1553, Etienne Jodelle began to write in this way, and was followed by Baïf, Passerat, Nicholas Rapin, and others, but without success. (See Pasquier, *Recherches*, l. vii. c. 12.) And in Italy this was attempted by Claudio Tolomei,[1] and other men of learning, to as little purpose. (See *Crescimbeni Coment.* vol. i. p. 21.)

THE MEASURES OF VERSE

THE measures which I find principally in use among our writers are as follow, being in all *fifty-nine*.

VERSE	ORDER OF THE RHYMES
Decasyllabic. As in Chaucer's Prologue to the Canterbury Tales, and many of the principal tales themselves: his Legende of Good Women, etc. Lydgate's Story of Thebes. Gawen Douglas's Translation of the Æneid, etc. Spenser, Mother Hubberd's Tale, and almost all our modern heroic poetry.	Successive, in Couplets; called by the old French writers *Rime plate*. (See Pasquier, Recherches de la France, l. vii. ch. 8.
Decasyllabic. Blank; as, The Death of Zoroas, The Death, of Cicero, } published with Lord Surrey's and Sir T. Wyatt's Poems in 1574, 8vo. Anonym.[2] Milton's Paradise Lost and Regained, etc.	Without Rhyme. (Versi [3] Sciolti of the Italians.) The invention [4] is attributed to Trissino, about the year 1525.

which were enlarged with Mr. Sydney's own judgment, and augmented with his (Spenser's) " Observations." This was in 1580.

[1] Bishop of Corsola; he flourished in 1540. He was five years ambassador from the Republic of Sienna in France, and died soon after his return in 1557.

[2] It appears that these poems were written by Nicholas Grimoald. See Ellis's *Specimens of English Poets*, vol. ii. p. 68, 3d edition.—*Mathias*.

[3] Thus Trissino's " Italia Liberata," the Georgic poems of L. Alamanni and Rucellai, the " Sette Giornate " of Tasso, etc., and many of the Italian tragedies are written. It was attempted too by the French in the sixteenth century, as Ronsard in some odes, Blaise Viginelle in his " Seven Psalms," etc., but was soon dropped again.

[4] *i.e.* As far as relates to the verse of eleven syllables, or Italian heroic measure. But in shorter verses it had been practised sometimes by the

VERSE	ORDER OF THE RHYMES
Stanzas of Four Lines.	

Lord Surrey's Verses written in Windsor Castle, Epitaph on Sir Thomas Wyatt, etc.

Dryden's Annus Mirabilis.

Spenser. Colin Clout's come Home again, and April. Gascoyne's Councel on Travelling. His Woodmanship.

Alternate: called by the French, Rime croisée, or entrelassée. Whether there were two or more rhymes which answered one another, as in all which we call Stanzas, see Pasquier, as above.

Stanza of Seven, on Three [1] Rhymes.

Chaucer's Man of Honour, Clerk of Oxenford, Second Nun and Prioress's Tales. Troilus and Cresseide. Assembly of Fowls. Annelida and Arcite. Flower and Leaf. Assembly of Ladies. Complaint of the Black Knight. Lamentation of Magdalen.

Remedy of Love. Several Ballads,[2] etc. John Hardynge's Chronicle.

Gower's Epistle to Henry the 4th.

Occleve, de Regimine Principis. Letter of Cupid. Ballade of our Lady. Of Pride, and wast [3] Clothing (in Camden's Remains.) Lydgate's Fall of Princes. Churl and Bird. Tale of the Merchants, Ballades, etc.

The 1st and 3d.
—2d 4th and 5th.
—6th and 7th.

most ancient writers of that nation, particularly in the beginning of the thirteenth century. St. Francis wrote an irregular ode, or canticle, without rhyme, for music, in no contemptible strain of poetry. It begins,

> " Altissimo Signore
> Vostre sono le lodi,
> La gloria, e gli onori," etc.
>   See *Crescimbeni Comentarj*, l. i. c. 10.

[1] There is also a rough stanza of seven, free in its feet, as Dingley's " Battle of Brampton," in the *Mirrour of Magistrates*.

[2] " The staff of seven verses hath seven proportions, whereof one only is the usual of our vulgar, and kept by our old poets, Chaucer and others, in their historical reports and other ditties." Puttenham, i. ii. c. 10.

[3] This is a part " De Regimine Principis."

VERSE	ORDER OF THE RHYMES

Stanzas of Seven, on Three Rhymes—
continued

Assemblé De Dyeus. Gawen Douglas, Prologue to the 2d and 4th Book of the Æneid. Sir David Lyndsay's Testament of the Papingo. His Dream. Complaint of Scotland. Prologue to Experience and the Courtier. Fabyan's Ballad Royal on Edward the First. W. Caxton's Work of Sapience. Angel's Song. Sir T. Wyatt's Complaint on Love. The Government of Kings and Princes, Anonymous.

Spenser's Hymns of Love and Beauty. Ruins of Time. Milton's Hymn on the Nativity, etc.

The 1st and 3d. —2d 4th and 5th. —6th and 7th.

Another Stanza of Seven Lines.

Some Poems of Chaucer. Spenser's Daphnaida.

The 1st and 3d. —2d 4th and 6th. —5th and 7th.

Stanza of Six, on Three Rhymes.

Chaucer, in some Envoys. Dr. Lodge, some Sonnets. Spenser, Tears of the Muses, Astrophel, December, and part of August. Gascoyne's Passion.

Four alternate, and the Two last together.

Another Stanza of Six, on Two Rhymes.

Spenser's October.

The 1st 4th and 6th.

Stanza of Eight, on Three Rhymes.

Chaucer, Monk's Tale. Belle Dame sans mercy. Envoys. His A. B. C. or Prayer to the Virgin. Lydgate's Ballads, etc.

Scogan's Letter to the Lords of the King's House. Spenser's November. G. Douglas's Prologue to the Sixth Æneid.

The 1st and 3d. —2d 4th 5th and 7th. —6th and 8th.

VERSE	ORDER OF THE RHYMES

Another.

Some Poems of Chaucer and Lydgate.
Gawen Douglas's Prologue to the Eleventh Æneid.

The 1st and 3d.
—2d 4th 5th and 8th.
—6th and 7th.

Another.[1]

Spenser's Muiopotmos and Culex.

The 1st 3rd and 5th.
—2d 4th and 6th.
—7th and 8th.

Another, on Two Rhymes.

Spenser's June.

The 1st 3d 6th and 8th.
—2d 4th 5th and 7th.

Stanza of Nine, on Three Rhymes.

G. Douglas's Prologue to the Fifth Æneid, and his Exclamation against Detractors. The Third Part of the Palice of Honour.
Sir D. Lindsay's Prologue to the Papingo's Testament.

The 1st 2d 4th and 5th.
—3d 6th and 7th.
—8th and 9th.

Another, on Two Rhymes.

Chaucer's Complaint of Annelida. G. Douglas's Prologue to the Third Æneid, and the two first Parts of the Palice of Honour.

The 1, 2, 4, 5, and 8.
—3, 6, 7, and 9.

Stanza of Five, on Two Rhymes.

Chaucer's Cuckoo and Nightingale. Gawen Douglas's Prologue to the Tenth Æneid.

The 1st 2d and 5th.
—3d and 4th.

Another.

Some of Sir Thomas Wyatt's Verses.

The 1st and 3d.
—2d 4th and 5th.

---

[1] This is the *Ottava Rima* of the Italians, the stanza of Ariosto and Tasso in their heroic poems, and that of an infinite number of authors. It was first introduced in Italy by Boccaccio, who wrote in this measure his "Teseide," "Filostrato," etc., in the fourteenth century; though he in reality appears to have borrowed it from Thibaut, King of Navarre and Count of Champagne, who had written in the same stanza in the year 1235. See *Crescembeni Comentarj*, vol. i. l. v. c. 7, p. 339.

VERSE	ORDER OF THE RHYMES

Terzetti,[1] or Terza Rima.

Lord Surrey's Restless State of a Lover. Sir T. Wyatt's [Epist.] to J. Poynes, and Sir Fr. Bryan. Milton, Second Psalm.

> The 1st and 3d rhyme. —2d 4th and 6th, and so on by threes alternate, till the last and last but two, which answer like those at first.

Sonnets of Fourteen,[2] on Five Rhymes.

Milton's 7th, 9th, 10th, and 13th Sonnets.

> The 1, 4, 5, and 8th. —2, 3, 6, and 7th. —9th and 12th. —10th and 13th. —11th and 14th.

Another.

Spenser's Amoretti.

> The 1st and 3rd. —2, 4, 5, and 7th. —6, 8, 9, and 11th. —10th and 12th. —13th and 14th.

Another.

Sir T. Wyatt's Sonnets of the Lover waxeth wiser, etc.

> 8 first lines, as of the first sort above. 4 next alternate. Couplet in the end.

Sonnets of Four Rhymes.

Milton's Sonnets, 8th, 11th, 12th, and 14th.

> Eight first lines as of the first sort, or else alternate: the six last alternate, or at pleasure.

---

[1] This is the measure of Dante in his " Inferno," etc., of Petrarch's " Trionfi," etc. The invention has usually been ascribed to the former, but there is a poem (called " Il Pataffio ") extant, written in this very measure by Ser Brunetto Latini, who was Dante's master, and who died in 1294. It was probably the invention of the Provençals, who used it in their syrvientes (or satires), whence the Italians have commonly called it *serventese*. See *Crescimbeni Coment.*, vol. i. l. 2, c. 13.

[2] This, and the fourth kind, are the true sonnet of the Italians. Petrarch uses only these two measures. The invention of the regular sonnet is ascribed to Fra Guittone d'Arezzo, who flourished about the year 1250; nor do we find any of this form among the Provençals till seventy years after. What they called *sonet* was only a short canzone, unconfined in the number of verses, the measure, and the order of the rhymes. *Crescimb. Coment.* l. ii. c. 14, 15.

VERSE	ORDER OF THE RHYMES

Another, of Two Rhymes.

Lord Surrey on the Spring: Complaint by Night, etc.

The 12 first alternate, and end with a couplet.

Another, of Seven Rhymes.

Lord Surrey's Vow to Love. On Sir T. Wyatt's Death, etc. Daniel's Delia.

The 12 first by 4 and 4 alternate.

Madrigals of Eight, on Three Rhymes.

Sir T. Wyatt.

Six first alternate; and end with a Couplet.

Madrigals on Two Rhymes.

Sir T. Wyatt.

The 1st 3d 6th and 8th.
—2, 4, 5, and 7th.

Stanza of Fourteen, on Seven Rhymes.

Spenser's Visions of Petrarch, Bellay, etc.

Like the last kind of Sonnet.

Another, on Five Rhymes.

Spenser, Visions of the World's Vanity.

The 1st and 3d.
—2, 4, 5, and 7th.
—6, 8, 9, and 11th.
—10th and 12th.
—13th and 14th.

Sestine, of six.[1]

Spenser, in his August.

No rhyme. The art consists in ringing changes on six words only, in the end of a line: the whole is finished in six stanzas only, and three verses over.

Decasyllabic, Mixed.

Stanza of Nine, with an Alexandrine at the end, on Three Rhymes. Spenser's Fairy Queen.[2]

The 1st and 3d.
—2, 4, 5, and 7th.
—6, 8, and 9th.

---

[1] The invention of the *Sestine* is ascribed to Arnauld Daniel in the middle of the twelfth century (see *Crescimb. Coment.* v. i. l. 2, c. 11), and from him the Italians borrowed it, though it must be always, both in sense and sound, a very mean composition.

[2] Spenser has also a stanza of eight, ending with an Alexandrine, where

VERSE	ORDER OF THE RHYMES
Stanza of Eighteen,[1] with 4 verses (the 5th, 10th, 15th, and 16th) of Six syllables, and the last an Alexandrine, on Seven Rhymes. Spenser's Prothalamion and Epithalamion.	The 1, 4, and 5th. — 2d and 3d. 4 next alternate (the 10th answers to the 9th). — 11, 12, and 14th. — 13, 15, and 16th. — 17th and 18th.
Stanza of Ten. The first an Alexandrine, the four next, and 9th, a decasyllabic, sixth and seventh octosyllabic, the eighth and tenth (being the Refrain or Burthen) tetrasyllabic. On four rhymes. Spenser's Lay, or Elegy of Dido, in the November.	The 1st and 3d. — 2, 4, 5, and 9th. — 6th and 7th. — 8th and 10th.
Stanza of Nine. The 1st, 3d, 5th, and 6th are decasyllabic, the 2d, 4th, 7th, and 8th are tetrasyllabic, the last octosyllabic. On four rhymes. Spenser's Lay to Eliza, in April.	The 1st and 3d. — 2d and 4th. — 5th 6th and 9th. — 7th and 8th.

the 1st and 3d rhyme; the 2d, 4th, and 5th; the 6th, 7th, and 8th, as in Britain's " Ida."

Sir Thomas Wyatt has a stanza of eight, where the 4th and 8th are of six syllables; it has three rhymes, the 1st, 2d, and 3d answering each other; the 4th and 8th; the 5th, 6th, and 7th.

[1] These resemble the canzoni of the Italians, which are in stanzas of 9, 12, 13, or 14 verses, etc., in unequal measure.   There is also a stanza (if it may be called so) not only of mixed measures but of an unequal number of verses, sometimes rhyming and sometimes not, as in Milton's " Lycidas," and in the choruses in his " Samson Agonistes."

The canzone is of very ancient date: the invention of it being ascribed to Girard de Borneil, of the school of Provence, who died in 1178.   He was of Limoges, and was called *Il Maestro d' Trovatori*.   The different kinds of canzoni are infinite, many new ones being introduced by the Italians.   The most ancient, which were extant in that tongue, were written by Folcacchio de' Folcacchieri, who lived before the year 1200. Nothing seems essential to this species of poetry, but that the measures of every stanza should answer to the first, whether they be of equal or of unequal measures.   It has generally been a rule that the stanzas should be not more than fifteen, and the verses in each stanza not fewer than nine, nor above twenty; but this rule is very often broken.   Dante esteemed it the noblest species of poetry, and adds, " Quicquid de cacuminibus illustrium Capitum poëtantium profluxit ad labia, in *solis Cantionibus* invenitur."   (" De Vulg. Eloquent." l. ii. c. 3, b. 3.)   He said they used all measures from eleven syllables to three, but particularly recommends the former, mixed with that of seven, which Petrarch has observed and approved.[1]

[1] Petrarch has used no other verses in his canzoni but the endecasillabi and the settenarj.—*Mathias*.

VERSE	ORDER OF THE RHYMES
Decasyllabic, free in their feet.	
Spenser, Proëme of his August. Baldwyn's Complaint of James the Fourth, King of Scotland. Donne's Satires.	In Couplets. With Trochees or Iambics in every foot indifferently.
The Same, Mixed, in Stanzas of thirteen, their four last verses are tetrasyllabic. On four rhymes. G. Douglas, Prologue to the Eighth Æneid.	The 1, 3, 5, and 7th. — 2, 4, 6, and 8th. — 9th and 13th. — 10, 11, and 12th. — I call them decasyllabic, and tetrasyllabic, because they have that effect on the ear: but as they admit of Anapæsts, etc., they have sometimes eleven or five syllables.
Octosyllabic.[1]	
The Lord's Prayer, by Pope Adrian, in Henry the Second's time. Chaucer's Romaunt of the Rose. House of Fame. Book of the Dutchess. His Dream. Poem of the Owl and Nightingale (as old as the time of Henry the Third). Gower's Confessio Amantis. Lydgate's Story of Thebes. Sir David Lyndsay's Dialogue between Experience and a Courtier. Romaunce of Merlin.	Successive in Couplets.

[1] This measure is borrowed from the Welch, or the Provençal and old French poets, with whom it was common. Robert Manning of Brunn, who towards the beginning of the fourteenth century translated Peter Langtoft's Chronicle out of the old French (or Romaun tongue as it was then called) has prefixed a prologue to it in octosyllabic rhymes, wherein he mentions different kinds of verse used in his days, as Entrelace, Baston, Couwe, Strangere, etc. The first of these is, as I suppose, the *rime croisée* or *entrelassée* of the French; the second are unequal verse in *staves* or stanzas, answering one to the other. The French still say *baston* de balade for *stance* de balade. (See Menage, *Dictionnaire Etymol.* v. Baston.) Couwe I take to be derived from the Welch cywydd (pronounced couwyth) which is a peculiar stanza and composition of rhyme, described by Dr. David ap Rhys, p. 186; it may perhaps be the same with Chaucer's "Tale of Sir Thopas."

VERSE	ORDER OF THE RHYMES
Another kind.	
Lord Surrey's Restless State of a Lover. Means of a happy Life. Gascoyne's Good Morrow. Wyatt's Prayer against Disdain; Lamentation, etc.	Alternate.
Another.	
Wyatt's Renunciation of Love.	Four successive rhymes.
Stanza of Eight, on Two Rhymes.	
Chaucer's Plowman's Tale and Prologue.	Alternate.
Stanza of Eight, on Three Rhymes.	
Chaucer's Ballade in praise of Women. Lydgate's Complaint of Tho. Chaucer.	The 1st and 3d. — 2, 4, 5, and 7th. — 6th and 8th.
Stanza of Seven, on Three Rhymes.	
Wyatt's Suit for Grace. Lover's Mistrust, etc.	The 1st and 3d. — 2d 4th and 5th. — 6th and 7th.
Stanza of Six, on Three Rhymes.	
Lord Surrey's Lover's Comfort. Complaint of Absence, etc. Gascoyne's Arraignement.	4 Alternate. 2 last together.
Stanza of Five, on Two Rhymes.	
Wyatt, to his Lute.	The 1st 2d and 4th. — 3d and 5th.
Octosyllabic, Mixed.	
Stanza of Six. The 3d and 6th are of six syllables; on Three Rhymes. (Doggerel.)	
Chaucer's Sir Thopas. Frere and Boy; Sir Eglamore; Sir Triamore; The Green Knight; Sir Lybius Disconius.	The 1st and 2d. — 4th and 5th. — 3d and 6th.

VERSE	ORDER OF THE RHYMES

Another. With Heptasyllabics mixed at pleasure. No Stanzas.

Milton's Allegro and Penseroso; Part of his Comus; Epitaph on the Marchioness of Winchester. } Successive.

Octosyllabics, with Verses of Six, alternate.

Spenser's July.   Alternate.

Another, with Verses of Six or Five Syllables, alternate.

Spenser's Roundelay, in August.   Alternate.

Octosyllabic, Free.

Spenser's February, May, and September. Bevis of Southampton. Sir Lambwell. Eger and Grime. Sir Degree. Earl of Carlisle. } Successive. The feet are Trochees, Spondees, Amphibrachys, and Anapæsts, indifferently with the Iambic.

Octosyllabic, Free.
Stanza of Six, Mixed and Free. On Three Rhymes.

Spenser, Proëme of March. } The 1st and 2d. — 4th and 5th. — 3d and 6th.

Octosyllabic, Blank.
Mixed with others of Six and Four Syllables.

Spenser's Mourning Muse of Thestylis. } No Rhyme.

Verses of Six Syllables.
Several Songs of Sir Tho. Wyatt and Lord Surrey.

Others in Stanzas of Eight, on Two Rhymes. } Alternate. 1, 3, 6, and 8th. 2, 4, 5, and 7th.

The same. On Three Rhymes. } The 1, 3, 5, and 7th. — 2d and 4th. — 6th and 8th.

Pentasyllabic and Tetrasyllabic.
These are rarely used alone.

VERSE	ORDER OF THE RHYMES

Alexandrines.[1]

Lord Surrey's Ecclesiastes.
Spenser's Envoy to the Shepherd's Kalendar.
Drayton's Polyolbion.

} Successive. There is also a Stanza of four Alexandrines with alternate rhyme as Phœbe's Sonnet in Lodge's Euphues' Gold. Legacy.

Alexandrines, mixed with Verses of Fourteen Syllables,[2] alternately.

Queen Elizabeth's Ditty on the Queen of Scots. Surrey's Description of Love. Complaint of a Lover. Dying Lover. The Warning. The careless Man, etc.
Wyatt's Complaint of Absence.
Song[3] of Iopas. Gascoyne's Gloze.

} Successive.

---

[1] The *Life of St. Margaret* in very old Saxon (cited hereafter), and written above one hundred and seventy years before Chaucer was born, is in a sort of free Alexandrine measure: as is the Chronicle of Robert of Gloucester, and Peter Langtoft's Chronicle translated by Robert Manning of Brunn, both of them older than Chaucer. The Alexandrine verse took its name from a poem written in this measure, called " La Vie d'Alexandre," by Jean li Nevelois and Pierre de St. Cloit, who lived in the thirteenth century. (Pasquier, l. vii. c. 3.) The "Roman d'Alexandre" was begun by Lambert li Cors and Alexandre de Paris; but some parts of it were executed by the two poets above mentioned. They all four (according to the President Fauchet) wrote between 1150 and 1193, in the reigns of Louis le Jeune and Philippe Auguste, and seem to have been of the trouveures or jongleurs, who then were in high esteem: their names appear in the work itself.

La verté de l'histoir, si com li Roy la fit,
Un Clers de Chateaudun, Lambert li Cors, l'escrit,
Qui de Latin *la*[1] *trest*, et en Roman la mit.

See Fauchet, *De la Langue et Poesie Françoise*, l. ii. (A.D. 1581.)

The Latin, whence they translated, was (I imagine) the Alexandréis of Gualterus (or Gautier de Châtillon, a native of Lisle in Flanders), a poet who lived about the same time, that is, in the middle of the twelfth century. It is observable, that none of these four jongleurs was a Provençal, nor do they write in that dialect, yet they are contemporary with the most ancient Provençal poets, mentioned by Nôtredame.

[2] " Some makers (says Puttenham) write in verses of fourteen syllables, giving the cesure at the first eight, which proportion is tedious, for the length of the verse keepeth the ear too long from its delight, which is, to hear the cadence of tuneable accent in the end of the verse."

[3] There is also a mixed stanza of four (as in Baldwin's " Complaint of Henry the Sixth," in the *Mirrour of Magistrates*), three verses of twelve and one of fourteen syllables. Rhymes in couplets.

[1] *tira.*

VERSE	ORDER OF THE RHYMES

Free Alexandrines, mixed in like manner.[1]

Chaucer's Tale of Beryn and Prologue. } Successive: but with various feet.

Free Verse,[2] of Fourteen Syllables.

Chaucer's Tale of Gamelin. Robin of Portingale; Ballade of Flodden Field; Adam Bell; Robin Hood; Nut-brown Maid; Childe Waters; Durham Field. } Successive. (Various.) There is also a verse of Sixteen, as Guy and Phillis, Thomas a Potts.

Of all these measures, which we may reduce to six, viz. the verse of fourteen, the Alexandrine, the decasyllabic, the octosyllabic,[3] the heptasyllabic, and verse of six; none are now used but the third and fourth; except it be interspersedly to vary our composition, and especially in lyric poetry. Our variety too in the rhyme is much circumscribed, never going further than the use of a triplet, and that rarely. As to any licence[4] in the feet, it is only permitted in the beginning of a long verse, where we sometimes use a trochee, and the same foot more freely in shorter measures.

The Provençal poets either invented or made use of all these measures, from verses of three syllables to those of eleven and thirteen; but of these last we find no example till about the year 1321, so that it is not certain that they were originally theirs, or borrowed from the French Alexandrine with the addition of a syllable, on account of the double rhyme. (See *Crescimbeni Comentarj*, vol. i. l. 2, c. 14, and l. 1, c. 6.)

---

[1] And thus is written Robert of Gloucester's Chronicle, a work of Henry the Third's time, but without any regularity, the Alexandrine sometimes wanting a syllable or two, and the verse of fourteen coming in at random, as the writer thought fit.

[2] It is the very same measure with the semi-Saxon moral poem (cited hereafter) written almost two hundred years after Chaucer's time.

There was also the regular verse of fourteen used in Queen Elizabeth's time, and in this measure is written Dr. Phaer's translation of the *Æneid* (see Lambarde's *Kent* and Weever's *Funeral Monuments*); Arthur Goldynge's *Ovid's Metamorphoses*, "Chevy Chase," "Gill Morrice," "Glasgerion," "Launcelot du Lake," etc.

[3] We now use this as well on serious subjects as comic: the latter *we* call doggerel, as *Hudibras*.

[4] We now and then in subjects of humour use a free verse of eleven or twelve syllables, which may consist of four amphibrachees, or four anapæsts, or the first may be an iambic, etc.; so Prior:

" As Chlŏe̋ căme ĭntŏ thĕ rőom t'ŏthĕr da̋y "—
" Tĭs enŏugh thăt 'tĭs loădĕd wĭth baűblĕs ănd sea̋ls," etc.

OBSERVATIONS ON THE PSEUDO-RHYTHMUS

THE most ancient instance of rhyming verse, as Sir W. Temple has observed, is that of the Emperor Adrian, about the 137th year of Christ.[1] It is undoubtedly borrowed from the barbarous nations, among whom, particularly in the east, it is said to have been in use from the remotest antiquity. The Welch still preserve the works of the ancient British bards, Taliessin, Benbeirdh, and Lomarkk, who lived towards the end of the sixth century, and wrote in rhyme. It is possible that our ancestors, the Anglo-Saxons, might borrow it from the Britons, but it is much more probable that they brought it from Germany with them.

It is true that we do not find any rhyming verses among them till towards the time of the Norman Conquest; all their poems now remaining being of a different contrivance, and their harmony consisting in alliteration,[2] or similar consonances in the beginning of three or more words in each distich; yet probably they might have had our *pseudo-rhythm* (as Dr. Hickes and Wormius call it), beside this, though their performances in it are now lost; which is no great wonder, considering that we have not any specimen of their poetry in any kind[3] for three

---

[1] There is a hymn of St. Augustine, who lived about the year 420, in which are interspersed several verses which rhyme in the middle; as,

" Abest limus, | deest fimus, | lues nulla cernitur,
Hyems horrens, | æstas torrens, | illic nunquam sæviunt.—
Virent prata, | vernant sata, | rivi mellis influunt," etc.
                                    Augustin. Meditat. c. 26.

And in a treatise written by Theodulus (who lived in 480 under the Emperor Zeno), " De Contemptu Mundi," are these lines:

" Pauper amabilis, | et venerabilis, | est benedictus,
Dives inutilis, | insatiabilis, | est maledictus," etc.

[2] This was the artifice of the skalds, or old Danish poets in their *Drotquæt* (or vulgar song) described by Wormius, and observed sometimes strictly, sometimes with more liberty, by our old Saxons, both before and after the coming of the Danes. As to the measure, Hickes imagines that they had feet and quantity, but, as he owns, we have lost the pronunciation, and neither know the power of the diphthongs, nor of the vowel *e* in the end of words; we cannot tell of how many syllables their verse consisted; it appears to have from four to fourteen indifferently, but most usually from four to eight or nine.

[3] That is, from the first settlement of the Saxons in Britain to the coming of the Danes. (See Hickes's *Gramm. Angl. Sax.* c. xix.) This

hundred and thirty-seven years now preserved, except that fragment of Cædmon the Monk, extant in King Alfred's Saxon translation of Bede's *History*, l. iv. c. 24, and the Harmony of the Evangelists paraphrased in verse, in the Cotton Library; nay, of these two it is doubtful if the latter be of that age or not.

What serves to confirm me in the opinion, that, beside their other species of verse, they might also use rhyme occasionally, is this: we have still extant in the language of the Franks a Paraphrase of the Gospels in rhyme, written by Otfrid, a monk of Weisenburgh, scholar to[1] Rhabanus Maurus, abbot of Fulde, before the year 876, and addressed[2] to Louis, the Germanic King of Austria (or East France), in stanzas, which begin thus:

Lodovig their snéllo	That is: Lewis the swift
Thes wisduames follo:	Of wisdom full,
Er Ostarichi rihtit al	He Austrasia rules all
So Francono Kuning scal.	So as a Frankish king becomes, etc.
Ubar Francono lant gizalt	
Se gengit ellu sin giuualt.	
Thas rihtit, so i thir zellu,	
Thiu sin giuualt ellu, etc.	

And as the Saxons and Franks[3] were near neighbours in Germany,

---

is his computation, I know not for what reason; for, from the arrival of Hengist, A.D. 449, to the settling of the Danes in Northumberland in 867, are 418 years. From that period to the Norman Conquest we have a good deal of their poetry preserved, but none of it in rhyme: the " Ransom of Eigil " (preserved by Olaus Wormius) written above one hundred and fifty years before the Conquest, is however in rhyme, as " Vestur kom eg om | ver | Enn eg vidris ber | Munstrindar mar | So er mitt offar | Dro eg eik a flot | Vid Isabrot | " etc.

[1] He was made Archbishop of Mentz in 847. His Latino-Theotische *Glossary of the Bible* is still preserved in the imperial library at Vienna. See Lambecius, *Comment. de Bibl.* l. ii. pp. 416 and 932.

[2] A specimen of it, with notes and a Latin version, was published in 1701 by Schilterus of Strasburgh. There are also extant the " Actions of Charlemagne " by Stricher, and the " Life of Anno, Archbishop of Cologne," both of them poems in rhyme, in the Franco-Theotische tongue, mentioned by Dr. Hickes in his grammar of that language, p. 109, and by Lambecius, l. ii. p. 422, who has published Otfrid's dedication of the work above-mentioned, in prose, which is very curious. In it he calls his own tongue " *barbara*, inculta, et *indisciplinabilis*," he complains of its roughness and of the variety of its sounds, which the letters of the alphabet could not at all express, and adds, " Lingua enim hæc velut agrestis habetur, dum a propriis nec scripturâ, nec arte aliquâ, ullis est temporibus expolita, quippe qui nec historias antecessorum suorum, ut multæ gentes cæteræ, commendant memoriæ, nec eorum gesta vel vitas exornant dignitatis amore. Quod si raro contigit, aliarum gentium linguâ, id est, Latinorum vel Græcorum, potius explanant." The President Fauchet had seen this poem and preface.

[3] The Franks under Clovis settled in Gaul about thirty-two years after the arrival of the Saxons in Kent. Hickes tells us that the Franco-Theotische and Anglo-Saxon (before the invasion of the Danes) were probably the same language. (*Gramm. Fr. Theot.* p. 6; see also Carte,

and spoke a language only differing in dialect, and alike derived from the old Gothic mother-tongue, it is likely that the same kinds of poetry were common to them both.

(N.B.—It is remarkable that Walafrid Strabo, who died in 840, and other writers of that age, call themselves *Barbari*, and their own language *Barbarica Locutio*. See Goldastus's Notes on Ekeckardus, *Res Alamannicæ*, tom. i. part 1, p. 113.)

vol. i. p. 221.) It seems to appear from the words of Otfrid, in his preface cited above, that the Franks of his time did still use some kind of meter distinct from rhyme, for he says: "Patitur quoque (Lingua Theotisca) nimiùm, non tamen assiduè, synalœphen, et hoc nisi legentes prævideant, rationis dicta deformius sonant, literas interdùm scriptione servantes, interdum vero Ebraicæ linguæ more vitantes, quibus ipsas literas ratione synalœphæ in lineis, ut quidam dicunt, penitus amittere et transilire moris habetur. Non quo series scriptionis hujus metricâ sit subtilitate constricta, sed schema homoioteleuton assiduè quærit," etc. *Apud Lambecium*, l. ii. c. 5, p. 425.

There are no verses extant in the Romaun, or old French tongue, which are known to be more ancient than the middle of the twelfth century, and accordingly Fauchet begins his catalogue of poets with Maistre Wistace, or Eustace, who wrote the "Romaunce of Brutt, the Trojan," in 1155: it is in octosyllabic rhymes.

The earliest of the Provençal writers (at least of those who have left any memorial behind them) lived about the middle of the same century. The Sicilian poets, who first taught Italy to write verse, lived very few years after, and in our own tongue, we have, I believe, nothing extant in rhyme that can be with certainty judged to be more ancient than the reign of Stephen or Henry the Second. The Germans have therefore preserved in their tongue the most ancient monument of rhyming poesy, perhaps in Europe, almost three hundred years older than any of those which I have mentioned. The Welch poetry only (if the remains of Taliessin and Lowarkk be not fictitious) can pretend to a superior antiquity.

As to the Provençal writers, Crescimbeni observes, "Avvi certezza, che incominciassero (i rimatori Provenzali) circa il 1100 sotto il Guglielmo VIII. duca d' Aquitania, e l' istesso duca fosse il primo verseggiatore, avendo composto in rima il viaggio di Gerusalemme, e qualche cosa amorosa.—Non si truovano però rime più antiche di quelle di Giusfredo Rudello, che molto scrisse in rima della Contessa di Tripoli, che amò, e appresso cui morì l' anno 1162." (*Crescimb. Istor. della Volg. Poesia*, l. i. p. 6).—Dante, who was born in 1265, ascribes the origin of the old romances in prose to the French nation, and that of the *volgare poesia* to the Provençale. "Allegat ergo pro se lingua Oïl (that is, the French) quod propter sui faciliorem et delectabiliorem vulgaritatem, quicquid redactum sive inventum est ad vulgare prosaicum, suum est, videlicet, biblia cum Trojanorum Romanorumque gestibus compilata, et Arturi Regis ambages pulcherrimæ, et quamplurimæ aliæ historiæ atque doctrinæ. Pro se vero argumentatur alia, scilicet *Oc* (he means the Provençale) quòd vulgares eloquentes in ea primitus poëtati sunt, tanquam in perfectiori dulciorique loquelâ, ut puto, Petrus de Alverniâ, et alii antiquiores doctores. Tertia, quæ Latinorum est (that is, the Italian), se duobus privilegiis attestatur præesse: primo quidem, qui subtilius dulciusque poëtati sunt *vulgariter*, hi familiares et domestici sui sunt, putà Cinus Pistoïensis et amicus ejus (Dante himself): secundo quia magis videntur initii *grammaticâ*, quæ communis est. (He means the Latin or mother tongue.) Dante, "De Vulgari Eloquentiâ," l. i. c. 10; see also *Scaligerana 2da*. vol. ii. p. 331.

However, we have not now among us any rhymes more ancient than that period, which extends from the Conquest in 1066 to the reign of Henry the Second, which begun in 1154; our tongue being then much mixed with the Norman-Gallic, and degenerating into what Hickes calls the semi-Saxon, as in the *Life of St. Margaret.*[1]

> Olde ant yonge, I preit ou oure folies for to *lete,*[2]
> (*Old and young, I pray you your follies for to leave*)
> Thenchet on God, that yef ou wit oure sunnes to *bete.*[3]
> (*Think on God, that gave you wit your sins to correct.*)
> Here I mai tellen ou wid wordes faire ant swete
> (*Here I may tell you with words fair and sweet*)
> The vie of one meidan was hoten Maregrete.
> (*The life of a maiden was hight Margaret.*)
> Hire fader was a patriac, as ic ou tellen may,
> (*Her father was a patriarch, as I you tell may,*)
> In Auntioge wif *eches*[4] i the false lay,
> (*In Antioch a wife he chose in the false law*)
> Deve godes and doumbe he served nitt ant day,
> (*Deaf gods and dumb he served night and day.*)
> So deden mony othere, that singet *weilaway.*[5]
> (*So did many others, that sing wellaway.*) Etc.

And in those verses preserved in some MSS. in the Bodleian Library, and in Trinity College, Cambridge.

> Ic am elder than ic wes, a wintre ant ec a lore,
> (*I am elder than I was, in winters and eke in learning.*)
> Ic ealdi more than ic dede: mi wit oghte to bi more,
> (*I grow old more than I did : my wit ought to be more*)
> Wel longe ic habbe childe ibien on worde ant on dede,
> (*Very long I have a child been in word and in deed*)
> Thegh ic bi on winter eald, to giung ic am on *rede,*[6] etc.
> (*Though I be in winters old, too young I am in counsel.*)

This is inscribed Parabolæ Regis Ælfredi. See J. Spelman's *Life of Alfred,* p. 98.

Other examples of ancient rhyme, within the period assigned, may be seen in Dr. Hickes, ch. xxiv., from whom I have transcribed the former. Yet though this kind of versification[7]

---

[1] See other examples in Wanley's *Catalogue,* in John's or Henry the Third's reign, p. 79.

[2] *Lætan,* Saxon, to let, or permit, whence to let alone, to let go.

[3] *Betan,* Saxon, to amend, to make better.

[4] *Gecas,* Saxon, he chose.

[5] *Wala-wa,* Saxon, Woe is me!

[6] *Rada,* Saxon, knowledge. *Ræd,* counsel.

[7] It was towards the end of this period, about ninety years after the Conquest, that the Provençal poetry began to flourish, and continued in the highest esteem above two hundred years. They wrote in rhyme, and were the inventors of a variety of measures. Dante, Petrarca, etc. in Italy; Helinand, William de Lorry, Jean de Mehun, Thibaud, Count of Champagne, in France; and Chaucer, in our own tongue, first caught their fire from these writers, and imitated their manner, style, and versification.

prevailed by degrees, and grew into general use, it is certain
that we retained, even so late as Edward the Third's reign, and
above a hundred years after, our old Saxon or Danish verse
without rhyme; for the "Vision of Peirce Plowman," a severe

(See Jean de Nôtredame, *Lives of the Provençal Poets*, Lyons, 1575, 8vo.)
The Sicilians, about the end of the twelfth century, under the reign of
Robert Guiscard the Norman, King of Naples, first began to imitate the
Provençal writers in their own tongue, and as the most judicious Italians
themselves inform us, such as Bembo, Varchi, Sansovini, Nicolo Villani,
and Crescimbeni. The last of these has given us the names of these first
Italian poets: "Le rime de' Siciliani a noi pervenute sono debolissime e
scipite ed infelici, a segno che non possono leggersi senza estrema noia e
rincrescimento, ancorche sieno de' più rinomati, cioè di Guido e d' Odo
delle Colonne, di Jacopo da Lentino, dell' Imperador Federigo, e d' altri
loro pari." (*Istor. Volg. Poes.*, vol. i. l. 1, c. 2, p. 91.) He also mentions
Ciullo dal Camo, and it appears that the art of versifying almost instan-
taneously diffused itself through Italy, from those verses inscribed in
Gothic letters on a marble at Florence by Ubaldino Ubaldini, as early as
the year 1184, which begin,

> "De favore isto
> Gratias refero Christo,
> Factus in festo serenæ
> Sanctæ Mariæ Magdalenæ;
> Ipsa peculiariter adori
> Ad Deum pro me peccatori.
> Con lo mio cantare
> Dallo vero vero narrare
> Nulla ne diparto, etc."

It is not written in distinct verses, as here, upon the marble, but like prose,
all confused together. (*Crescimb. Coment.* vol. i. l. 1, c. 4, p. 100.) Dante
observes, "Videtur *Sicilianum Vulgare* sibi famam præ aliis asciscere;
eò quòd, quicquid poëtantur Itali, *Sicilianum* vocatur.—Quòd (*i.e.* tempore
illustrium heroum Frederici Cæsaris et benegeniti ejus Manfredi), quicquid
excellentes Latinorum nitebantur, primitùs in tantorum coronatorum
aulâ prodibat, et quia regale solium erat Sicilia, factum est, quicquid
nostri predecessores *vulgariter* protulerunt, *Sicilianum* vocatur." Dante,
"De Vulg. Eloq." l. i. c. 12.
   The President Fauchet takes pains to prove that the people of Normandy, of Provence, of Sicily, of Italy, of Spain, etc., all borrowed their
rhyme from the Franks; and, I own, it wears a face of probability: but
then it may be equally probable that the Franks borrowed it from the
Latin church. He cites also the "Life of Sancta Fides," in the Catalan
dialect of the Spanish tongue (it is, he says, as old as the year 1100, and
in rhyme), which calls the rhyming verses *a lei Francesca, i.e.* a la Françoise
(see *Acad. des Inscript.* vol. xxvi. p. 638), which is, with allowance for
some changes (which length of time will inevitably introduce in all languages), the true *Romaun*-tongue generally spoken throughout all the
Roman Gaul, for many years before and after it fell into the hands of the
Franks. This appears from the famous treaty, in A.D. 843, between the
sons of Lodovicus Pius, where the oaths in the original tongues (*i.e.* the
Romaun, which was then the language of all who lay west of the Meuse,
and the Theotiscic, or Frankish, spoken by all the people, who lived east
of that river), are preserved to us by Nitard, the historian, grandson to
Charlemagne: the first of these still nearly resembling the Provençal
dialect, was then called *Rustica Romana*. The Council of Tours, assembled
in the year 812, has this article: "Quilibet Episcopus habeat Omilias,

satire on the times, written by Robert Langland in 1350, is
wholly in such measure, as, for instance:

> I *l*oked on my *l*eft halfe,
> As the *l*ady me taught,
> And *w*as *w*are of a *w*oman
> *W*orthlyith clothed.
> Purfiled [1] with *p*elure,[2]
> The finest u*p*on erthe,
> Crowned with a *c*rowne
> The king hath no better;
> Fetislich [3] her *f*ingers,
> Were *f*retted with gold wiers,
> And thereon *r*ed *r*ubies,
> As *r*ed as any glede,[4]
> And *d*iamonds of *d*earest price,
> And *d*ouble maner saphirs, etc.
>
> *Passus* 2dus *in princip.*

and thus through the whole poem, which is a long one, with very
few exceptions, the triple consonance is observed in every distich.

Robert Crowley, who printed the first edition of " Peirce
Plowman's Vision " in 1550 (dated by mistake 1505), says that
Robert Langland, the author of it, " wrote altogether in meter,
but not after the maner of our rimers that write now-a-days, for
his verses end not alike, for the nature of his meter is to have
at least thre wordes in every verse, which begin with some one,
and the same, letter.   The author was a Shropshire man, born
in Cleybirie, about eight miles from Malverne-Hills: his worke
was written between 1350 and 1409."

In the same measure is the poem called " Death and Life in
two fitts; " and another named " Scottish Field," which describes
the action at Flodden in Henry the Eighth's time, who was
present in the action, and dwelt at Bagily. (I read them in a
MS. collection belonging to the Rev. Mr. Thomas Piercy [5] in
1761.)

etc., et easdem quisque apertè traducere studeat *in Rusticam Romanam
linguam et Theotiscam* ; " as being then the two languages most generally
understood.   The Provençal was only the Latin tongue corrupted and
altered a little in its terminations by a mixture of the Celtic or Gaulish
idiom, and afterwards of the Visigoth and Frankish.   In the more northern
provinces of Gaul it received a still stronger tincture of the latter, and of
the Norman or Danish tongue, and formed the *Valonne,* or what is now
called in France Vieille Gauloise, out of which time produced the modern
French.   But both this and the Provençale retained alike, till the fourteenth century, the name of *Langue Romande.* See Fauchet, l. i. c. 3
and 4; *Duclos Mem.* vol. xv. p. 565, *et* vol. xvii. p. 171; *De l' Acad. des
Inscript. et Huetiana,* pp. 41 and 189.

[1] *Pourfilè,* Fr. bordered.   [2] *Pelure,* furs, from pellis, Lat.
[3] *Fetislich,* handsomely.   [4] *Gled,* Sax. a burning coal.
[5] Mr. (afterwards Dr.) Percy, Bishop of Dromore in Ireland, who edited
the " *Relicks of Antient Poetry,* in three volumes, in the year 1765." Dr.
Percy was a man of learning and accomplishments, and of an elegant

It cannot be supposed possible to fix exactly the time when rhyme was first introduced and practised in a country; but if we trace it back to the remotest monuments of the kind now extant, we shall find the æras nearly as follows:

	Anno Xti.
At Rome before the introduction of Christianity	137
In the Latin Church	420
In use among the Welch . . .	590
Among the Arabs earlier than . . .	622
Among the Franks, in the old German tongue .	873
In Provence, in the dialect of the country . .	1100
In Italy, in the Latin tongue, after the coming of the Normans	1032
In England, in our own tongue, before the year	1154
In France, in the French tongue . . .	1155
In Sicily, and in the rest of Italy, in the Italian tongue, before	1187

Any one who considers these several dates, and sees that the fathers and priests of the Roman church wrote Latin rhyme early in the fifth century, and that the Franks did the same in their own tongue in the ninth, will scarcely give credit to P. Huet, who affirms that the Provençals borrowed the art of rhyme from the Arabs. For though it is true that the Arabs had practised it before Mahomet's time, and perhaps from the remotest antiquity, and that they were in possession of part of Aquitaine from 732 to 738; which is the most probable of the two, that the Provençals should imitate the taste of a nation wholly different from themselves in language, religion, and manners, who were but for a small time conversant among them? or, that they should copy the Franks, who had reigned over them above two hundred years before the arrival of the Arabs, and still continue to do so to this day? Indeed, for my own part, I do believe, that neither the one nor the other of these nations was the immediate object of their imitation, but rather the hymns of the church, and the monkish Latin verses, which were even then[1] in vogue all over France at the time, when the earliest Provençal writers attempted to rhyme in their own tongue.

mind, whose curious researches into our ancient literature were directed by judgment, which he displayed in these pleasing and most gratifying volumes, published by him in his early life.—*Mathias.*

[1] Crescimbeni observes that rhyming verses in Latin epitaphs, inscriptions, etc., first appeared in Italy, upon the arrival of the Normans, who served under Guimaro, Prince of Salerno, in 1032. In that city were

This is the opinion of Crescimbeni (*Istor. della Poesia*, l. i. p. 13), and it will appear very natural, if we consider the near affinity of the Latin and Provençal tongues; and that they were accustomed to Latin rhymes in their books of religion, epitaphs, inscriptions, and other compositions of the learned in those days. Besides that in many old Provençal poems the rhyme not only appears at the end, but in the middle of a verse,[1] which manner was often imitated by the old Italians, Rinaldo d'Aquino, Dante da Majano, Guido Cavalcanti, and others, and is known by the name of "*Rima alla Provenzale*" (see *Crescimbeni Comentarj*, vol. i. l. 2, c. 19, p. 178); and that this

composed, about the year 1100, the famous medical precepts of the "Schola Salernitana," addressed to Robert, Duke of Normandy, son to William the Conqueror. They are in Latin rhyme, thus:

> "Cœna brevis, | vel cœna levis, | fit raro molesta,
> Magna nocet, | medicina docet, | res est manifesta," etc.

See also Fauchet (l. i. c. 7) and Maffei (*Journal Italien*, t. i.) "On ne peut nier que la rime ne tire son origine des vers rimés et Leonins de la basse Latinité, connus uniquement dans des siecles barbares."

[1] Latin rhymes, as it may be well imagined, were nothing the less esteemed when people began to rhyme in their own tongue; indeed they flourished most when the Provençale poetry was in its dawn. In the year 1154 lived Leonius, a Canon of St. Benedict at Paris, and afterwards a religious of St. Victor, who, for the age he lived in, wrote Latin verse in the regular way not contemptibly, as appears both in his elegies and in his heroics on sacred subjects; but he too gives into the taste of those times, and writes epistles in rhyme to Pope Adrian the Fourth and Alexander the Third, which begin,

> "Papa, meas, Adriane, preces, si postulo *di*gna,
> Suscipe tam vultu placido, quam mente be*ni*gnâ," etc.

And,

> "Summe Parens hominum, Christi devote Mi*ni*ster,
> Pastorum pastor, præceptorumque Ma*gi*ster," etc.

and upon such verses as these (it seems) he built his reputation; so that they have ever since borne the name of Leonine verses; and the *rime riche* (or double rhyme) even in French verses was of old called *ryme Leonine*, or *Leonime*. The ancient "Fabliau des trois Dames" has these lines:

> "Ma peine mettray, et m'entente,
> A conter un fabliau par ryme
> Sans coulour, et sans *Leonime*," etc.

So that the rhyme-female was not looked upon as a rhyme of two syllables. An old book, printed in 1493, intitled, *L'Art et Science de Rhetorique pour faire Rhymes et Ballades*, says, "Ryme Leonisme est, quand deux dictions sont semblables et de pareille consonance en syllabes, comme au chapitre de jalousie, de Jean de Meung:

> "Preude femmes, par St. Denis,
> Autant est, que de Fenis," etc.

But the word *Leonimeté* was more particularly applied (it seems) to such rhymes as run uninterrupted for many lines together; for the *Life of*

was the manner of the Latin rhymers is plain from the " Schola Salernitana," the epitaph of Roger, Duke of Sicily, in 1101;

> Linquens terrenas | migravit dux ad amœnas
> Rogerius sedes, | nam cæli detinet ædes:

and the poem " De Contemptu Mundi," written by Benard, a monk of Cluny, about 1125, in this measure:

> Hora novissima, tempora pessima sunt, vigilemus:
> Ecce minaciter imminet arbiter ille Supremus! etc.—Fauchet, l. i. c. 7.

Observe, that if the date of this poem be true, the general opinion, that the Leonine verse owes its name to Leonius, seems to be false; for Benard, in a preface prefixed to his own work, calls his own measure " genus metricum, dactylum continuum, exceptis finalibus, trochæo vel spondæo, tum etiam sonoritatem *Leoninicam* servans: " and he mentions Hildebert de Laverdin, Bishop of Mans and afterwards of Tours, and Wichard, a canon of Lyons, as having written a few things in this measure before him. It is not therefore very likely, as Leonius flourished in 1154, that he should give name to such Latin verses upwards of thirty years before. Indeed some people have thought that it was called after Leo, probably the Second, who lived in 684, a pope who is said to have reformed the hymns and the music of the church. (See Fauchet, l. i. c. 16.)

What makes it still more probable that the ancient verses in Latin rhyme might give rise to the Provençal and Italian poetry is that mixture of different languages which appears in some old compositions, namely, the canzone of Rambald de Vacheres (before the year 1226) in five several tongues, the Provençal, Tuscan, French, Gascon, and Spanish; the strange rhymes of Ubaldino the Florentine; the canzone of Dante, which begins,

> Provenç.   Ahi, faulx ris, qe trai haves
> Lat.   Oculos meos! et quid tibi feci?
> Ital.   Che fatto m' hai così spietata fraude, etc.[1]

and the great work, or " La Divina Comedia," of the same poet.

St. Christina, written about the year 1300, after rhyming in couplets throughout, finishes with these lines:

> " Seigneurs, qui en vos livres par maistrie metez
>   Equivocations et *leonismetéz*,
>   Si je tel ne puis faire, ne deprisiez mon livre,
>   Car qui a trouver n'a soubtil cuer et delivre,
>   Et *leonismete* veult par tout a consuivre
>   Moult souvent entrelest, ce qu'il devoit en suivre."

See Fauchet, l. i. c. 8, and Pasquier, l. vii. c. 2; Menage, *Dictionnaire Etymol.* v. Leonins; Jul. Scaliger Poetice, *Naude Mascurat*, p. 332.

[1] *V. le Opere di Dante*, 8vo, vol. iv. p. 300, della bella ed utilissima edizione in Londra, 1809, dall' erudito Sig. Zotti, benemerito della Letteratura Toscana per le sue edizioni del Petrarca, del Tasso, etc., con note e spiegazioni, el comodo e vantaggio de' studiosi ed anche de' dotti.—*Mathias*.

SOME OBSERVATIONS ON THE USE OF RHYME [1]

THE oldest instance which we have of rhyme in our tongue (if it be genuine) is that Tenure of the manor of Cholmer and Dancing, preserved in the Exchequer Rolls de anno 17 Edw. 2di (at which time I suppose it was lodged there), being the Grant of Edward the Confessor to Randolph Paperking. It begins:

> " Iche, Edward Konyng,
> Have geven of my forest the keeping
> Of the hundred of Cholmer and Dancing
> To Randolph Paperking, and his kindling.
> With heort and hynd, doe and bocke,
> Hare and fox, cat and brocke,
> Wilde fowell, with his flocke,
> Partridge, Fesaunt-hen, and Fesaunt-cocke,
> With grene and wild stob and stocke,
> To kepen and to yemen by all her might," etc.

That king began his reign in 1043, and this grant must have been made before 1051, when Earl Godwyn rebelled; for Swein, the eldest son of Godwyn, and brother to Edward's wife, is named as a witness to it. From that time he was in arms against the king till he went to the Holy Land, whence he never returned. It is to be observed, that he is here called *Swein of Essex* (see Camden); yet in reality not he, but his brother Harold, was earl of that county and East Anglia: which is a circumstance that may give cause to suspect the antiquity of this rhyming donation.

There is another of the same sort preserved by Stow in his *Chronicle*, and transcribed more perfectly by Blount (in his *Ancient Tenures*, p. 102), from a manuscript belonging to Robert Glover in Com. Salop:

> " To the heyrs male of the Hopton lawfully begotten," etc.

There is also a poetical History of Great Britain extant, about

---

[1] If any apology could be conceived to be necessary for the minuteness of these discussions by Mr. Gray, we might adapt the words of the prima poet of Italy to such laborious and happy investigations:

> " Senti ben *la virtù di quella corda*
> Che ciò che scocca drizza in segno lieto:
>   E vero, che la forma non s' accorda
> Molte fiate all' intention dell' arte,
> Piochè a risponder la materia è sorda."
>
> Dante, " Parad." c. i. v. 125.—*Mathias.*

Honour, p. i. c. 3. The same may be seen in Weever's *Funeral Monuments*, p. 152; see also Scotch rhyme on Edward the First, and the answer (*ibid.* p. 458); Robert of Gloucester's *Chronicle*.

Note.—It appears from a story told by Ekkehardus junior, a monk of St. Gall, in his history of that monastery, that early in the *tenth* century the children who were educated there were taught to make Latin rhymes without regard to quantity and metre, and also verses strictly metrical in the same tongue. Ekkehardus says, that when Solomon, Bishop of Constance, a little before his death, came into their school, the boys addressed him in both these manners: " Parvuli Latinè *pro nosse* (perhaps *prosaicè*), medii rhythmicè, cæteri vero metricè, quasi pro rostris rhetoricè etiam affantur; quorum duorum (quoniam a patribus verba recepimus) unus inquit,

> Quid tibi fecimus *tale*, | ut nobis facias *male ?*
> Appellamus *regem*, | quia nostram fecimus *legem :*

at alter versificator inquit,

> Non nobis pia *spes* | fuerat, cum sis novus ho*spes,*
> Ut vetus in pe*jus* | transvertere tute velis *jus :* "

this prelate died in the year 919.

As to those rhyming epitaphs of Ethelbert, King of Kent, Laurentius the second Archbishop of Canterbury, etc., said by Weever (pp. 241 and 246) to be inscribed on their monuments, in the church of St. Austin's at Canterbury, they would carry back the date of Latin rhyme as far as the beginning of the seventh century, in England, but I suspect they are of a later date, written perhaps in the time of Abbot Scotland, soon after the Conquest; who, I find, rebuilt a great part of the church, and removed many of the ancient kings and abbots from the place in which they were first interred into the choir, where he erected princely monuments over them. (Weever, p. 253.)

ADDITIONAL OBSERVATIONS AND CONJECTURES ON RHYME [1]

In the most ancient of the British poets and others, it appears that the *Cambri*, or Welch, originally called themselves *Prydhain*, and their country Inis Prydhain, the Isle of Britain. The inhabitants of Wales removing their cattle and habitations from place to place (which is still practised in some mountainous parts, and was so universally in former ages), after the custom was disused in England, were called Wallenses, from *Walen*, a word synonymous to that of Normades. (See Carte's *Hist.* vol. i. p. 5, and p. 108.)

The Druidical compositions, which served as a model to Taliessin, Llywark, and others of the most ancient and best of the British poets, whose works are preserved, and have since served for the foundation of that excellent prosodia which they have in the Welch grammar, and which is perhaps the finest that any language affords, were admirably contrived for assisting the memory. They were all adapted to music, every word being harmonious, the strongest and most expressive repeated in a beautiful manner, and all of them ranged in an order established by rules well known and universally received in such compositions; each verse so connected with, and dependent on, those which either preceded or followed it, that, if any one line in a stanza be remembered, all the rest must of course be called to mind, and it is almost impracticable to forget or to mistake in any. " The British poetry, as well as the language, hath a peculiarity which no other language perhaps in the world hath; so that the British poets in all ages, and to this day, call their art *Cyfrinach y Beirdd*, or ' The Secret of the Poets.' Knowing this art of the poets, it is impossible that any one word of the language, which is to be found in poetry, should be pronounced in any other manner than is there used; so that without a transformation of the whole language, not one word could be altered."

These are the words of a very judicious antiquary, Mr. Lewis Morris, perfectly well versed in the ancient British poets. He adds, though at first sight it may be naturally thought that their poetry is clogged with so many rules, that it is impossible

[1] From an article entitled " Cambri " these remarks are selected as relating to the subject of Rhyme.

to write a poem of common sense in the language, yet the vast number of flexions of consonants in it, and the variations of declensions, etc., make it almost as copious as four or five languages added together; and consequently a poet in the Cambrian language, notwithstanding the strictness of his rules, hath as great a scope and use of words as in any other tongue whatsoever, as will appear from a perusal of the British poets. (*Ibid.* p. 33.)

This "*Secret of the Poets*" is explained to us at large by Dr. David ap Rhys (or Rhæsus) in his *Linguæ Cambro-Britannicæ Institutiones*, p. 146, Lond. 1592, 4to. They had nine different measures from verses of three to those of eleven syllables, each distinguished by its proper appellation. Some of them have been from a very remote antiquity common among us in the English tongue, and not improbably might have been borrowed from the Britons, as I am apt to believe that the use of rhyme itself was. I was once, I own, of Crescimbeni's opinion, that it was derived from the Roman Church in its hymns, and thence passed to the people of Provence. But if we consider that, some few slight traces of rhyme among the Romans excepted, there is nothing of their hymns, or sequentiæ, written in that manner earlier than the time of Pope Gregory the Great, in the end of the sixth century; and at the same time that it was regularly and very artificially practised among the Britons in a variety of measures, and these too of a peculiar contrivance, and (as men of letters acquainted with the language assure us) full of poetical spirit and enthusiasm: if we consider also how well adapted the division and rhyme of their poetry is to assist the memory, and that the British Druids (once the priesthood of the nation) delivered all the precepts of their doctrine in verse, which never was to be committed to writing; we may easily enough be induced to believe that these bards of the sixth century practised an art which they had received by tradition from the times of the Druids, and, though the precepts of their superstition had been laid aside and forgotten at the introduction of Christianity, yet the traces of their harmony did remain.

That the Saxons, who had no rhyme among them, might borrow both that and some of the measures still in use from their neighbours the Britons, seems probable to me, though at what time they did it is very uncertain. For above one hundred and fifty years after the Saxon invasion the two nations had no other commerce than in the rough intercourse of war, and seemed to breathe nothing but inextinguishable hatred and mutual defiance. But Christianity (it is likely) something softened their spirits, and brought the Britons to regard their bitter enemies, who were now no longer pagans, as their brethren and their fellow-creatures.

If any one ask, why (supposing us to have first borrowed our rhyme from the Britons) no memorial of it is left in England earlier than the Conquest, nay, perhaps than Henry the Second's reign, which is about four hundred and fifty years after our connection with the Welch; I answer, the fact is not certainly true; for there are some few rhymes recorded as old as the beginning of the tenth century, witness Athelstan's donation to Beverley Minster; and, in the succeeding century, the freedom of Coventry granted to Earl Leofric, and the Tenure of Cholmer and Dancing in Essex, attributed to Edward the Confessor. But if these should be only the fictions of after ages, can any one tell me why the Franks, who, as we know, wrote rhyme in their own tongue [1] in the ninth century, should have nothing to produce of rhyme in the French or Provençal language till almost two hundred and fifty years afterwards? Why have they no monument at all, preserved in their ancient tongue, of the Gothic poetry, though for so many years they bordered on the Anglo-Saxons in Germany who practised it, a people of like origin and manners, and who probably spoke the same tongue? Why have these Saxons themselves, for above three hundred years after they landed in this island, no verses of this sort remaining, but a small fragment of Cædmon, preserved in a book of King Alfred's? Why have the Normans nothing at all of this kind extant among them after their arrival in France? Who can account for the caprice of time, and

---

[1] As we have no reason to imagine that the Gothic nations of the north made any use of rhyme in their versification, and as the Franks appear to be the first who practised it (three hundred and fifty years after they conquered Gaul), it seems highly probable that they borrowed it from the natives of this country, to whom it must have been familiar at least three hundred years before. For, as we know that the Britons had it so early, who spoke the same tongue with the Gauls, and delivered to them the precepts of their religion and philosophy in verse, these latter could not possibly be ignorant of their poetry, which they imitated in their own country. Nor is it probable that the government of the Romans had obliterated all traces of their ancient arts and learning in the minds of the Gauls, since it had not made them forget their ancient language. It is plain, that in the fifth century the Arverni still spoke the Celtic tongue, from a letter of Sidonius Apollinaris (l. iii. ep. 3), and that it was still understood in the ninth century, appears from the *Life of St. Germain,* written in the reign of Charles the Bald, by Heric, a monk of Auxerre, wherein he interprets the names of several cities in Gaul. See *Mémoires de l'Academie des Inscriptions,* vol. **xx.** pp. 43 and 44.

shew why one monument has, and another has not, escaped the wreck of ages? Perhaps rhyme might begin among the common people, and be applied only to the meaner species of poetry, adages, songs, and vulgar histories, passing by tradition from one to another; while the clergy and others, who possessed what literature there was in the nation, either wrote in the Latin tongue, or in the measures peculiar to their country and language, which by a very natural prejudice they would prefer to those of a conquered people, especially as poesy had been cultivated among them, and in the highest esteem for ages past; and their *Scalds* were as necessary in their armies, and in the courts of their princes, as either Druid or bard among the Britons. After the Normans came over, and had introduced so much of the French (or Roman) tongue among us, rhyme must of course grow prevalent and familiar in England, especially when Henry the Second (himself an Angevin, and educated in France) had married the heiress of Aquitaine, where the Provençal school first began about fifty years before, and was at that time in the highest reputation.[1]

[1] The reader will probably regret that the disquisitions on the subject of metre and rhythmus are here closed; but the editor has great pleasure in being able to present him with a few remarks on the poet Lydgate by Mr. Gray, some of which are curious, profound, and philosophic, and in *his* best manner. There can be no greater commendation of them.

For more copious information concerning Lydgate, see Warton's *History of English Poetry*, 4to, vol. ii. pp. 31 to 100.—*Mathias*.

SOME REMARKS ON THE POEMS OF JOHN
LYDGATE

JOHN LYDGATE was born at a place of that name in Suffolk, about the year 1370.

> I followed after, fordulled for rudenèss,
> More than three scorè yerès set my date.
> Lustè of youth, passed his freshènesse,
> Colours of rhetorike, to help me translate,
> Were faded away; I was born in Lydgate
> Where Bacchus' licour doth ful scarsely flete,
> My dry soul for to dewè and to wete.
>
> Prologue to Book viii. by Bochas on the Fall of Princes.

This work, he tells us, was begun while Henry the Sixth was in France, where that king never was but when he went to be crowned at Paris in 1432, so that if Lydgate were then upwards of threescore, he must have been born at the time I have assigned; and Tanner says that he was ordained a deacon in 1393, which is usually done in the twenty-third year of a man's age. He was a monk of the Benedictine order at St. Edmund's Bury, and in 1423 was elected prior of Hatfield-Brodhook, but the following year had licence to return to his convent again. His condition, one would imagine, should have supplied him with the necessaries of life, yet he more than once complains to his great patron the protector, Humphry, Duke of Gloucester, of his wants, and he shews, particularly in the passage above, that he did not dislike a little more wine than the convent allowed him.

After enumerating the principal English poets who lived before him, whose merit he does not pretend to equal, he says,

> But I, who stand low downè in the vale,
> So grete a booke in Englyshe to translate,
> Did it by constrainte, and no presumption,
> Born in a village, which is called Lydgate
> By oldè time a famous castel towne,
> In Danès time it was beatè down,
> Time what St. Edmund's martir, maid and king,
> Was slaine at Oxford, récorde of writing, etc.
>
> Epilogue.

There are a few other things in this work of Lydgate's which have no connection with his merit as a poet, but are curious as they relate to the history and manners of the times in which he lived. Thus in book viii. c. 24, we see that wine was still made in England in Henry the Sixth's reign, and that Hampshire was famous for it; so that the reason assigned for neglecting the culture of vines, I mean, that we could have so much better wines from our French dominions, is not true; and indeed a few years after this we lost all our conquests and territories in that country.

> [1] London hath shippis by the sea to saile,
> Bacchus at Winchester greatly doth availe,
> Worcester with fruits aboundeth at the full,
> Hertford with beastis, Cotiswold with wooll.
>   Bath hath hot bathes holesome for medicine,
> Yorke mighty timber for great ávauntage,
> Cornëwall miners in to mine,—
> And Salisbury has beastès full savàge,
> Wheate meale and hony plentie for every age:
> Kent and Canterbury hath great commoditie,
> Of sondrie fishes there taken in the sea.

We may remark too the notion then current in Britain, that King Arthur was not dead, but translated to fairy-land, and should come again to restore the Round Table:

> This errour [2] abideth yet among Britons,
> Which founded is upon the prophesie
> Of old Merlin, like their opinion;
> He as a king is crowned in faërie,
> With sceptre and sworde, and with his regalie
> Shall resort as lord and soveraine
> Out of faerie, and reigne in Britaine, etc.
>
>   B. viii. c. 24.

[1] It may be worth while to compare this passage with a similar one in Robert of Gloucester, who wrote (near two hundred years before) in the days of Henry the Third.

> In the country of Canterbury most plenty of fish is,
> And most chase of wild beasts about Salisbury, I wis,
> And London ships most, and wine at Winchester,
> At Hartford sheepe and oxe, and fruit at Worcester,
> Soape about Coventry, and iron at Glocester,
> Metall, lead, and tinne in the countie of Exeter,
> Everwicke [1] of fairest wood, Lincolne [2] of fairest men,
> Cambridge and Huntingdon most plentie of deep venne,
> Elie of fairest place, of fairest sight Rochester, etc.
>
>   In Camden's *Remains*, p. 8.

[2] Peter of Glois, who lived in 1170, says ironically, in his *Epistles*, 57:

> Quibus si credideris
> Expectare poteris
> Arturum cum Britonibus.

> [1] *Eboracum*, York.

> [2] Testis Lincolnie, gens infinita decore,
> Testis Ely formosa situ, Roucestria visu.
>
>   *Liber Costumorum.*

And we may remark also the opinion, then prevailing, that a decisive victory was a certain proof of the justice of the conqueror's cause, which was but natural among a people which for ages had been taught to refer even civil causes to a decision by combat.

It seems that Lydgate was little acquainted with the Latin tongue, whatever he might be with the Italian and French, in which Bishop Tanner says he was well skilled, having travelled in both those countries; for he says himself,

> I never was acquaintedde with Virgile,
> Nor with the sugared ditties of Homère,
> Nor Dares Phrygius withe his goldenne stile,
> Nor with Ovide in poetry most entère,
> Nor with the sovereign ballades of Chaucère,
> Which, amonge all that ever were redde or sunge,
> Excelled all other in our Englishe tungue.
>   I cannot ben a judge in this mattère,
> As I conceive, following my fantaisie;
> In moral matter notable was Gowère,
> And so was Strode [1] in his philosophie,
> In perfite living, which passith poesie,
> Richard Hermite, contemplatif of sentènce,
> Drough in Englishe, *the Pricke of Conscience.*
>   As the gold-crested brightè summer-sunne
> Passith other sterres with his bemès cleare,
> And as Lucina chases setès downe
> The frostie nights when Hesperus doth appere,
> Righte soe my master haddè never peere,
> I mean Chaucère in stories, that he tolde,
> And he also wrote tragedïes olde.

But this perhaps [2] is only an affectation of great humility and modesty, which was common to all these ancient writers; for however little he might be *acquainted* with Homer and Virgil, it is certain that he was very much so with Chaucer's compositions, whom he calls his master, and who (as I imagine) was so in a literal sense. It is certain that Lydgate was full thirty years of age when Chaucer died.[3]   But whatever his skill were

[1] Chaucer mentions these two writers with the same species of commendation:

> " Oh moralle Gowere, this bokè I dirècte
> To thee, and to the philosophicke Strode."
>   *Troilus and Cresseide*, Book v. v. 1855.—*Mathias.*

[2] So in Machabrées " Daunce of Death," paraphrased from the French, he says:

> Have me excused, my name is John Lydgate,
> Rude of languàge, I was not born in France,
> Her curious metres in Englishe to translate:
> Of other tongue I have noe suffisaunce.

[3] See Lydgate's *Life of the Virgin Mary*, cap. xxxiv. and in the *Pylgrimage of the Soul*, printed by Caxton, 1483, c., xxxiv., which is the same, and seems to show this latter translation to be Lydgate's also.

in the learned languages, it is sure that he has not taken his
"Fall of Princes" from the original Latin prose of Boccaccio,[1]
but from a French translation of it by one Laurence, as he tells
us himself in the beginning of his work. It was indeed rather
a paraphrase than a translation, for he took the liberty of making
several additions, and of reciting more at large many histories,
which Boccaccio had slightly passed over:

> And he [2] sayeth eke, that his entencyon
> Is to amend, correcten, and declare,
> Not to condemne of no presumpcyon,
> But to supportè plainly and to spare
> Thing touched shortly of the storie bare,
> Under a stile briefe and compendious,
> Them to prolong when they be virtuous.
>   For a storye which is not plainly tolde,
> But constreyned under wordes few,
> For lacke of truth, wher they ben new or olde,
> Men by reporte cannot the matter shewe
> These oakès greatè be not down yhewe
> First at a stroke, but by a *long processe*,
> Nor long stories a word may not expresse.

These " *long processes* " indeed suited wonderfully with the
attention and simple curiosity of the age in which Lydgate
lived. Many *a stroke* have he and the best of his contemporaries
spent upon a *sturdy old story*, till they had blunted their own
edge and that of their readers; at least a modern reader will
find it so: but it is a folly to judge of the understanding and
of the patience of those times by our own. They loved, I will
not say tediousness, but length and a train of circumstances in
a narration. The vulgar do so still: it gives an air of reality
to facts, it fixes the attention, raises and keeps in suspense their
expectation, and supplies the defects of their little and lifeless
imagination; and it keeps pace with the slow motion of their
own thoughts. Tell them a story as you would tell it to
a man of wit, it will appear to them as an object seen in
the night by a flash of lightning; but when you have placed
it in various lights and in various positions, they will come at
last to see and feel it as well as others. But we need not
confine ourselves to the vulgar, and to understandings beneath
our own. *Circumstance* ever was, and ever will be, the life and

---

[1] *Boccacius de Casibus Illustrium Virorum* is (like the rest of his Latin
works and those of his master Petrarch) now little read or esteemed by
anybody; it is written in a kind of poetical prose; the parties concerned
are introduced as passing in review before him, as in a vision, and recount-
ing their own catastrophe, and it is interspersed with the author's moral
reflections upon each of their histories.

[2] *i.e.* Laurence.

the essence both of oratory and of poetry. It has in some sort the same effect upon every mind that it has upon that of the populace; and I fear the quickness and delicate impatience of these polished times, in which we live, are but the forerunners of the decline of all those beautiful arts which depend upon the imagination.

Whether these apprehensions are well or ill grounded, it is sufficient for me that Homer, the father of *circumstance*, has occasion for the same apology which I am making for Lydgate and for his predecessors. Not that I pretend to make any more comparison between his beauties and theirs, than I do between the different languages in which they wrote. Ours was indeed barbarous enough at that time, the orthography unsettled, the syntax very deficient and confused, the metre [1] and the number of syllables left to the ear alone; and yet, with all its rudeness, our tongue had then acquired an energy and a plenty by the adoption of a variety of words borrowed from the

---

[1] I am inclined to think (whatever Mr. Dryden says in the preface to his *Tales*), that their metre, at least in serious measures and in heroic stanzas, was uniform; not indeed to the eye, but to the ear, *when rightly pronounced*. We undoubtedly destroy a great part of the music of their versification by laying the accent of words, where nobody *then* laid it; for example, in the lines cited above, if we pronounce enténcion, presúmpcion, compéndious, vértuous, prócesse, etc., in the manner in which we do in our own age, it is neither verse nor rhyme; but Lydgate and his contemporaries undoubtedly said, entenciōn, compendioūs, procēsse, etc., as the French (from whom those words were borrowed) do at this day, *intentiōn, compendieūx, procēs*.

We may every day see instances of this: the better sort of people affect to introduce many words from that language, some of which retain their original accent for many years, such as *fracās, eclāt, ennūi*, etc.; others, by coming more into vulgar use, lose it and assume the English accent, as rīdicule, rāillery, éclāircissement, advértisement, hāutgout, etc. Another peculiarity in the old pronunciation was that of liquefying two syllables into one, especially where there was a liquid consonant in either of them, as,

"Which among all that *ever* were redde or sunge"—

Or,

"Of right *consid'red* of truth and equitè."

Here undoubtedly " *ever* " in the first line was pronounced as one syllable, and " *consid'red*," in the second line, as two syllables. We cannot wonder at this, because we do it still; " *memory, heavenly, every*," etc., naturally of three syllables, are, when spoken, of two only; " *given, driven*," etc., which should be of two, are reduced only to one syllable. It is true that we are uniform in this, and pronounce such words always alike in prose and verse, and we have thrown out the vowel (to the great detriment of our language) in the end of all participles-past, as " awaken'd, bless'd, damag'd, troubl'd," etc., by which they either lose a syllable quite, or (what is worse) that syllable is pronounced, and yet consists of nothing but consonants. The ancients, I imagine, did the same, but not uniformly, either opening or contracting such words to suit the necessities of *their*

French, the Provençal, and the Italian, about the middle of the fourteenth century, which at this day our best writers seem to miss and to regret; for many of them have gradually dropped into disuse, and are only now to be found in the remotest counties of England.

Another thing which perhaps contributed in a degree to the making our ancient poets so voluminous, was the great facility of rhyming, which is now grown so difficult; words of two or three syllables, being then newly taken from foreign languages, did still retain their original accent, and that accent (as they were mostly derived from the French) fell, according to the genius of that tongue, upon the last syllable;[1] which, if it had still continued among us, had been a great advantage to our poetry. Among the Scotch this still continues in many words; for they say, envȳ, practīse, pensīve, positīve,[2] etc.: but we, in process of time, have accustomed ourselves to throw back all our accents upon the antepenultima, in words of three or more syllables, and of our dissyllables comparatively but a few are left, as despāir, disdāin, repēnt, pretēnd, etc., where the stress is not laid on the penultima. By this mean we are almost reduced to find our rhymes among the monosyllables, in which our tongue too much abounds, a defect which will for ever hinder it from adapting itself well to music, and must be con-

measure. They also at pleasure united two syllables, where one ended and the other begun with a vowel; as,

> " In pērfīt līvǐng, whǐch pǎssīth poësǐe "—

Or,

> " Nor with Ŏvīde, ǐn pŏetrȳ mŏst ēntēre."

Poesie and *poetry* were dissyllables: and this they did even where the syllables were in two different words, as,

> " Shall follŏw *a* sprǐng-floŏde ŏf grācǐoŭs plēntǐe."

The syllables I have marked were melted into one, as well in " follŏw *a*," as in " grācǐoŭs." They carried it still further, and cut off a syllable where the accent did not fall upon it, even before a consonant, as,

> " Cause ŏf mȳ sŏrrowe, roŏte ŏf mȳ hēavǐnēsse; "

here " sorrow " lost its last syllable entirely. These liberties may be justified by our use of the particle " *the* " in verse, which we sometimes sink, and sometimes pronounce distinctly before a vowel; and not many years ago it was frequently cut off even before a consonant.

[1] Except in words which end with an *e* mute, which being always pronounced in verse by the French, and making a distinct syllable, the accent is laid upon the penultima: in such words our ancestors either pronounced the finishing *e*, or dropped it entirely, as the French themselves do in common conversation. This, I conceive, was one of our poetical licenses.

[2] In Waller's time only we said commērce, triūmph, etc., with the accent on the last syllable.

sequently no small impediment to the sweetness and harmony of versification. I have now before me Pope's ethic epistles, the first folio edition, which I open at random, and find in two opposite pages (beginning with

" Who but must laugh, the master when he sees," etc.

in the " Epistle on Taste to Lord Burlington ") in the compass of forty lines only seven words at the end of a verse which are not monosyllables: there is indeed one which is properly a dissyllable, hĕavĕn, but cruel constraint has obliged our poets to make it but one syllable (as indeed it is in common pronunciation), otherwise it would not have been any single rhyme at all. Thus our too numerous monosyllables are increased, and consonants crowded together till they can hardly be pronounced at all; a misfortune which has already happened to the second person singular perfect in most of our verbs, such as thou stood'st, gav'st, hurt'st, laugh'dst, uprear'dst, built'st, etc., which can scarcely be borne in prose. Now as to trisyllables, as their accent is very rarely on the last, they cannot properly be any rhymes at all: yet nevertheless I highly commend those who have judiciously and sparingly introduced them as such. Dryden, *in whose admirable ear the music of our old versification still sounded*, has frequently done it in his tales and elsewhere. Pope does it now and then, but seems to avoid it as licentious. If any future Englishman can attain that height of glory to which *these two poets* have risen, let him be less scrupulous, upon reflecting, that to poetry languages owe their first formation, elegance, and purity; that our own, which was naturally rough and barren, borrowed from thence its copiousness and its ornaments; and that the authority of such a poet may perhaps redress many of the abuses which time and ill custom have introduced, the poverty of rhyme, the crowd of monosyllables, the collision of harsh consonants, and the want of picturesque expression, which, I will be bold to say, our language labours under *now* more than it did a hundred years ago.

To return to Lydgate. I do not pretend to set him on a level with his master, Chaucer, but he certainly comes the nearest to him of any contemporary writer that I am acquainted with. His choice of expression, and the smoothness of his verse, far surpass both Gower and Occleve. He wanted not art in raising the more tender emotions of the mind, of which I might give several examples. The first is, of that sympathy which we feel for humble piety and contrition: Constantine is introduced

making his confession and returning thanks to heaven in sight
of the Roman people, after he had been cured of a grievous
malady by the water of baptism:

> His crown he tooke, and kneeling thus he said,
> With wepinge eyen and voice lamentàble,
> And for sobbnȳge so as he might abbrayde;
> " O blessed Jesu, O Lord most merciàble,
> Lettè my teares to thee be acceptàble,
> Receive my prayer, my rèquest not refuse,
> As man most sinful, I may not me excuse.
>   " I occupied the state of the emperòur,
> Of thy martȳrs I shedde the holye blood,
> Sparèd no saintes in my cruel erròur,
> Them to pursue most furious and woode;
> Now blessed Jesu, gracious and most good,
> Peysed [1] and considred mine importàble' [2] offènce,
> I am not worthy to come in thy presènce,
>   " Nor for to enter into this holy place,
> Upon this ground unable for to dwell,
> To open my eyen, or lift up my face;
> Butte of thy mercy (so thou mee not repell)
> As man most sinfull I come unto the welle,
> Thy welle of grace and merciful pitye,
> For to be washed of mine iniquity."
>   This example in open hath he showed,
> His state imperial of mekeness laid aside,
> His purple garment with teares all bedewed,
> Sworde, nor sceptèrre, ne horse whereon to ride,
> There was none seen, nor banners splayed wide,
> Of martial triumphs was no token founde,
> But, crying mercy, the emperour lay plat on the ground.
>   The people's gladness was meddled with wepinge,
> And theire wepynge was meddled with gladness,
> To see an emperour and so noble a king,
> Of his free choyce to shew soe great mekenèss;
> Thus intermeddled was joy and heavyness,
> Heavyness far passed oldè vengĕaünce,
> With newe rejoising of ghostly repentaunce.

Book viii. fol. 184.

Of the same kind is the prayer of Theodosius before he
engaged in battle with Arbogastes (in the same book, fol. 188).
A second instance of the pathetic, but in a different way, I shall
transcribe from the first book, fol. 39, to shew how far he could
enter into the distresses of love and of maternal fondness.
Canace, condemned to death by Æolus her father, sends to her
guilty brother, Macareus, the last testimony of her unhappy
passion:

> Out of her swoonè when she did abbraide,
> Knowing no mean but death in her distrèsse,
> To her brother full piteouslie she said,
> " Cause of my sorrowe, roote of my heavinesse,

---

[1] *Pesè*, weighed.   [2] Insupportable.

That whilom were the sourse of my gladnèsse
When both our joyes by wille were so disposed,
Under one key our hearts to be inclosed.

.   .   .   .   .

This is mine end, I may it not astarte;
O brother mine, there is no more to saye;
Lowly beseeching with all mine whole hearte
For to remember specially, I praye,
If it befall my littel sonne to dye,
That thou mayst after some mynd on us have,
Suffer us both be buried in one grave.

I hold him streitly twene my armès twein,
Thou and natùre laidè on me this charge;
He, guiltlesse, mustè with me suffer paine:
And sith thou art at freedome and at large
Let kindnesse oure love not so discharge,
But have a minde, wherever that thou be,
Once on a day upon my child and me.

On thee and me dependeth the trespàce,
Touching our guilt and our great offence,
But, welaway! most àngelik of face
Our childè, young in his pure innocence,
Shall agayn right suffer death's violence,
Tender of limbes, God wote, full guiltĕless,
The goodly faire, that lieth here speechlèss.

A mouth he has, but wordis hath he none:
Cannot complaine, alas! for none outràge,
Nor grutcheth not, but lies here all alone,
Still as a lambe, most meke of his visàge.
What heart of stele could do to him damàge,
Or suffer him dye, beholding the manere
And looke benigne of his tweine eyen clere?

                                        B. i. fol. 39.

I stop here, not because there are not great beauties in the
remainder of this epistle, but because Lydgate, in the three last
stanzas of this extract, has touched the very heart-springs of
compassion with so masterly a hand, as to merit a place among
the greatest poets.   The learned reader will see the resemblance
they bear to one of the most admirable remnants of all antiquity,
I mean the fragment of Simonides (unhappily it is but a fragment) preserved to us by Dionysius Halicarnassensis; and yet,
I believe, that no one will imagine that Lydgate had ever seen
or heard of it.   As to Ovid, from whom Boccaccio might borrow
many of his ideas in this story, it will be easily seen, upon comparison, how far our poet has surpassed him.   He finishes his
narration in this manner:

Writing her letter, awhapped all in drede,
In her right hand her penne ygan to quake,
And a sharp sword to make her heartè blede,
In her left hand her father hath her take,
And most her sorrowe was for her childes sake,
Upon whose facè in her barme sleepȳnge
Full many a tere she wept in cōmplȳnȳng.

> After all this, so as she stoode and quoke,
> Her child beholding mid of her peines smart,
> Without abode the sharpè sword she tooke,
> And rove herselfè even to the hearte;
> Her child fell down, which mightè not astert,
> Having no help to succour him, nor save,
> But in her blood the selfe began to bathe.
>
> B. i. fol. 39.

A third kind of pathos arises from magnanimity in distress, which, managed by a skilful hand, will touch us even where we detest the character which suffers. Of this too I shall produce an example in Olympias, the mother of Alexander, betrayed into the hands of the perfidious Cassander. It begins:

> His faith was laidè that time for hostàge—

And for five stanzas following.

And his reflections, after this, upon the fortitude of so cruel and imperious a woman shew something of penetration and insight into the human heart:

> But froward rancour and wode melancholie
> Gave her a sprite of feignèd patience,
> A false pretence of high magnificence;
> A scauncè she had been in virtue stronge,
> For truthe to have enduredde every wrong.
>   Contrarious force made her dispiteous
> Stronge in her errour to endure her payne,
> Of obstinate heart she was, fell and yròus,
> In death's constreintè list not to complaine:
> Counterfeit suffrance made her for to feigne,
> Nothing of virtue plainly to termine,
> Nor of no manners that be feminine.
>
> B. iv. fol. 114.

Of the same kind are his description of Mithridates surrounded by the troops of Pompey in Armenia (b. vi. fol. 153), the Speech of Regulus to the Senate (b. v.), and that of Lucrece to her husband and father determining on death (b. ii. fol. 48), and the same story repeated, for he has told it twice in a different manner (b. iii. fol. 74).

It is observable that in images of horror, and in a certain terrible greatness, our author comes far behind Chaucer. Whether they were not suited to the genius or to the temper of Lydgate, I do not determine; but it is certain that, though they naturally seemed to present themselves, he has almost generally chosen to avoid them: yet is there frequently a stiller kind of majesty both in his thought and expression, which makes one of his principal beauties. The following instance of it (I think) approaches even to sublimity:

> God hath a thousand handès to chastÿse,
> A thousand dartès of punicìon,
> A thousand bowès made in uncouthe wyse,
> A thousand arblastes bent in his doungeon,[1]
> Ordeind each one for castigacìon;
> But where he fyndes mekeness and repentaùnce
> Mercy is mystresse of his ordinaunce.
>
> B. i. f. 6.

There is also a particular elegance in his grave and sententious
reflections, which makes a distinguishing part of his character:
of this I shall give some examples out of a multitude. B. i. f. 6,
etc., on pride; on literature, in the prologue to the fourth book;
and on contented poverty (b. i. f. 34); and on the vices of
persons meanly born, when raised to power (b. iv. f. 118); but
examples of this kind are too many and too prolix for me to
transcribe. I shall refer, however, also to those verses which
recommend gentleness and mercy to women (f. 115); on the
mischiefs of flattery (f. 44); on ingratitude (f. 139); on patience
(f. 211); on avarice (f. 93); on the duties of a king (f. 190); and
the allegorical combat between fortune and glad poverty (f. 69).

Lydgate seems to have been by nature of a more serious and
melancholy turn of mind than Chaucer; yet one here and there
meets with a stroke of satire and irony which does not want
humour, and it usually falls (as was the custom of those times)
either upon the women or on the clergy. As the religious were
the principal scholars of these ages, they probably gave the tone
in writing or in wit to the rest of the nation. The celibacy
imposed on them by the church had soured their temper, and
naturally disposed them (as is observed of old bachelors in our
days) to make the weaknesses of the other sex their theme; and
though every one had a profound respect for his own particular
order, yet the feuds and bickerings between one order and
another were perpetual and irreconcileable. These possibly
were the causes which directed the satire of our old writers
principally to those two objects. On the first may be produced
the passage (b. i. f. 26),

> But Bochas here, etc.

for three stanzas.

In the dispute between Brunichilde, Queen of France, and
Boccaccio, he is more direct and explicit:

> Soothely, quoth he, this is the condicion,
> Of you women, almostè everywhere, etc.

(b. ix. f. 198), and so for three stanzas: and surely his reflections

---

[1] *Doungeon* is a castle or palace: so in B. viii. c. 24, he calls heaven
" the riche sterry bright doungeon."

on Orpheus, when he had lost Euridice, are neither deficient in spirit nor in expression (b. i. f. 32):

> If some husbands had stonden in the case
> To have lost their wives for a looke sodeine, etc.

and for five stanzas.

This kind of satire will, I know, appear to modern men of taste a little stale and unfashionable; but our reflections should go deeper, and lead us to consider the fading and transitory nature of wit in general. I have above attempted to shew the source whence the two prevailing subjects of our ancestors' severity were derived: let us also observe their different success and duration from those times to our own.

The first, I mean the frailties of women, are now become the favourite theme of conversation among country-gentlemen, fellows of colleges, and the lower clergy. Upon these (if we attend to it) commonly turns the archness and pleasantry of farmers, peasants, and the meanest of the people; for to them it is that modes of wit, as well as of dress and manners, gradually descend; and there (as they came to them by a very slow and insensible progress) from a peculiar sullenness and aversion in their nature to everything which seems new; so, when they are once established, do they continue and obstinately adhere for ages; for, as it has been said of justice, it is in the country that

> *Fashion* lingers, ere she leaves the land.

Go but into some county at a distance from the capital; observe their table, their furniture, their habits; and be sure that there was a time (which a person of curiosity in the original and antiquity of national customs may frequently discover) when those meats with which they serve you, and those moveables which they use, were delicacies and conveniences of life, only seen in the houses of people of high distinction; and when those forms of dress, at which you now laugh, were newly imported or invented by some "ruffling gallant," or by some lofty dame of honour in the court of Elizabeth, perhaps, or, at latest, of Charles the Second. In the same manner, in their expressions of civility and compliment, and in their turn of reflection, their stories and their jokes all savour of a former age, and once belonged to the most polished and gayest people of our nation. Sometimes they were originally ridiculous and absurd, sometimes far more proper and more sensible than what has been since introduced in their room; and here it is only the misapplication of them, and somewhat of awkwardness which they may have contracted in the country, that can with justice make them objects of ridicule.

That general satire upon the female sex, of which I am speaking, is now banished from good company; for which there may be several reasons given. Celibacy is no more enjoined to our clergy, and as knowledge and writing diffused themselves among the body of the people, the clergy grew no longer to be the leaders of their taste and humour; and lastly, we have (as in most things) adopted in some measure that extreme politeness and respect which the French *pretend* to shew to their women. The case is nearly the same in that nation as in this, in one point; the clergy have less influence there than in any other catholic country, and, as erudition has spread among the laity, they are no more the models of wit and good sense to their countrymen. Their old *Fabliaux* and *Romans* were just as severe upon the women, and in the same way, as ours; and just so that humour has imperceptibly worn out with them. Yet we need but look into the tales of Fontaine in that tongue, borrowed from those old stories which I have mentioned, and from Boccaccio, Machiavel, Ariosto, and others, where all the naïveté and sly simplicity of the ancient writers are preserved and heightened with the correctness, elegance, and graces of the moderns; and (though far the greater part of their humour runs upon this very subject) we shall soon be convinced that it is a topic not to be exhausted, and full as susceptible of wit and of true ridicule as it was four hundred years ago. Instances of this in our own language may be seen in most of Dryden's tales, in Pope's " January " and " May," the " Wife of Bath's " prologue, and in other compositions.

But raillery on the priesthood has continued through every age, and remains almost as fashionable as ever. It was in its full force about the time of the Reformation, and a little before, upon the revival of learning and the invention of printing: afterwards it turned upon our established church, and the variety of sects produced the same effect that the variety of the religious orders had done formerly; not to mention the struggles for power between the Church and the Commonwealth in Charles the First's and in Charles the Second's reign, and at the Revolution, and in the last years of Queen Anne, and in the beginning of George the First, which have produced a lasting bitterness and rancour, which keeps this kind of satire alive and in countenance even to this day. Addison, who formed and influenced the national taste in a thousand instances, could not with all his efforts do it in this case; yet perhaps we may, in no long time, see the end of this fashion, for, if I am not greatly mistaken, the spirit is already subsiding.

The examples of this second kind of wit are much more frequent in Chaucer than in Lydgate: there are, however, some, as in b. ix. fol. 202, of the "Fall of Princes":

> The poorè staff, and potent of doctrine,
> When it was chaungèd, and listè not abide
> In wilful povertie; but gan anon decline
> On statelie palfreys and highe horse to ride;
> Sharpe hairès then were also laidè asyde,
> Turned to copes of purple and sanguine,
> Gownès of scarlet furrèd with ermine.
>
> Slenderè fare of wine and water clere,
> With abstinence of bread ymade of wheat,
> Chaunged the days to many fat dinère
> With confit drink and Ippocrasè swete;
> All sobernessè did his boundès lete:
> Scarsness of foode leftè his olde estate,
> With new excess gan wexè delicate.

And in b. ix. f. 217.

> Priestès, prelàtes, and well-fed fat parsòns
> Richly avauncèd, and clerkès of degree
> Reken up religions with all their brode crowns,
> And patriarches, that have great sovereigntie,
> Bishops, abbòts, confirmed in their see,
> Secular canons, with many a great prebènd,
> Behold of fortune the mutabilitie,
> How sodeinly she made them to descend.

And in the "Daunce of Machabree,"[1] where Death is introduced as leading a measure, and compelling all sorts and degrees of mankind to join the dance, men of the church arè represented as more loth and unwilling to die, than any other profession whatever.

The Pope, indeed, out of respect to his dignity, and the Chartreux and the Hermit (who were entirely abstracted from worldly affairs, and exposed therefore to no one's malignity, shew less repugnance to death, and the latter even welcomes him with great cheerfulness.

Lydgate, however, makes his apology to the ladies very handsomely for the hard things he has said of them:

> The richè rubye, nor the sapphire Ynde,
> Be not appairèd of their freshe beautèe,
> Thoughe amonge stones men counterfeitès finde:
> And semblaby, though some women be
> Not well govèrned after their degre,

---

[1] It is a translation, or rather a paraphrase from the French of Doctor Machabrée, and the subject of it was expressed on the wall of St. Innocent's at Paris in painting, where Lydgate had seen it. It is printed by Tothill at the end of *Boccace* in 1554, fol.

It not defaceth, nor doth violence
To them, that never did in their life offence.
  The whitè lilie, nor the wholesom rose,
Nor violettès spredde on bankis thick
Their swetènesse, which outward they unclose,
Is not appaired with no wedès wicke, etc.

B. i. f. 37.

He defends the honour of his country with a laudable spirit
against Boccaccio, who, though speaking of the victory when
John, King of France, was made prisoner, calls the English
" inertissimos et nullius valoris homines " :

Though the said Boccace flowred in poetrie,
His partialle writinge gave no mortal wounde,
Caughtè a quarrel in his melancholie,
Which to his shame did afterwardes redounde, etc.
  Held them but smale of reputation,
In his report: men may his writings see:
His fantasie, nor his opinion
Stode in that case of no authoritie:
Their kinge was took; their knightès all did flee:
Where was Bochas to help them at such nede?
Save with his pen, he made no man to blede.

B. ix. f. 216.

The epilogue addressed to the Duke of Gloucester, and the
three envoyes which follow it, have much poetical expression in
them, which was Lydgate's [1] peculiar merit. However his name

---

[1] Lydgate composed a great number of ballads, one of which I shall
here transcribe, as, I imagine, it never was printed.

Let no man boaste of cunnyng, ne virtù,
Of tresour, richesse, nor of sapience,
Of worldly sùpport, alle cummith of Jesù,
Counsel, comfòrt, discretion, and prudènce,
Promotion, foresighte, and providence;
Like as the lord of grace lyst to dispose,
Som man hath wisdom, som hath eloquence.
All stand on chaunge, like a midsòmer rose.
  Holsome in smellyng be the sotè flowers,
Full delectàble outwarde to the syght;
The thorn is sharpe, endued with freshe colòurs;
All is not gold, that outwarde sheweth bryght.
A stockfysch bone in darkeness giveth light,
Twene faire and fowle, as God list to dispose,
A difference atwyx the day and nyght.
All stand on chaunge, like a midsòmer rose.
  Flowerrès open upon every greene
Whannè the larkè, mesangere of day,
Saleweth the' upryst of the sunnis shene
Most amorosely in April and in May;
And Aurora, agayne the morrow gray,
Causith the daysy his crowne to unclose,
Worldly gladnèsse is medlyd with affray:
All stand on chaunge, like a midsòmer rose.
  Atwene the cukkow and the nightyngale
There is amayde a straungè difference.

be now almost lost in oblivion, yet did his reputation continue flourishing above a hundred years after his death, and particularly we may see the esteem in which this work of " The Fall of Princes " was in, for eight poets in Queen Elizabeth's

> On freschè branchys singyth the wood-wayle; [1]
> Jays in musicke have small experience;
> Chattering pyes, whan they cum in presènce,
> Most malapert theire verdyte to propose.
> All thyng hath favour brevely in sentènce
> Of soft or sharp, like a midsòmer rose.
>
> The royal lion let call a parlament,
> All beastis soone aboute him ènviron;
> The wolf of malice being ther presènt
> Upon the lambe complayns again resòn
> Saidè, he made his water ùnholsumè,
> Hys tendyr stomak to' hinder and undispose;
> Ravenors ravyne, the' innocent is borne downe.
> All stand on chaunge, like a midsòmer rose.
>
> All worldly thyngè braidyth upon time;
> The sunnè chaungith, so does the pale moone;
> The aureat noumbre in kalenders for prime:
> Fortune is double, doth favour for no boone;
> And who that hath with that qwene [2] to done,
> Contrariosely she will his chaunge dispose;
> Who sitteth hyghest, most like to fall sone.
> All stands on chaunge, like a midsòmer rose.
>
> The golden carr of Phebus in the aire
> Causith mists blake that they dare not appere,
> At whose upryst mountains be made so faire
> As they were new gylt with his bemys clere,
> The nyght doth follow, appallith all his chere,
> When westerne waves his stremys over-close;
> Recken all beawty, all fresheness, that is here:
> All stand on chaunge, like a midsòmer rose.
>
> Constreynt of cold makith the fowlis dare [3]
> With wynter frost, that they dare not appere;
> All cladde in russett soil of greene is bare,
> Tellus and Juno dullyd of their chere
> By revolution turnyng of the yere;
> As grayè March his stoundys [4] doth disclose,
> Now rayne, now storme, now Phebus bright and clere.
> All stand on chaunge, like a midsòmer rose.
>
> Where is now David, the most worthy king,
> Of Juda and Israel famous and notàble?
> And where is Solomon, soveraine of cunning,
> Richest of buylding, of tresour incomparàble?
> Face of Absalom most faire most amiable?
> Recken up echone, of truth make no close;
> Recken up Jonathas of friendship immutable.
> All stand on chaunge, like a midsòmer rose.
>
> Where Julius, proudest in his empìre,
> With his triumphis most imperial?
> And where is Porus, that was lord and sire
> Of Indè in hys hygh estate royàl?

[1] Wood-pigeon. Some say it is the witwall or golden thrush.
[2] Harlot.   [3] Lie hid. From the A. Saxon dearn, dearnan, to hide.
[4] Times, weathers. Saxon.

reign, and at the head of them Thomas Sackville, afterwards
Lord Buckhurst, joined their forces to write a supplement to it,
called "The Mirror of Magistrates." (See W. Baldwyn's
preface, fol. 109 of the edition in 1587, in 4to.)

> And where is Alisaund, that conquer'd all?
> Fayld laisour his testament to dispose,
> Nabucodnosor, or Sardanapal?
> All stand on chaunge, like a midsòmer rose.
>   And where is Tullius wyth hys sugyrd tungue,
> Or Chrisostomus with his golden mouthe?
> The aureate ditties that were redde or sunge
> Of Hòmerus in Grece both north and south?
> The tragedìes divers and unkouth
> Of moral Seneck the misteries to unclose?
> By many' examplys this *matt* [1] is full kowth:
> All stand on chaunge as a midsòmer rose.
>   Where ben of Fauncè all the dousèperes [2]
> Which over allè had the governance?
> (Wowis of the pecok with her prowdè chères!)
> The worthy [3] nine with allè their beaunce
> The Trojan knightes, greatest of àllyaunce?
> The flece of gold conquered in Colchòse?
> Rome and Carthàge most soverein of puissaùnce?
> All stand on chaunge, like a midsòmer rose.
>   Putt in a summe all martial policye,
> Compleat in Afrik, and bowndis of Cartàge,
> The Theban legion, example' of chivalry,
> At Jordain's river was expert their coràge,
> There thousand knightis born of hygh paràge,
> There martyrd, redde in metre and in prose;
> The golden crownes made in the heavenly stage,
> Fresher than lily', or the midsòmer rose.
>   The rémembraunce of every famose knyght,
> Grownd considerd, is buylt on ryghtwysnesse.
> Rase out eche quarrell that' is not buylt on right.
> Withouten trouthe what vaylith high noblèsse?
> Lawrer of martyrs foundyd on holynesse,
> White was made rede their triumphs to disclose;
> The whitè lilie was theire chast cleannèsse,
> Theire bloody sufferaunce no midsòmer rose:
>   It was the rosè of the bloodye field,
> The rose of Jericho, that grew in Bethlèmm,
> The fine posìes, purtreyed on the sheelde
> Splayd in the banner at Jerusalem.
> The sunne was clypsd and darke in every reame, [4]
> When Jesu Crist five wellis list unclose
> Toward Paradyse, and callid the rede streme,
> Of whose five woundes print in your heart a rose.

> From a MS. in the Public Library in the University
> of Cambridge.

[1] *i.e.* This motto is well known.
[2] Douze pairs; the twelve peers of Charlemagne.
[3] The nine worthies: they are Joshua, David, Judas Machabeus, Hector,
Alexander, Julius Cæsar, Arthur, Charlemagne, and Godfrey of Boulogne.
[4] Realm.

INDEX